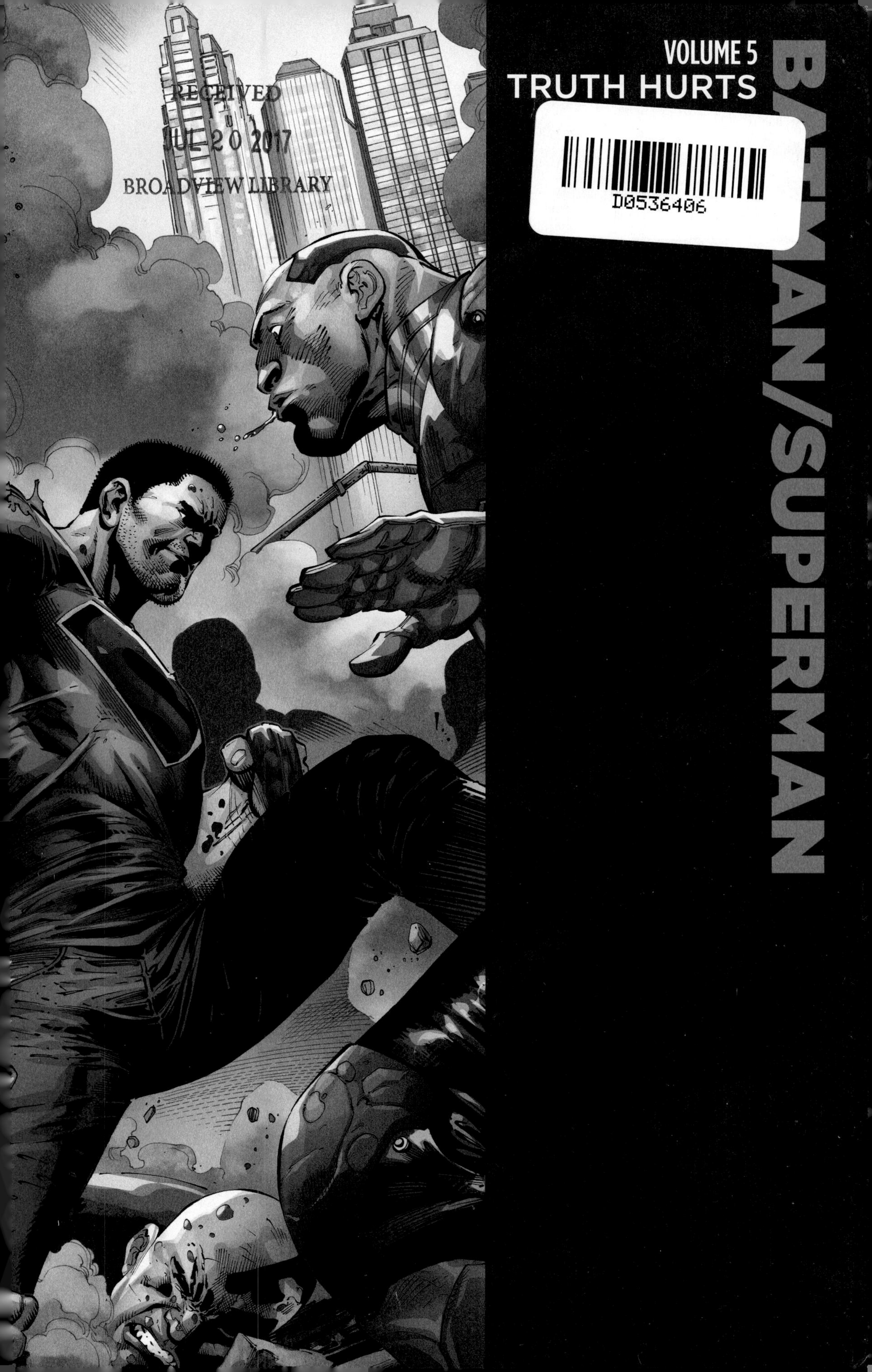

VOLUME 5

TRUTH HURTS

BATMAN/SUPERMAN

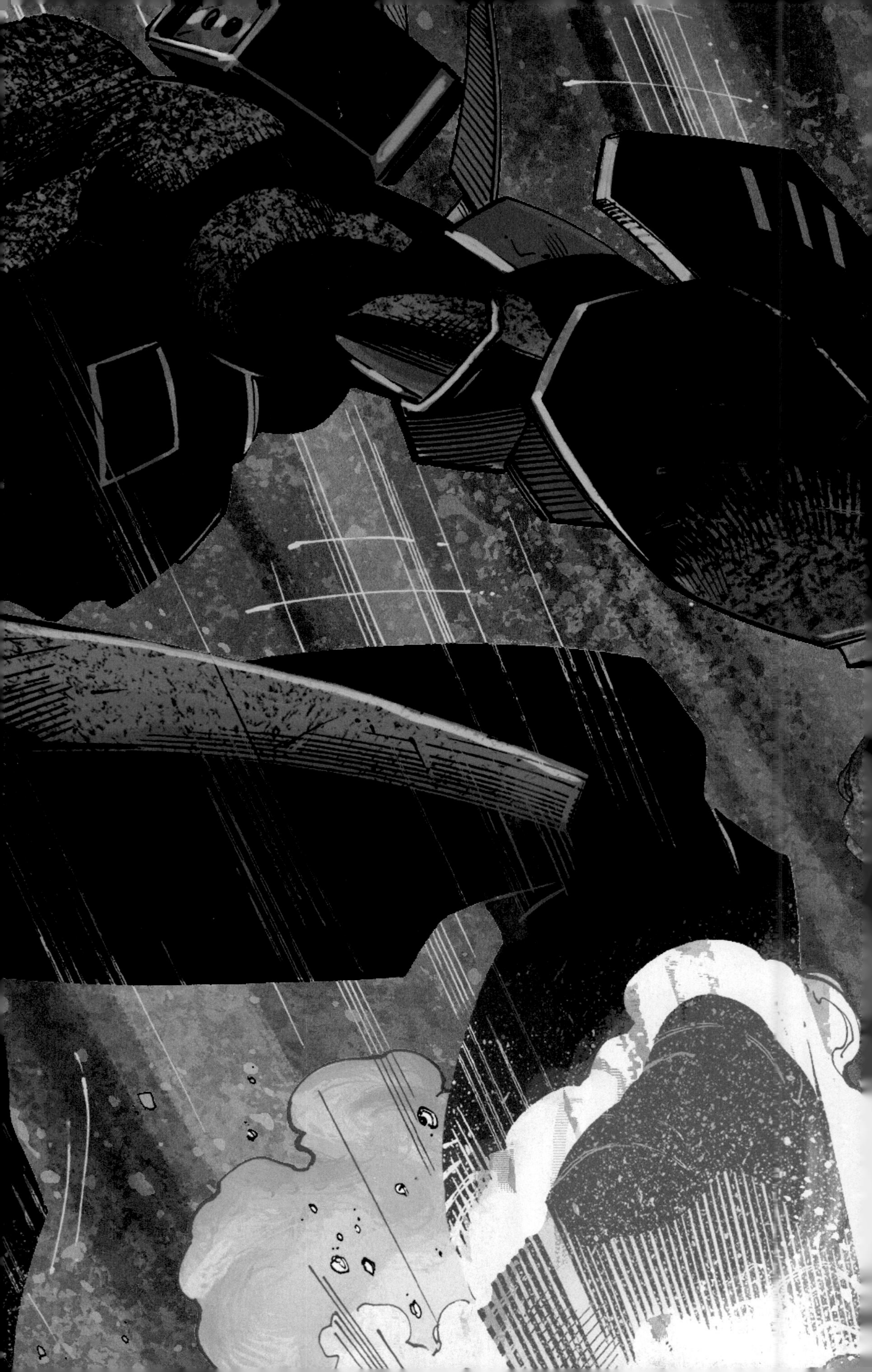

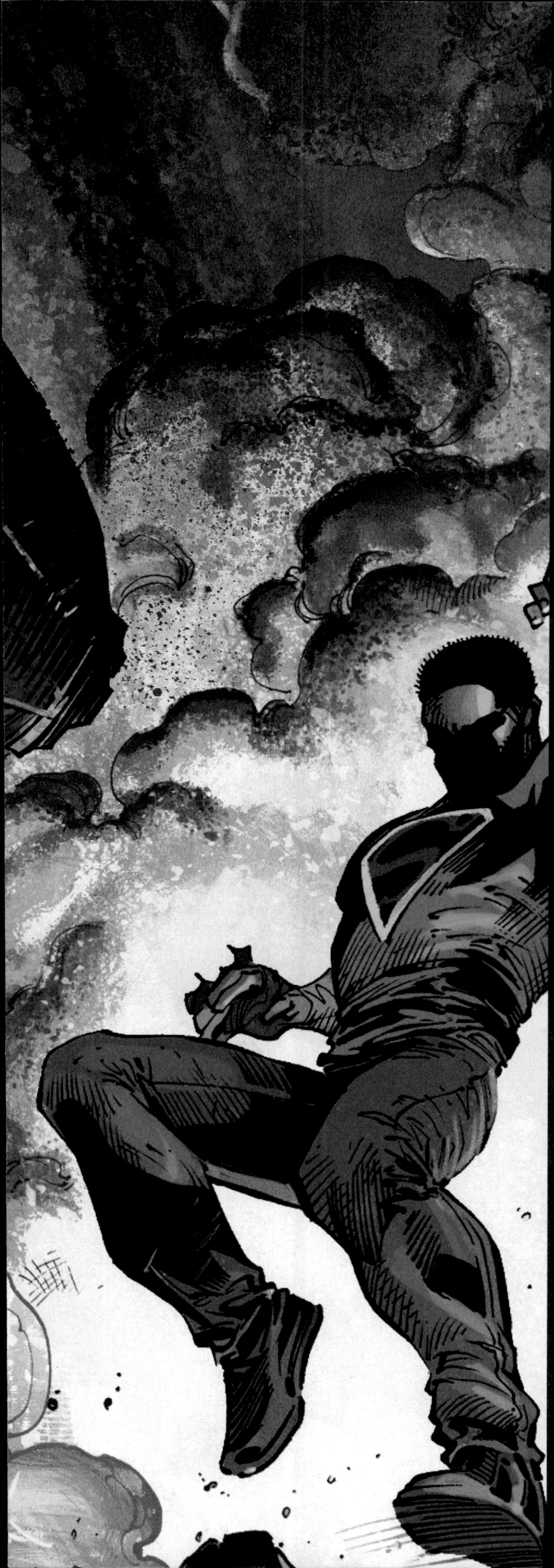

BATMAN/SUPERMAN

VOLUME 5
TRUTH HURTS

WRITTEN BY
GREG PAK

PENCILS BY
ARDIAN SYAF
CLIFF RICHARDS
YILDIRAY CINAR
HOWARD PORTER
JACK HERBERT

INKS BY
VICENTE CIFUENTES
CLIFF RICHARDS
YILDIRAY CINAR
HOWARD PORTER
JACK HERBERT

COLOR BY
BETH SOTELO
ULISES ARREOLA
DEAN WHITE
WIL QUINTANA
BLOND

LETTERS BY
ROB LEIGH

COLLECTION COVER BY
ARDIAN SYAF
DANNY MIKI
ULISES ARREOLA

SUPERMAN CREATED BY
JERRY SIEGEL & **JOE SHUSTER**
BY SPECIAL ARRANGEMENT WITH
THE JERRY SIEGEL FAMILY

BATMAN CREATED BY
BOB KANE
WITH **BILL FINGER**

BATMAN/SUPERMAN VOLUME 5: TRUTH HURTS

Published by DC Comics. All new material Copyright © 2017. Compilation originally published © 2016 DC Comics. All Rights Reserved.
Originally published online as BATMAN/SUPERMAN Sneak Peek and in single magazine form in BATMAN/SUPERMAN 2–27.
Copyright © 2015, 2016 DC Comics. All Rights Reserved. All characters, their distinctive likenesses and related elements featured in this
publication are trademarks of DC Comics. The stories, characters and incidents featured in this publication are entirely fictional.
DC Comics does not read or accept unsolicited submissions of ideas, stories or artwork.

DC Comics, 2900 West Alameda Ave., Burbank, CA 91505
Printed by LSC Communications, Salem, VA. 3/3/17. First Printing.

ISBN: 978-1-4012-6818-3

Library of Congress Cataloging-in-Publication Data is available.

PEFC Certified

Printed on paper from
sustainably managed
forests, controlled
sources

PEFC™

PEFC/29-31-337   www.pefc.org

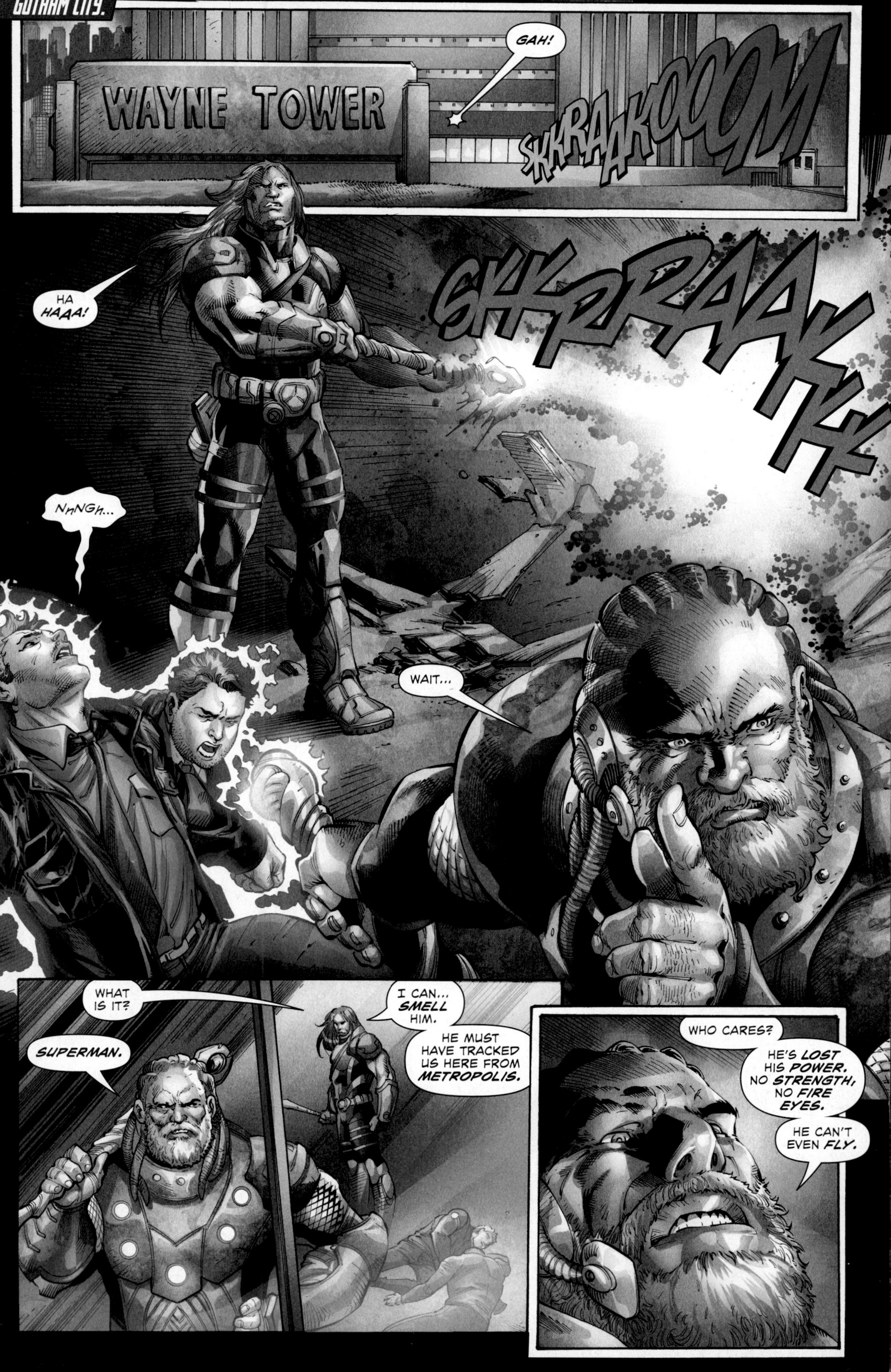
GOTHAM CITY.
WAYNE TOWER
GAH!
SKKRAAKOOOM
HA HAAA!
SKKRAAKKK
NnNGh...
WAIT...
WHAT IS IT?
SUPERMAN.
I CAN... SMELL HIM.
HE MUST HAVE TRACKED US HERE FROM METROPOLIS.
WHO CARES?
HE'S LOST HIS POWER. NO STRENGTH, NO FIRE EYES.
HE CAN'T EVEN FLY.

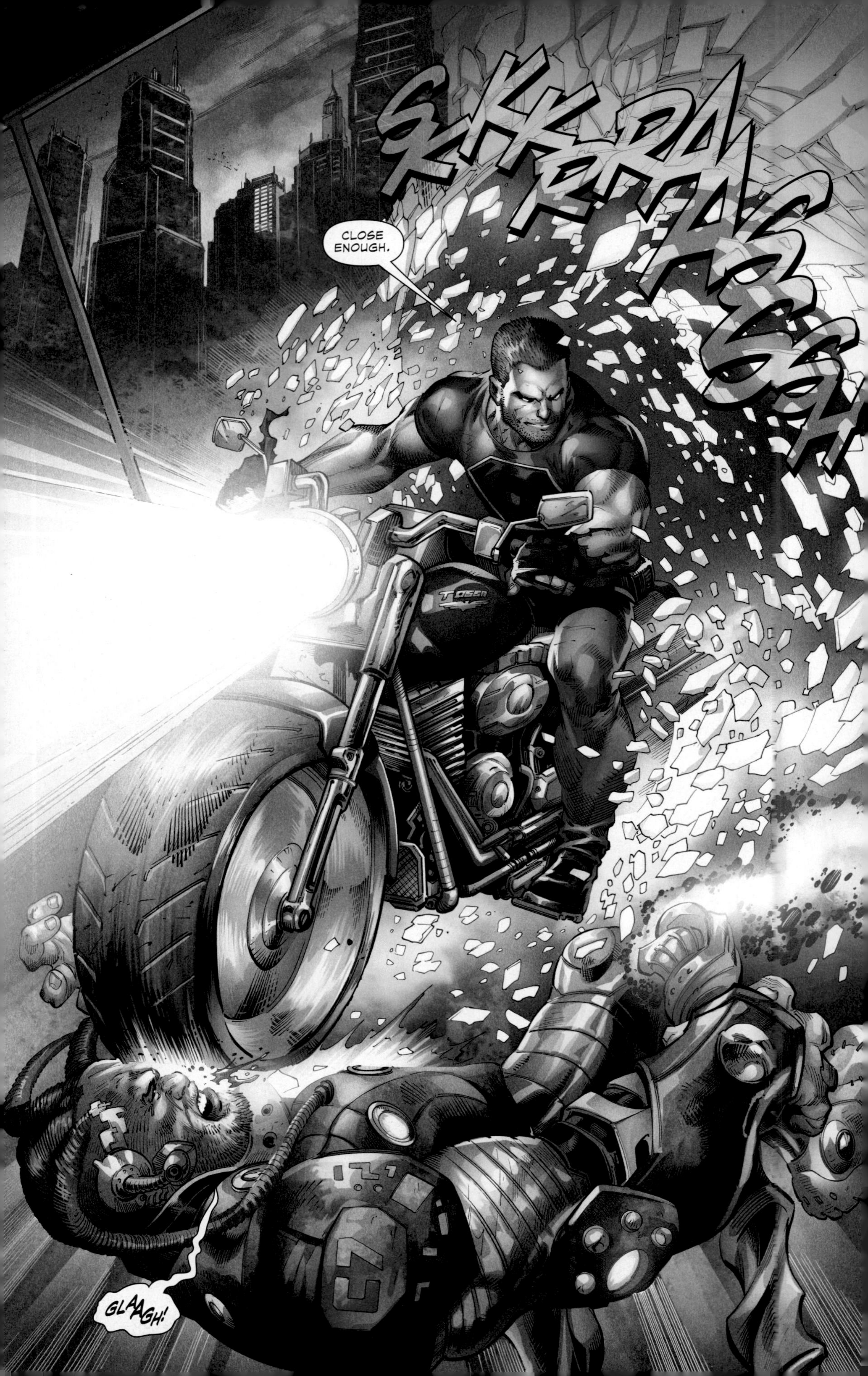
CLOSE ENOUGH.
GLAAGH!

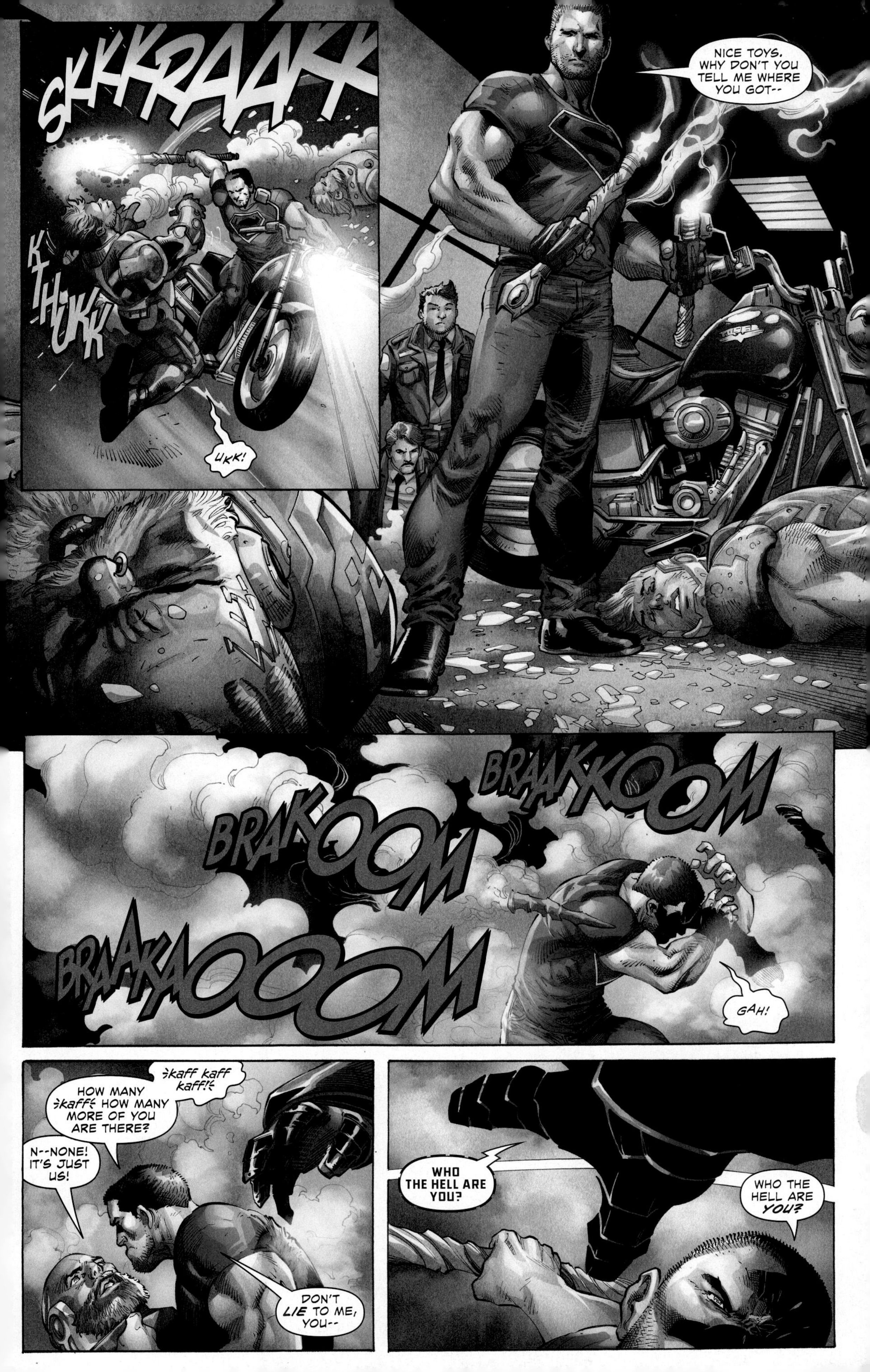
SKKRAAKK
KTHUKK
UKK!
NICE TOYS. WHY DON'T YOU TELL ME WHERE YOU GOT--
BRAKOOM
BRAAKKOOM
BRAAKAOOOOM
GAH!
HOW MANY ⊰kaff⊱ HOW MANY MORE OF YOU ARE THERE?
⊰kaff kaff kaff!⊱
N--NONE! IT'S JUST US!
DON'T LIE TO ME, YOU--
WHO THE HELL ARE YOU?
WHO THE HELL ARE YOU?

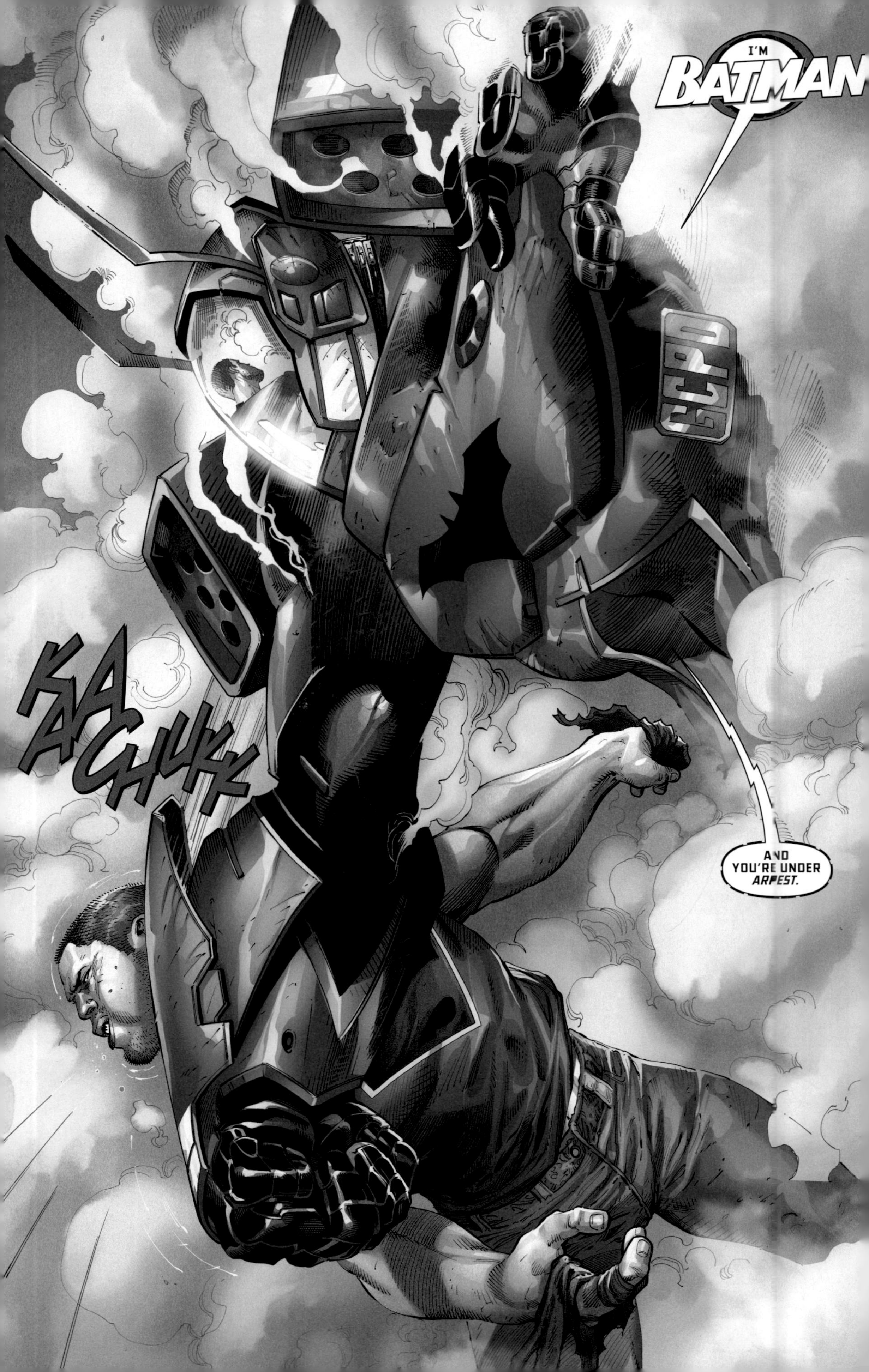
I'M BATMAN
KA-A-CHUKK
AND YOU'RE UNDER ARREST.

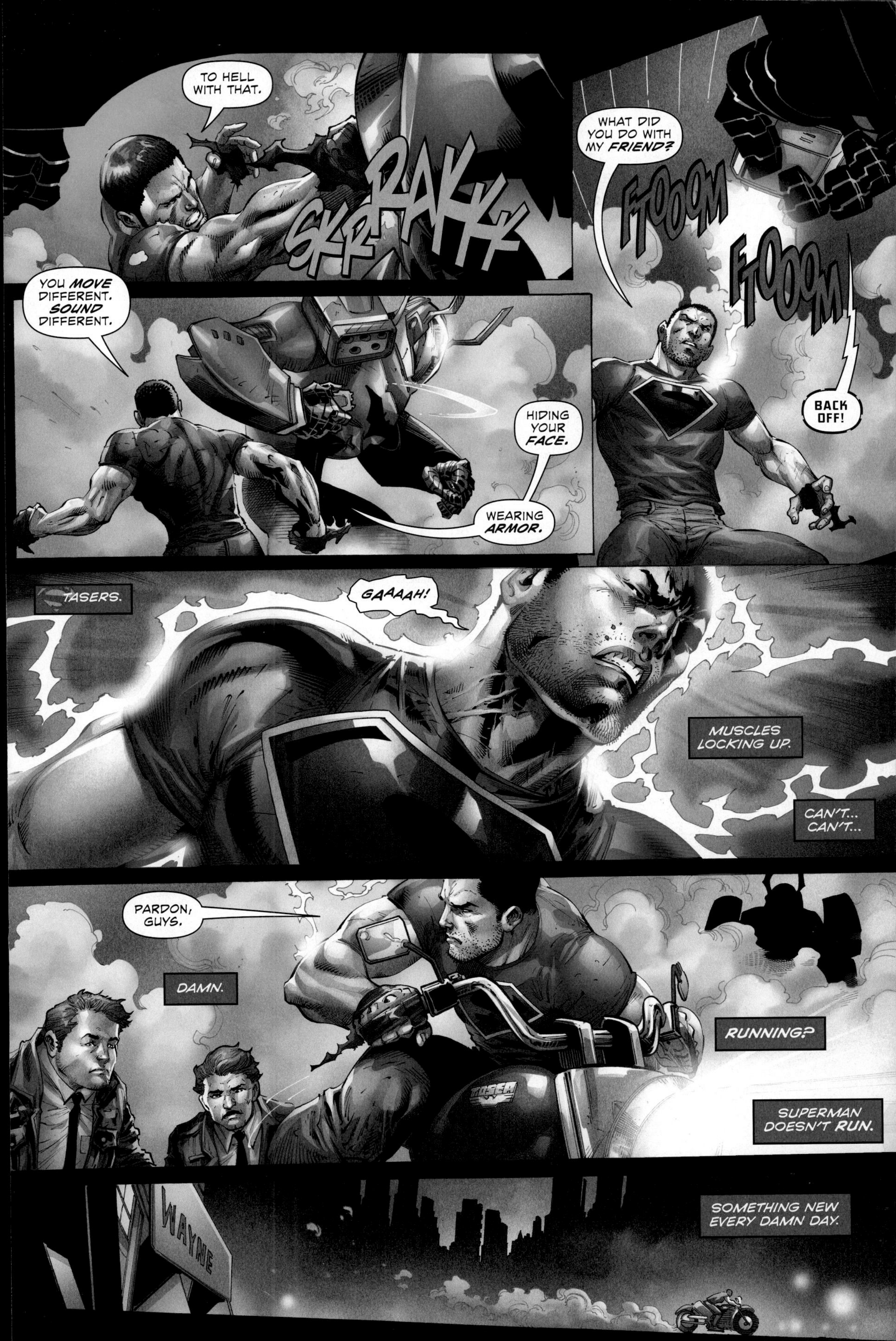
TO HELL WITH THAT.
SKRRAKKK
WHAT DID YOU DO WITH MY FRIEND?
FTOOOM
FTOOOM
YOU MOVE DIFFERENT. SOUND DIFFERENT.
HIDING YOUR FACE.
WEARING ARMOR.
BACK OFF!
TASERS.
GAAAAH!
MUSCLES LOCKING UP.
CAN'T... CAN'T...
PARDON, GUYS.
DAMN.
RUNNING?
SUPERMAN DOESN'T RUN.
WAYNE
SOMETHING NEW EVERY DAMN DAY.

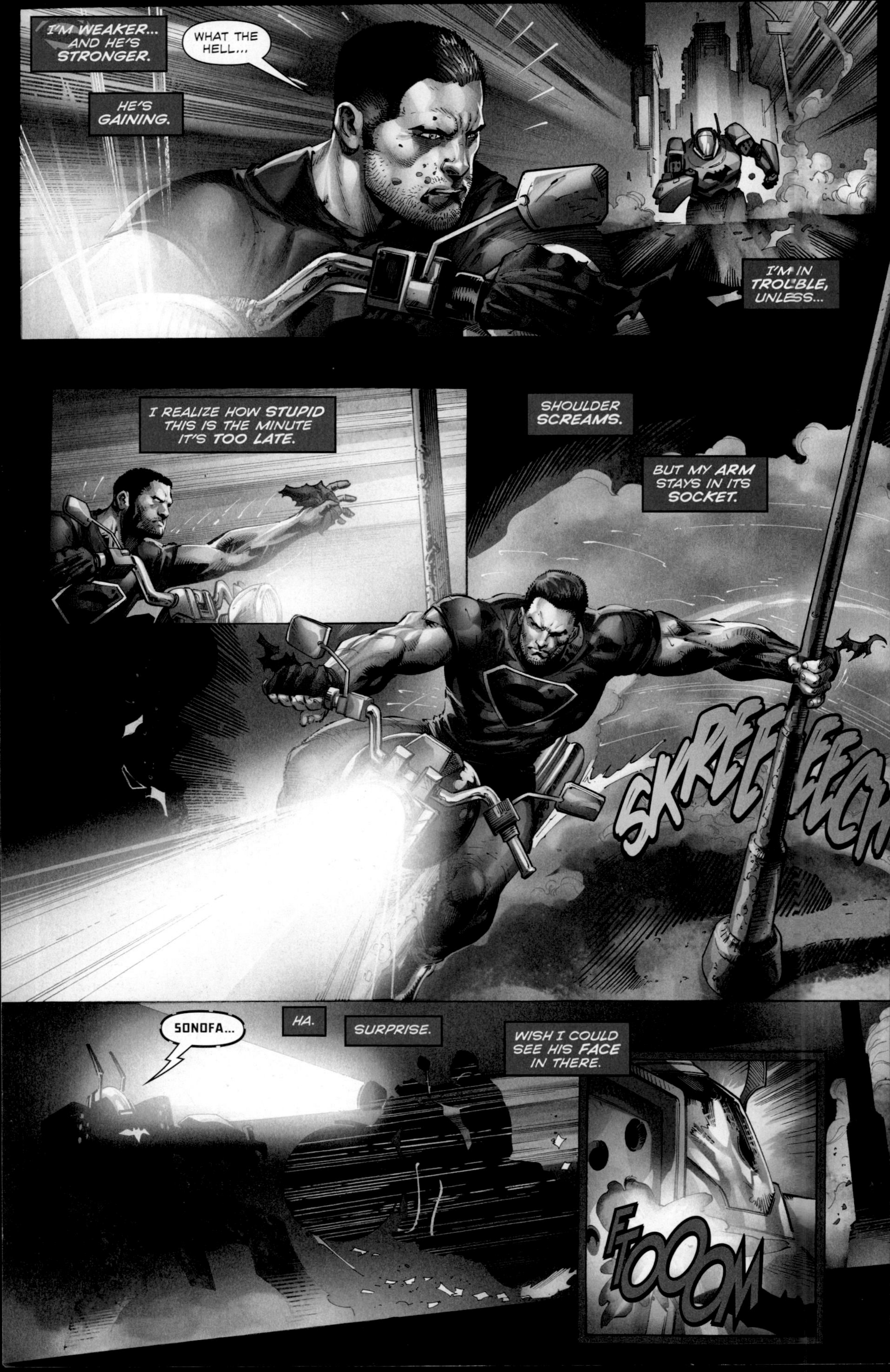
I'M WEAKER... AND HE'S STRONGER.
WHAT THE HELL...
HE'S GAINING.
I'M IN TROUBLE, UNLESS...
I REALIZE HOW STUPID THIS IS THE MINUTE IT'S TOO LATE.
SHOULDER SCREAMS.
BUT MY ARM STAYS IN ITS SOCKET.
SKREEEEECH
SONOFA...
HA.
SURPRISE.
WISH I COULD SEE HIS FACE IN THERE.
FTOOOM

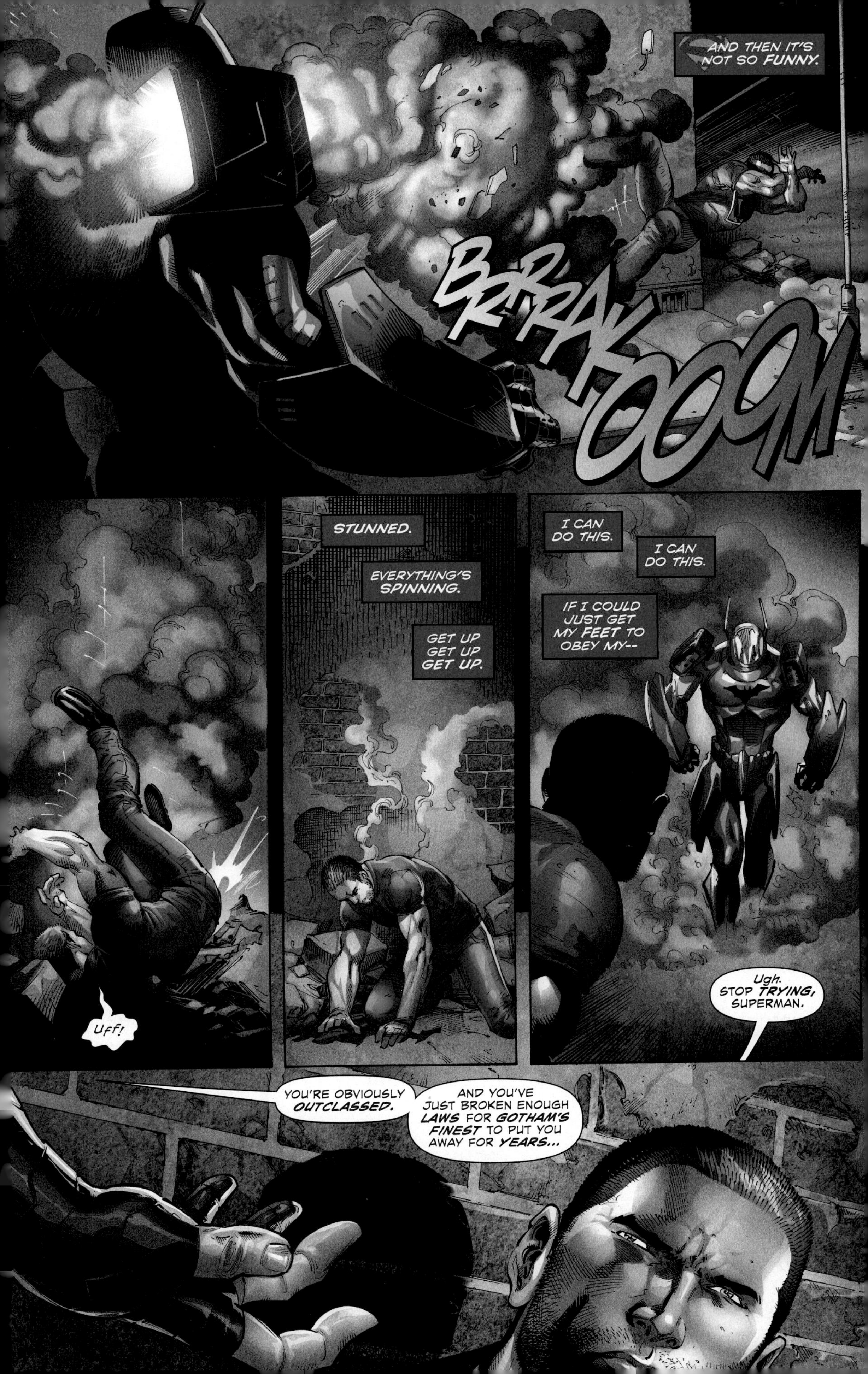
AND THEN IT'S NOT SO FUNNY.
BRRRAKOOOM
STUNNED.
EVERYTHING'S SPINNING.
GET UP GET UP GET UP.
Uff!
I CAN DO THIS.
I CAN DO THIS.
IF I COULD JUST GET MY FEET TO OBEY MY--
Ugh. STOP TRYING, SUPERMAN.
YOU'RE OBVIOUSLY OUTCLASSED.
AND YOU'VE JUST BROKEN ENOUGH LAWS FOR GOTHAM'S FINEST TO PUT YOU AWAY FOR YEARS...

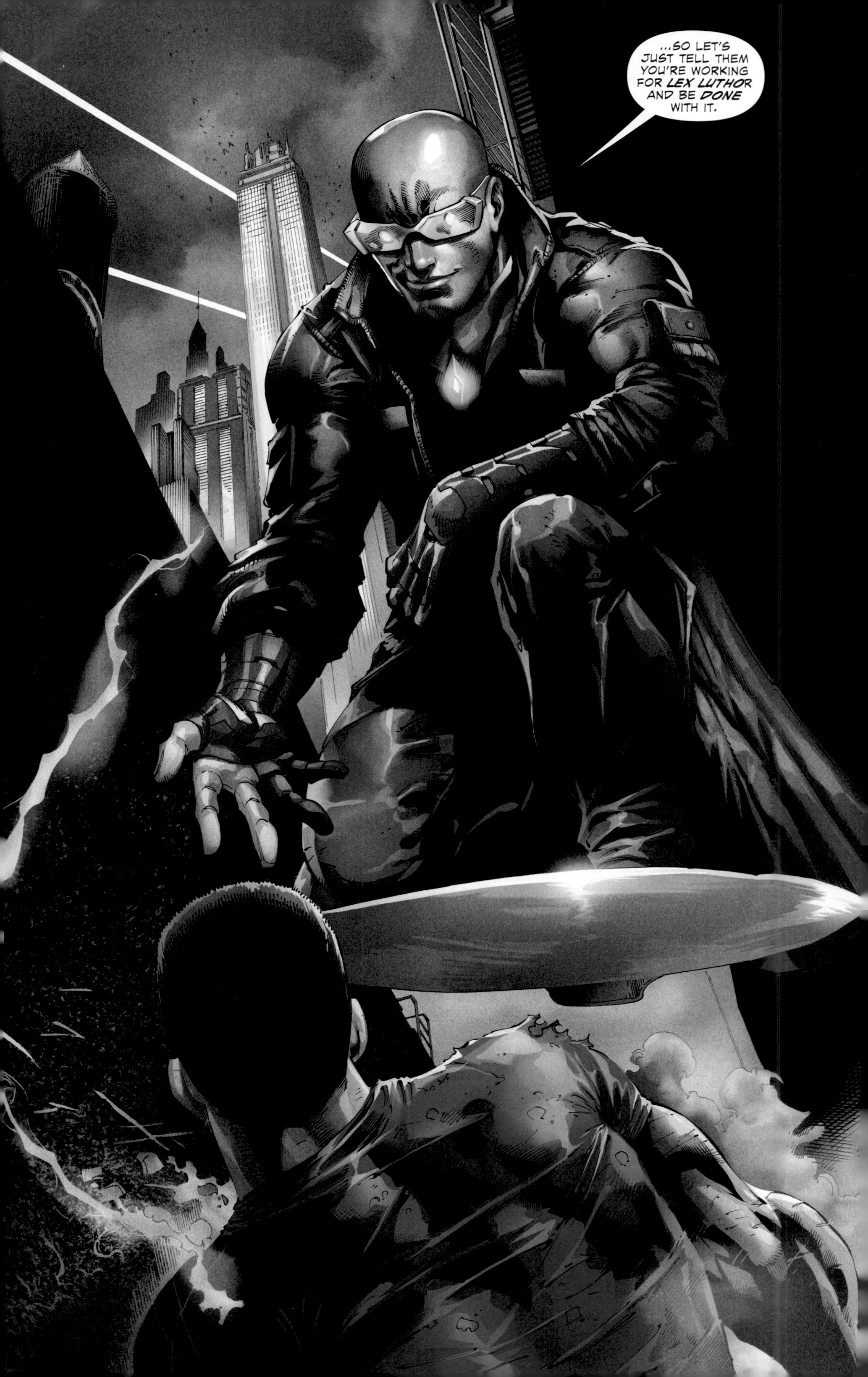
...SO LET'S JUST TELL THEM YOU'RE WORKING FOR LEX LUTHOR AND BE DONE WITH IT.

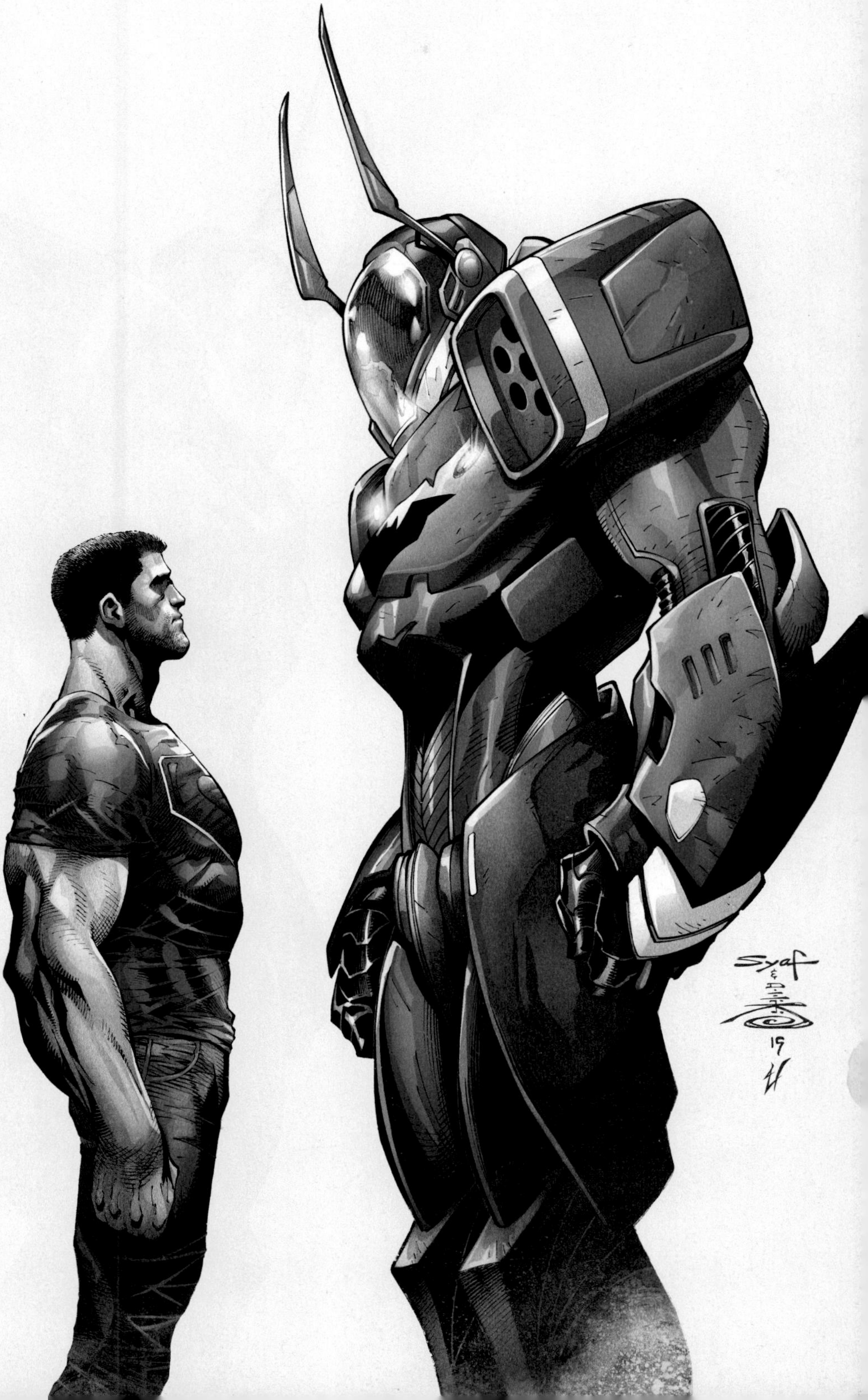
Syaf

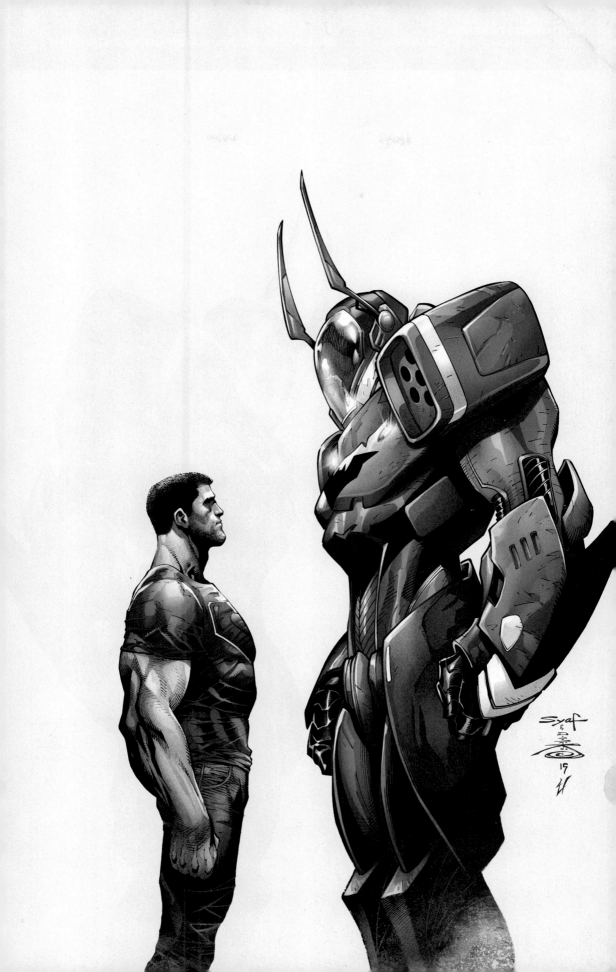

TRUTH HURTS PART ONE

GREG PAK writer **ARDIAN SYAF** penciller **VICENTE CIFUENTES** inker **ULISES ARREOLA** colorist **ROB LEIGH** letterer **ARDIAN SYAF DANNY MIKI ULISES ARREOLA** cover

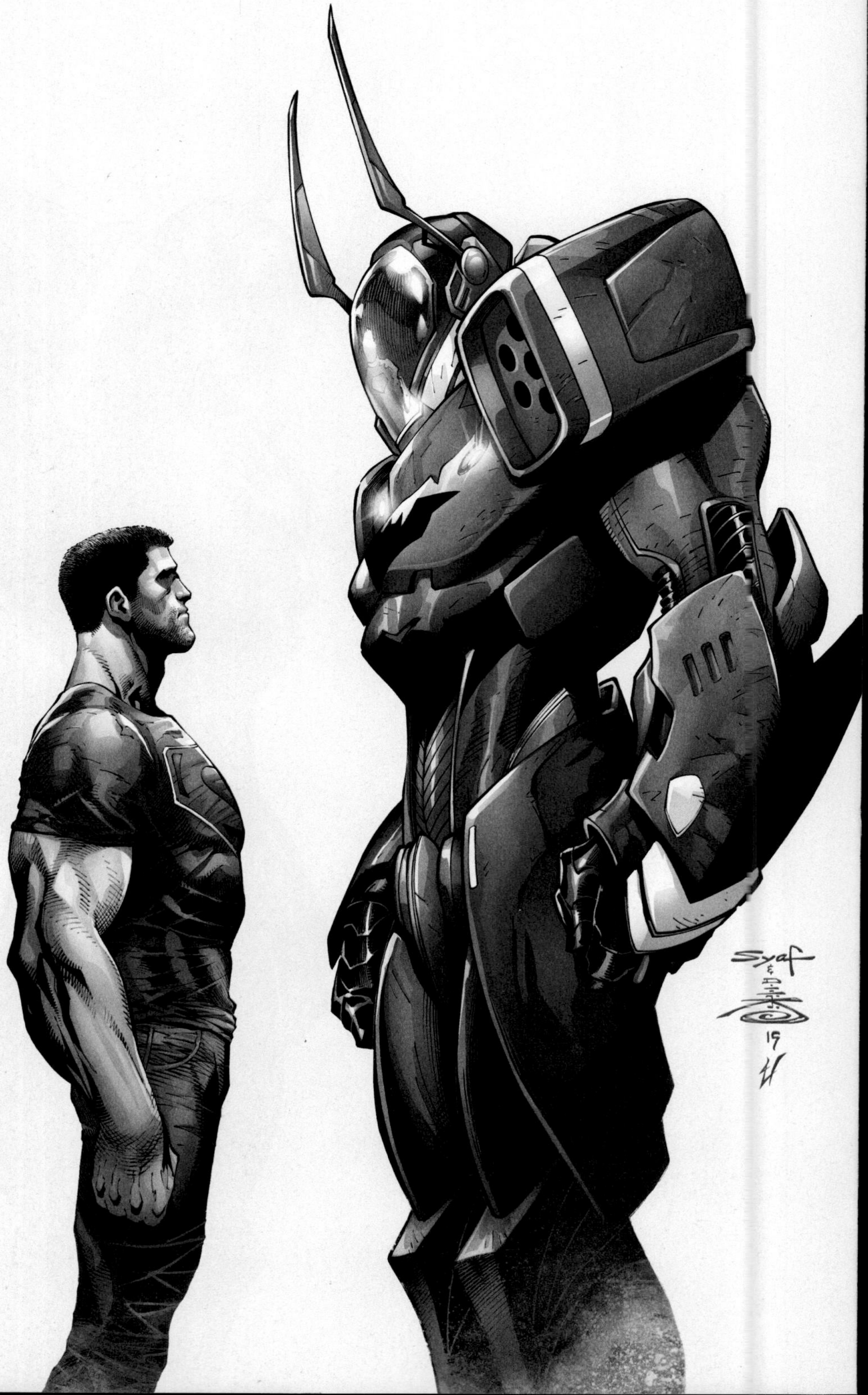

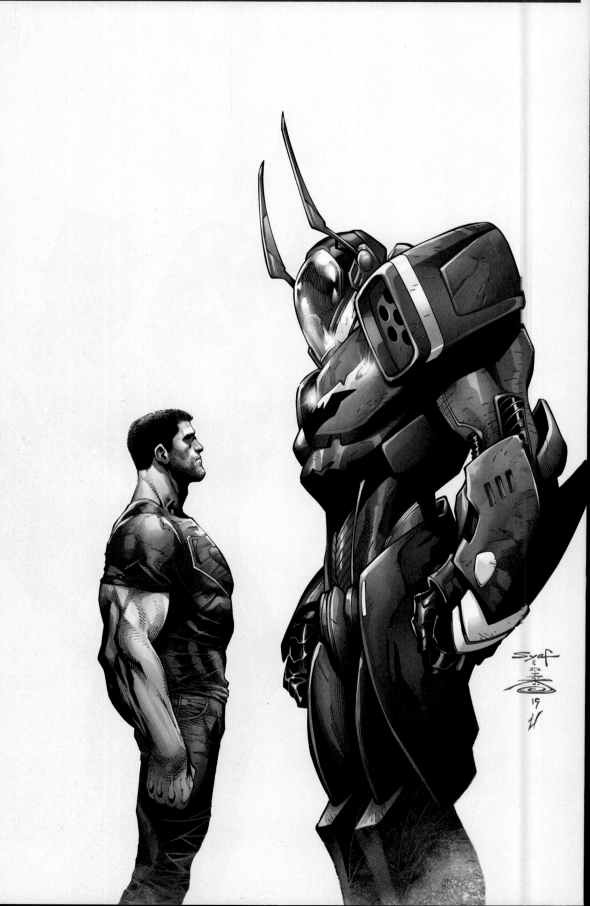

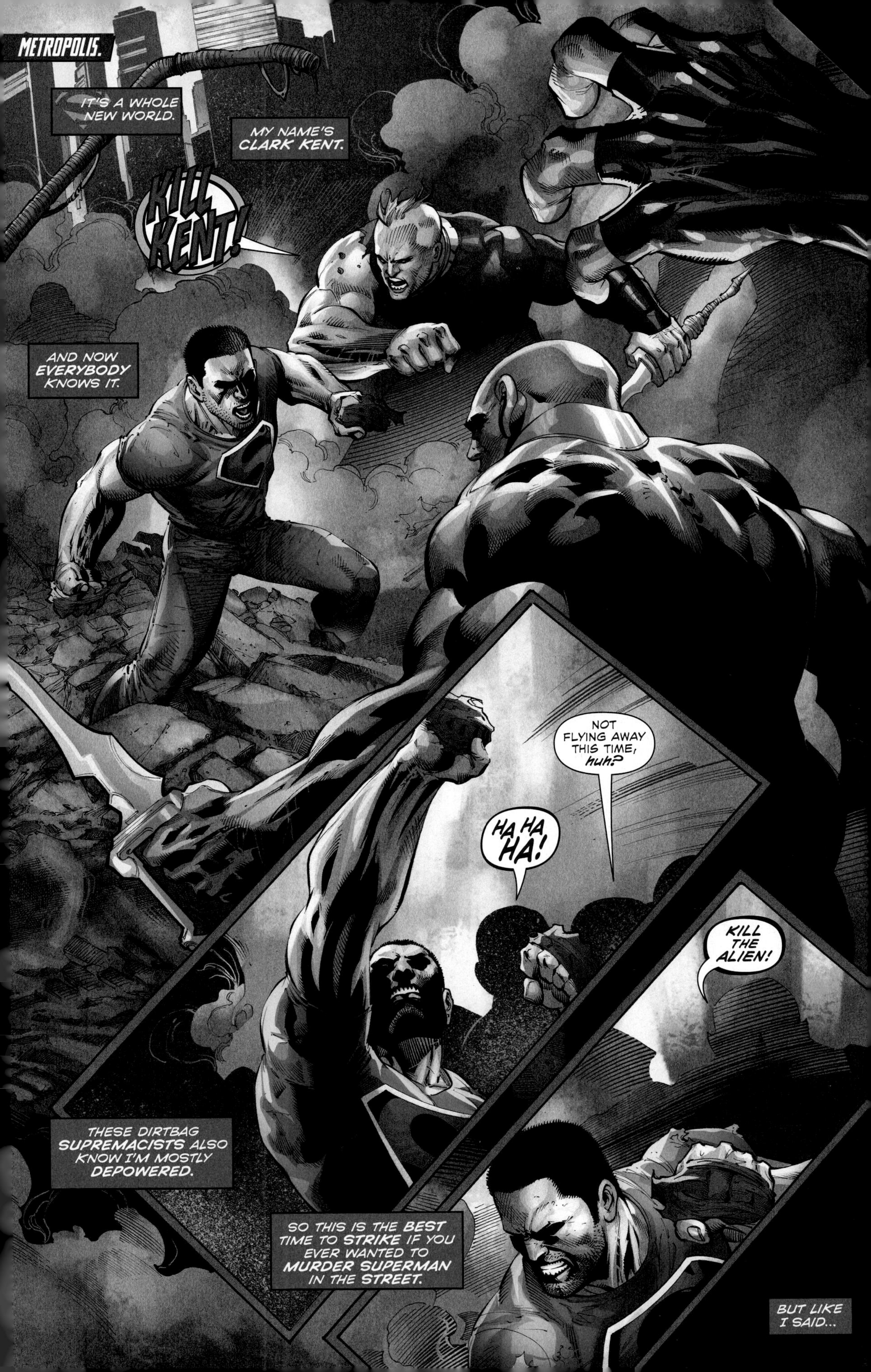
METROPOLIS.
IT'S A WHOLE NEW WORLD.
MY NAME'S CLARK KENT.
KILL KENT!
AND NOW EVERYBODY KNOWS IT.
NOT FLYING AWAY THIS TIME, huh?
HA HA HA!
KILL THE ALIEN!
THESE DIRTBAG SUPREMACISTS ALSO KNOW I'M MOSTLY DEPOWERED.
SO THIS IS THE BEST TIME TO STRIKE IF YOU EVER WANTED TO MURDER SUPERMAN IN THE STREET.
BUT LIKE I SAID...

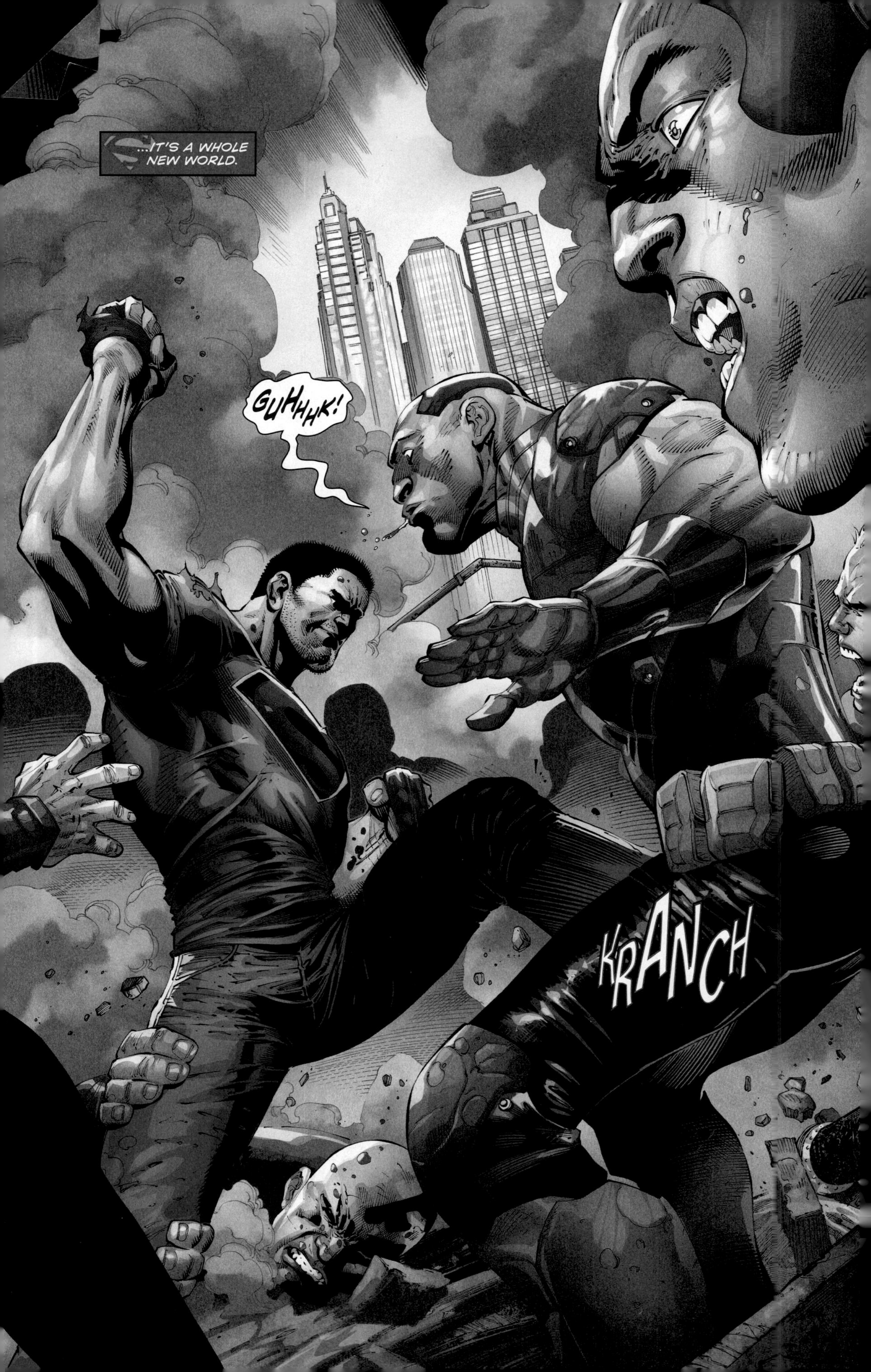
...IT'S A WHOLE NEW WORLD.
GUHHHK!
KRANCH

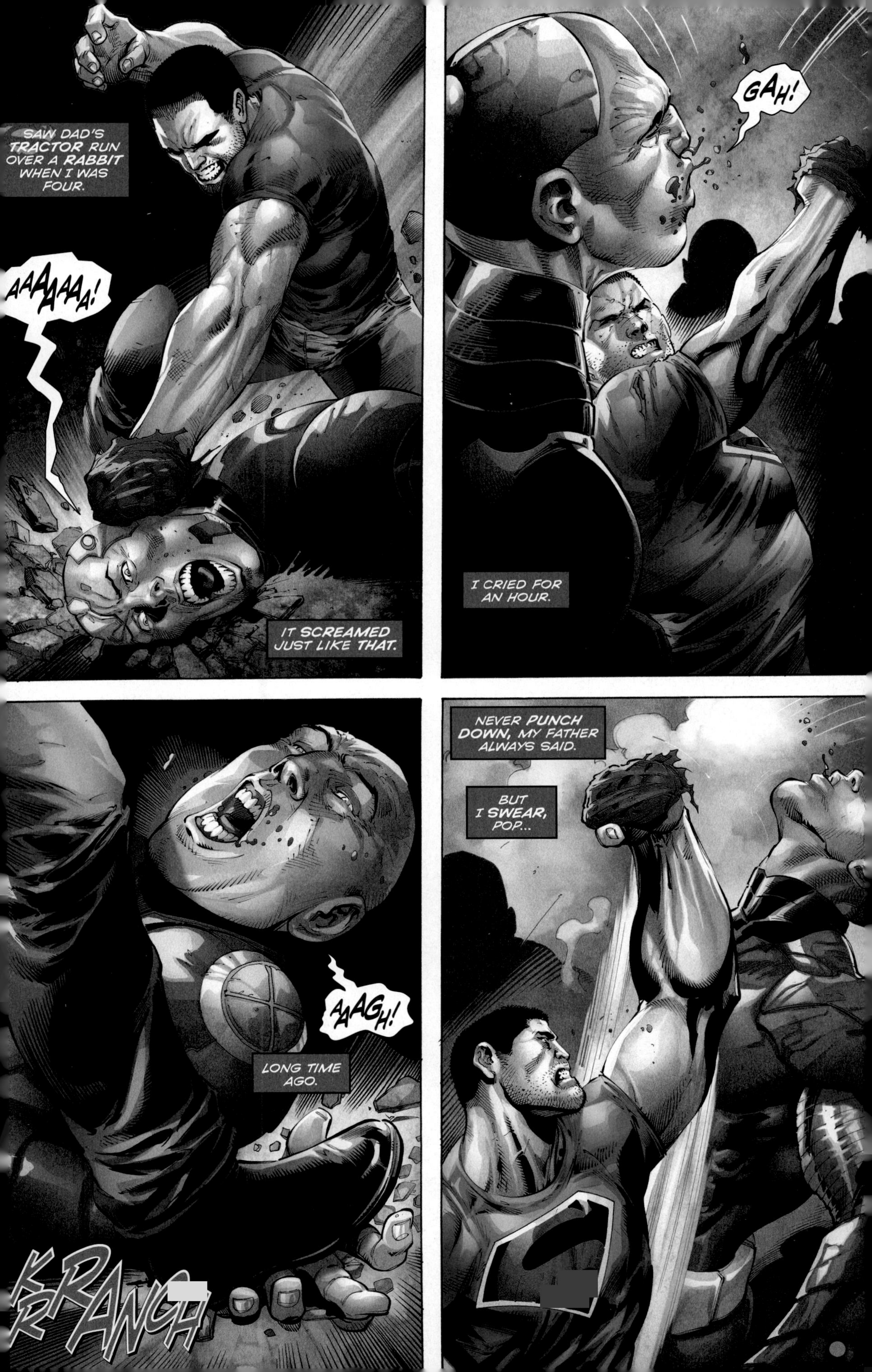
SAW DAD'S TRACTOR RUN OVER A RABBIT WHEN I WAS FOUR.
AAAAAAA!
IT SCREAMED JUST LIKE THAT.
GAH!
I CRIED FOR AN HOUR.
AAAGH!
LONG TIME AGO.
KRRANCH
NEVER PUNCH DOWN, MY FATHER ALWAYS SAID.
BUT I SWEAR, POP...

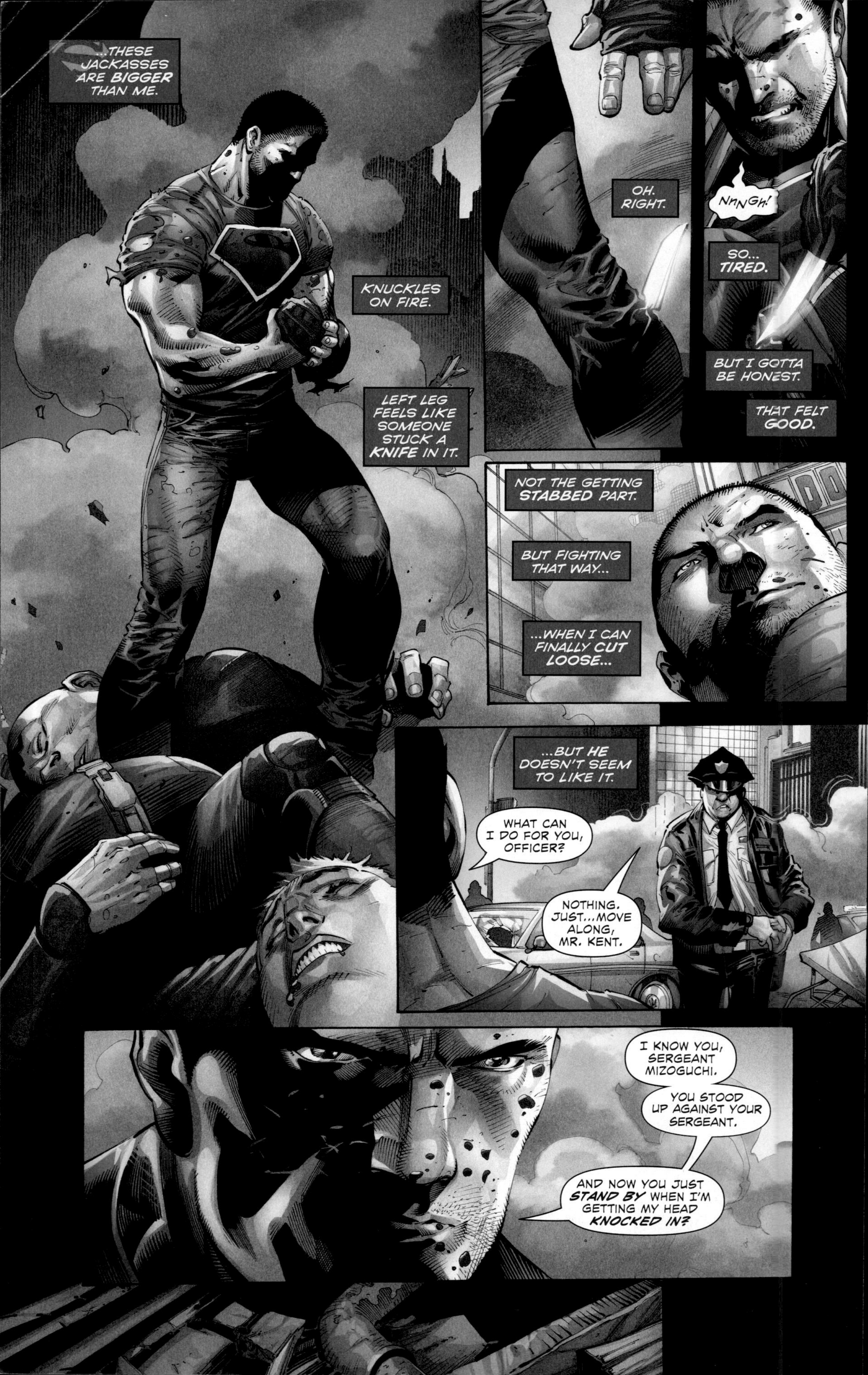
...THESE JACKASSES ARE BIGGER THAN ME.
KNUCKLES ON FIRE.
LEFT LEG FEELS LIKE SOMEONE STUCK A KNIFE IN IT.
OH. RIGHT.
NNNGH!
SO... TIRED.
BUT I GOTTA BE HONEST.
THAT FELT GOOD.
NOT THE GETTING STABBED PART.
BUT FIGHTING THAT WAY...
...WHEN I CAN FINALLY CUT LOOSE...
...BUT HE DOESN'T SEEM TO LIKE IT.
WHAT CAN I DO FOR YOU, OFFICER?
NOTHING. JUST...MOVE ALONG, MR. KENT.
I KNOW YOU, SERGEANT MIZOGUCHI.
YOU STOOD UP AGAINST YOUR SERGEANT.
AND NOW YOU JUST STAND BY WHEN I'M GETTING MY HEAD KNOCKED IN?

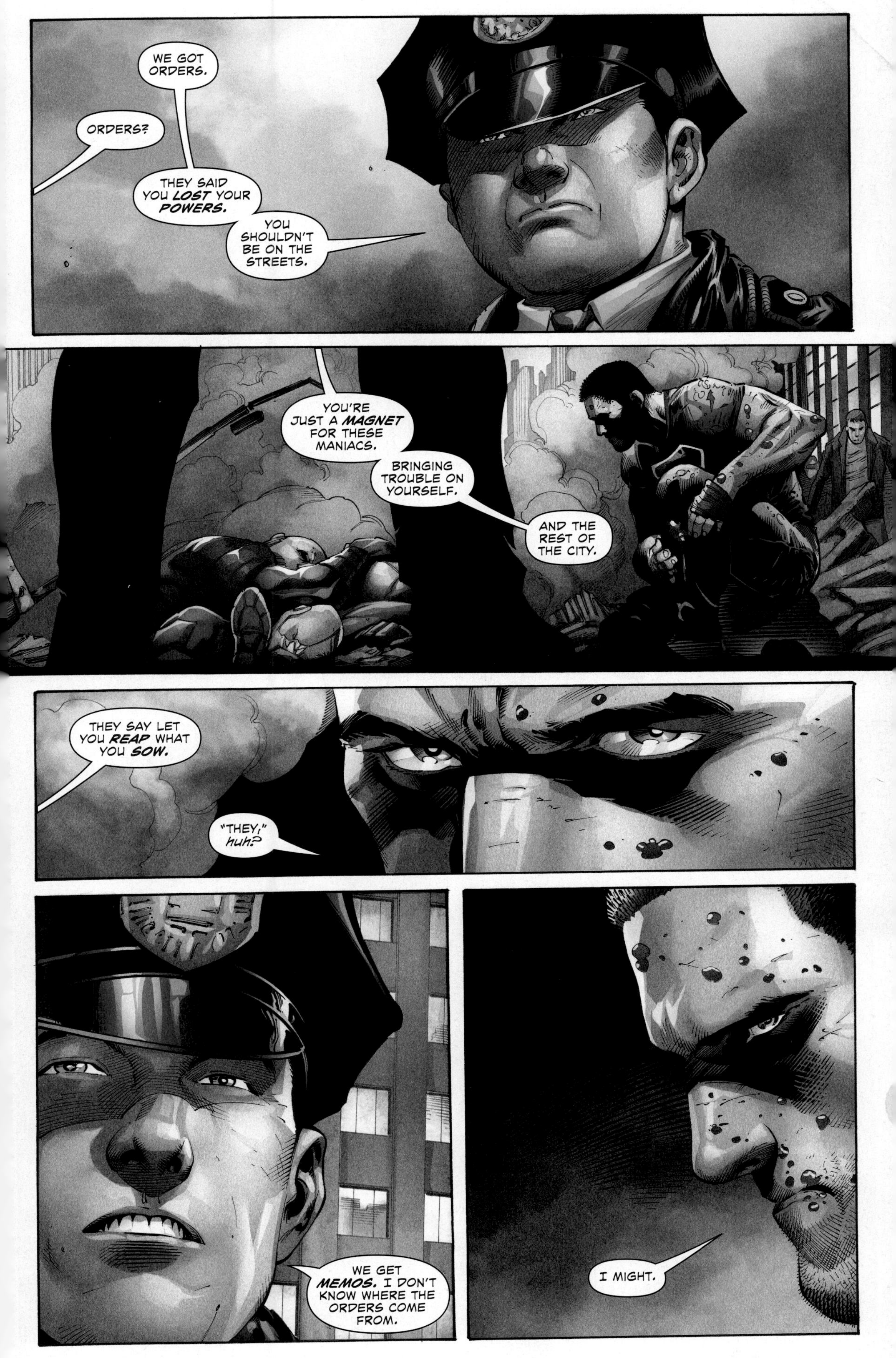
WE GOT ORDERS.
ORDERS?
THEY SAID YOU *LOST* YOUR *POWERS.*
YOU SHOULDN'T BE ON THE STREETS.
YOU'RE JUST A *MAGNET* FOR THESE MANIACS.
BRINGING TROUBLE ON YOURSELF.
AND THE REST OF THE CITY.
THEY SAY LET YOU *REAP* WHAT YOU *SOW.*
"THEY," *huh?*
WE GET *MEMOS.* I DON'T KNOW WHERE THE ORDERS COME FROM.
I MIGHT.

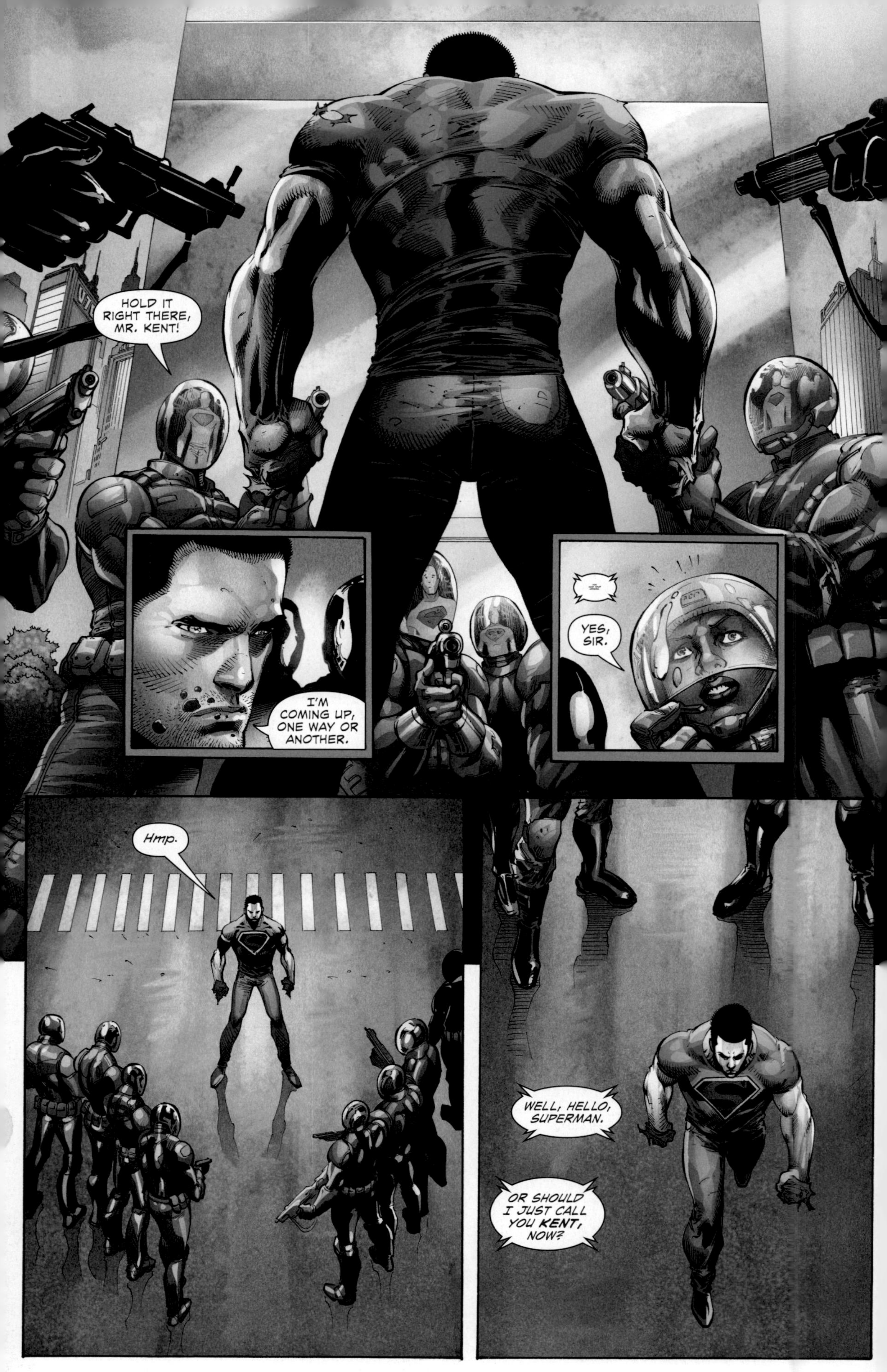
HOLD IT RIGHT THERE, MR. KENT!
I'M COMING UP, ONE WAY OR ANOTHER.
YES, SIR.
Hmp.
WELL, HELLO, SUPERMAN.
OR SHOULD I JUST CALL YOU KENT, NOW?

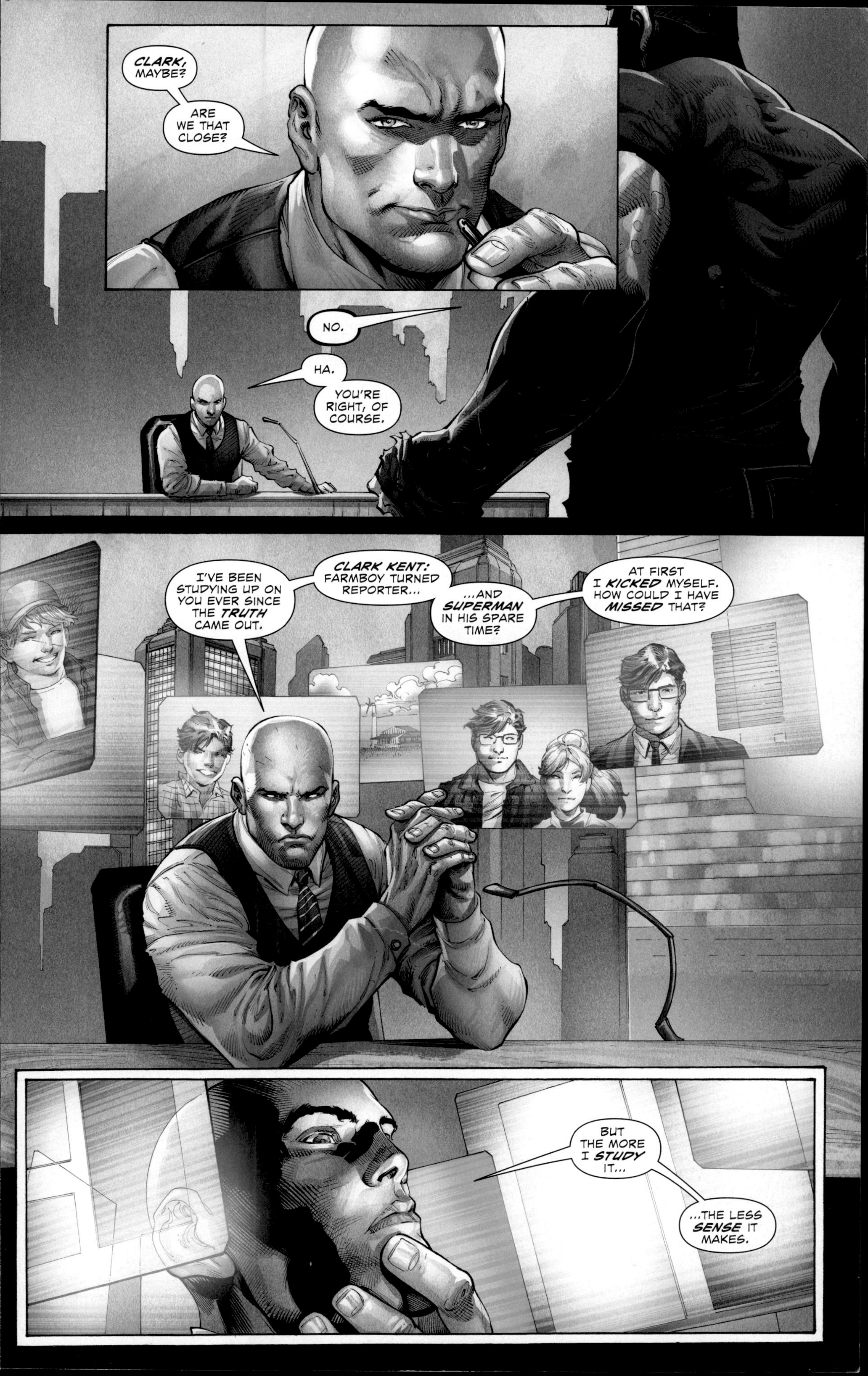
CLARK, MAYBE?
ARE WE THAT CLOSE?
NO.
HA.
YOU'RE RIGHT, OF COURSE.
I'VE BEEN STUDYING UP ON YOU EVER SINCE THE TRUTH CAME OUT.
CLARK KENT: FARMBOY TURNED REPORTER...
...AND SUPERMAN IN HIS SPARE TIME?
AT FIRST I KICKED MYSELF. HOW COULD I HAVE MISSED THAT?
BUT THE MORE I STUDY IT...
...THE LESS SENSE IT MAKES.

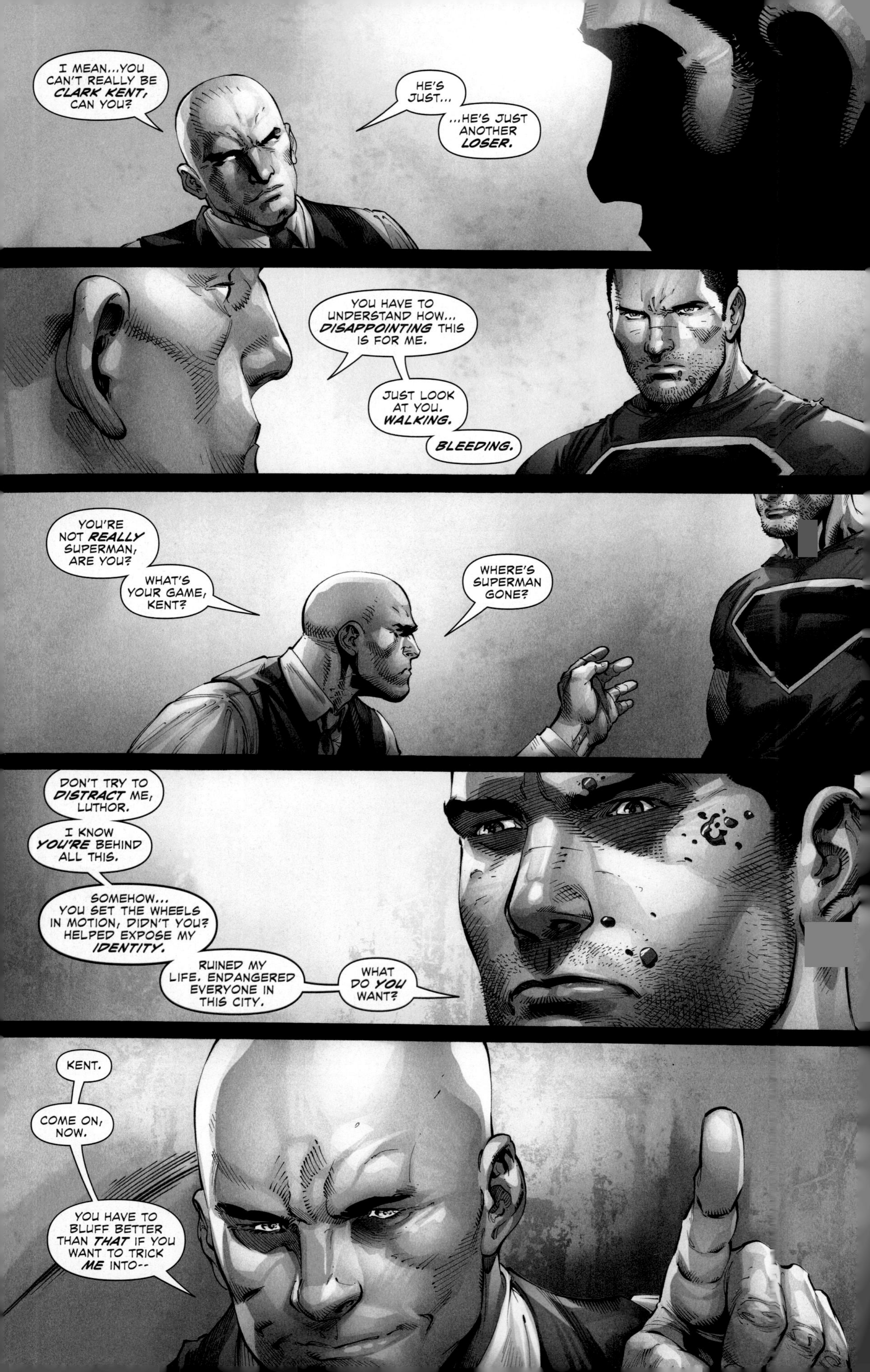

I MEAN...YOU CAN'T REALLY BE CLARK KENT, CAN YOU?
HE'S JUST...
...HE'S JUST ANOTHER LOSER.
YOU HAVE TO UNDERSTAND HOW... DISAPPOINTING THIS IS FOR ME.
JUST LOOK AT YOU. WALKING.
BLEEDING.
YOU'RE NOT REALLY SUPERMAN, ARE YOU?
WHAT'S YOUR GAME, KENT?
WHERE'S SUPERMAN GONE?
DON'T TRY TO DISTRACT ME, LUTHOR.
I KNOW YOU'RE BEHIND ALL THIS.
SOMEHOW... YOU SET THE WHEELS IN MOTION, DIDN'T YOU? HELPED EXPOSE MY IDENTITY.
RUINED MY LIFE. ENDANGERED EVERYONE IN THIS CITY.
WHAT DO YOU WANT?
KENT.
COME ON, NOW.
YOU HAVE TO BLUFF BETTER THAN THAT IF YOU WANT TO TRICK ME INTO--

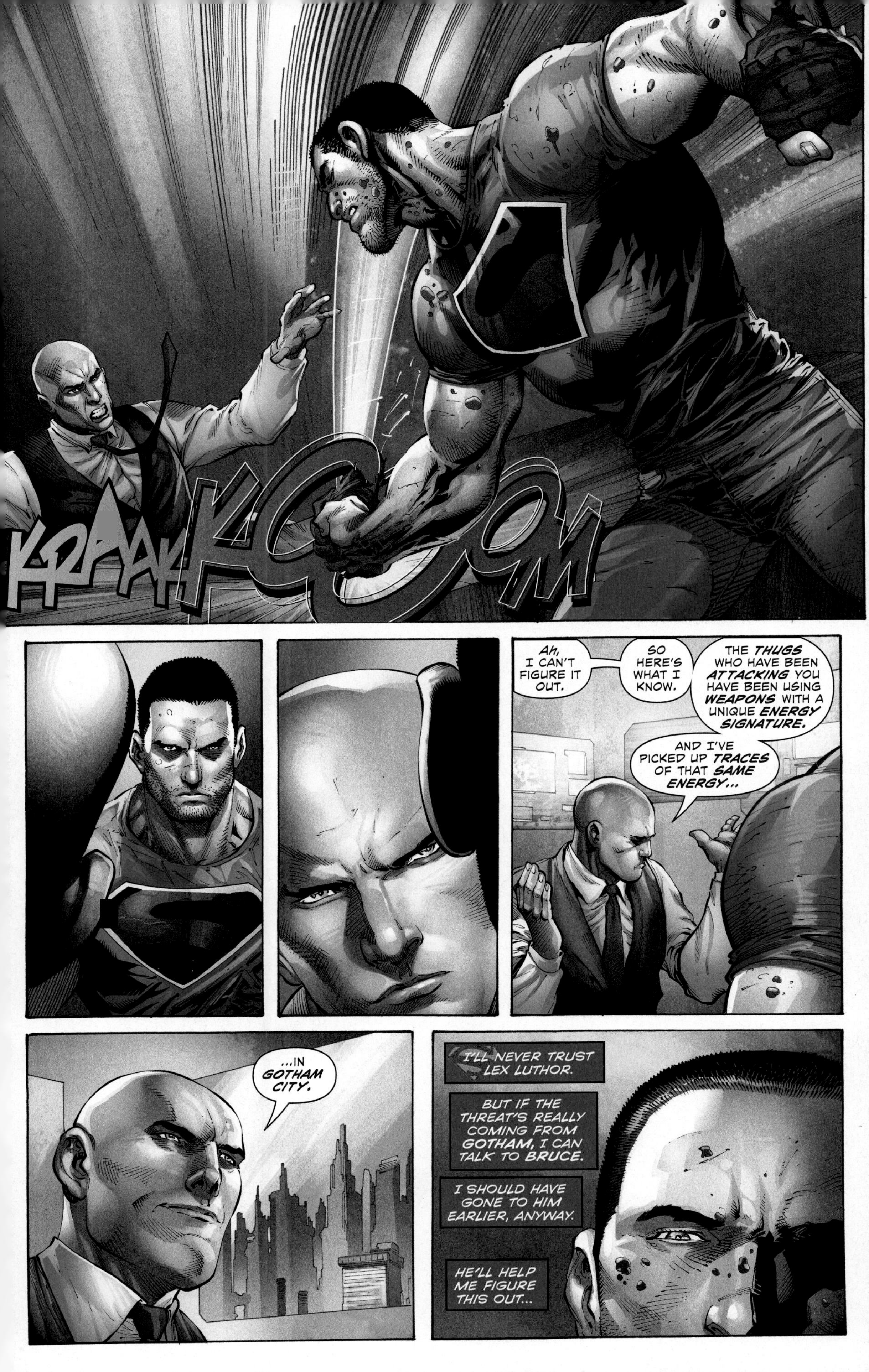
KRAAK KOOM
Ah, I CAN'T FIGURE IT OUT.
SO HERE'S WHAT I KNOW.
THE THUGS WHO HAVE BEEN ATTACKING YOU HAVE BEEN USING WEAPONS WITH A UNIQUE ENERGY SIGNATURE.
AND I'VE PICKED UP TRACES OF THAT SAME ENERGY...
...IN GOTHAM CITY.
I'LL NEVER TRUST LEX LUTHOR.
BUT IF THE THREAT'S REALLY COMING FROM GOTHAM, I CAN TALK TO BRUCE.
I SHOULD HAVE GONE TO HIM EARLIER, ANYWAY.
HE'LL HELP ME FIGURE THIS OUT...

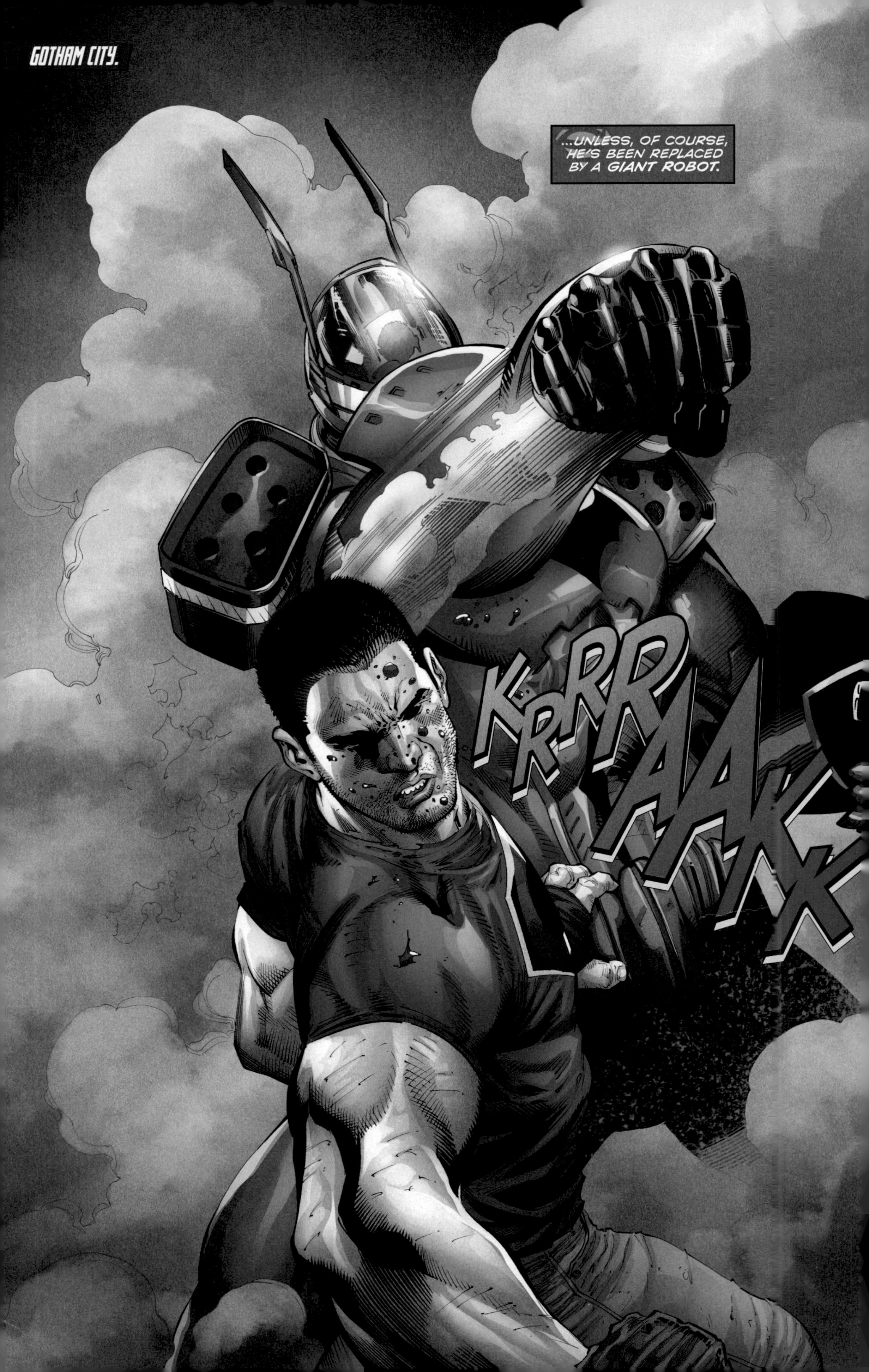
GOTHAM CITY.
...UNLESS, OF COURSE, HE'S BEEN REPLACED BY A GIANT ROBOT.
KRRRAAKK

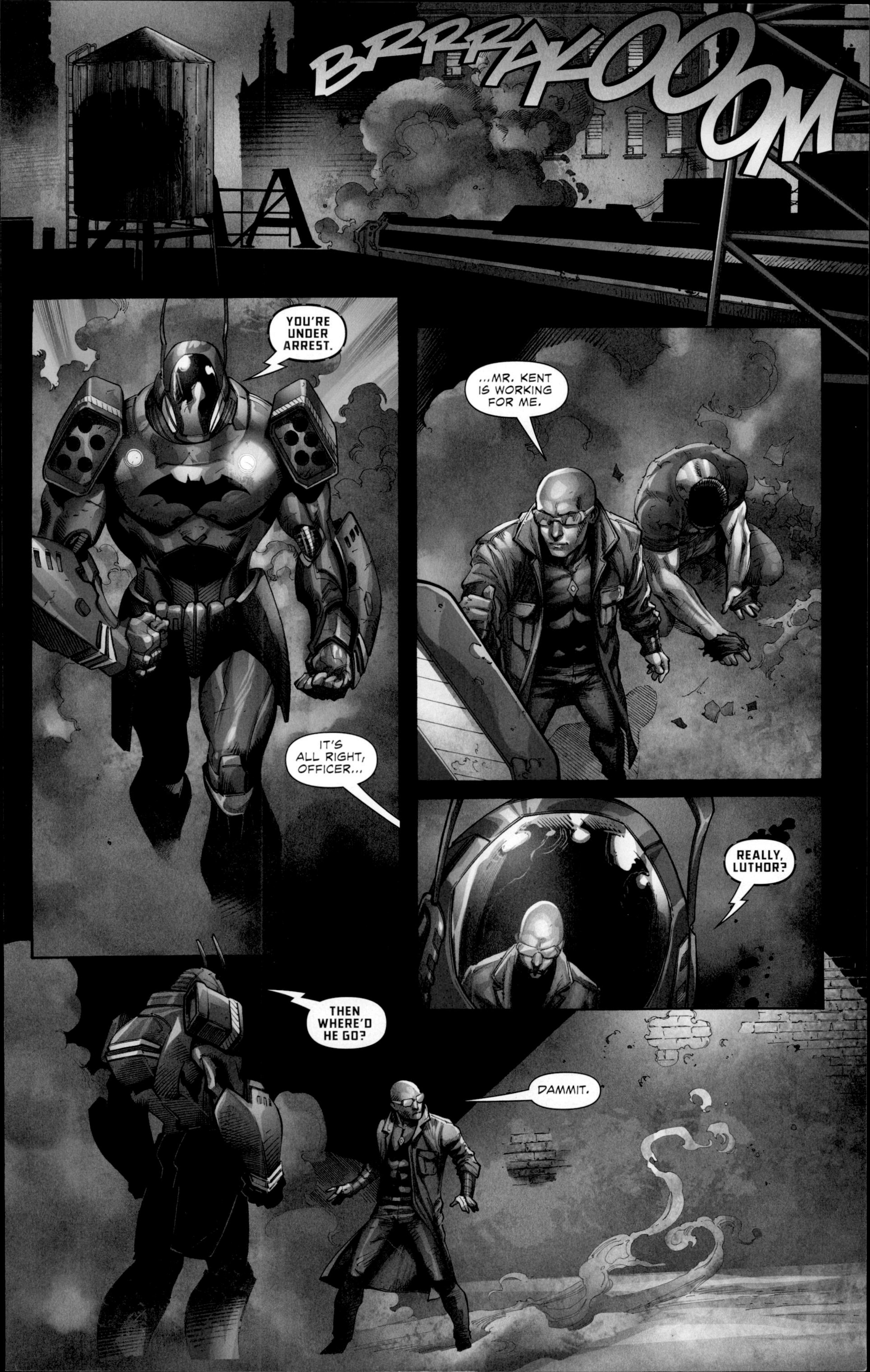
BRRRRAKOOOOM
YOU'RE UNDER ARREST.
IT'S ALL RIGHT, OFFICER...
...MR. KENT IS WORKING FOR ME.
REALLY, LUTHOR?
THEN WHERE'D HE GO?
DAMMIT.

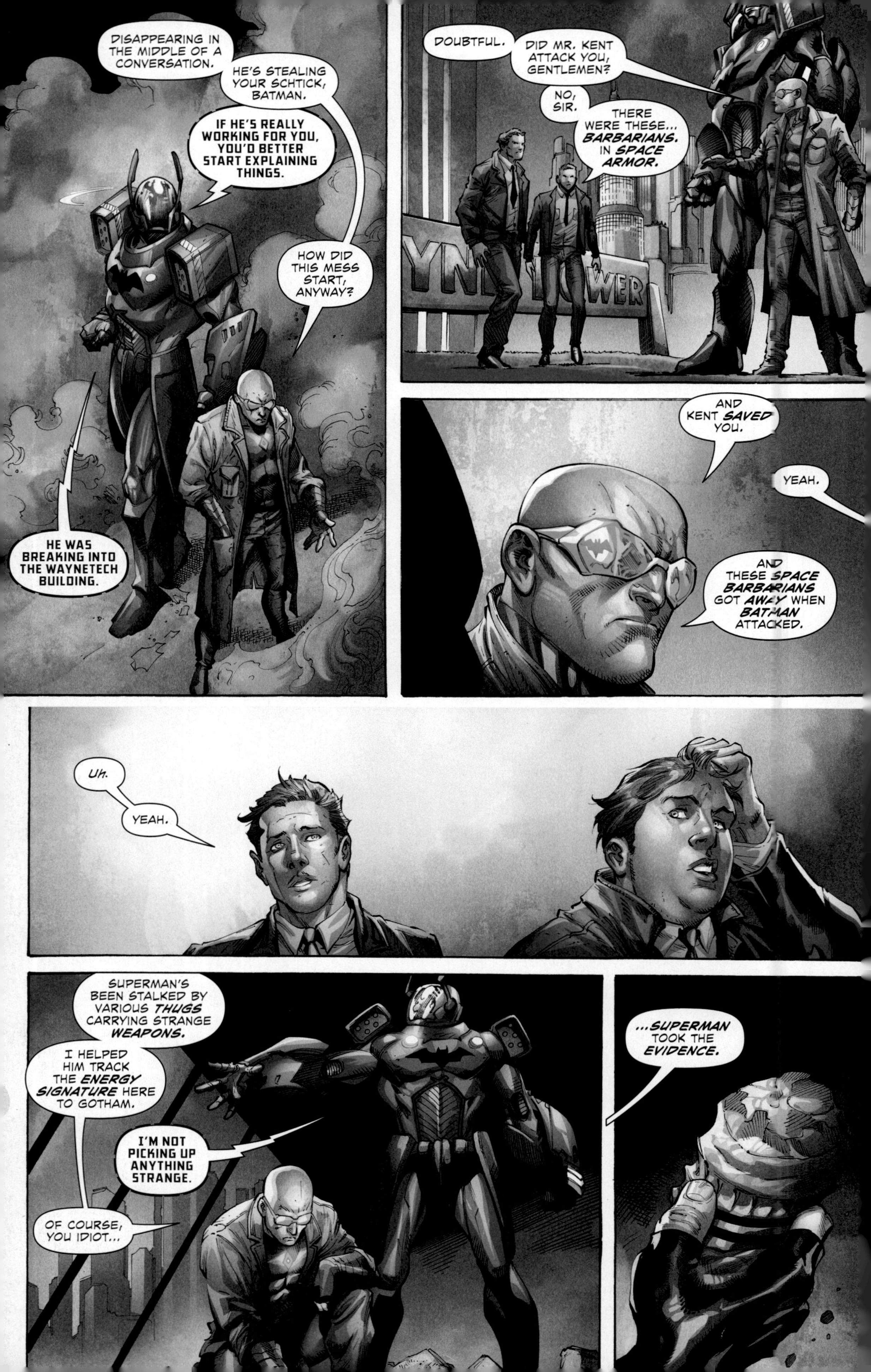
DISAPPEARING IN THE MIDDLE OF A CONVERSATION.
HE'S STEALING YOUR SCHTICK, BATMAN.
IF HE'S REALLY WORKING FOR YOU, YOU'D BETTER START EXPLAINING THINGS.
HOW DID THIS MESS START, ANYWAY?
HE WAS BREAKING INTO THE WAYNETECH BUILDING.
DOUBTFUL.
DID MR. KENT ATTACK YOU, GENTLEMEN?
NO, SIR.
THERE WERE THESE... BARBARIANS. IN SPACE ARMOR.
AND KENT SAVED YOU.
YEAH.
AND THESE SPACE BARBARIANS GOT AWAY WHEN BATMAN ATTACKED.
Uh.
YEAH.
SUPERMAN'S BEEN STALKED BY VARIOUS THUGS CARRYING STRANGE WEAPONS.
I HELPED HIM TRACK THE ENERGY SIGNATURE HERE TO GOTHAM.
I'M NOT PICKING UP ANYTHING STRANGE.
OF COURSE, YOU IDIOT...
...SUPERMAN TOOK THE EVIDENCE.

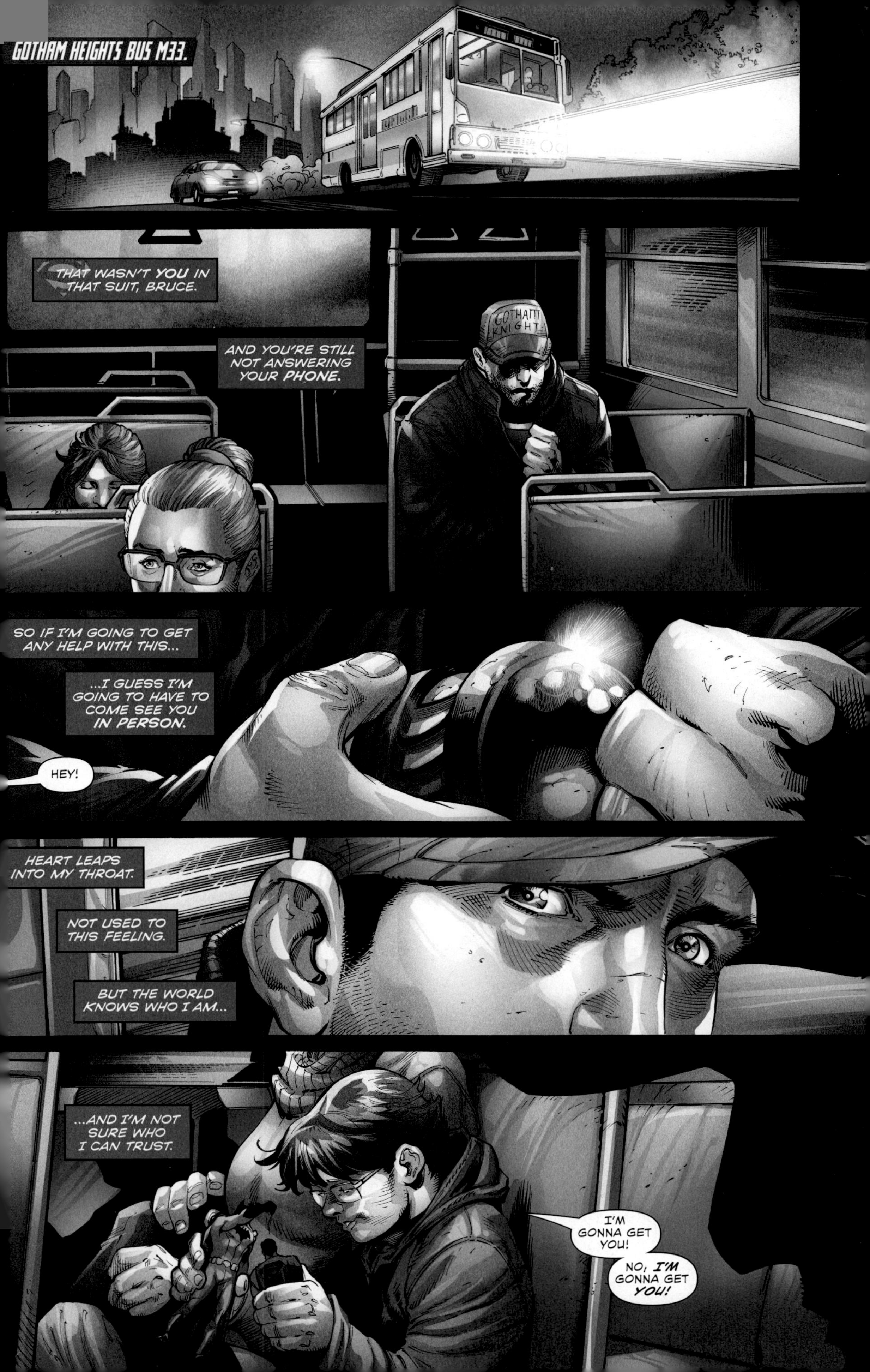
GOTHAM HEIGHTS BUS M33.
THAT WASN'T YOU IN THAT SUIT, BRUCE.
AND YOU'RE STILL NOT ANSWERING YOUR PHONE.
GOTHAM KNIGHT
SO IF I'M GOING TO GET ANY HELP WITH THIS...
...I GUESS I'M GOING TO HAVE TO COME SEE YOU IN PERSON.
HEY!
HEART LEAPS INTO MY THROAT.
NOT USED TO THIS FEELING.
BUT THE WORLD KNOWS WHO I AM...
...AND I'M NOT SURE WHO I CAN TRUST.
I'M GONNA GET YOU!
NO, I'M GONNA GET YOU!

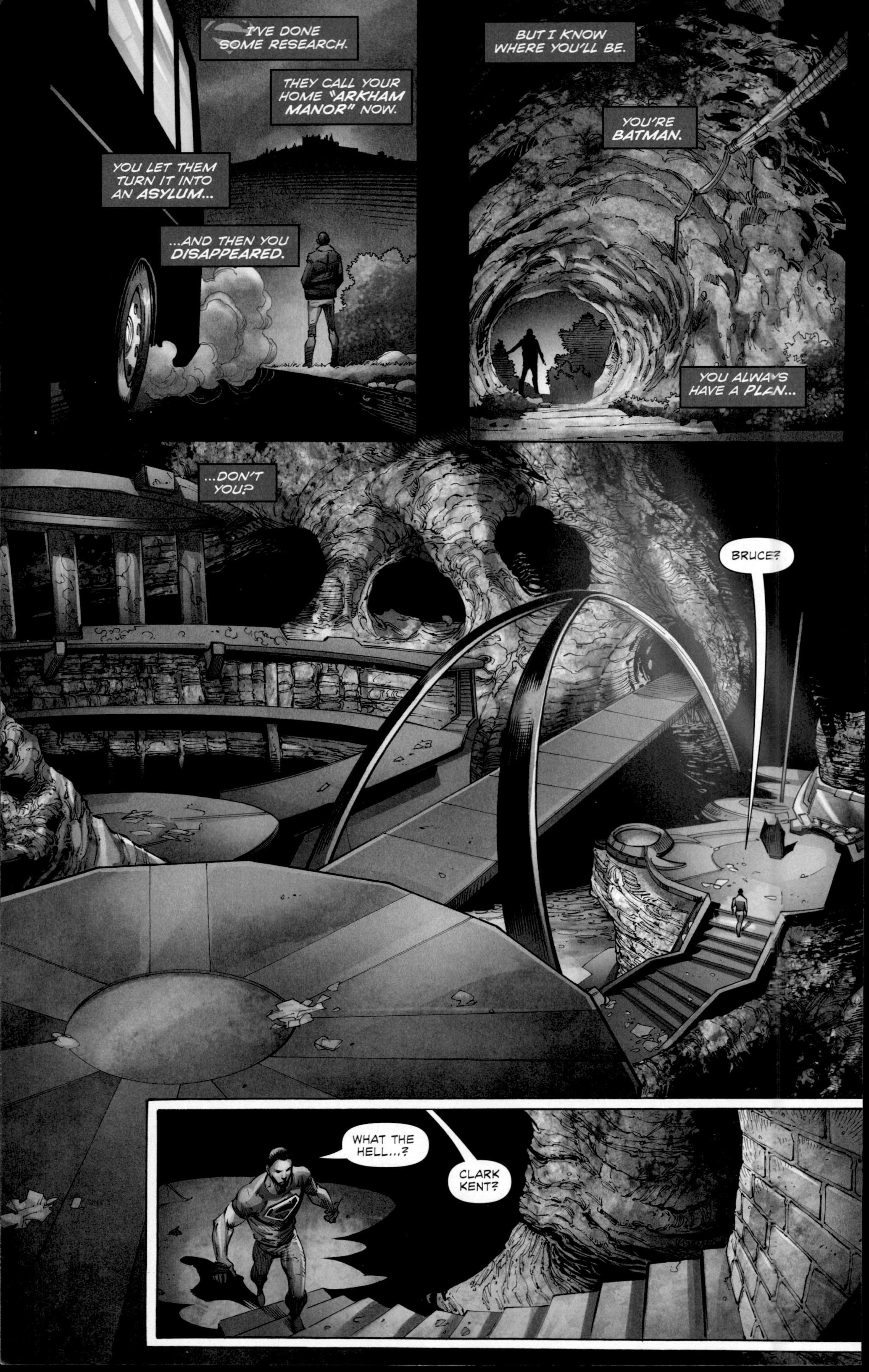
I'VE DONE SOME RESEARCH.
THEY CALL YOUR HOME "ARKHAM MANOR" NOW.
YOU LET THEM TURN IT INTO AN ASYLUM...
...AND THEN YOU DISAPPEARED.
BUT I KNOW WHERE YOU'LL BE.
YOU'RE BATMAN.
YOU ALWAYS HAVE A PLAN...
...DON'T YOU?
BRUCE?
WHAT THE HELL...?
CLARK KENT?

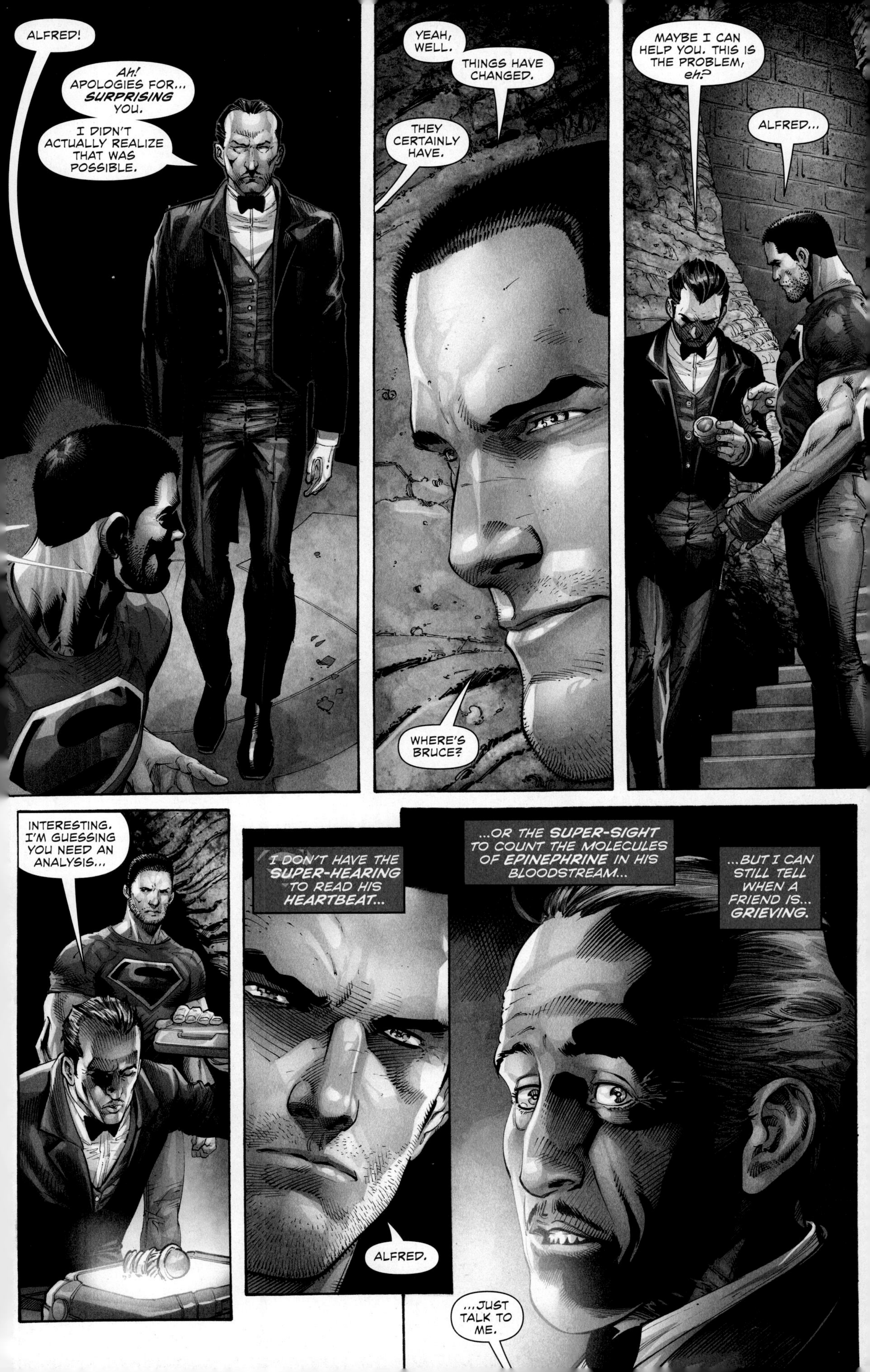
ALFRED!
Ah! APOLOGIES FOR... SURPRISING YOU.
I DIDN'T ACTUALLY REALIZE THAT WAS POSSIBLE.
YEAH, WELL.
THINGS HAVE CHANGED.
THEY CERTAINLY HAVE.
WHERE'S BRUCE?
MAYBE I CAN HELP YOU. THIS IS THE PROBLEM, eh?
ALFRED...
INTERESTING. I'M GUESSING YOU NEED AN ANALYSIS...
I DON'T HAVE THE SUPER-HEARING TO READ HIS HEARTBEAT...
...OR THE SUPER-SIGHT TO COUNT THE MOLECULES OF EPINEPHRINE IN HIS BLOODSTREAM...
...BUT I CAN STILL TELL WHEN A FRIEND IS... GRIEVING.
ALFRED.
...JUST TALK TO ME.

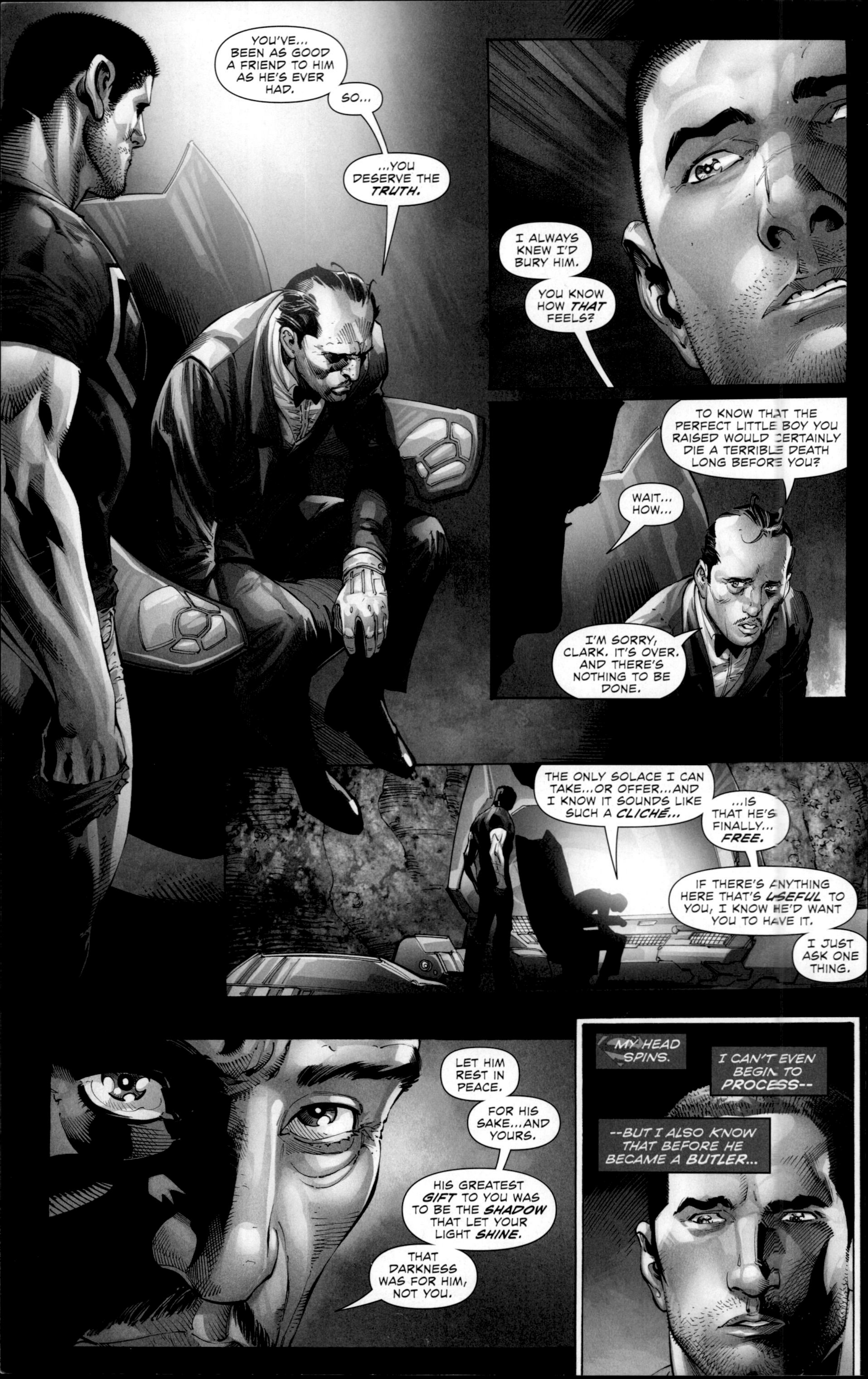

YOU'VE... BEEN AS GOOD A FRIEND TO HIM AS HE'S EVER HAD.
SO...
...YOU DESERVE THE TRUTH.
I ALWAYS KNEW I'D BURY HIM.
YOU KNOW HOW THAT FEELS?
TO KNOW THAT THE PERFECT LITTLE BOY YOU RAISED WOULD CERTAINLY DIE A TERRIBLE DEATH LONG BEFORE YOU?
WAIT... HOW...
I'M SORRY, CLARK. IT'S OVER. AND THERE'S NOTHING TO BE DONE.
THE ONLY SOLACE I CAN TAKE...OR OFFER...AND I KNOW IT SOUNDS LIKE SUCH A CLICHÉ...
...IS THAT HE'S FINALLY... FREE.
IF THERE'S ANYTHING HERE THAT'S USEFUL TO YOU, I KNOW HE'D WANT YOU TO HAVE IT.
I JUST ASK ONE THING.
LET HIM REST IN PEACE.
FOR HIS SAKE...AND YOURS.
HIS GREATEST GIFT TO YOU WAS TO BE THE SHADOW THAT LET YOUR LIGHT SHINE.
THAT DARKNESS WAS FOR HIM, NOT YOU.
MY HEAD SPINS.
I CAN'T EVEN BEGIN TO PROCESS--
--BUT I ALSO KNOW THAT BEFORE HE BECAME A BUTLER...

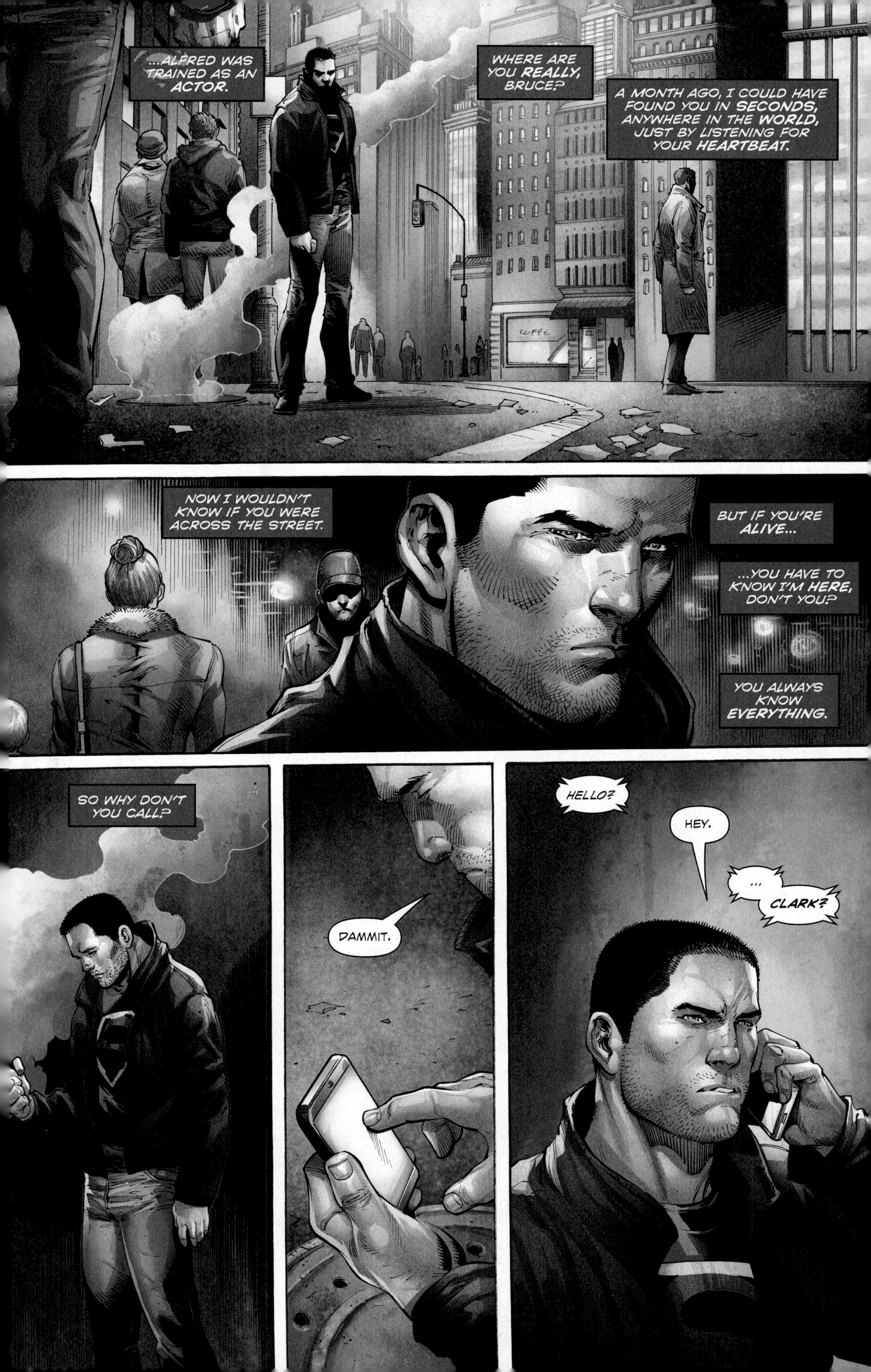
...ALFRED WAS TRAINED AS AN ACTOR.
WHERE ARE YOU REALLY, BRUCE?
A MONTH AGO, I COULD HAVE FOUND YOU IN SECONDS, ANYWHERE IN THE WORLD, JUST BY LISTENING FOR YOUR HEARTBEAT.
COFFEE
NOW I WOULDN'T KNOW IF YOU WERE ACROSS THE STREET.
BUT IF YOU'RE ALIVE...
...YOU HAVE TO KNOW I'M HERE, DON'T YOU?
YOU ALWAYS KNOW EVERYTHING.
SO WHY DON'T YOU CALL?
DAMMIT.
HELLO?
HEY.
...
CLARK?

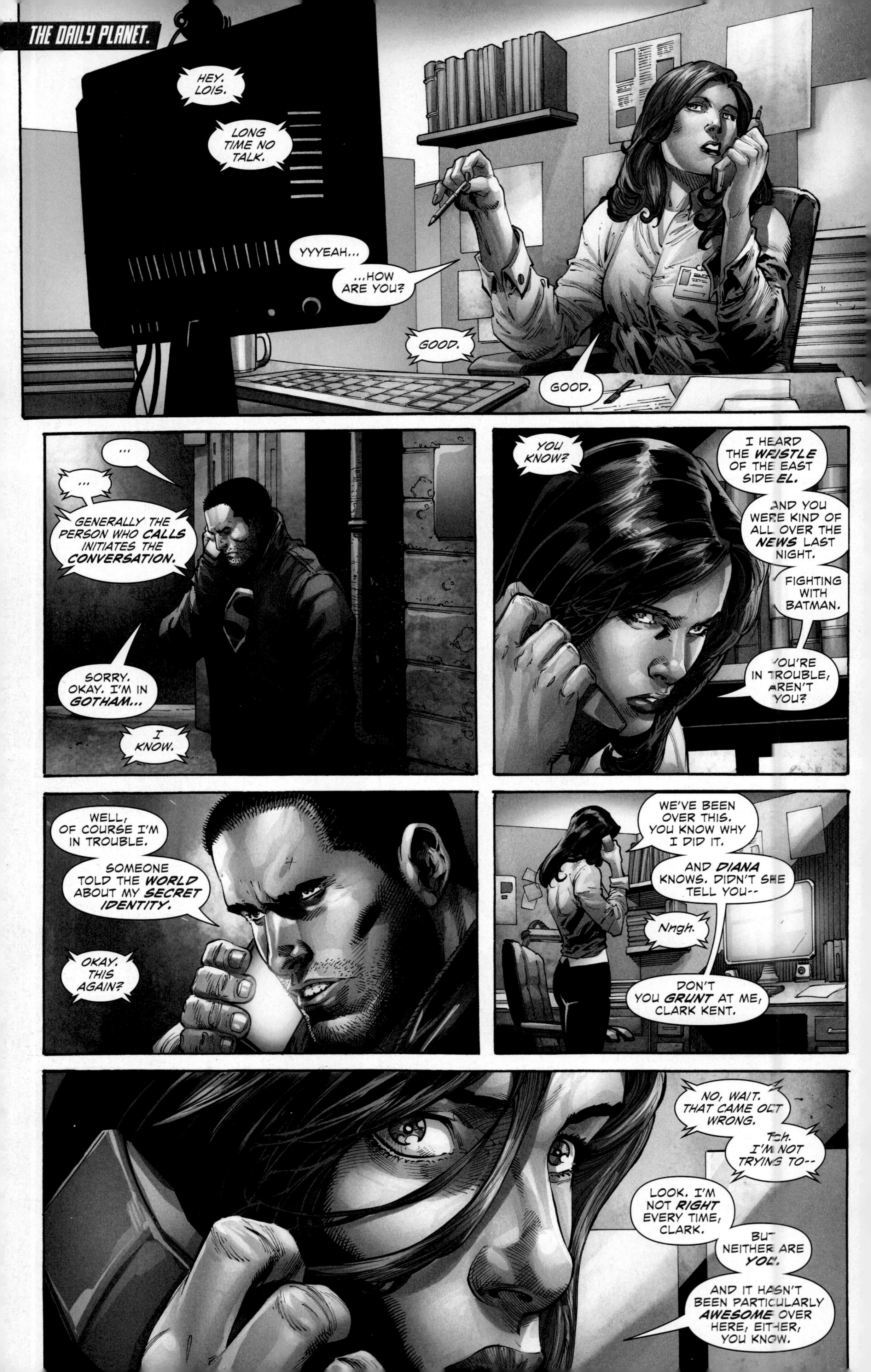
THE DAILY PLANET.
HEY. LOIS.
LONG TIME NO TALK.
YYYEAH... ...HOW ARE YOU?
GOOD.
GOOD.
...
...
GENERALLY THE PERSON WHO CALLS INITIATES THE CONVERSATION.
SORRY. OKAY. I'M IN GOTHAM...
I KNOW.
YOU KNOW?
I HEARD THE WHISTLE OF THE EAST SIDE EL.
AND YOU WERE KIND OF ALL OVER THE NEWS LAST NIGHT.
FIGHTING WITH BATMAN.
YOU'RE IN TROUBLE, AREN'T YOU?
WELL, OF COURSE I'M IN TROUBLE.
SOMEONE TOLD THE WORLD ABOUT MY SECRET IDENTITY.
OKAY. THIS AGAIN?
WE'VE BEEN OVER THIS. YOU KNOW WHY I DID IT.
AND DIANA KNOWS. DIDN'T SHE TELL YOU--
Nngh.
DON'T YOU GRUNT AT ME, CLARK KENT.
NO, WAIT. THAT CAME OUT WRONG.
Tch. I'M NOT TRYING TO--
LOOK. I'M NOT RIGHT EVERY TIME, CLARK.
BUT NEITHER ARE YOU.
AND IT HASN'T BEEN PARTICULARLY AWESOME OVER HERE, EITHER, YOU KNOW.

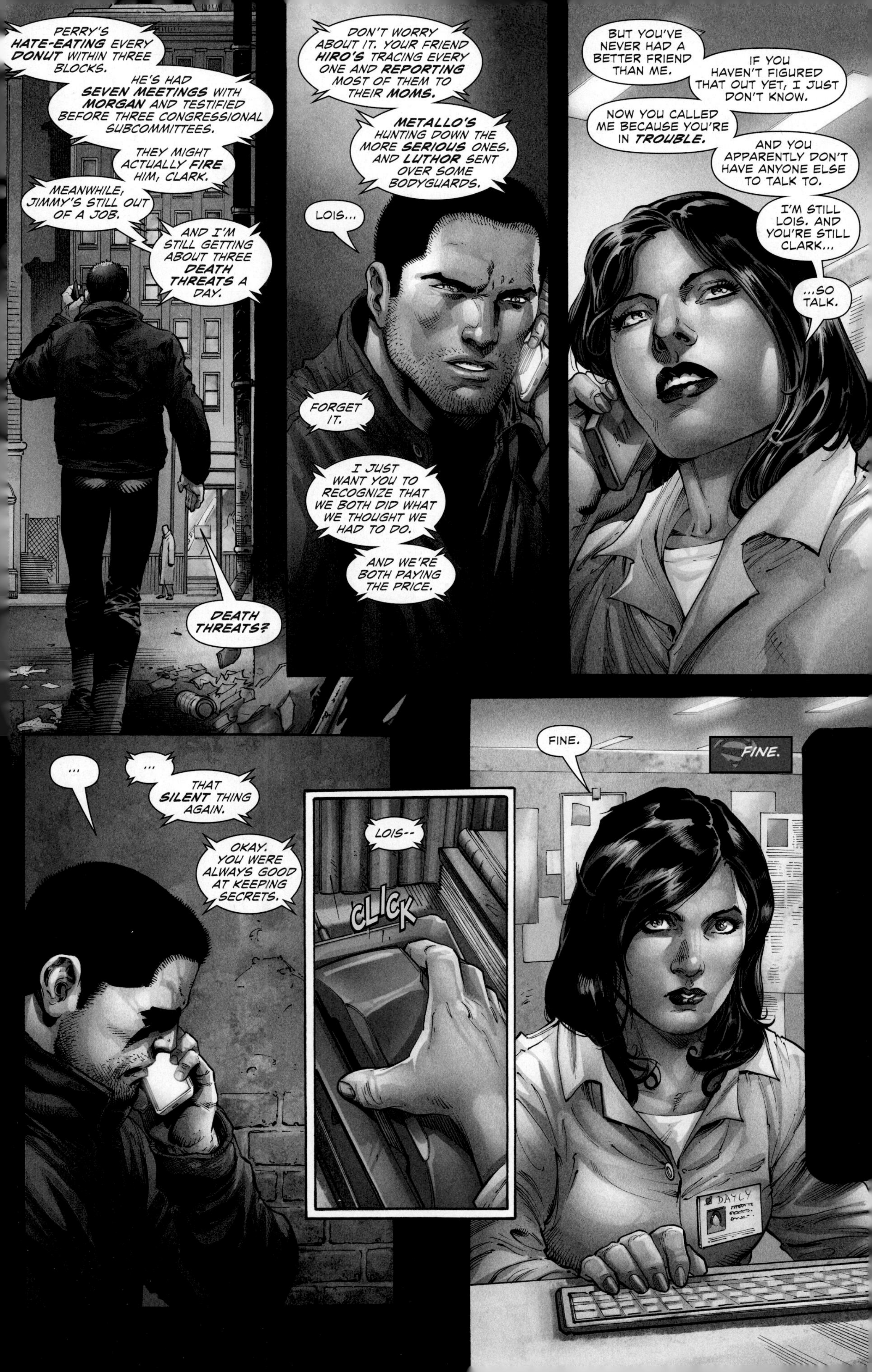
PERRY'S HATE-EATING EVERY DONUT WITHIN THREE BLOCKS.
HE'S HAD SEVEN MEETINGS WITH MORGAN AND TESTIFIED BEFORE THREE CONGRESSIONAL SUBCOMMITTEES.
THEY MIGHT ACTUALLY FIRE HIM, CLARK.
MEANWHILE, JIMMY'S STILL OUT OF A JOB.
AND I'M STILL GETTING ABOUT THREE DEATH THREATS A DAY.
DEATH THREATS?
DON'T WORRY ABOUT IT. YOUR FRIEND HIRO'S TRACING EVERY ONE AND REPORTING MOST OF THEM TO THEIR MOMS.
METALLO'S HUNTING DOWN THE MORE SERIOUS ONES. AND LUTHOR SENT OVER SOME BODYGUARDS.
LOIS...
FORGET IT.
I JUST WANT YOU TO RECOGNIZE THAT WE BOTH DID WHAT WE THOUGHT WE HAD TO DO.
AND WE'RE BOTH PAYING THE PRICE.
BUT YOU'VE NEVER HAD A BETTER FRIEND THAN ME.
IF YOU HAVEN'T FIGURED THAT OUT YET, I JUST DON'T KNOW.
NOW YOU CALLED ME BECAUSE YOU'RE IN TROUBLE.
AND YOU APPARENTLY DON'T HAVE ANYONE ELSE TO TALK TO.
I'M STILL LOIS. AND YOU'RE STILL CLARK...
...SO TALK.
...
...
THAT SILENT THING AGAIN.
OKAY. YOU WERE ALWAYS GOOD AT KEEPING SECRETS.
LOIS--
CLICK
FINE.
FINE.
DAYLY

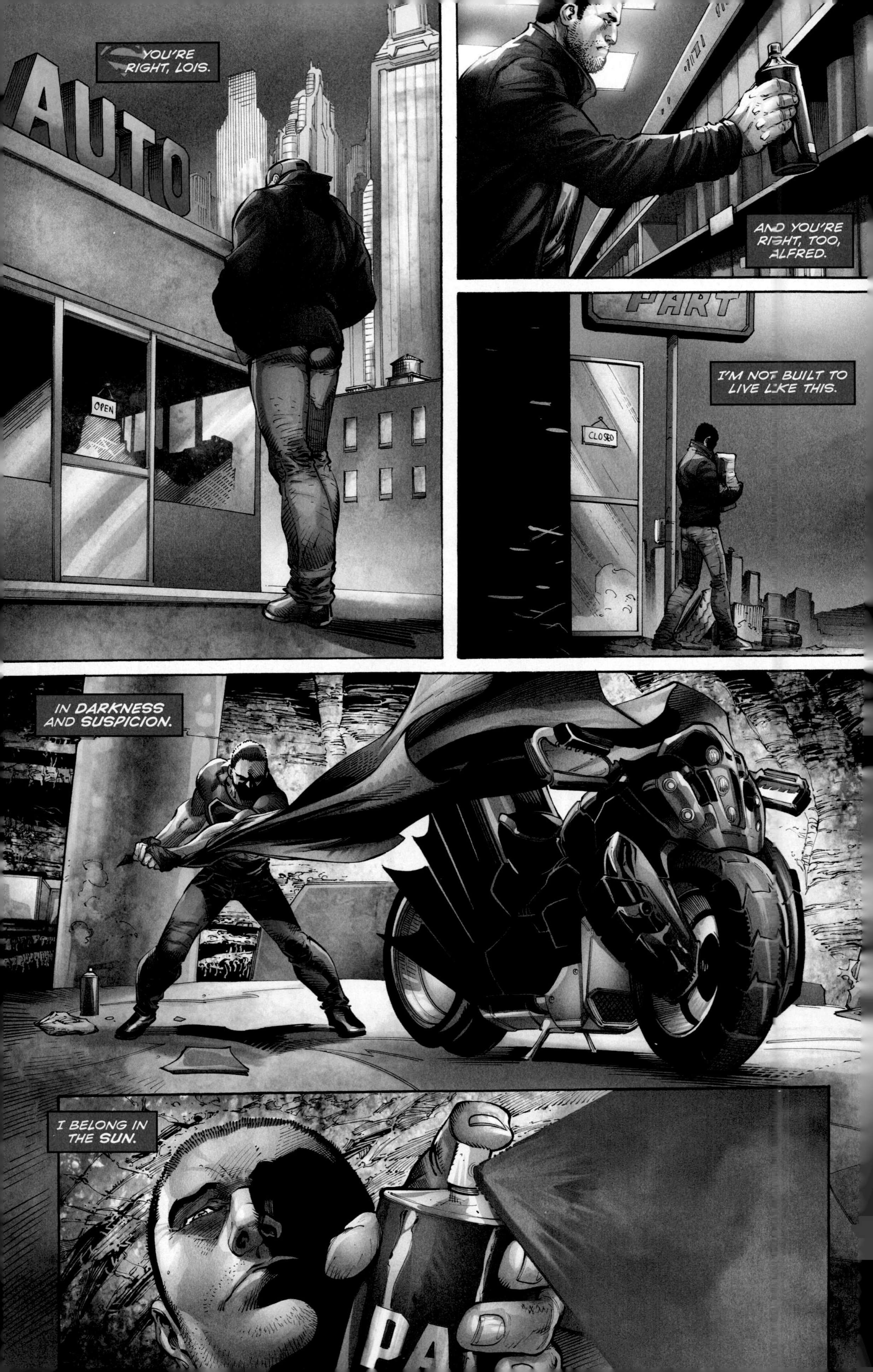
YOU'RE RIGHT, LOIS.
AUTO
OPEN
AND YOU'RE RIGHT, TOO, ALFRED.
PART
I'M NOT BUILT TO LIVE LIKE THIS.
CLOSED
IN DARKNESS AND SUSPICION.
I BELONG IN THE SUN.

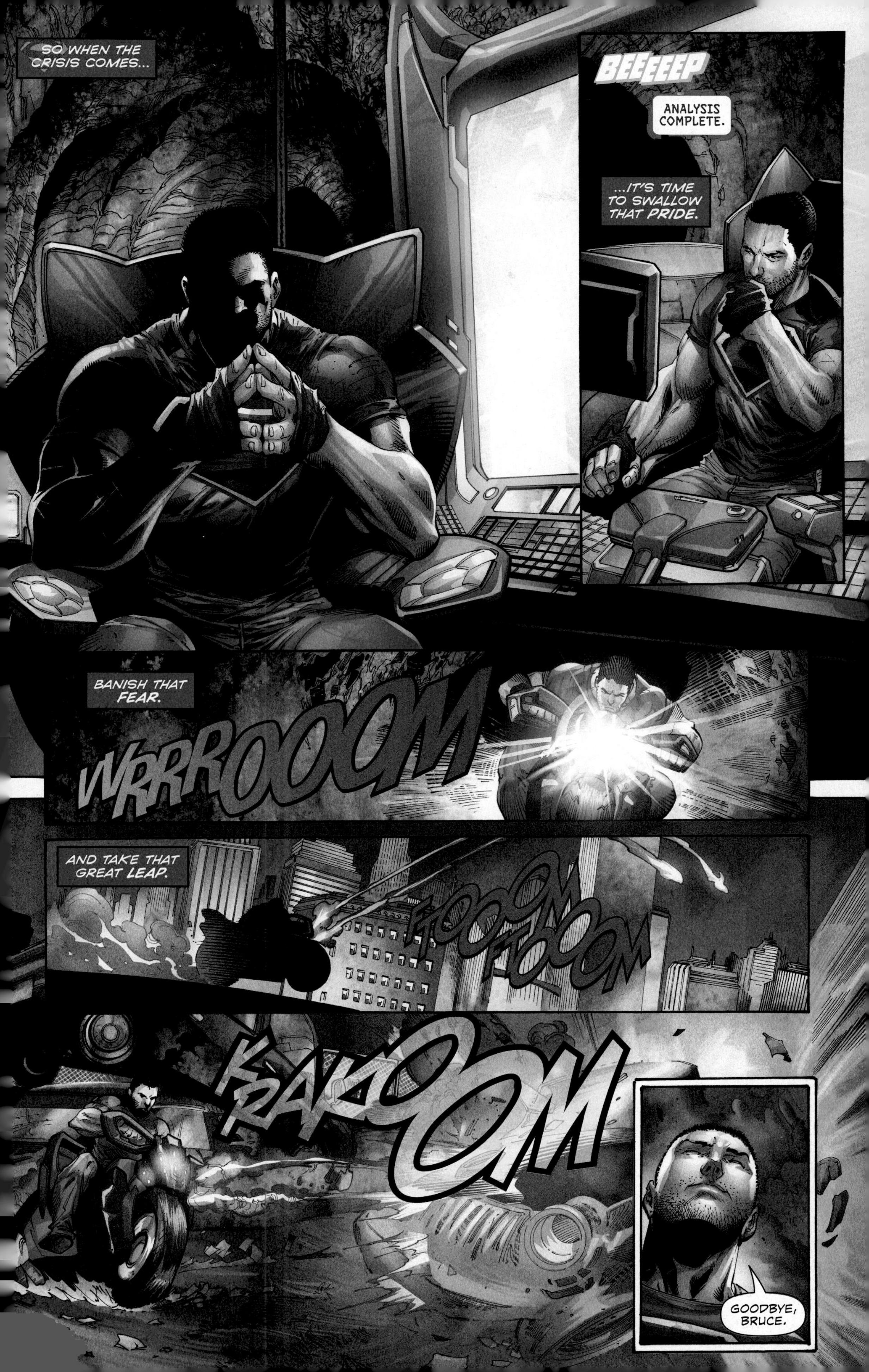
SO WHEN THE CRISIS COMES...
BEEEEEP
ANALYSIS COMPLETE.
...IT'S TIME TO SWALLOW THAT PRIDE.
BANISH THAT FEAR.
VVRRROOOM
AND TAKE THAT GREAT LEAP.
FOOOM
FOOOM
KRAKOOM
GOODBYE, BRUCE.

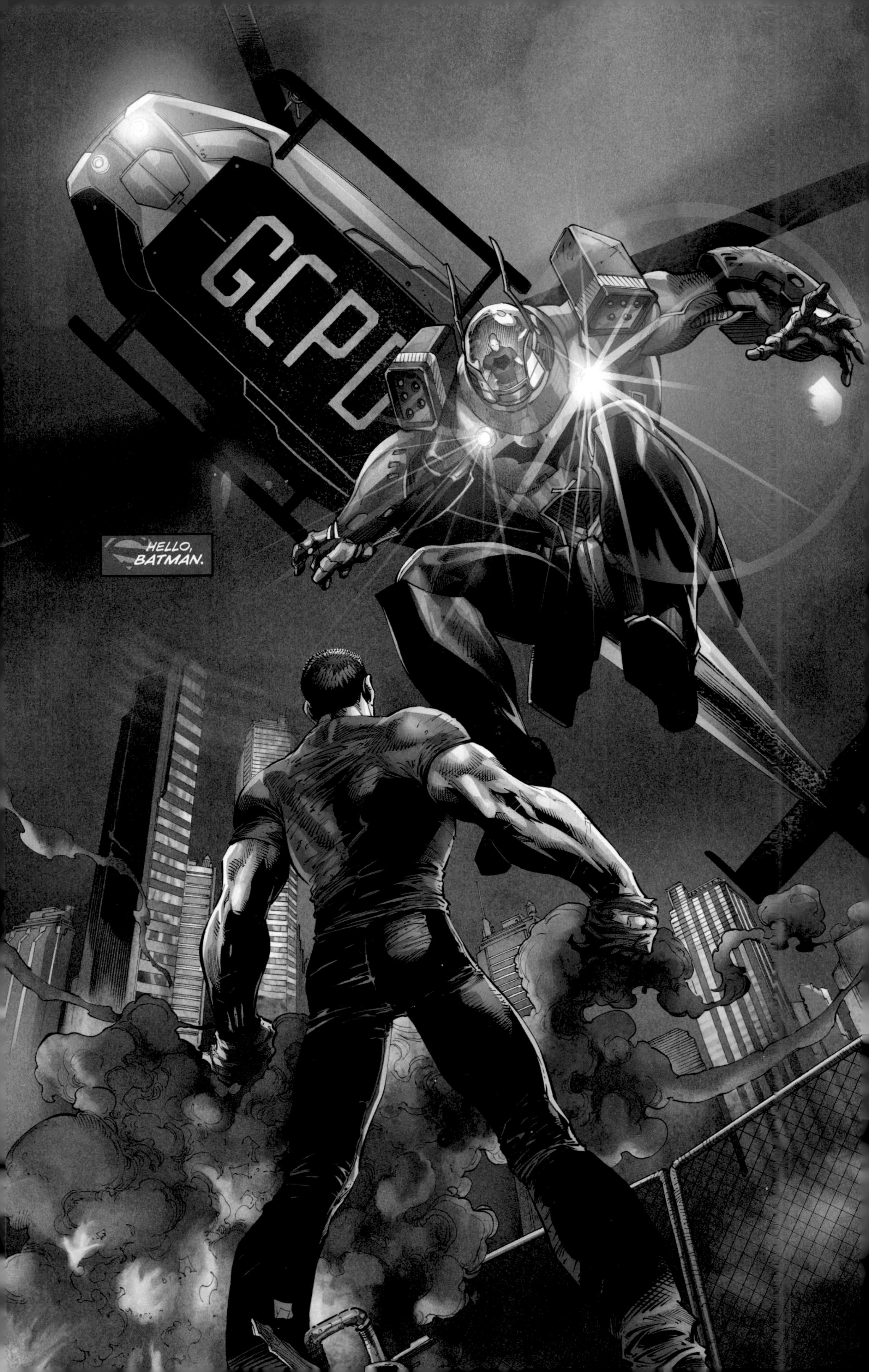

HELLO, BATMAN.
GCPD

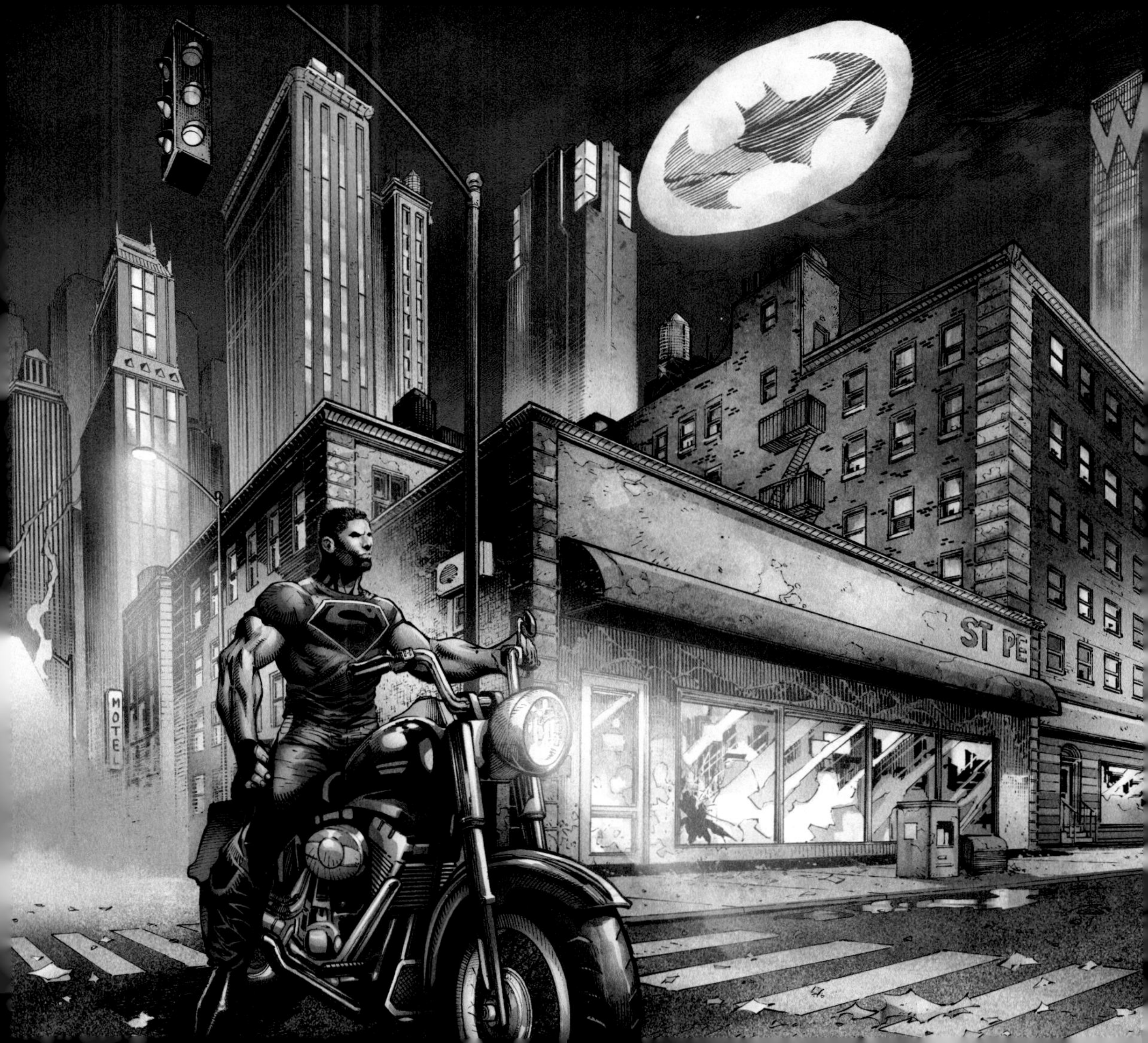
MOTEL
ST PE

TRUTH HURTS PART TWO

GREG PAK writer **ARDIAN SYAF** penciller **VICENTE CIFUENTES** inker **DEAN WHITE BETH SOTELO BLOND** colorists **ROB LEIGH** letterer
ARDIAN SYAF DANNY MIKI ULISES ARREOLA cover

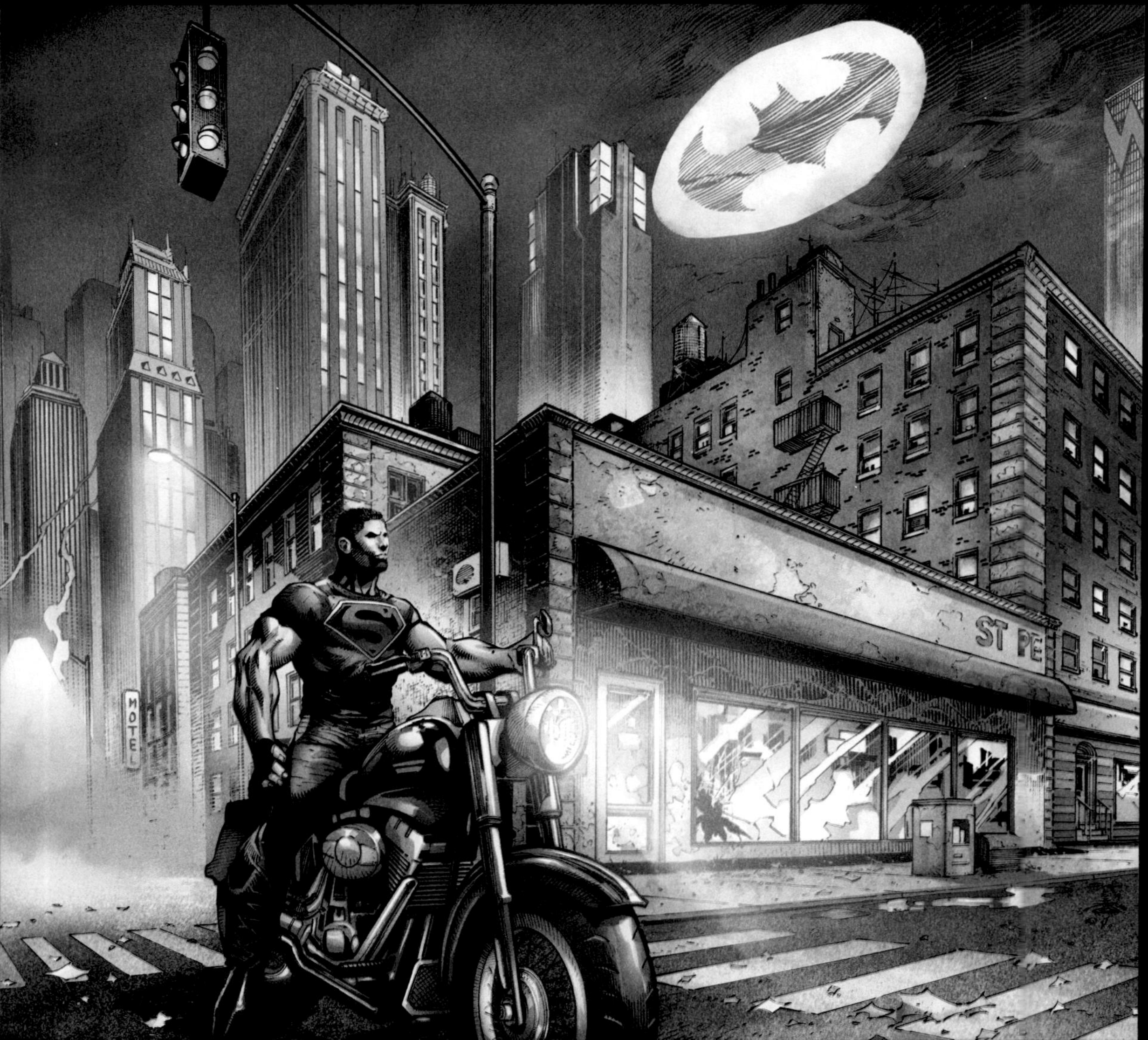
MOTEL
ST PE

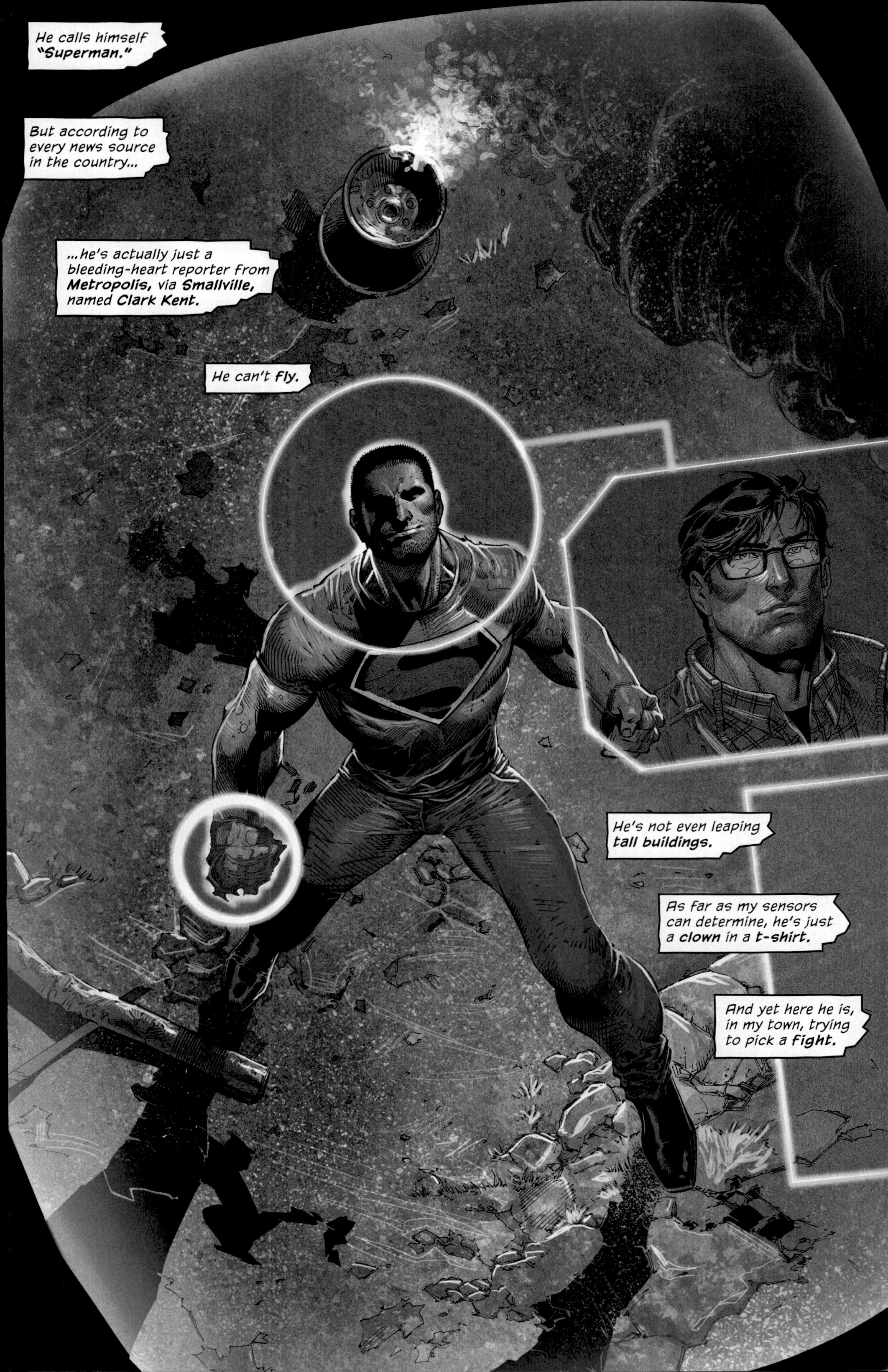
He calls himself "Superman."
But according to every news source in the country...
...he's actually just a bleeding-heart reporter from Metropolis, via Smallville, named Clark Kent.
He can't fly.
He's not even leaping tall buildings.
As far as my sensors can determine, he's just a clown in a t-shirt.
And yet here he is, in my town, trying to pick a fight.

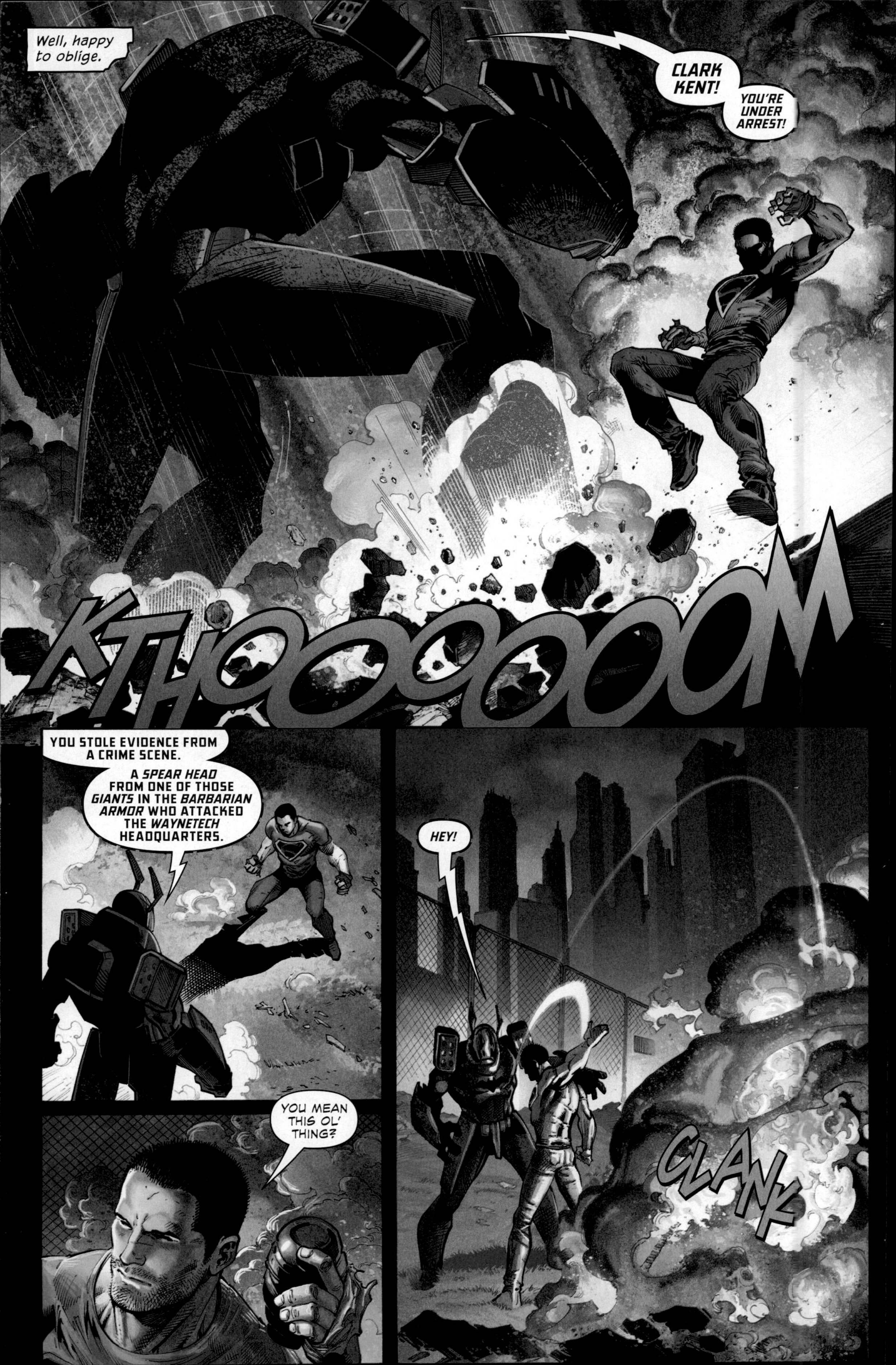
Well, happy to oblige.
CLARK KENT!
YOU'RE UNDER ARREST!
KTHOOOOOOOM
YOU STOLE EVIDENCE FROM A CRIME SCENE.
A SPEAR HEAD FROM ONE OF THOSE GIANTS IN THE BARBARIAN ARMOR WHO ATTACKED THE WAYNETECH HEADQUARTERS.
YOU MEAN THIS OL' THING?
HEY!
CLANK

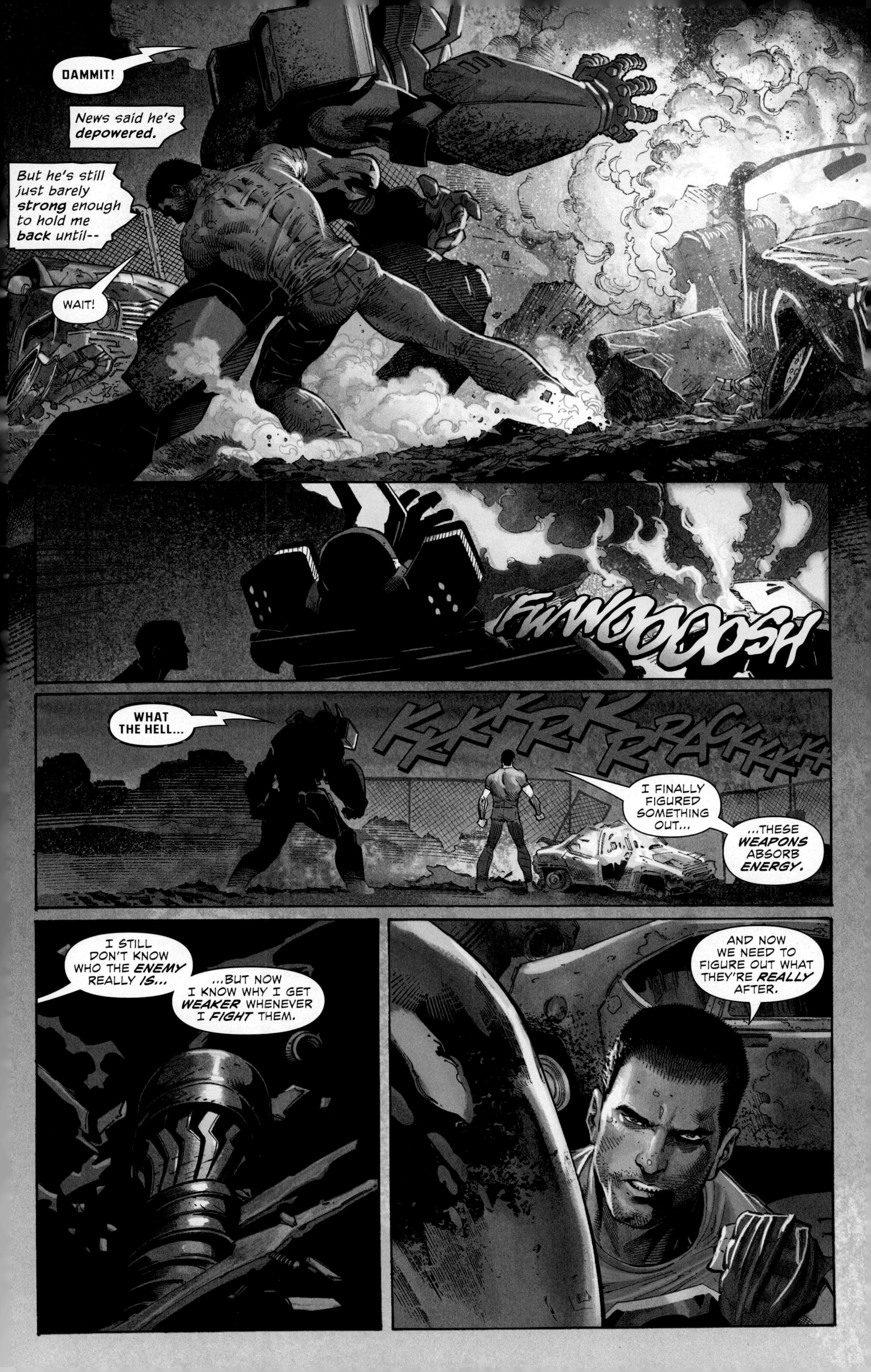
DAMMIT!
News said he's **depowered.**
But he's still just barely **strong** enough to hold me **back** until--
WAIT!
FWWOOOOOSH
WHAT THE HELL...
KKKRK RRACKKKK
I FINALLY FIGURED SOMETHING OUT...
...THESE ***WEAPONS*** ABSORB ***ENERGY.***
I STILL DON'T KNOW WHO THE ***ENEMY*** REALLY ***IS...***
...BUT NOW I KNOW WHY I GET ***WEAKER*** WHENEVER I ***FIGHT*** THEM.
AND NOW WE NEED TO FIGURE OUT WHAT THEY'RE ***REALLY*** AFTER.

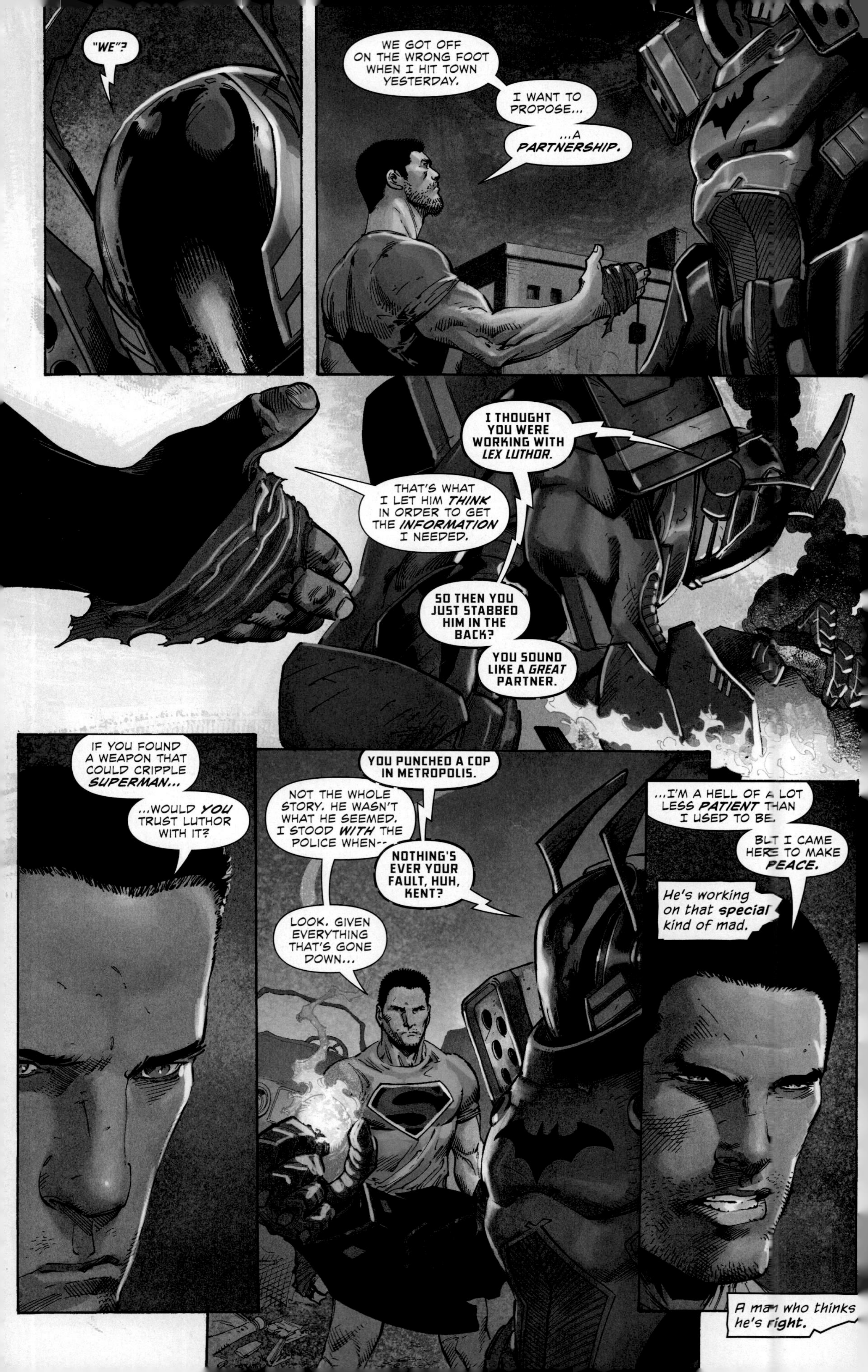
"WE"?
WE GOT OFF ON THE WRONG FOOT WHEN I HIT TOWN YESTERDAY.
I WANT TO PROPOSE...
...A PARTNERSHIP.
I THOUGHT YOU WERE WORKING WITH LEX LUTHOR.
THAT'S WHAT I LET HIM THINK IN ORDER TO GET THE INFORMATION I NEEDED.
SO THEN YOU JUST STABBED HIM IN THE BACK?
YOU SOUND LIKE A GREAT PARTNER.
IF YOU FOUND A WEAPON THAT COULD CRIPPLE SUPERMAN...
...WOULD YOU TRUST LUTHOR WITH IT?
YOU PUNCHED A COP IN METROPOLIS.
NOT THE WHOLE STORY. HE WASN'T WHAT HE SEEMED. I STOOD WITH THE POLICE WHEN--
NOTHING'S EVER YOUR FAULT, HUH, KENT?
LOOK. GIVEN EVERYTHING THAT'S GONE DOWN...
...I'M A HELL OF A LOT LESS PATIENT THAN I USED TO BE.
BUT I CAME HERE TO MAKE PEACE.
He's working on that special kind of mad.
A man who thinks he's right.

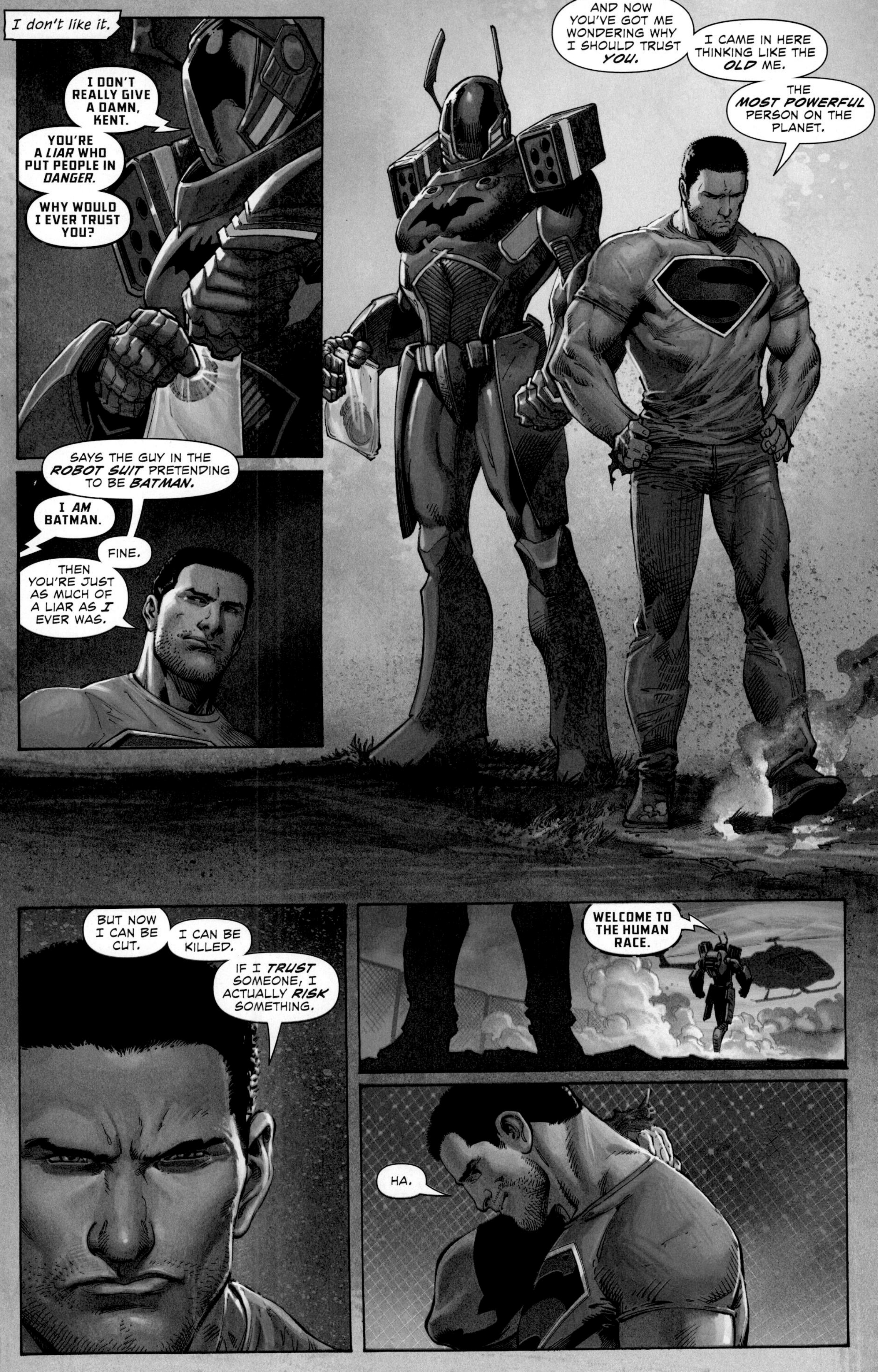
I don't like it.
I DON'T REALLY GIVE A DAMN, KENT.
YOU'RE A LIAR WHO PUT PEOPLE IN DANGER.
WHY WOULD I EVER TRUST YOU?
SAYS THE GUY IN THE ROBOT SUIT PRETENDING TO BE BATMAN.
I AM BATMAN.
FINE.
THEN YOU'RE JUST AS MUCH OF A LIAR AS I EVER WAS.
AND NOW YOU'VE GOT ME WONDERING WHY I SHOULD TRUST YOU.
I CAME IN HERE THINKING LIKE THE OLD ME.
THE MOST POWERFUL PERSON ON THE PLANET.
BUT NOW I CAN BE CUT.
I CAN BE KILLED.
IF I TRUST SOMEONE, I ACTUALLY RISK SOMETHING.
WELCOME TO THE HUMAN RACE.
HA.

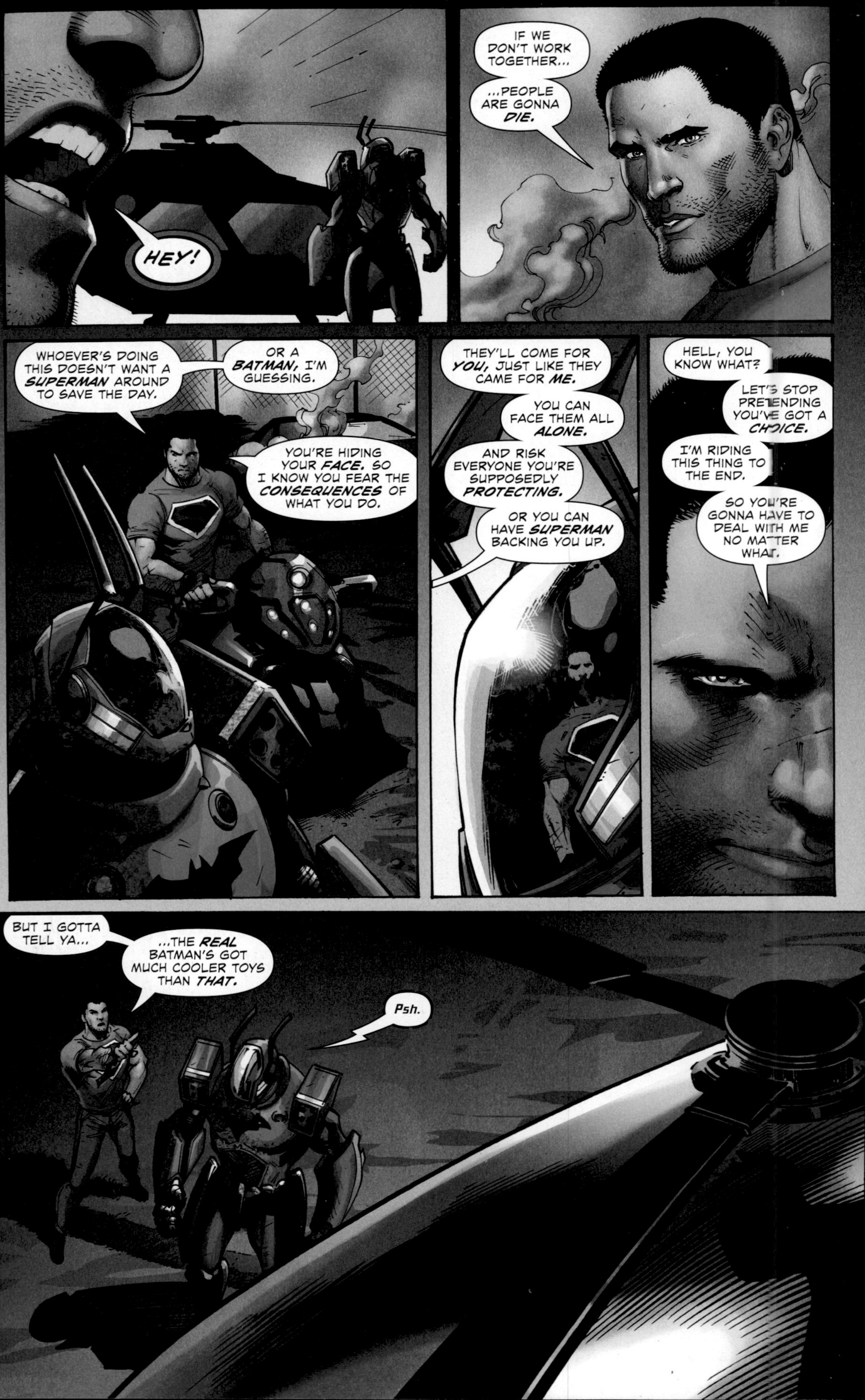
HEY!
IF WE DON'T WORK TOGETHER...
...PEOPLE ARE GONNA DIE.
WHOEVER'S DOING THIS DOESN'T WANT A SUPERMAN AROUND TO SAVE THE DAY.
OR A BATMAN, I'M GUESSING.
YOU'RE HIDING YOUR FACE. SO I KNOW YOU FEAR THE CONSEQUENCES OF WHAT YOU DO.
THEY'LL COME FOR YOU, JUST LIKE THEY CAME FOR ME.
YOU CAN FACE THEM ALL ALONE.
AND RISK EVERYONE YOU'RE SUPPOSEDLY PROTECTING.
OR YOU CAN HAVE SUPERMAN BACKING YOU UP.
HELL, YOU KNOW WHAT?
LET'S STOP PRETENDING YOU'VE GOT A CHOICE.
I'M RIDING THIS THING TO THE END.
SO YOU'RE GONNA HAVE TO DEAL WITH ME NO MATTER WHAT.
BUT I GOTTA TELL YA...
...THE REAL BATMAN'S GOT MUCH COOLER TOYS THAN THAT.
Psh.

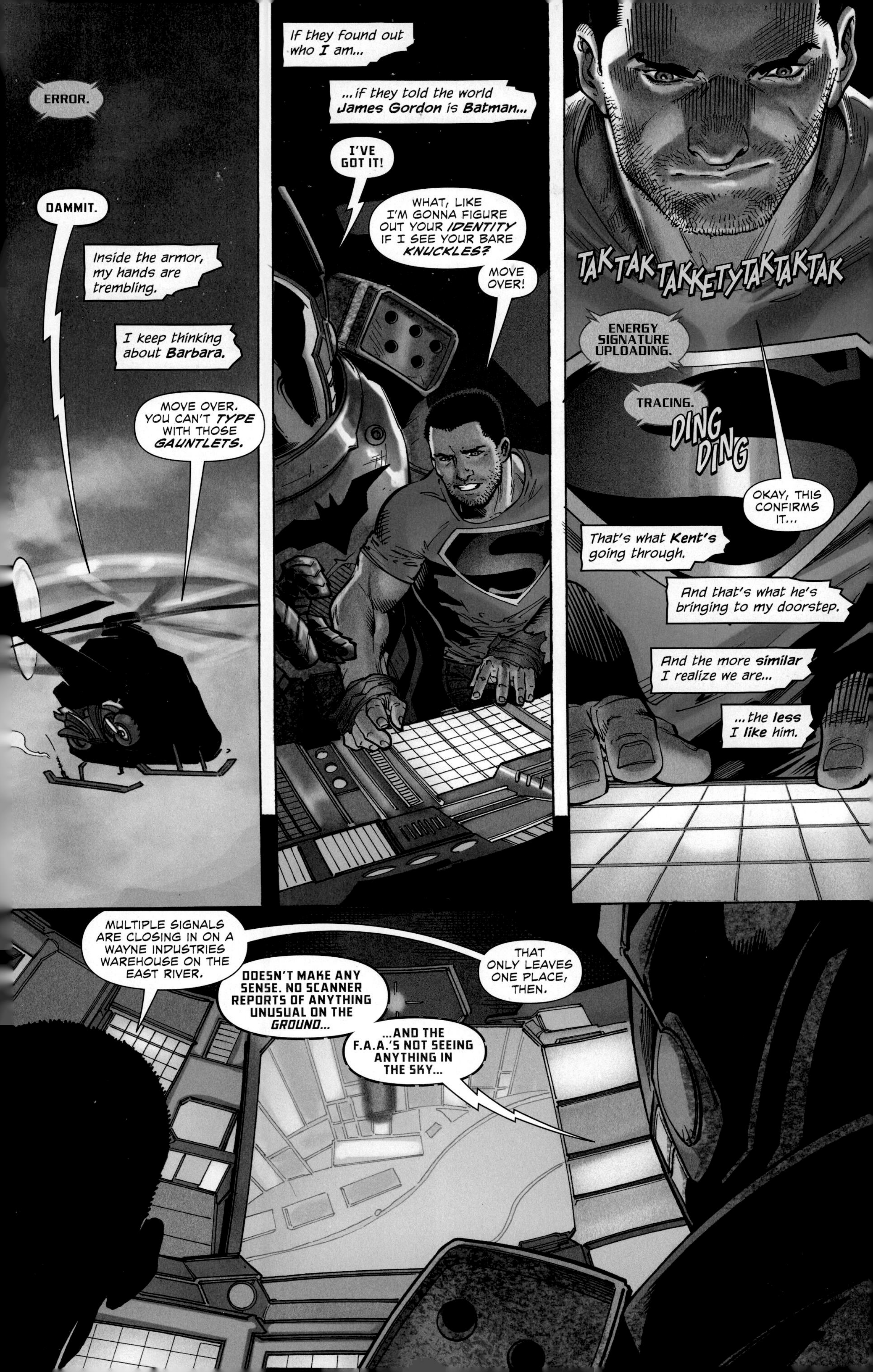
ERROR.
DAMMIT.
Inside the armor, my hands are trembling.
I keep thinking about Barbara.
MOVE OVER. YOU CAN'T TYPE WITH THOSE GAUNTLETS.
If they found out who I am...
...if they told the world James Gordon is Batman...
I'VE GOT IT!
WHAT, LIKE I'M GONNA FIGURE OUT YOUR IDENTITY IF I SEE YOUR BARE KNUCKLES?
MOVE OVER!
TAKTAKTAKKETYTAKTAKTAK
ENERGY SIGNATURE UPLOADING.
TRACING.
DING DING
OKAY, THIS CONFIRMS IT...
That's what Kent's going through.
And that's what he's bringing to my doorstep.
And the more similar I realize we are...
...the less I like him.
MULTIPLE SIGNALS ARE CLOSING IN ON A WAYNE INDUSTRIES WAREHOUSE ON THE EAST RIVER.
DOESN'T MAKE ANY SENSE. NO SCANNER REPORTS OF ANYTHING UNUSUAL ON THE GROUND...
...AND THE F.A.A.'S NOT SEEING ANYTHING IN THE SKY...
THAT ONLY LEAVES ONE PLACE, THEN.

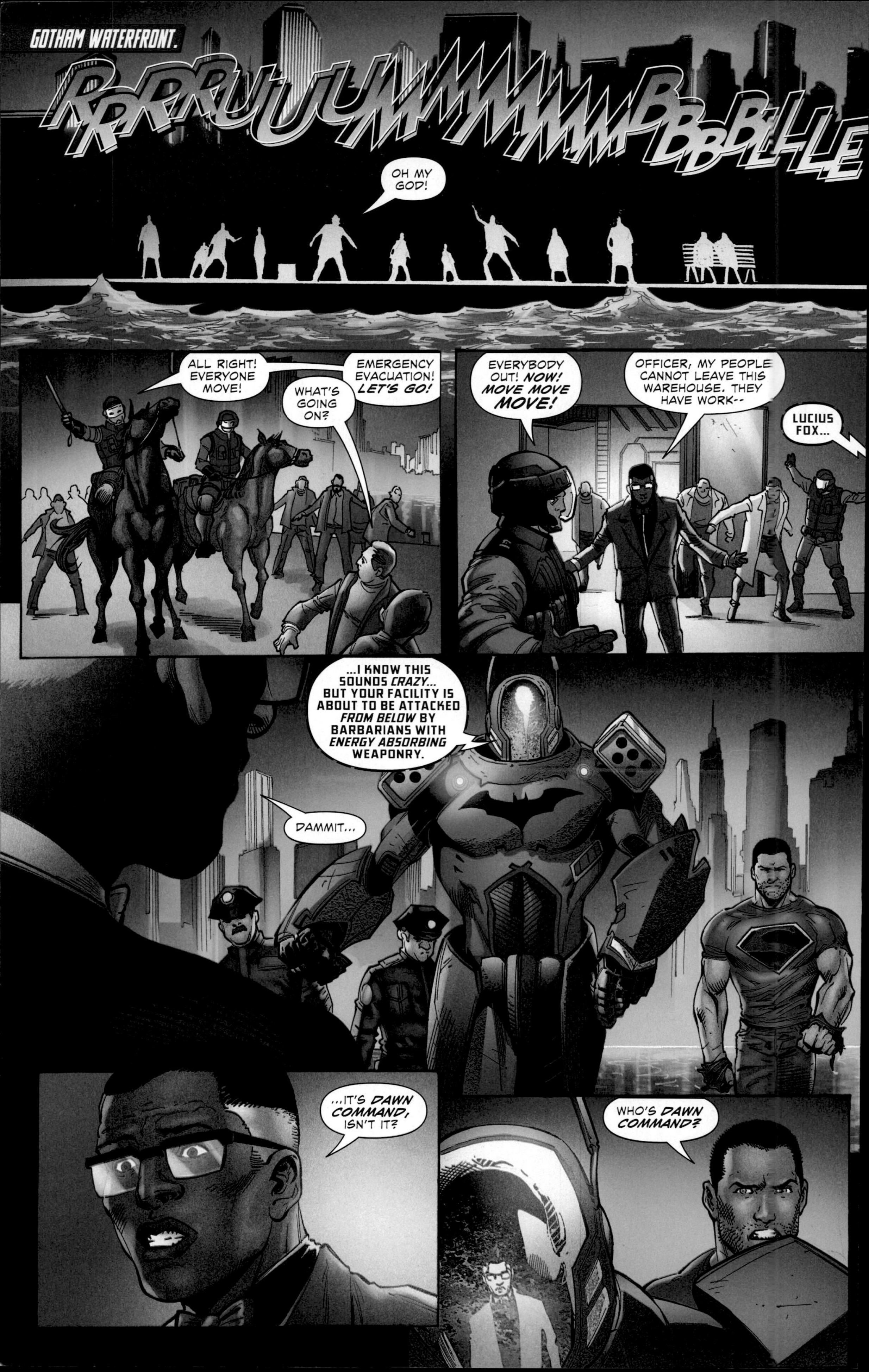
GOTHAM WATERFRONT.
RRRRRUUUUMMMMMMMMBBBBLLLE
OH MY GOD!
ALL RIGHT! EVERYONE MOVE!
EMERGENCY EVACUATION! LET'S GO!
WHAT'S GOING ON?
EVERYBODY OUT! NOW! MOVE MOVE MOVE!
OFFICER, MY PEOPLE CANNOT LEAVE THIS WAREHOUSE. THEY HAVE WORK--
LUCIUS FOX...
...I KNOW THIS SOUNDS CRAZY... BUT YOUR FACILITY IS ABOUT TO BE ATTACKED FROM BELOW BY BARBARIANS WITH ENERGY ABSORBING WEAPONRY.
DAMMIT...
...IT'S DAWN COMMAND, ISN'T IT?
WHO'S DAWN COMMAND?

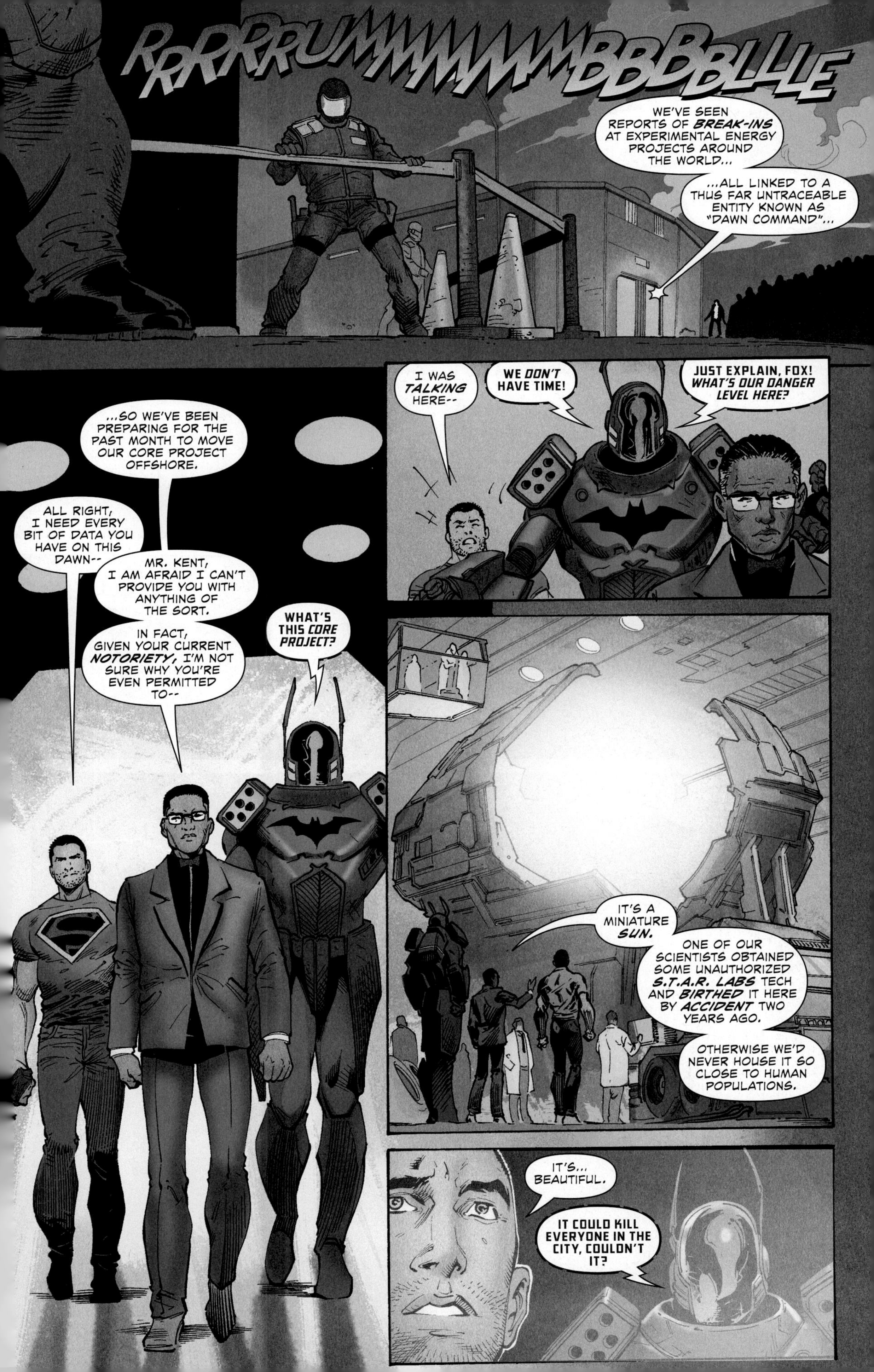
RRRRRUMMMMMMMBBBBBLLLE
WE'VE SEEN REPORTS OF BREAK-INS AT EXPERIMENTAL ENERGY PROJECTS AROUND THE WORLD...
...ALL LINKED TO A THUS FAR UNTRACEABLE ENTITY KNOWN AS "DAWN COMMAND"...
...SO WE'VE BEEN PREPARING FOR THE PAST MONTH TO MOVE OUR CORE PROJECT OFFSHORE.
ALL RIGHT, I NEED EVERY BIT OF DATA YOU HAVE ON THIS DAWN--
MR. KENT, I AM AFRAID I CAN'T PROVIDE YOU WITH ANYTHING OF THE SORT.
IN FACT, GIVEN YOUR CURRENT NOTORIETY, I'M NOT SURE WHY YOU'RE EVEN PERMITTED TO--
WHAT'S THIS CORE PROJECT?
I WAS TALKING HERE--
WE DON'T HAVE TIME!
JUST EXPLAIN, FOX! WHAT'S OUR DANGER LEVEL HERE?
IT'S A MINIATURE SUN.
ONE OF OUR SCIENTISTS OBTAINED SOME UNAUTHORIZED S.T.A.R. LABS TECH AND BIRTHED IT HERE BY ACCIDENT TWO YEARS AGO.
OTHERWISE WE'D NEVER HOUSE IT SO CLOSE TO HUMAN POPULATIONS.
IT'S... BEAUTIFUL.
IT COULD KILL EVERYONE IN THE CITY, COULDN'T IT?

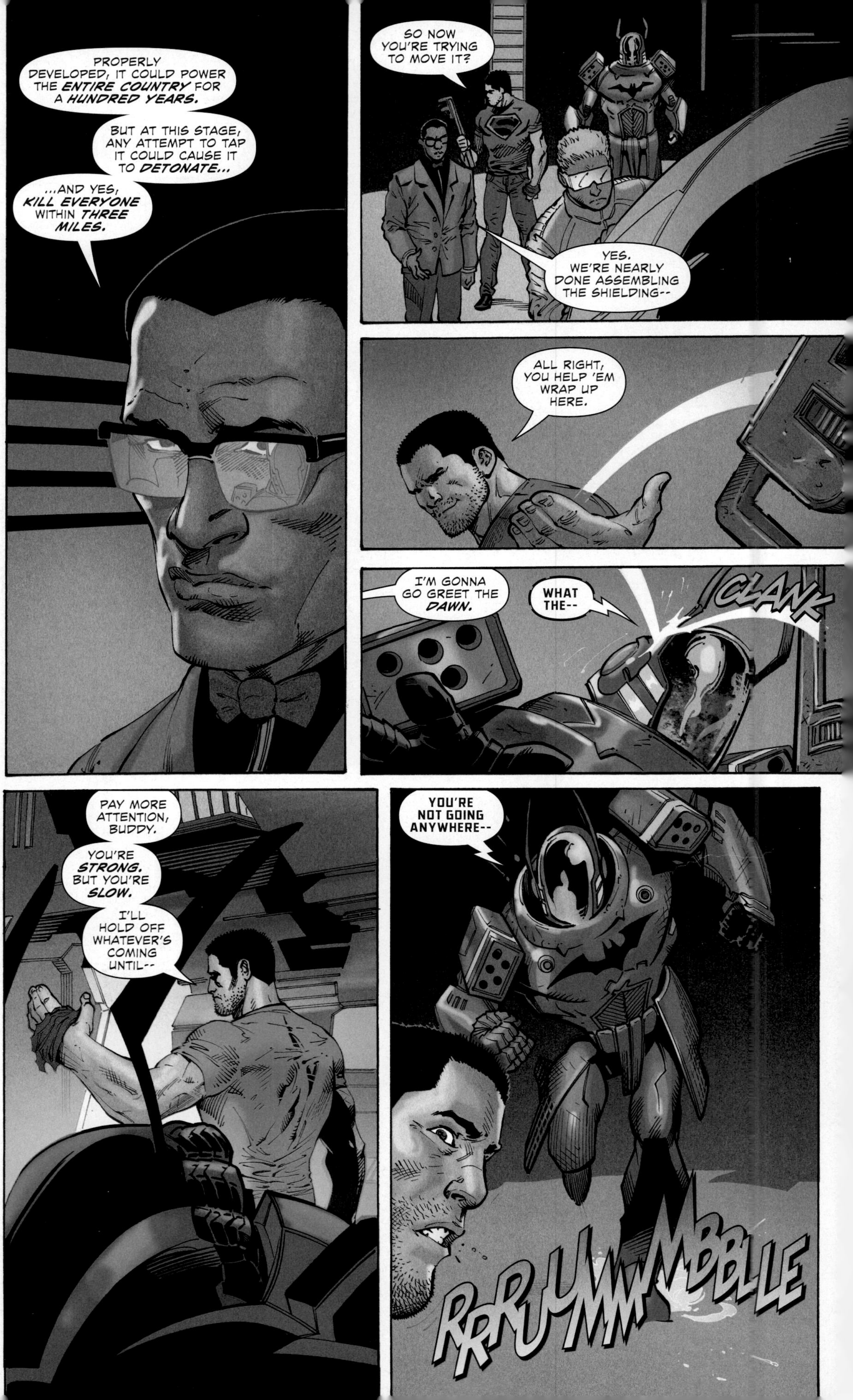
PROPERLY DEVELOPED, IT COULD POWER THE ENTIRE COUNTRY FOR A HUNDRED YEARS.
BUT AT THIS STAGE, ANY ATTEMPT TO TAP IT COULD CAUSE IT TO DETONATE...
...AND YES, KILL EVERYONE WITHIN THREE MILES.
SO NOW YOU'RE TRYING TO MOVE IT?
YES. WE'RE NEARLY DONE ASSEMBLING THE SHIELDING--
ALL RIGHT, YOU HELP 'EM WRAP UP HERE.
I'M GONNA GO GREET THE DAWN.
WHAT THE--
CLANK
PAY MORE ATTENTION, BUDDY.
YOU'RE STRONG. BUT YOU'RE SLOW.
I'LL HOLD OFF WHATEVER'S COMING UNTIL--
YOU'RE NOT GOING ANYWHERE--
RRRUMMMBBLLE

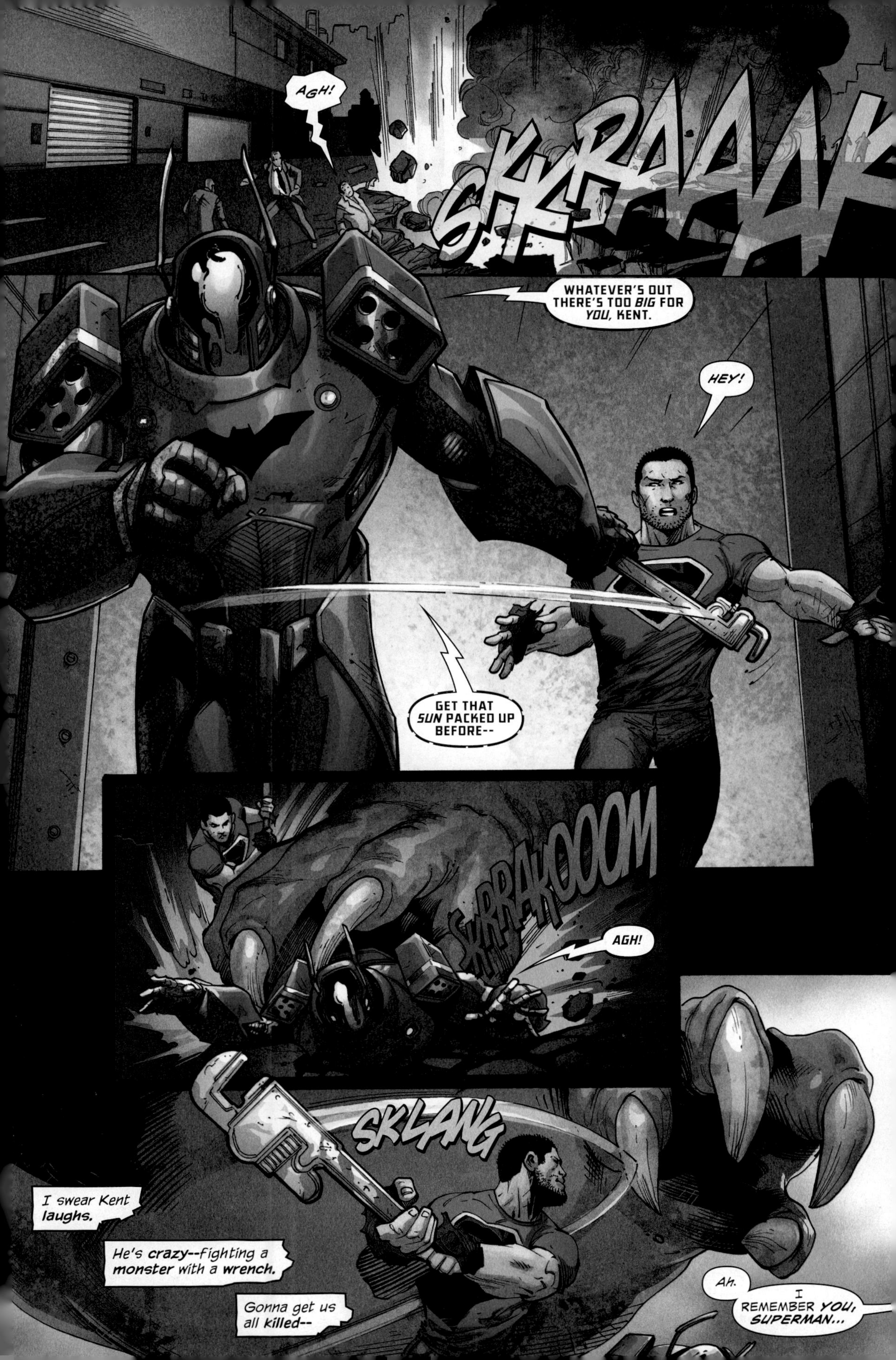
AGH!
SKRAAAK
WHATEVER'S OUT THERE'S TOO BIG FOR YOU, KENT.
HEY!
GET THAT SUN PACKED UP BEFORE--
SKRRAKOOOM
AGH!
SKLANG
I swear Kent laughs.
He's crazy--fighting a monster with a wrench.
Gonna get us all killed--
Ah.
I REMEMBER YOU, SUPERMAN...

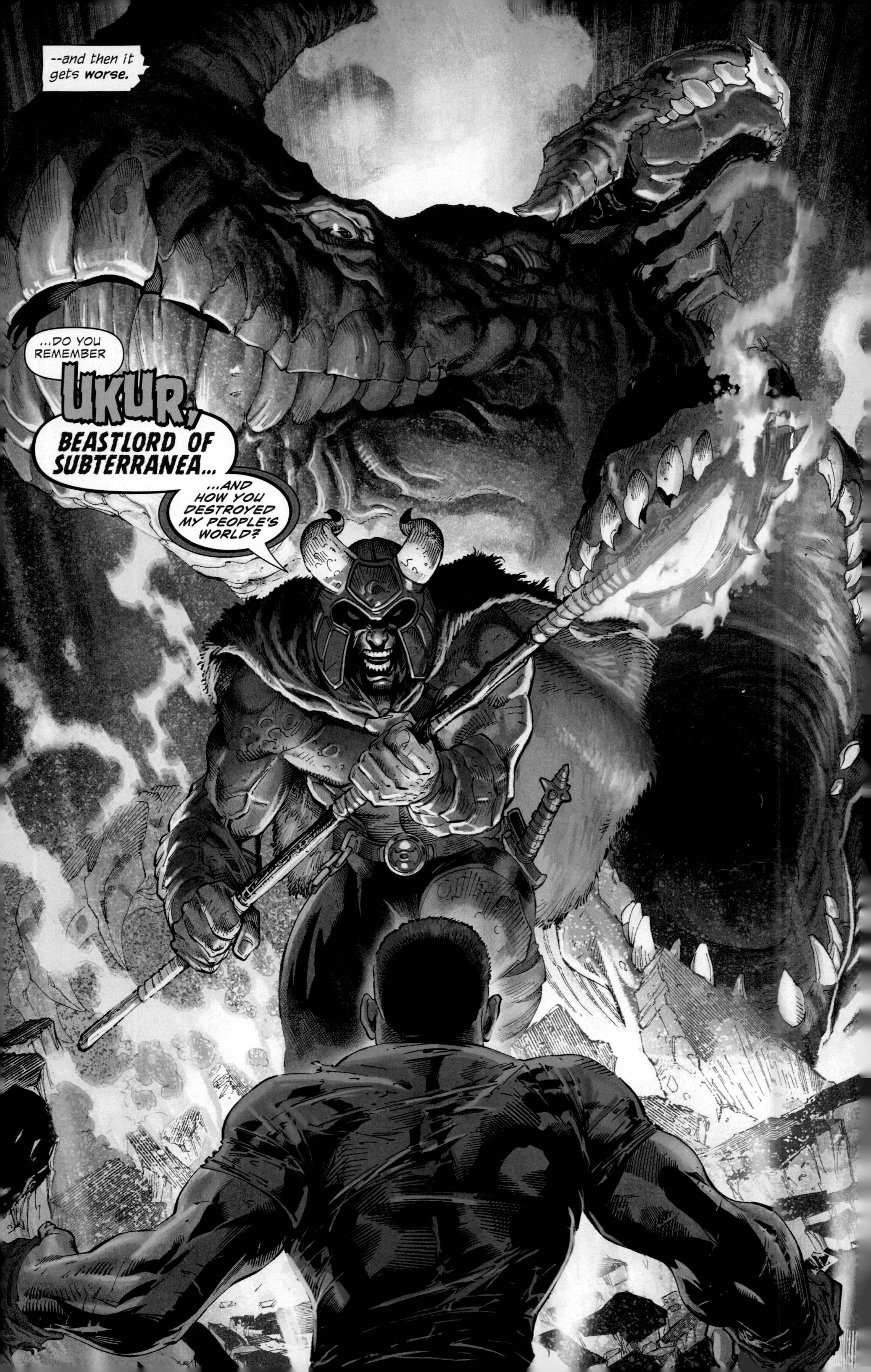
--and then it gets worse.
...DO YOU REMEMBER
UKUR,
BEASTLORD OF SUBTERRANEA...
...AND HOW YOU DESTROYED MY PEOPLE'S WORLD?

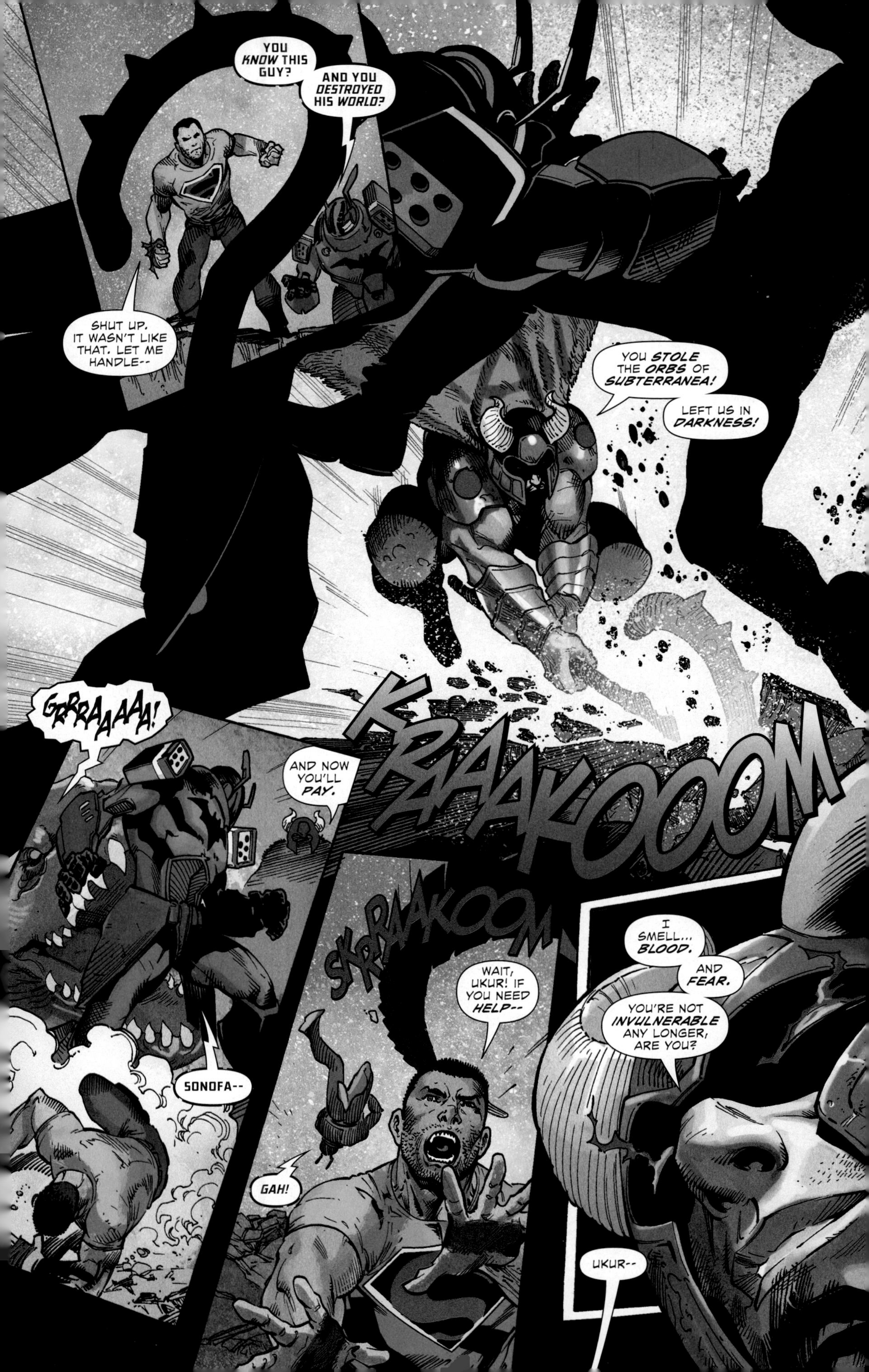
YOU KNOW THIS GUY?
AND YOU DESTROYED HIS WORLD?
SHUT UP. IT WASN'T LIKE THAT. LET ME HANDLE--
YOU STOLE THE ORBS OF SUBTERRANEA!
LEFT US IN DARKNESS!
GRRRAAAAA!
AND NOW YOU'LL PAY.
KRAAAKOOOOM
SONOFA--
SKRRAAKOOM
WAIT, UKUR! IF YOU NEED HELP--
GAH!
I SMELL... BLOOD.
AND FEAR.
YOU'RE NOT INVULNERABLE ANY LONGER, ARE YOU?
UKUR--

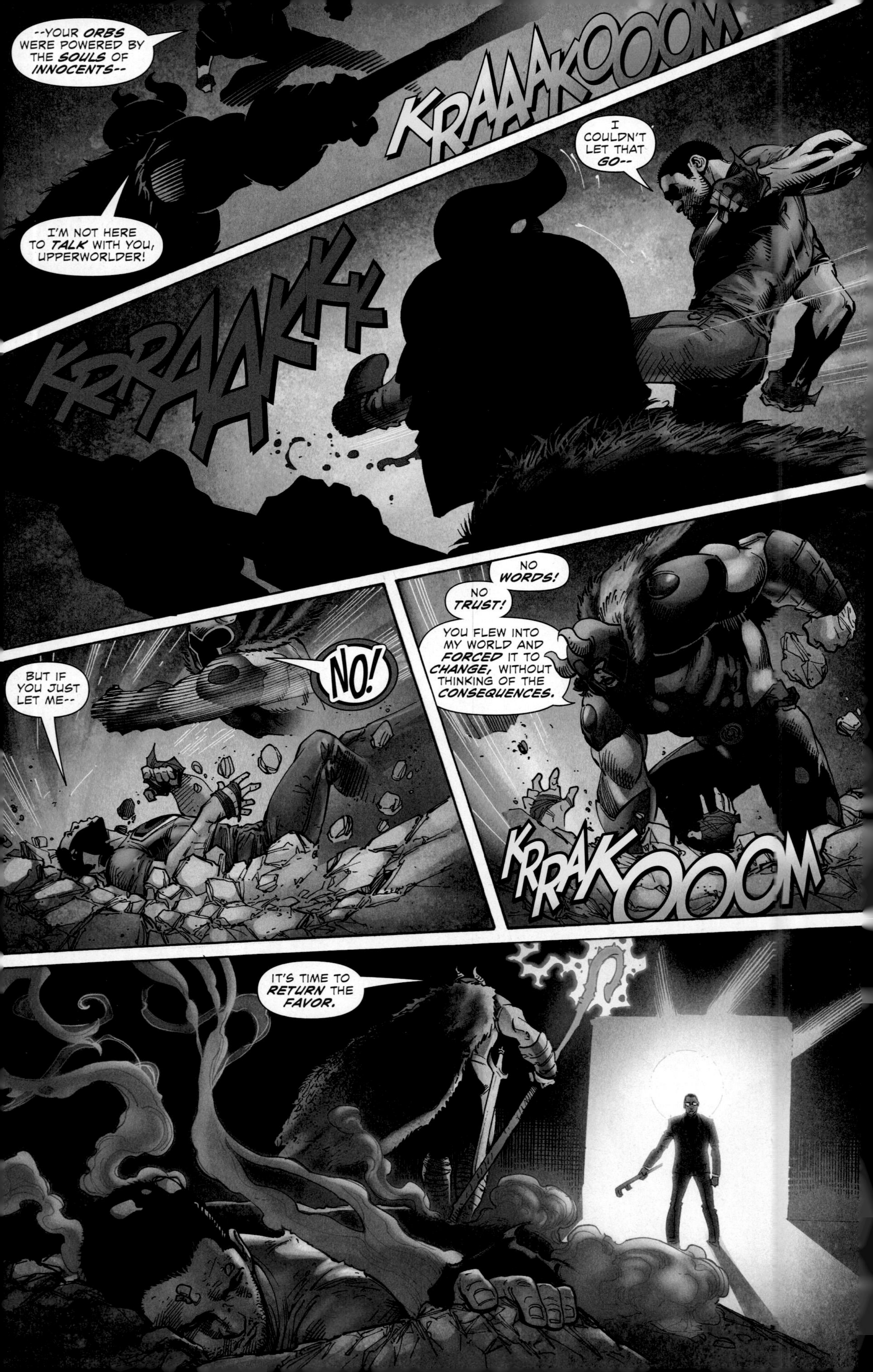
--YOUR ORBS WERE POWERED BY THE SOULS OF INNOCENTS--
KRAAAKOOOM
I COULDN'T LET THAT GO--
I'M NOT HERE TO TALK WITH YOU, UPPERWORLDER!
KRRAAKKK
BUT IF YOU JUST LET ME--
NO!
NO WORDS!
NO TRUST!
YOU FLEW INTO MY WORLD AND FORCED IT TO CHANGE, WITHOUT THINKING OF THE CONSEQUENCES.
KRRAKOOOM
IT'S TIME TO RETURN THE FAVOR.

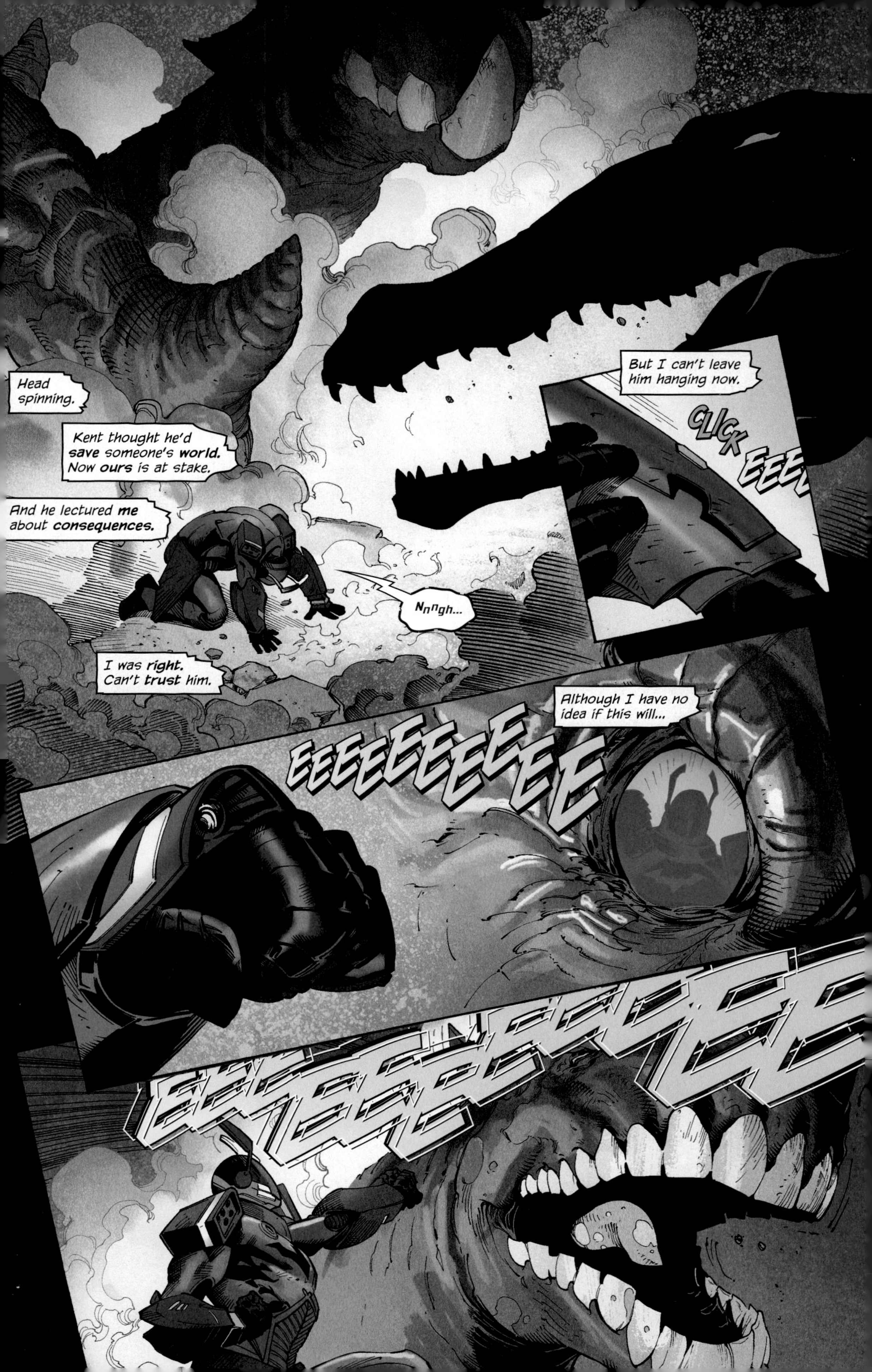

Head spinning.
Kent thought he'd save someone's world. Now ours is at stake.
And he lectured me about consequences.
Nnngh...
I was right. Can't trust him.
But I can't leave him hanging now.
CLICK
EEEE
Although I have no idea if this will...
EEEEEEEEEEEE
EEEEEEEEEEEEE

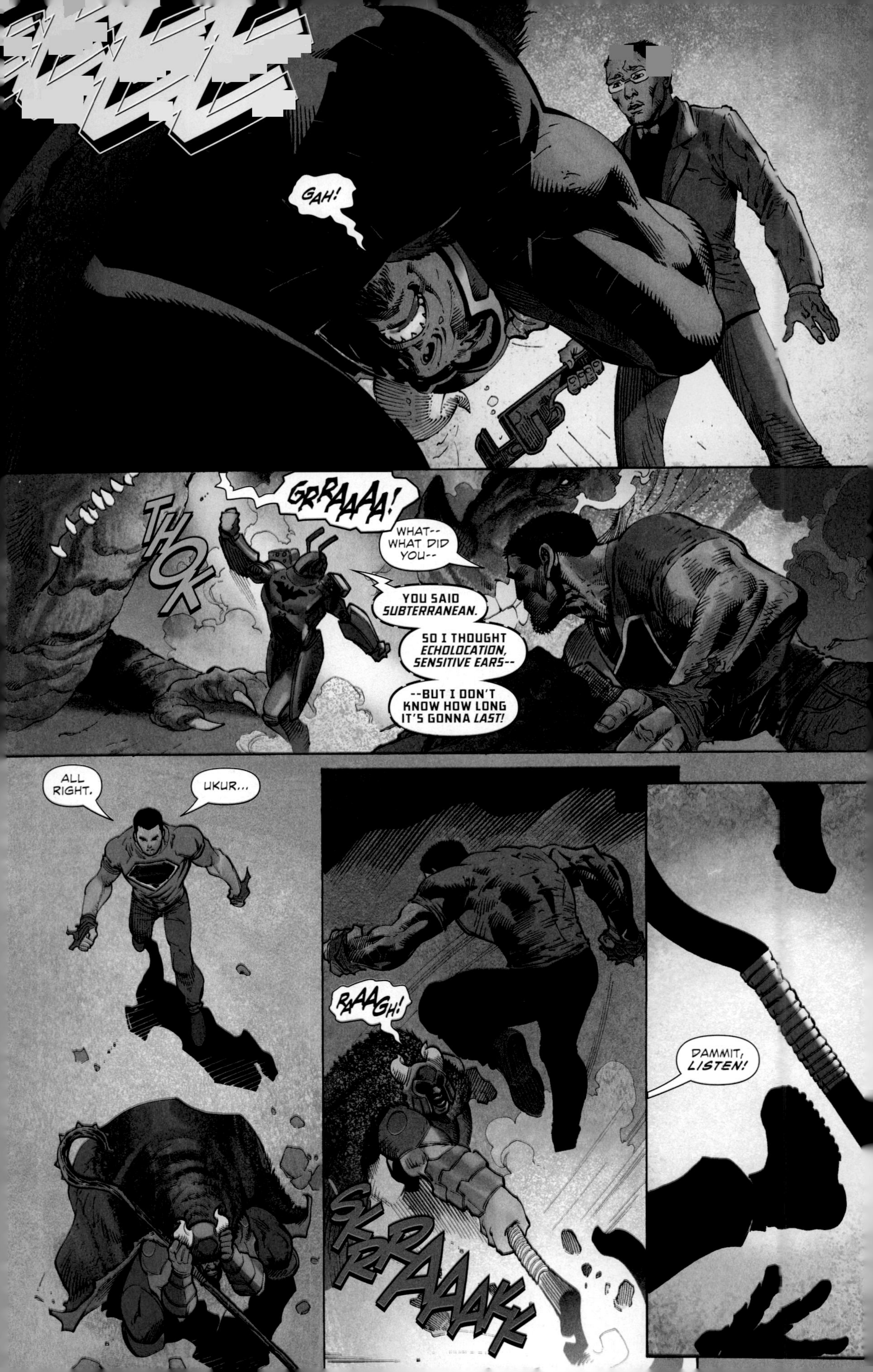
GAH!
GRRAAAAA!
THOK
WHAT-- WHAT DID YOU--
YOU SAID *SUBTERRANEAN.*
SO I THOUGHT *ECHOLOCATION, SENSITIVE EARS--*
--BUT I DON'T KNOW HOW LONG IT'S GONNA *LAST!*
ALL RIGHT.
UKUR...
RAAAGH!
SKRRAAAAKK
DAMMIT, *LISTEN!*

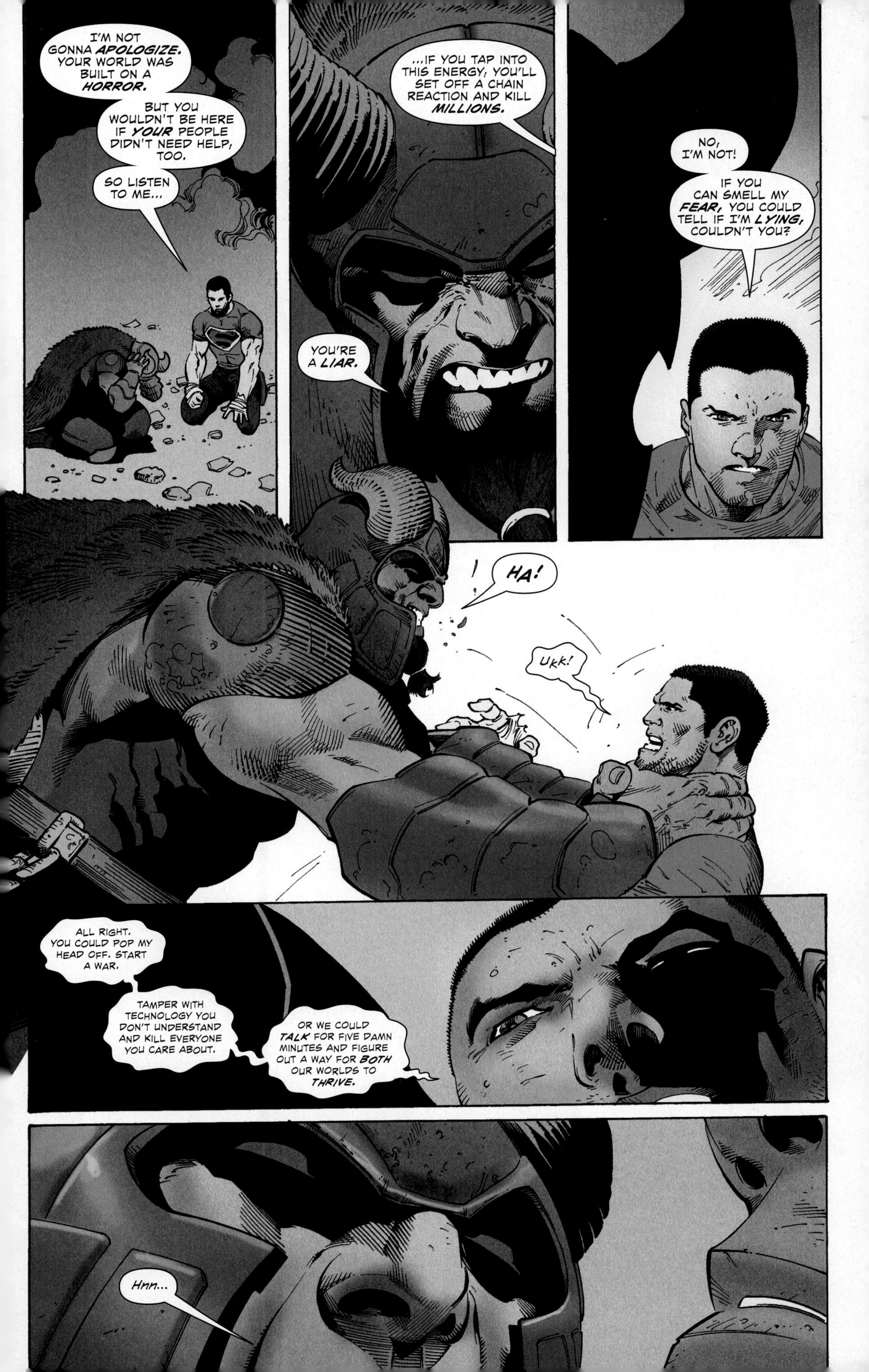
I'M NOT GONNA APOLOGIZE. YOUR WORLD WAS BUILT ON A HORROR.
BUT YOU WOULDN'T BE HERE IF YOUR PEOPLE DIDN'T NEED HELP, TOO.
SO LISTEN TO ME...
...IF YOU TAP INTO THIS ENERGY, YOU'LL SET OFF A CHAIN REACTION AND KILL MILLIONS.
YOU'RE A LIAR.
NO, I'M NOT!
IF YOU CAN SMELL MY FEAR, YOU COULD TELL IF I'M LYING, COULDN'T YOU?
HA!
Ukk!
ALL RIGHT. YOU COULD POP MY HEAD OFF. START A WAR.
TAMPER WITH TECHNOLOGY YOU DON'T UNDERSTAND AND KILL EVERYONE YOU CARE ABOUT.
OR WE COULD TALK FOR FIVE DAMN MINUTES AND FIGURE OUT A WAY FOR BOTH OUR WORLDS TO THRIVE.
Hnn...

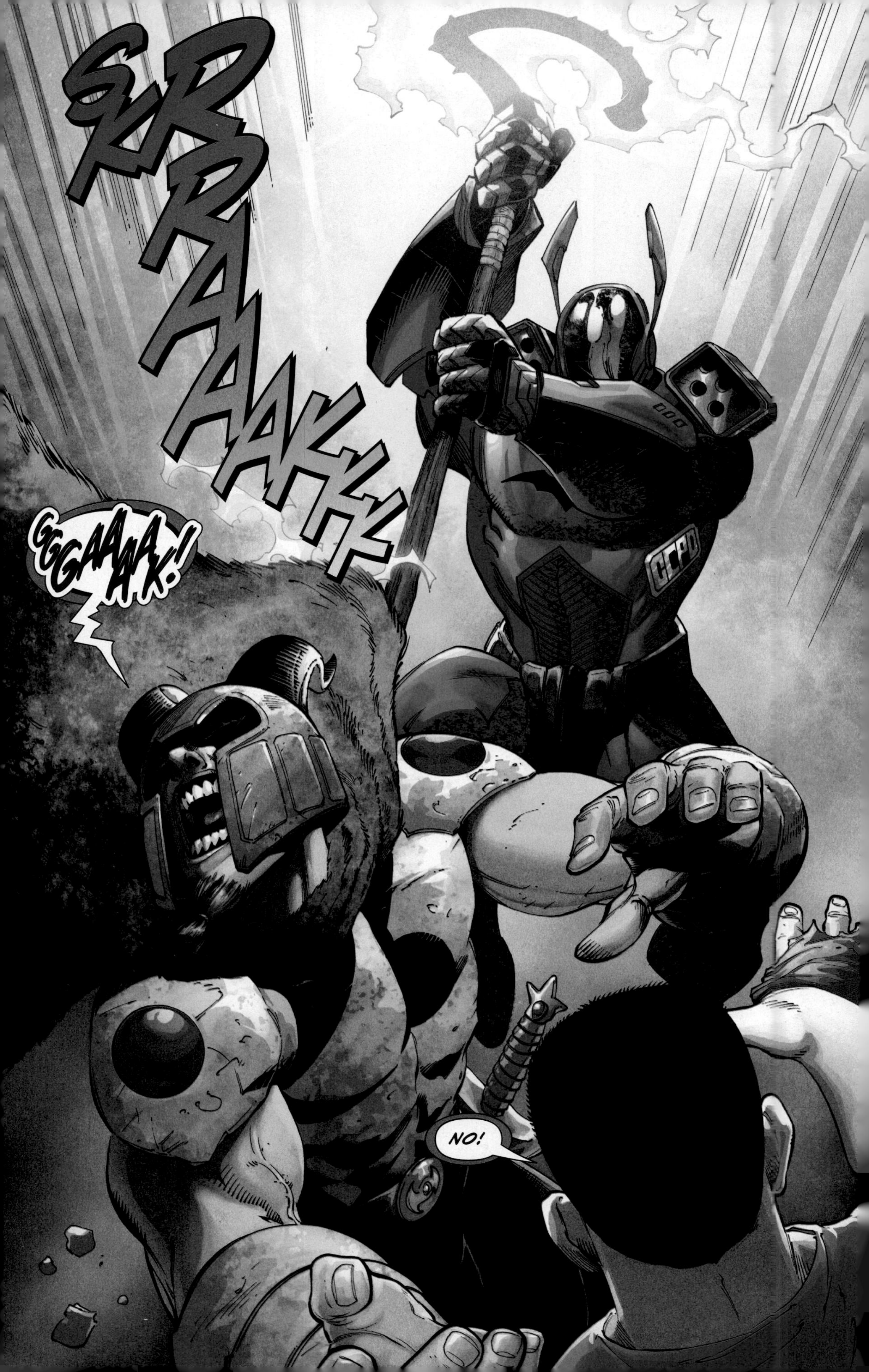
SKRRAAKKK
GGGAAAAAK!
NO!

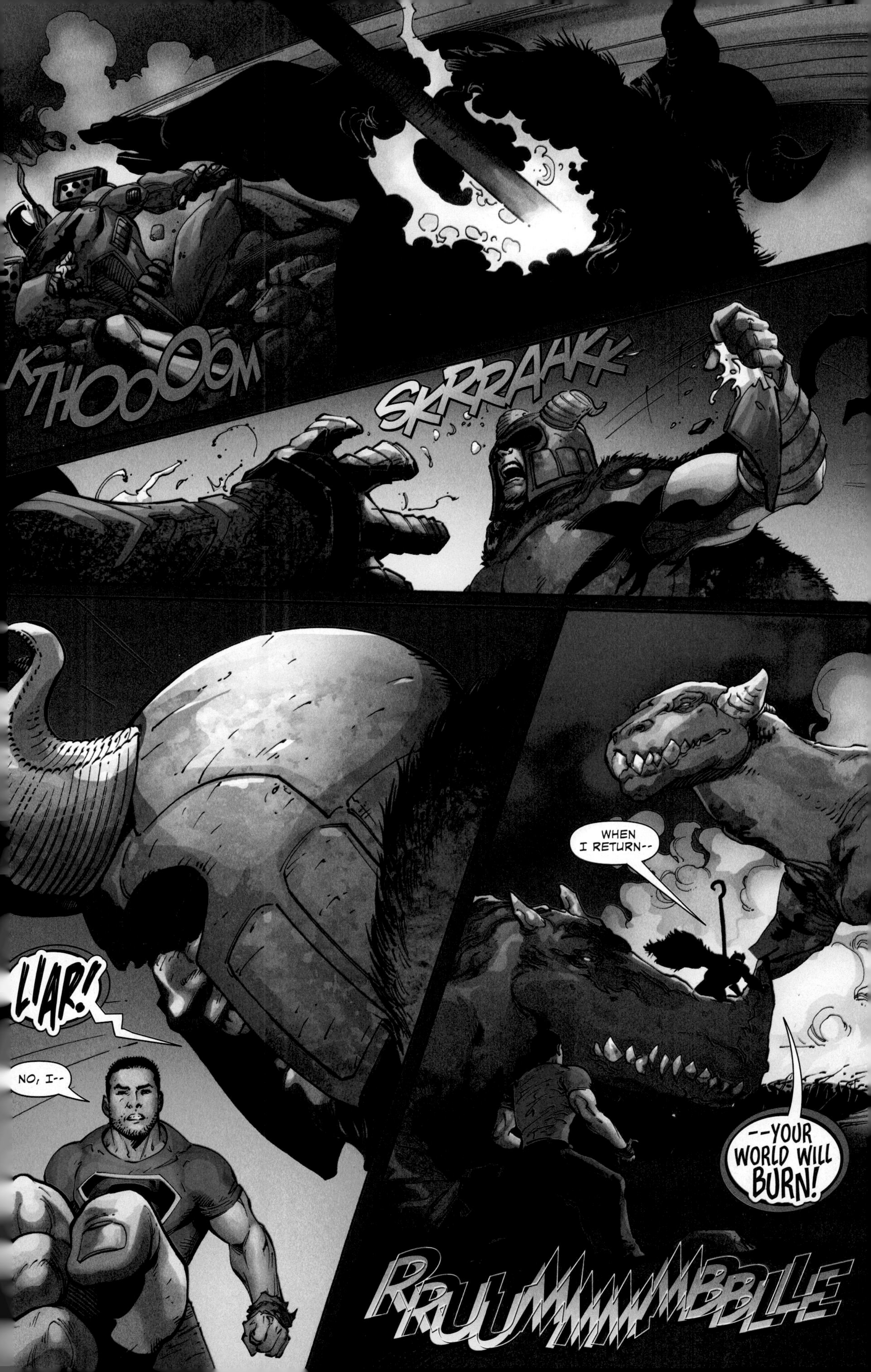
KTHOOOOM
SKRRAAKK
LIAR!
NO, I--
WHEN I RETURN--
--YOUR WORLD WILL BURN!
RRUUMMMMBBLLE

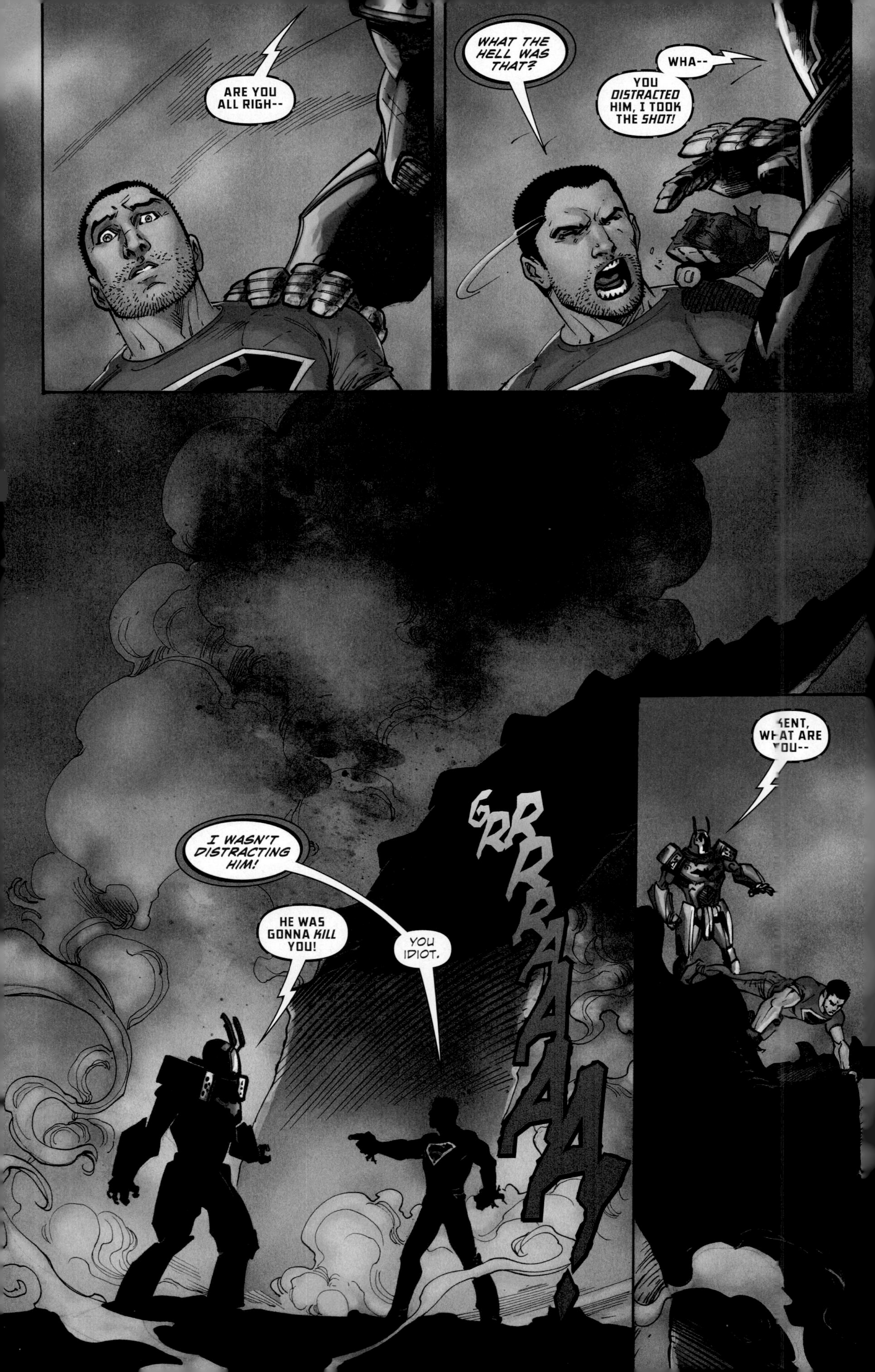

ARE YOU ALL RIGH--
WHAT THE HELL WAS THAT?
WHA--
YOU DISTRACTED HIM, I TOOK THE SHOT!
GRRRAAAA
KENT, WHAT ARE YOU--
I WASN'T DISTRACTING HIM!
HE WAS GONNA KILL YOU!
YOU IDIOT.

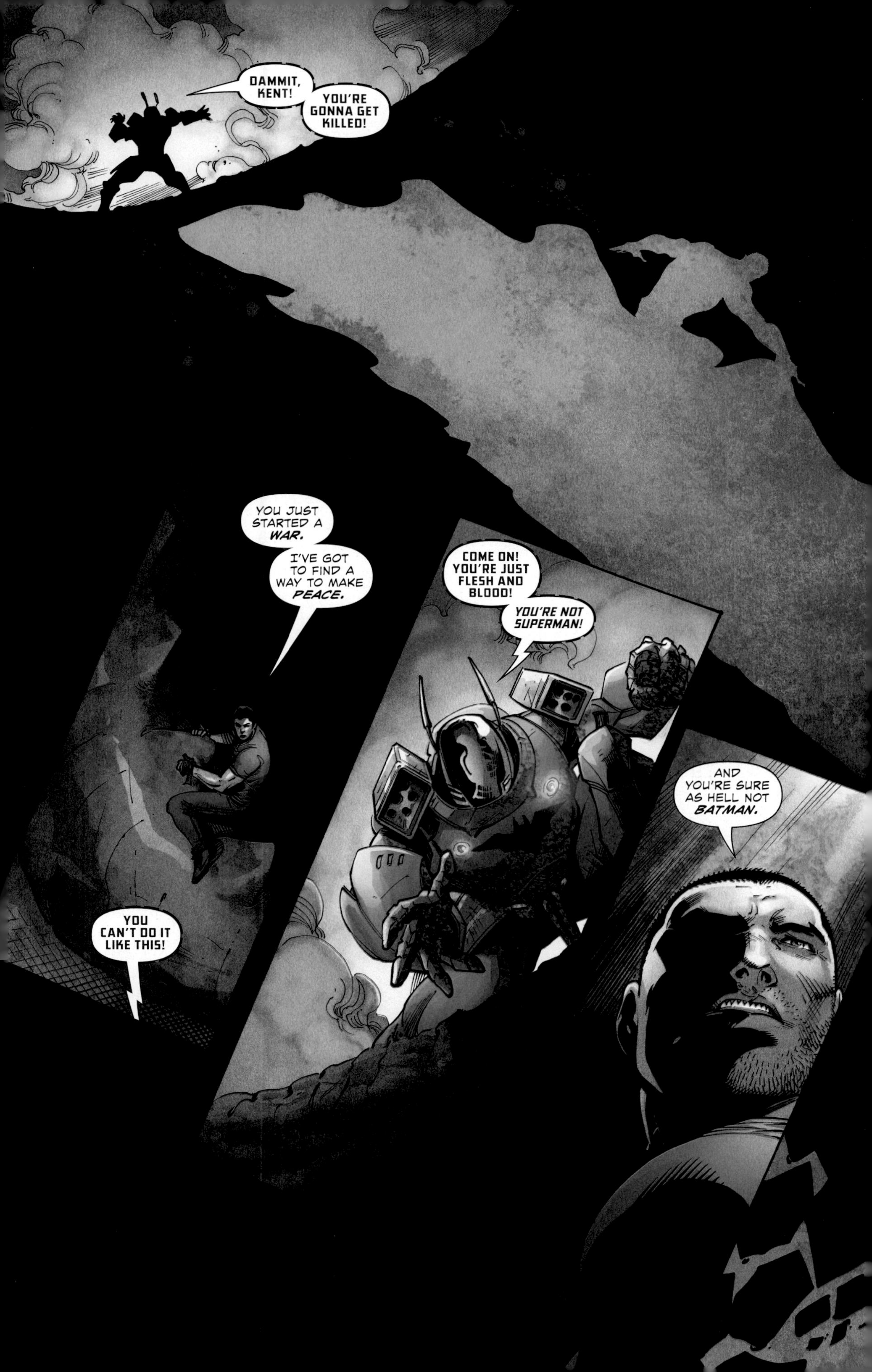
DAMMIT, KENT!
YOU'RE GONNA GET KILLED!
YOU JUST STARTED A *WAR.*
I'VE GOT TO FIND A WAY TO MAKE *PEACE.*
YOU CAN'T DO IT LIKE THIS!
COME ON! YOU'RE JUST FLESH AND BLOOD!
YOU'RE NOT SUPERMAN!
AND YOU'RE SURE AS HELL NOT *BATMAN.*

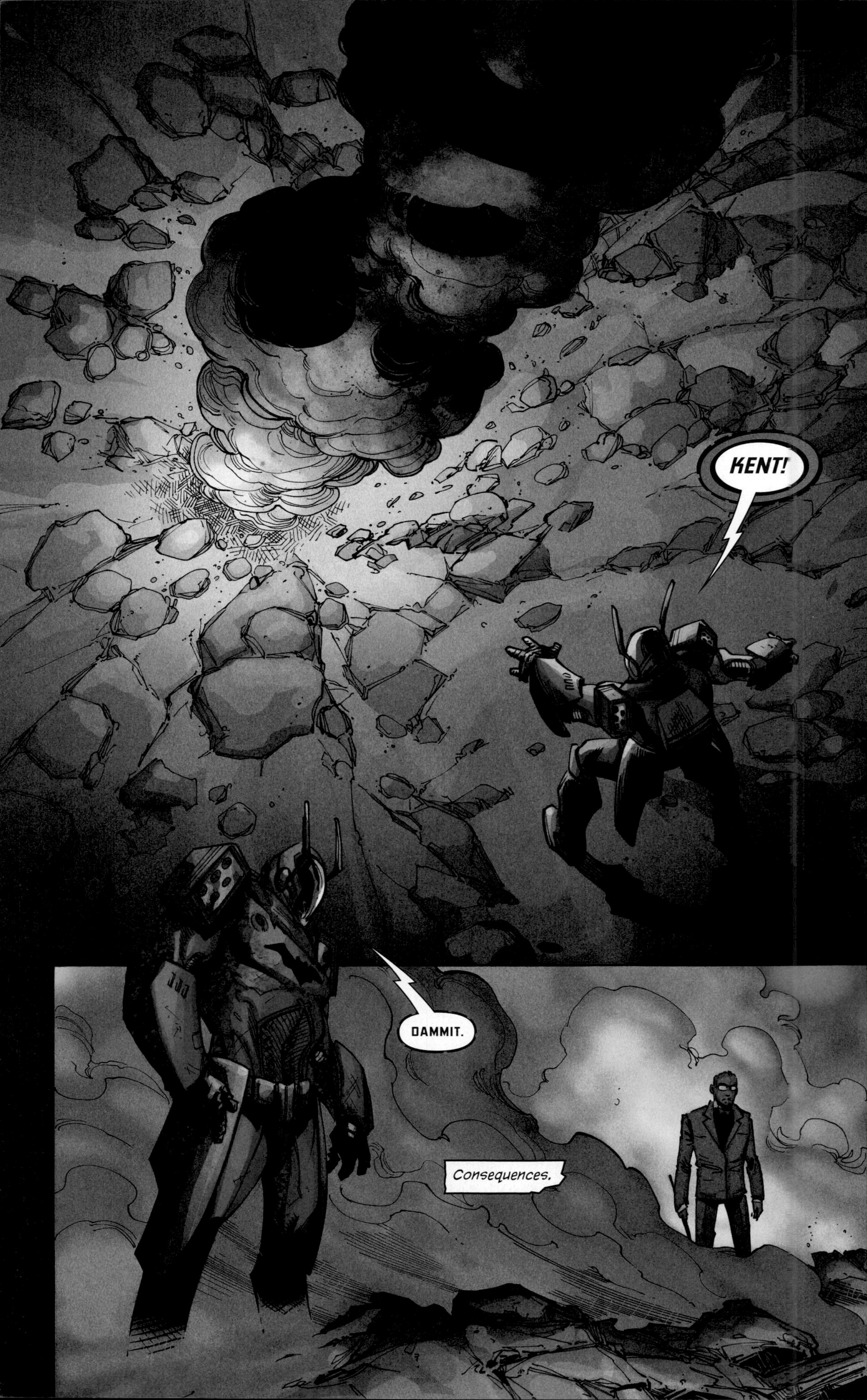
KENT!
DAMMIT.
Consequences.

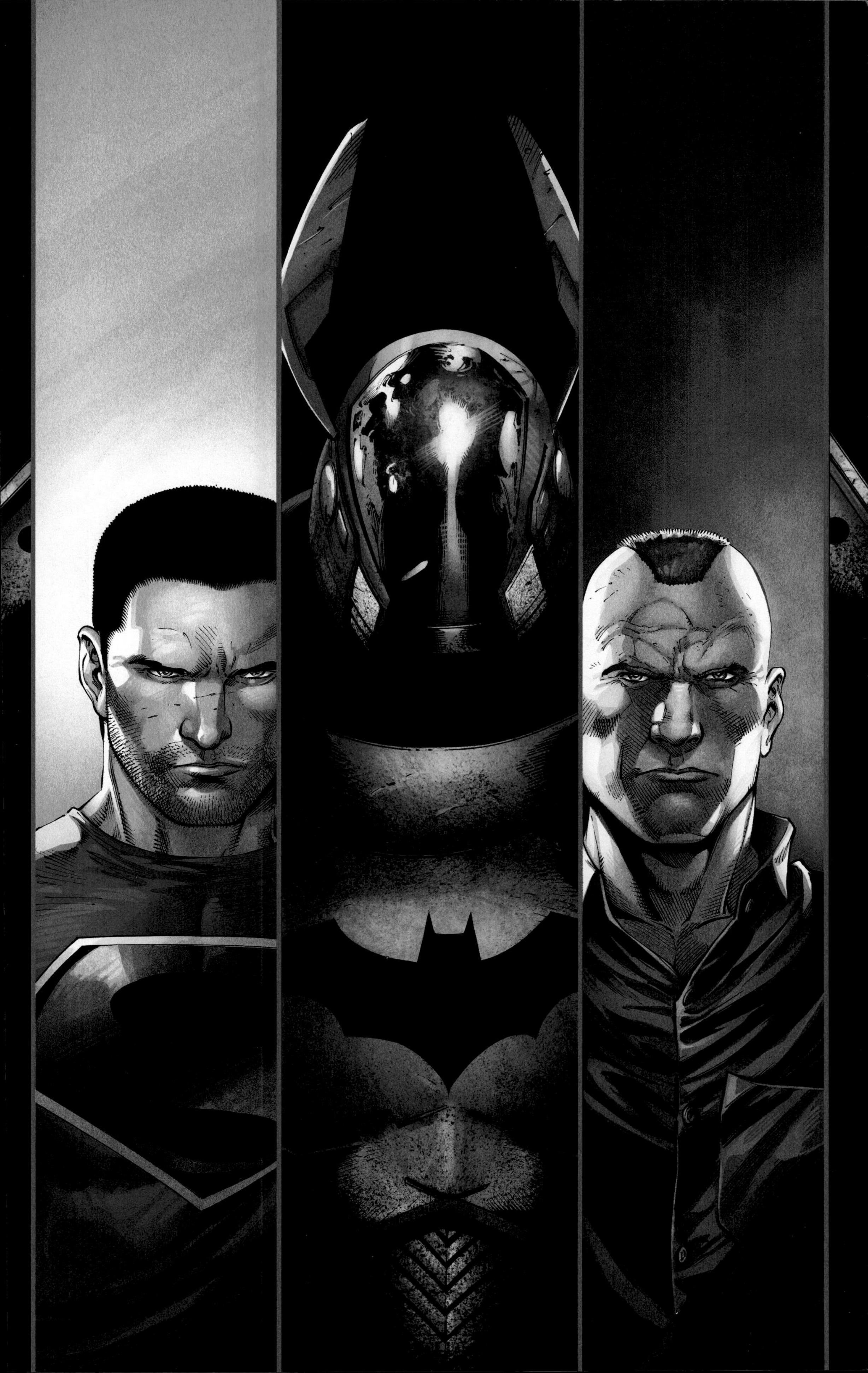

TRUTH HURTS PART THREE

GREG PAK writer **ARDIAN SYAF** penciller **VICENTE CIFUENTES** inker **BETH SOTELO** colorist **ROB LEIGH** letterer **ARDIAN SYAF DANNY MIKI ULISES ARREOLA** cover

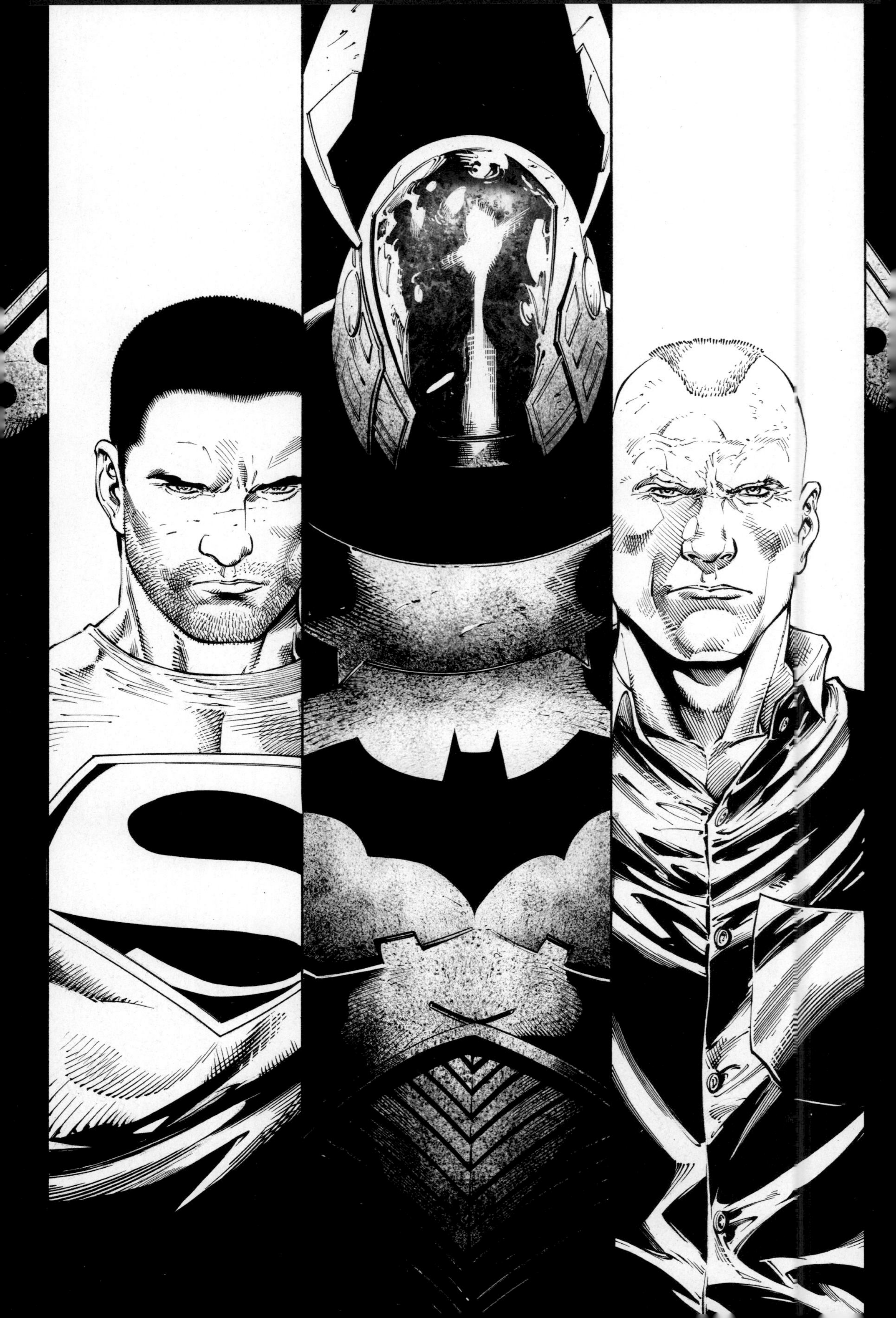

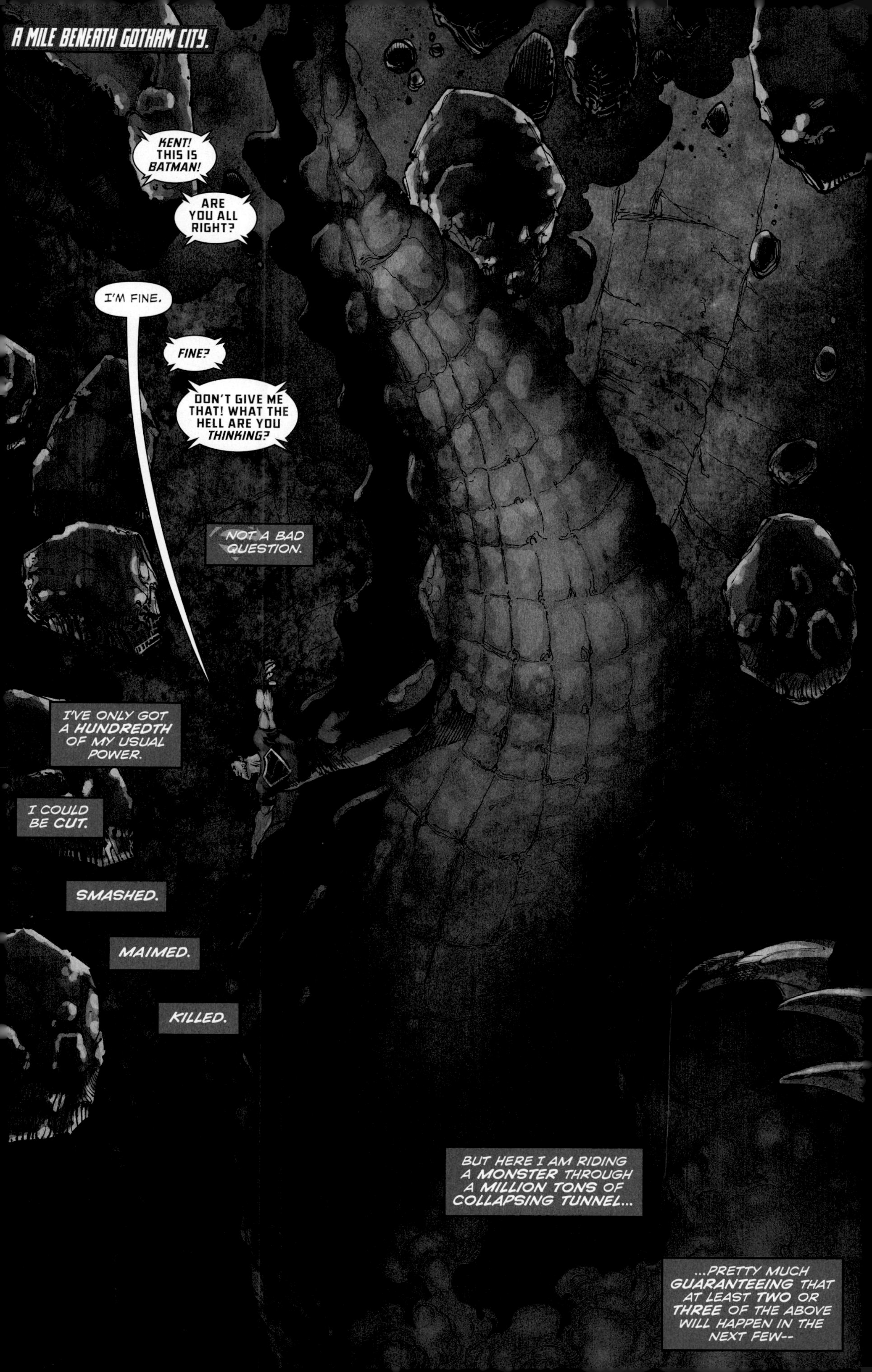
A MILE BENEATH GOTHAM CITY.
KENT! THIS IS BATMAN!
ARE YOU ALL RIGHT?
I'M FINE.
FINE?
DON'T GIVE ME THAT! WHAT THE HELL ARE YOU THINKING?
NOT A BAD QUESTION.
I'VE ONLY GOT A HUNDREDTH OF MY USUAL POWER.
I COULD BE CUT.
SMASHED.
MAIMED.
KILLED.
BUT HERE I AM RIDING A MONSTER THROUGH A MILLION TONS OF COLLAPSING TUNNEL...
...PRETTY MUCH GUARANTEEING THAT AT LEAST TWO OR THREE OF THE ABOVE WILL HAPPEN IN THE NEXT FEW--

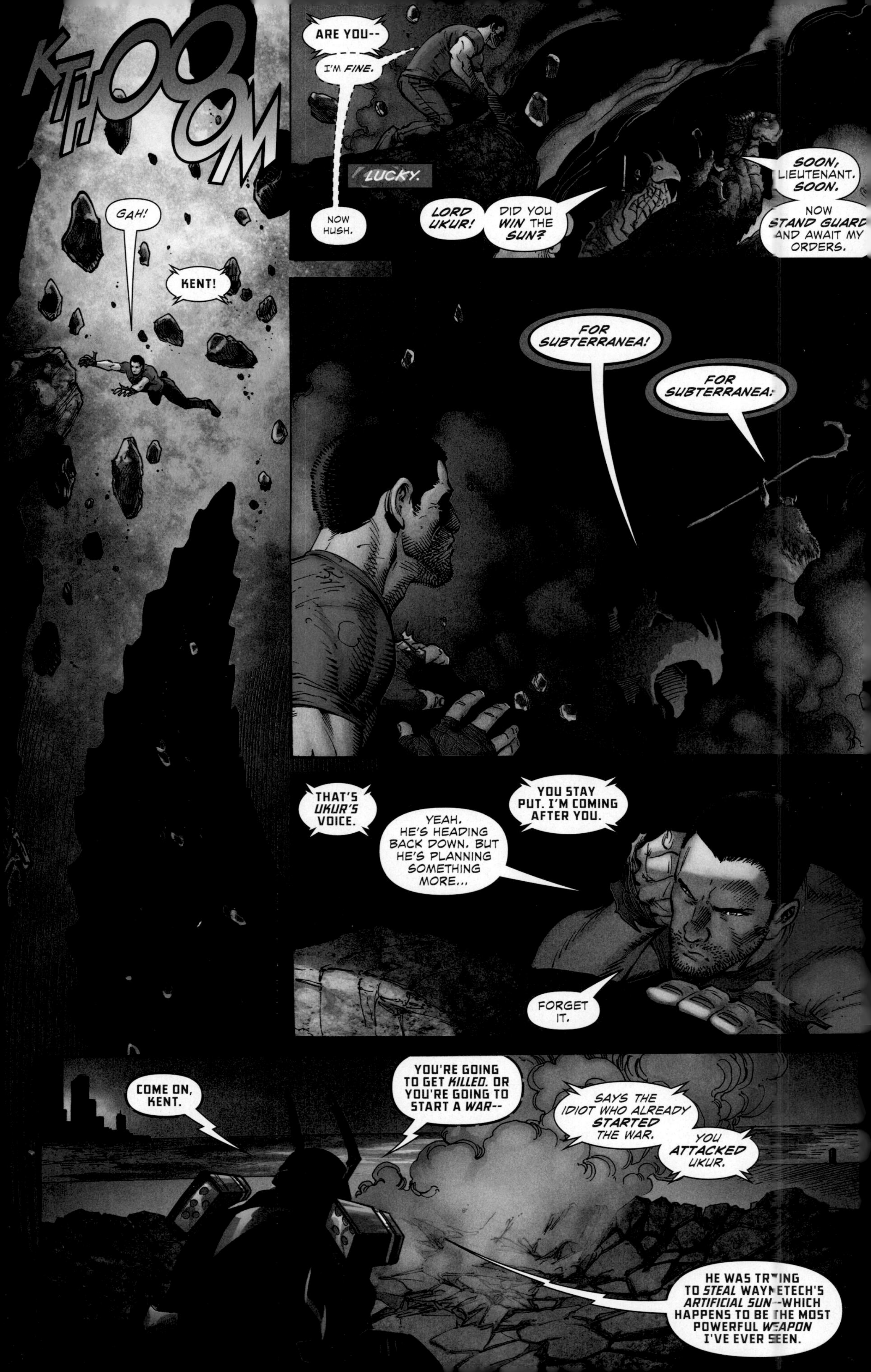
KTHOOOM
GAH!
KENT!
ARE YOU--
I'M FINE.
LUCKY.
NOW HUSH.
LORD UKUR!
DID YOU WIN THE SUN?
SOON, LIEUTENANT. SOON.
NOW STAND GUARD AND AWAIT MY ORDERS.
FOR SUBTERRANEA!
FOR SUBTERRANEA!
THAT'S UKUR'S VOICE.
YEAH. HE'S HEADING BACK DOWN. BUT HE'S PLANNING SOMETHING MORE...
YOU STAY PUT. I'M COMING AFTER YOU.
FORGET IT.
COME ON, KENT.
YOU'RE GOING TO GET KILLED. OR YOU'RE GOING TO START A WAR--
SAYS THE IDIOT WHO ALREADY STARTED THE WAR.
YOU ATTACKED UKUR.
HE WAS TRYING TO STEAL WAYNETECH'S ARTIFICIAL SUN--WHICH HAPPENS TO BE THE MOST POWERFUL WEAPON I'VE EVER SEEN.

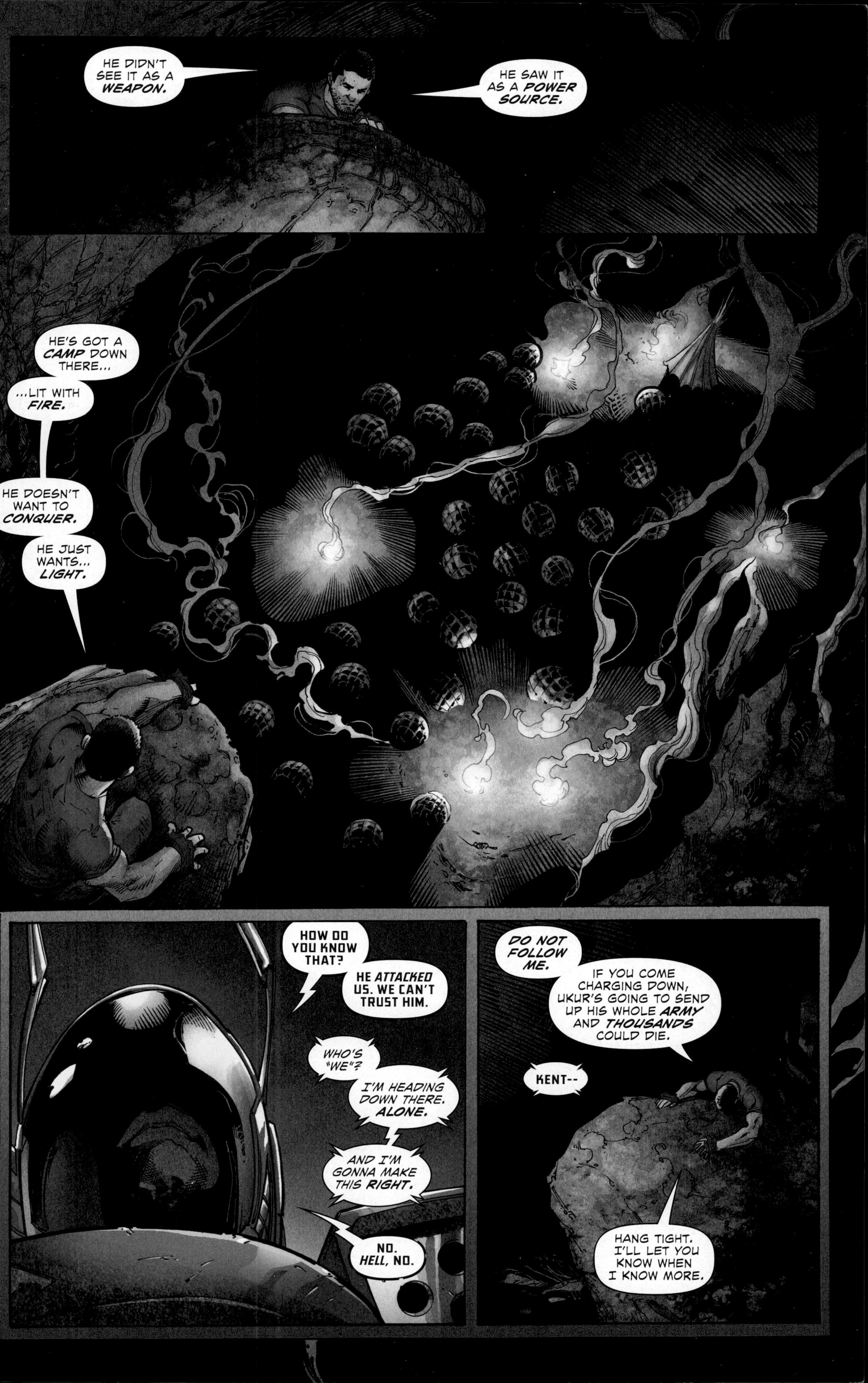
HE DIDN'T SEE IT AS A WEAPON.
HE SAW IT AS A POWER SOURCE.
HE'S GOT A CAMP DOWN THERE...
...LIT WITH FIRE.
HE DOESN'T WANT TO CONQUER.
HE JUST WANTS... LIGHT.
HOW DO YOU KNOW THAT?
HE ATTACKED US. WE CAN'T TRUST HIM.
WHO'S "WE"?
I'M HEADING DOWN THERE. ALONE.
AND I'M GONNA MAKE THIS RIGHT.
NO. HELL, NO.
DO NOT FOLLOW ME.
IF YOU COME CHARGING DOWN, UKUR'S GOING TO SEND UP HIS WHOLE ARMY AND THOUSANDS COULD DIE.
KENT--
HANG TIGHT. I'LL LET YOU KNOW WHEN I KNOW MORE.

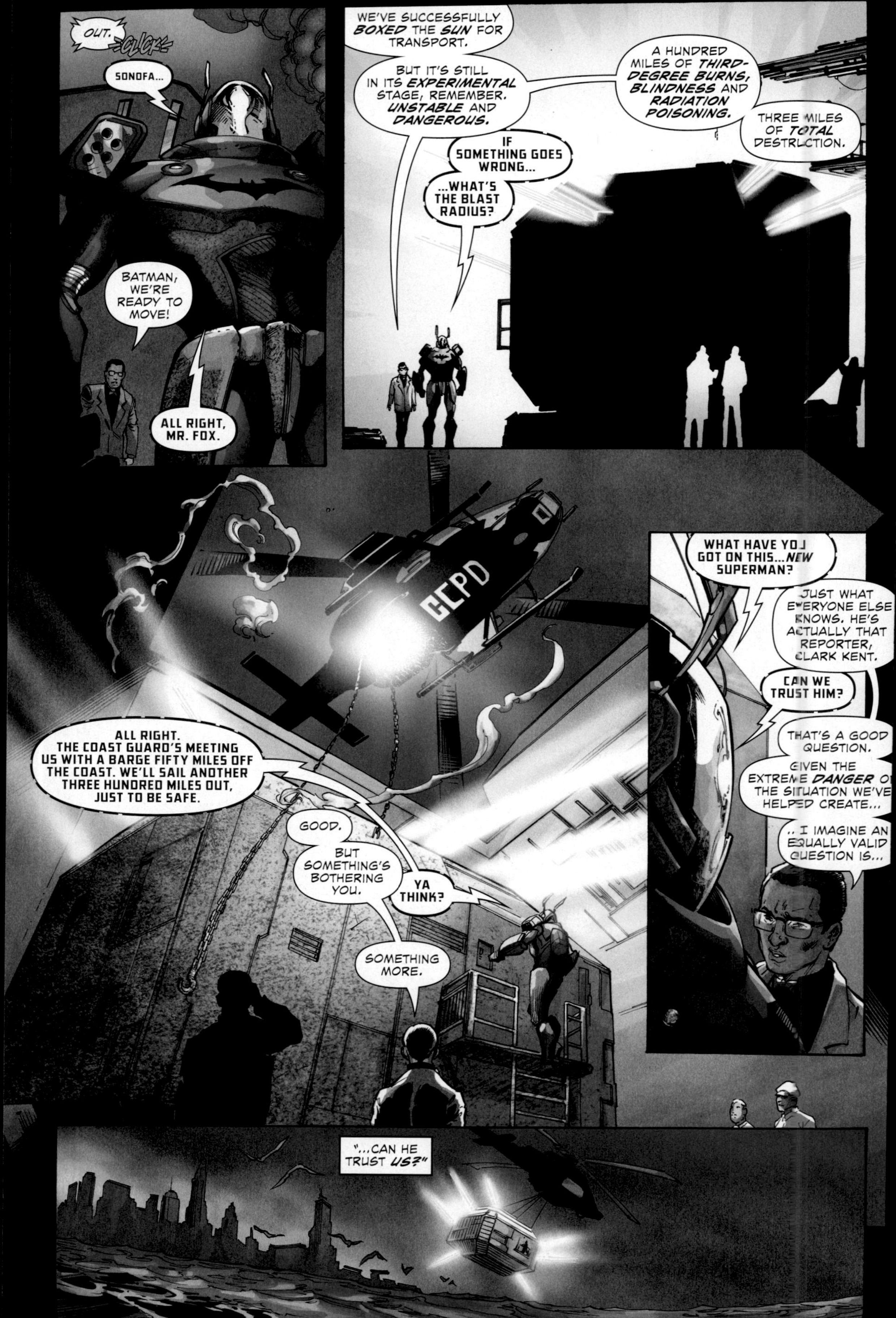
OUT.
CLICK
SONOFA...
BATMAN, WE'RE READY TO MOVE!
ALL RIGHT, MR. FOX.
WE'VE SUCCESSFULLY BOXED THE SUN FOR TRANSPORT.
BUT IT'S STILL IN ITS EXPERIMENTAL STAGE, REMEMBER. UNSTABLE AND DANGEROUS.
IF SOMETHING GOES WRONG...
...WHAT'S THE BLAST RADIUS?
A HUNDRED MILES OF THIRD-DEGREE BURNS, BLINDNESS AND RADIATION POISONING.
THREE MILES OF TOTAL DESTRUCTION.
GCPD
ALL RIGHT. THE COAST GUARD'S MEETING US WITH A BARGE FIFTY MILES OFF THE COAST. WE'LL SAIL ANOTHER THREE HUNDRED MILES OUT, JUST TO BE SAFE.
GOOD.
BUT SOMETHING'S BOTHERING YOU.
YA THINK?
SOMETHING MORE.
WHAT HAVE YOU GOT ON THIS...NEW SUPERMAN?
JUST WHAT EVERYONE ELSE KNOWS. HE'S ACTUALLY THAT REPORTER, CLARK KENT.
CAN WE TRUST HIM?
THAT'S A GOOD QUESTION.
GIVEN THE EXTREME DANGER OF THE SITUATION WE'VE HELPED CREATE...
...I IMAGINE AN EQUALLY VALID QUESTION IS...
"...CAN HE TRUST US?"

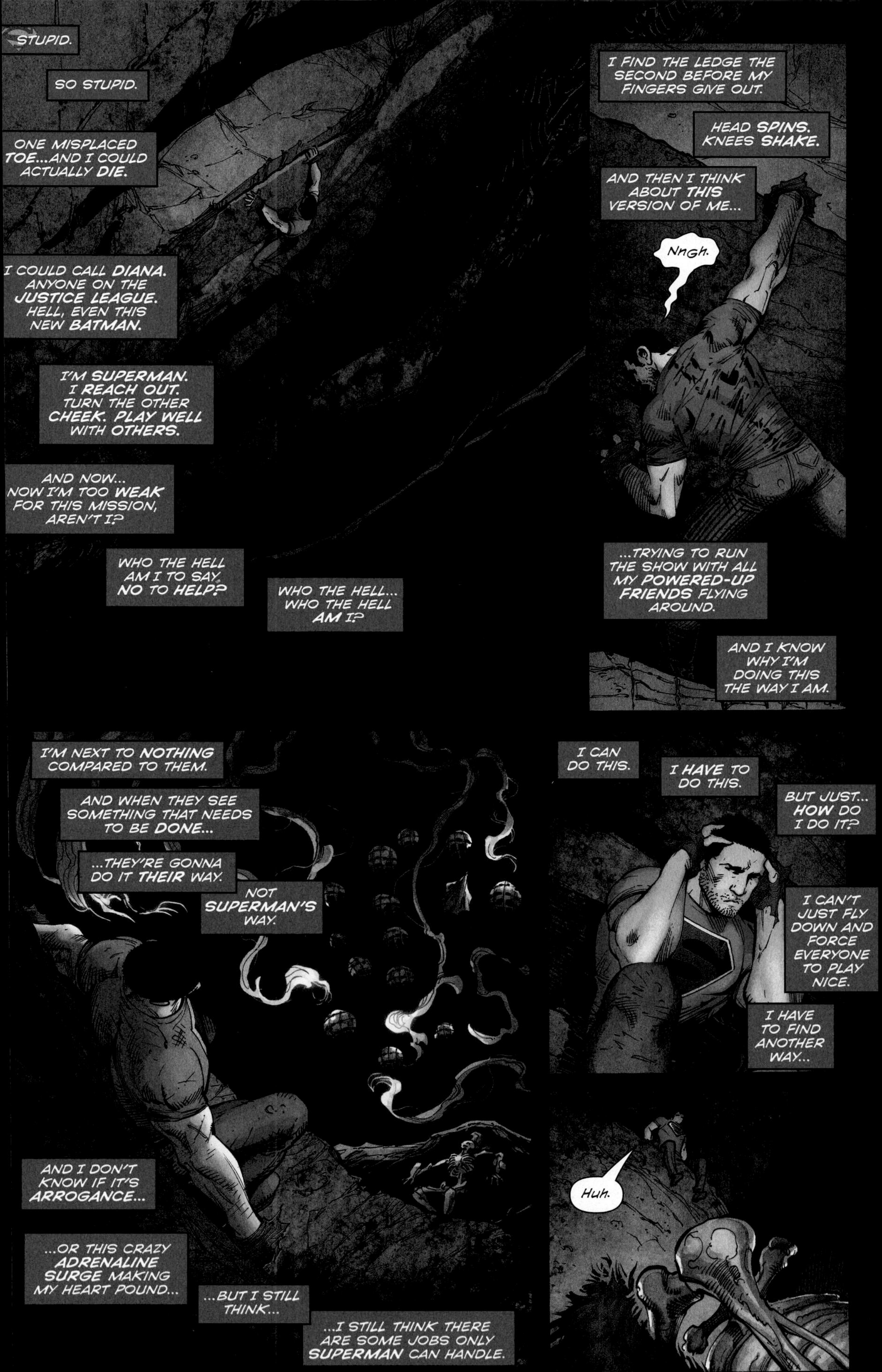
STUPID.
SO STUPID.
ONE MISPLACED TOE...AND I COULD ACTUALLY DIE.
I COULD CALL DIANA. ANYONE ON THE JUSTICE LEAGUE. HELL, EVEN THIS NEW BATMAN.
I'M SUPERMAN. I REACH OUT. TURN THE OTHER CHEEK. PLAY WELL WITH OTHERS.
AND NOW... NOW I'M TOO WEAK FOR THIS MISSION, AREN'T I?
WHO THE HELL AM I TO SAY NO TO HELP?
WHO THE HELL... WHO THE HELL AM I?
I FIND THE LEDGE THE SECOND BEFORE MY FINGERS GIVE OUT.
HEAD SPINS. KNEES SHAKE.
AND THEN I THINK ABOUT THIS VERSION OF ME...
Nngh.
...TRYING TO RUN THE SHOW WITH ALL MY POWERED-UP FRIENDS FLYING AROUND.
AND I KNOW WHY I'M DOING THIS THE WAY I AM.
I'M NEXT TO NOTHING COMPARED TO THEM.
AND WHEN THEY SEE SOMETHING THAT NEEDS TO BE DONE...
...THEY'RE GONNA DO IT THEIR WAY.
NOT SUPERMAN'S WAY.
AND I DON'T KNOW IF IT'S ARROGANCE...
...OR THIS CRAZY ADRENALINE SURGE MAKING MY HEART POUND...
...BUT I STILL THINK...
...I STILL THINK THERE ARE SOME JOBS ONLY SUPERMAN CAN HANDLE.
I CAN DO THIS.
I HAVE TO DO THIS.
BUT JUST... HOW DO I DO IT?
I CAN'T JUST FLY DOWN AND FORCE EVERYONE TO PLAY NICE.
I HAVE TO FIND ANOTHER WAY...
Huh.

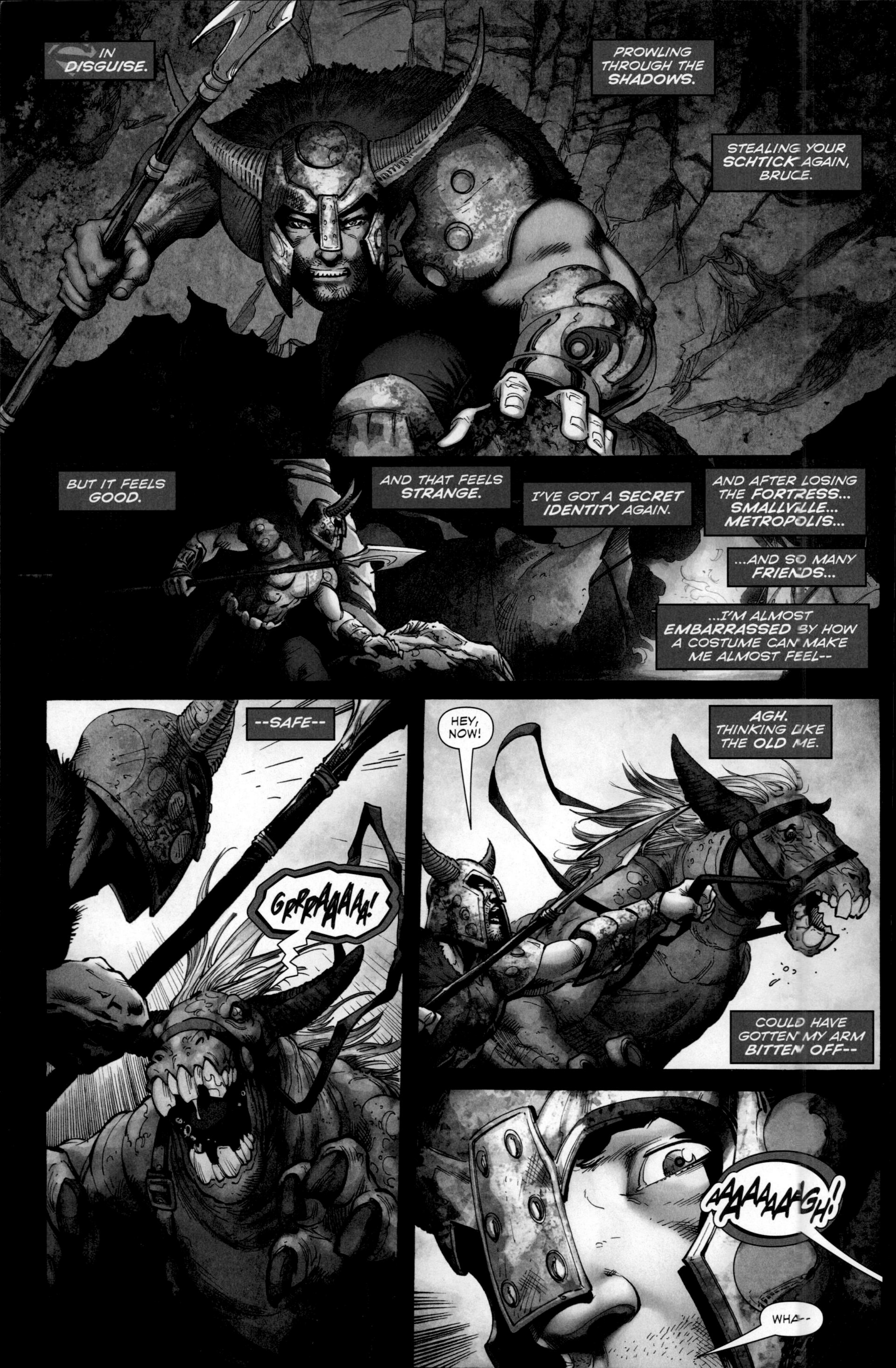
IN DISGUISE.
PROWLING THROUGH THE SHADOWS.
STEALING YOUR SCHTICK AGAIN, BRUCE.
BUT IT FEELS GOOD.
AND THAT FEELS STRANGE.
I'VE GOT A SECRET IDENTITY AGAIN.
AND AFTER LOSING THE FORTRESS... SMALLVILLE... METROPOLIS...
...AND SO MANY FRIENDS...
...I'M ALMOST EMBARRASSED BY HOW A COSTUME CAN MAKE ME ALMOST FEEL--
--SAFE--
GRRRAAAAAA!
HEY, NOW!
AGH. THINKING LIKE THE OLD ME.
COULD HAVE GOTTEN MY ARM BITTEN OFF--
AAAAAAAAGH!
WHA--

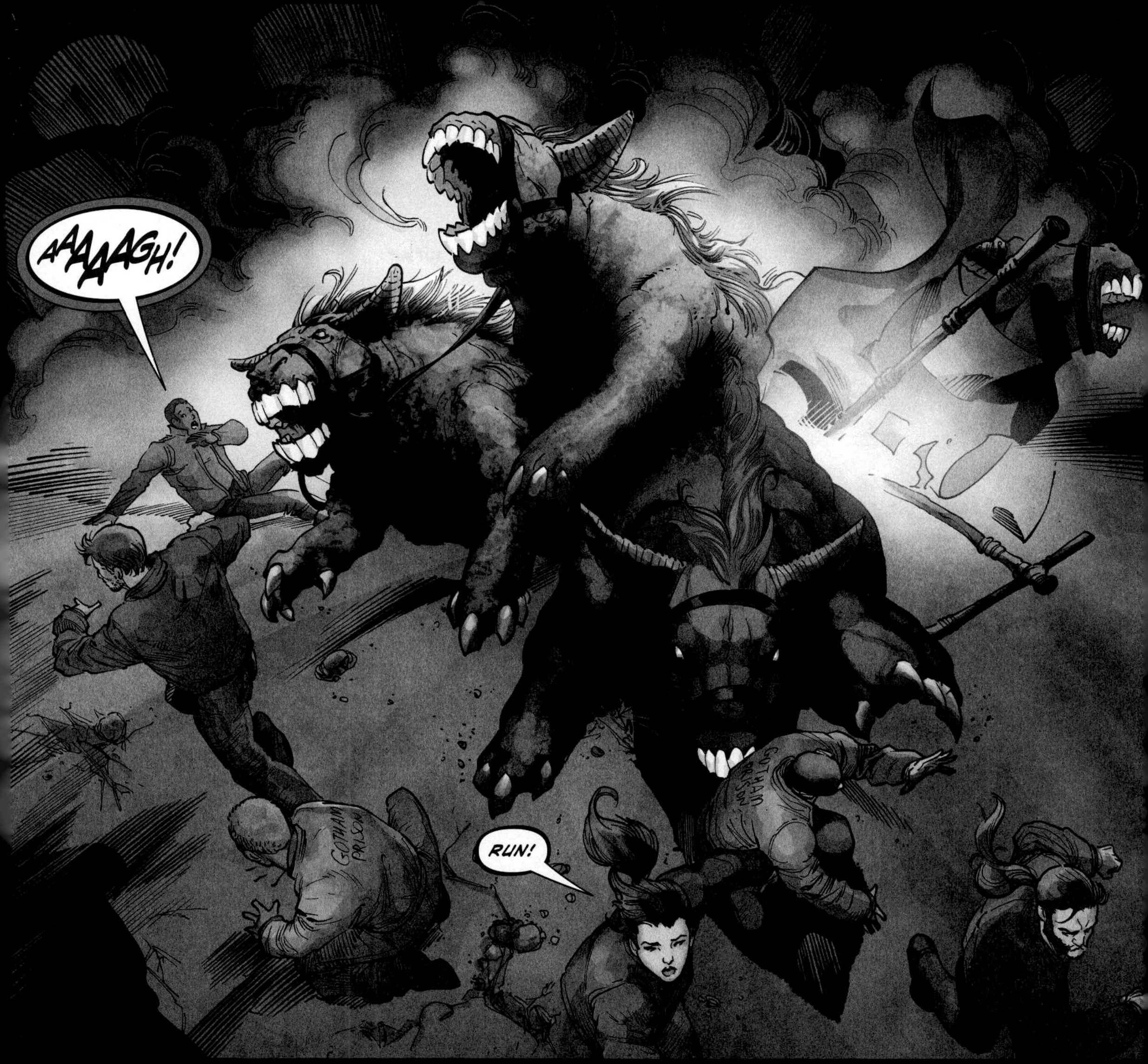
AAAAAGH!
GOTHAM PRISON
RUN!
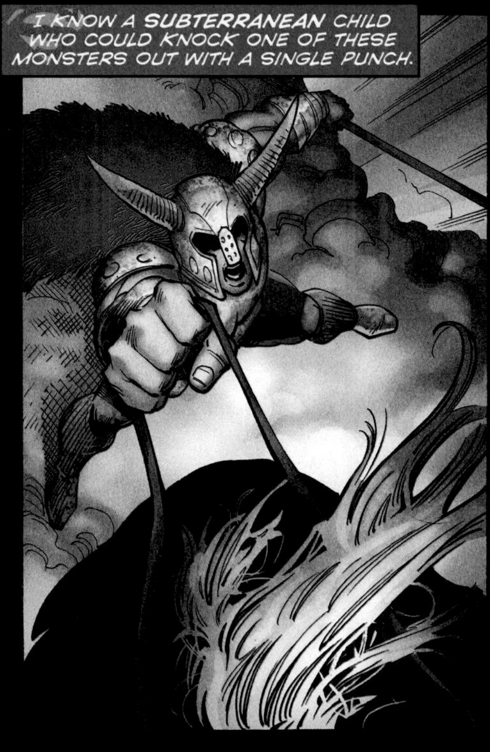
I KNOW A SUBTERRANEAN CHILD WHO COULD KNOCK ONE OF THESE MONSTERS OUT WITH A SINGLE PUNCH.
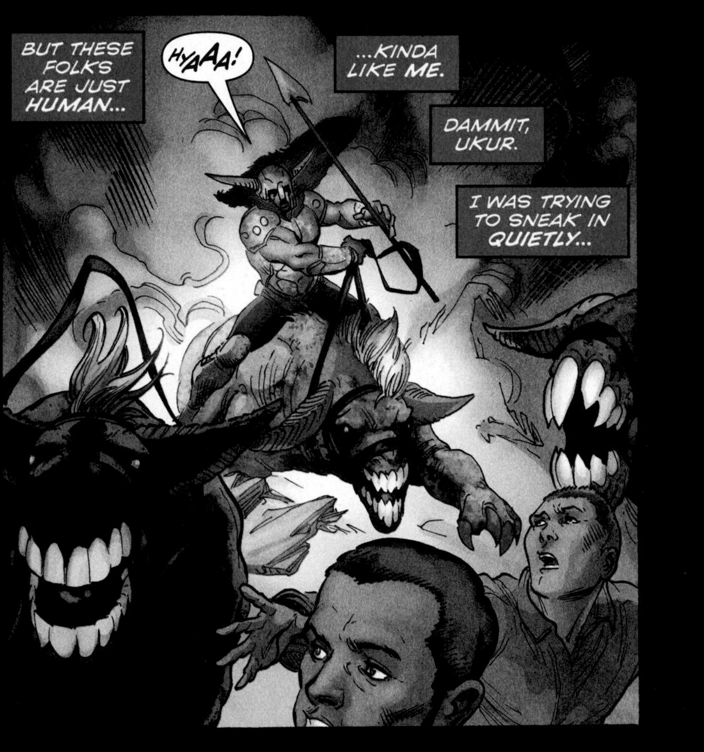
BUT THESE FOLK'S ARE JUST HUMAN...
HYAAA!
...KINDA LIKE ME.
DAMMIT, UKUR.
I WAS TRYING TO SNEAK IN QUIETLY...

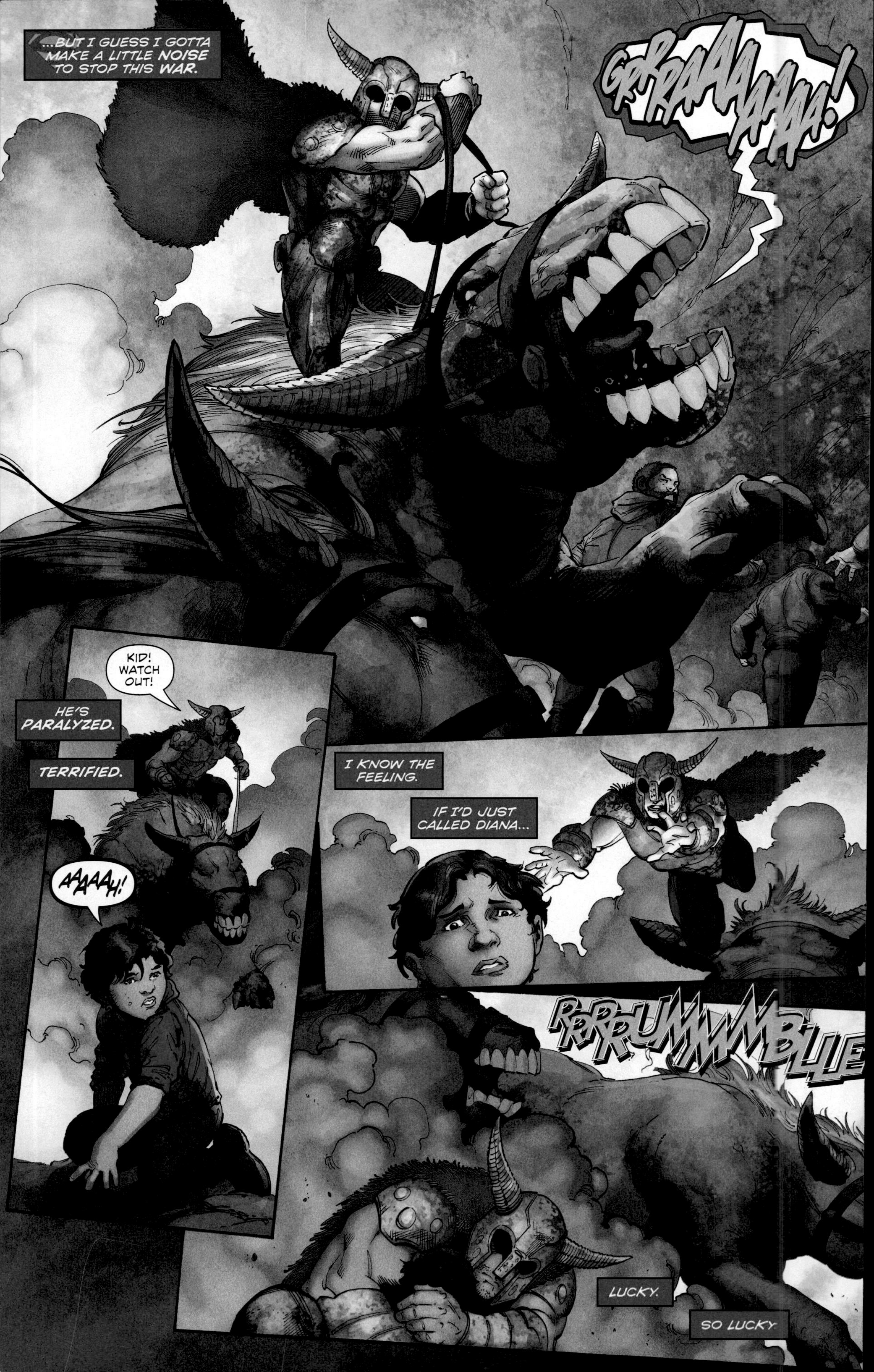
...BUT I GUESS I GOTTA MAKE A LITTLE NOISE TO STOP THIS WAR.
GRRAAAAAAAAA!
KID! WATCH OUT!
HE'S PARALYZED.
TERRIFIED.
AAAAAH!
I KNOW THE FEELING.
IF I'D JUST CALLED DIANA...
RRRRUMMMBLLE
LUCKY.
SO LUCKY.

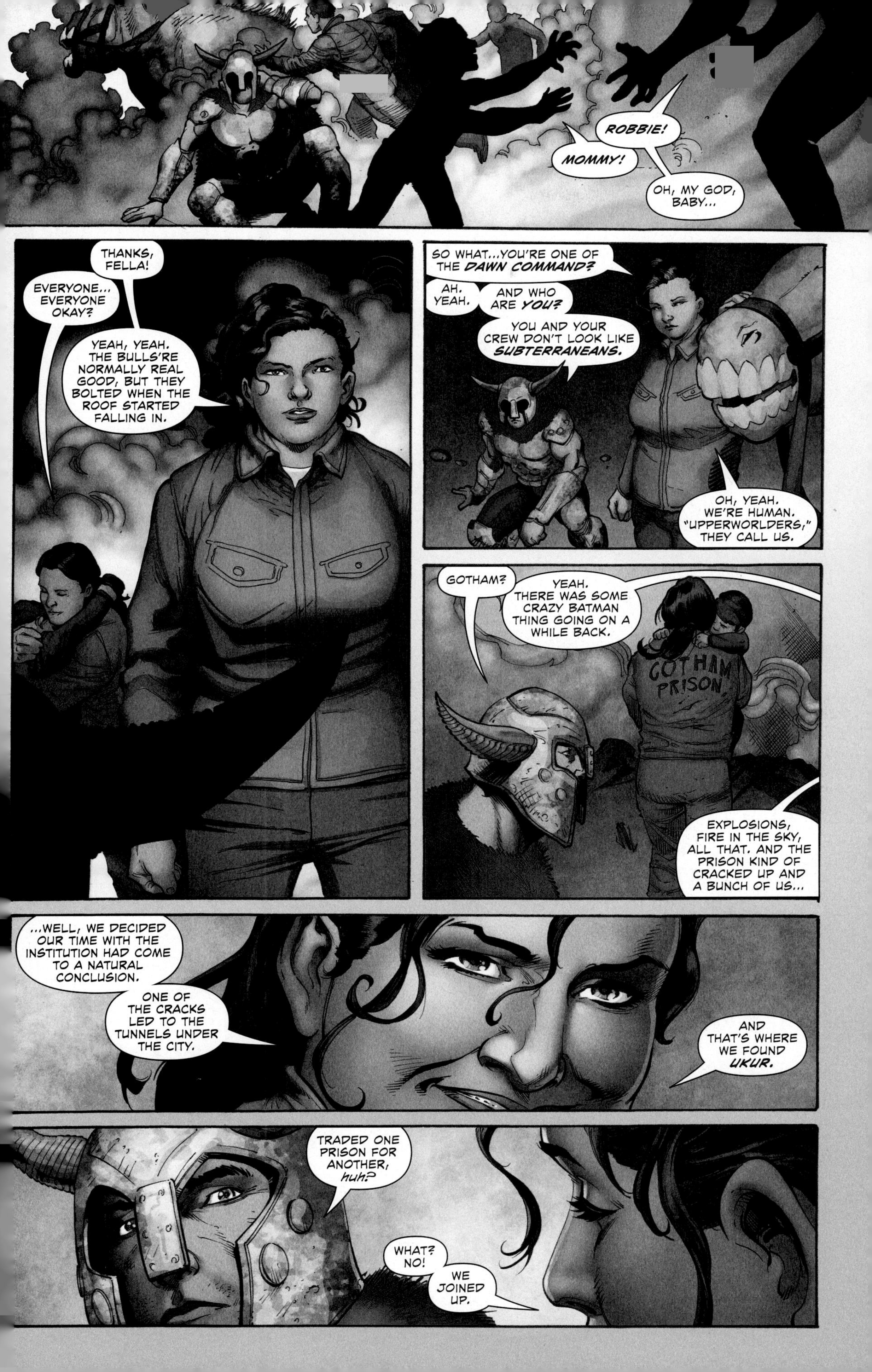
ROBBIE!
MOMMY!
OH, MY GOD, BABY...
EVERYONE... EVERYONE OKAY?
THANKS, FELLA!
YEAH, YEAH. THE BULLS'RE NORMALLY REAL GOOD, BUT THEY BOLTED WHEN THE ROOF STARTED FALLING IN.
SO WHAT...YOU'RE ONE OF THE DAWN COMMAND?
AH. YEAH.
AND WHO ARE YOU?
YOU AND YOUR CREW DON'T LOOK LIKE SUBTERRANEANS.
OH, YEAH. WE'RE HUMAN. "UPPERWORLDERS," THEY CALL US.
GOTHAM?
YEAH. THERE WAS SOME CRAZY BATMAN THING GOING ON A WHILE BACK.
GOTHAM PRISON
EXPLOSIONS, FIRE IN THE SKY, ALL THAT. AND THE PRISON KIND OF CRACKED UP AND A BUNCH OF US...
...WELL, WE DECIDED OUR TIME WITH THE INSTITUTION HAD COME TO A NATURAL CONCLUSION.
ONE OF THE CRACKS LED TO THE TUNNELS UNDER THE CITY.
AND THAT'S WHERE WE FOUND UKUR.
TRADED ONE PRISON FOR ANOTHER, huh?
WHAT? NO!
WE JOINED UP.

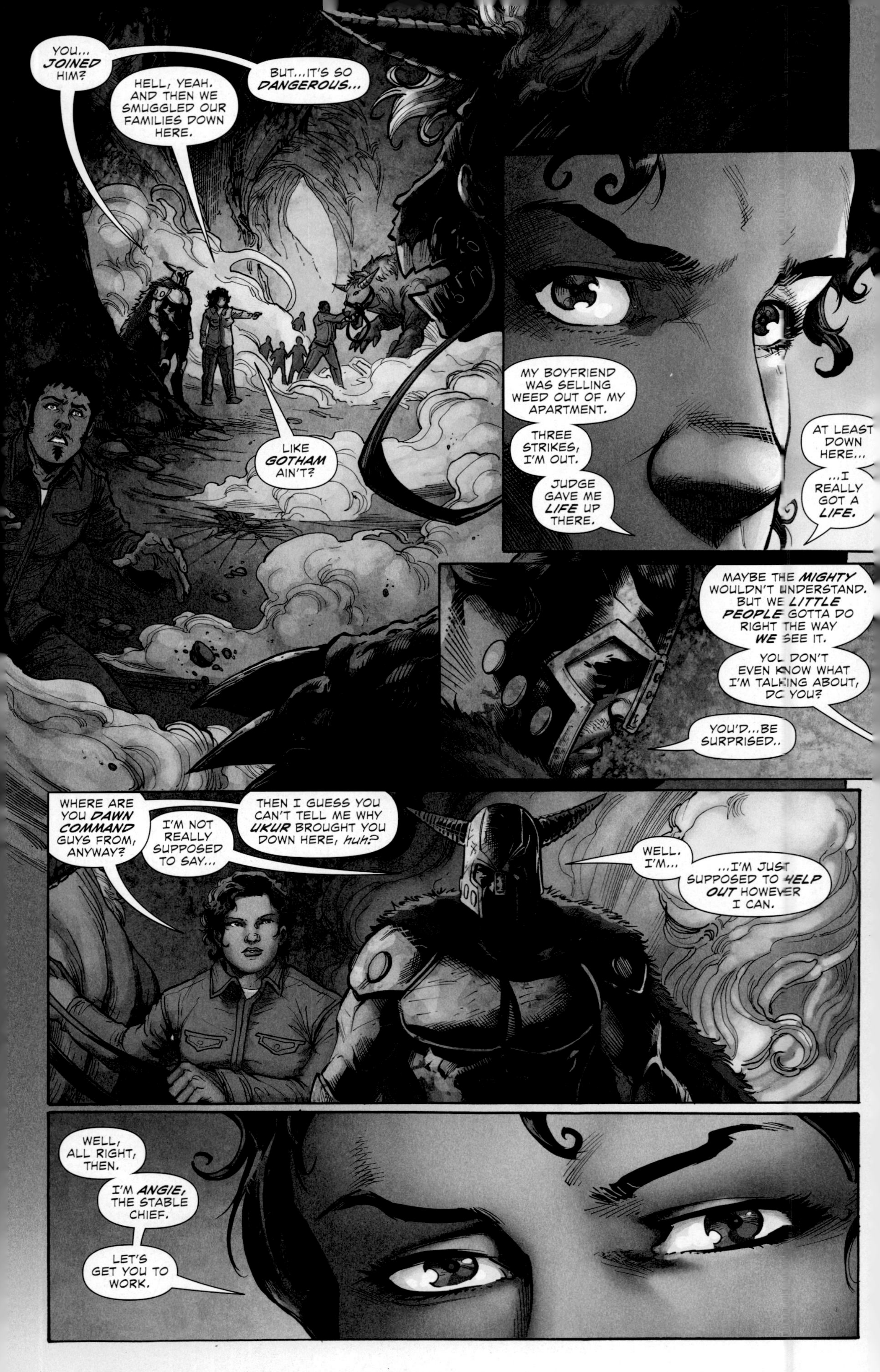
YOU... JOINED HIM?
HELL, YEAH. AND THEN WE SMUGGLED OUR FAMILIES DOWN HERE.
BUT...IT'S SO DANGEROUS...
LIKE GOTHAM AIN'T?
MY BOYFRIEND WAS SELLING WEED OUT OF MY APARTMENT.
THREE STRIKES, I'M OUT.
JUDGE GAVE ME LIFE UP THERE.
AT LEAST DOWN HERE...
...I REALLY GOT A LIFE.
MAYBE THE MIGHTY WOULDN'T UNDERSTAND. BUT WE LITTLE PEOPLE GOTTA DO RIGHT THE WAY WE SEE IT.
YOU DON'T EVEN KNOW WHAT I'M TALKING ABOUT, DO YOU?
YOU'D...BE SURPRISED..
WHERE ARE YOU DAWN COMMAND GUYS FROM, ANYWAY?
I'M NOT REALLY SUPPOSED TO SAY...
THEN I GUESS YOU CAN'T TELL ME WHY UKUR BROUGHT YOU DOWN HERE, HUH?
WELL. I'M...
...I'M JUST SUPPOSED TO HELP OUT HOWEVER I CAN.
WELL, ALL RIGHT, THEN.
I'M ANGIE, THE STABLE CHIEF.
LET'S GET YOU TO WORK.

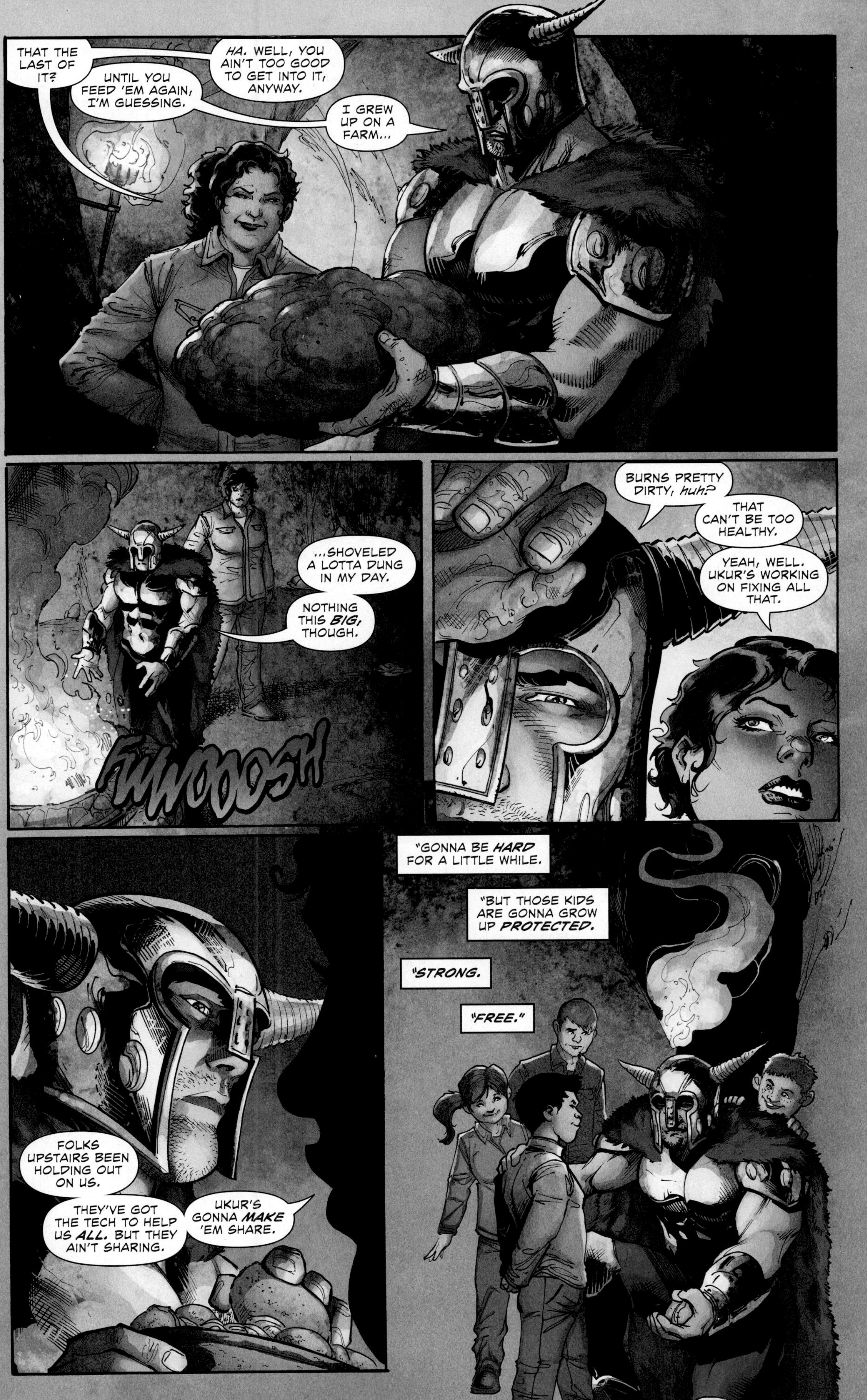
THAT THE LAST OF IT?
HA. WELL, YOU AIN'T TOO GOOD TO GET INTO IT, ANYWAY.
UNTIL YOU FEED 'EM AGAIN, I'M GUESSING.
I GREW UP ON A FARM...
...SHOVELED A LOTTA DUNG IN MY DAY.
NOTHING THIS BIG, THOUGH.
FWOOOSH
BURNS PRETTY DIRTY, huh?
THAT CAN'T BE TOO HEALTHY.
YEAH, WELL. UKUR'S WORKING ON FIXING ALL THAT.
FOLKS UPSTAIRS BEEN HOLDING OUT ON US.
THEY'VE GOT THE TECH TO HELP US ALL. BUT THEY AIN'T SHARING.
UKUR'S GONNA MAKE 'EM SHARE.
"GONNA BE HARD FOR A LITTLE WHILE.
"BUT THOSE KIDS ARE GONNA GROW UP PROTECTED.
"STRONG.
"FREE."

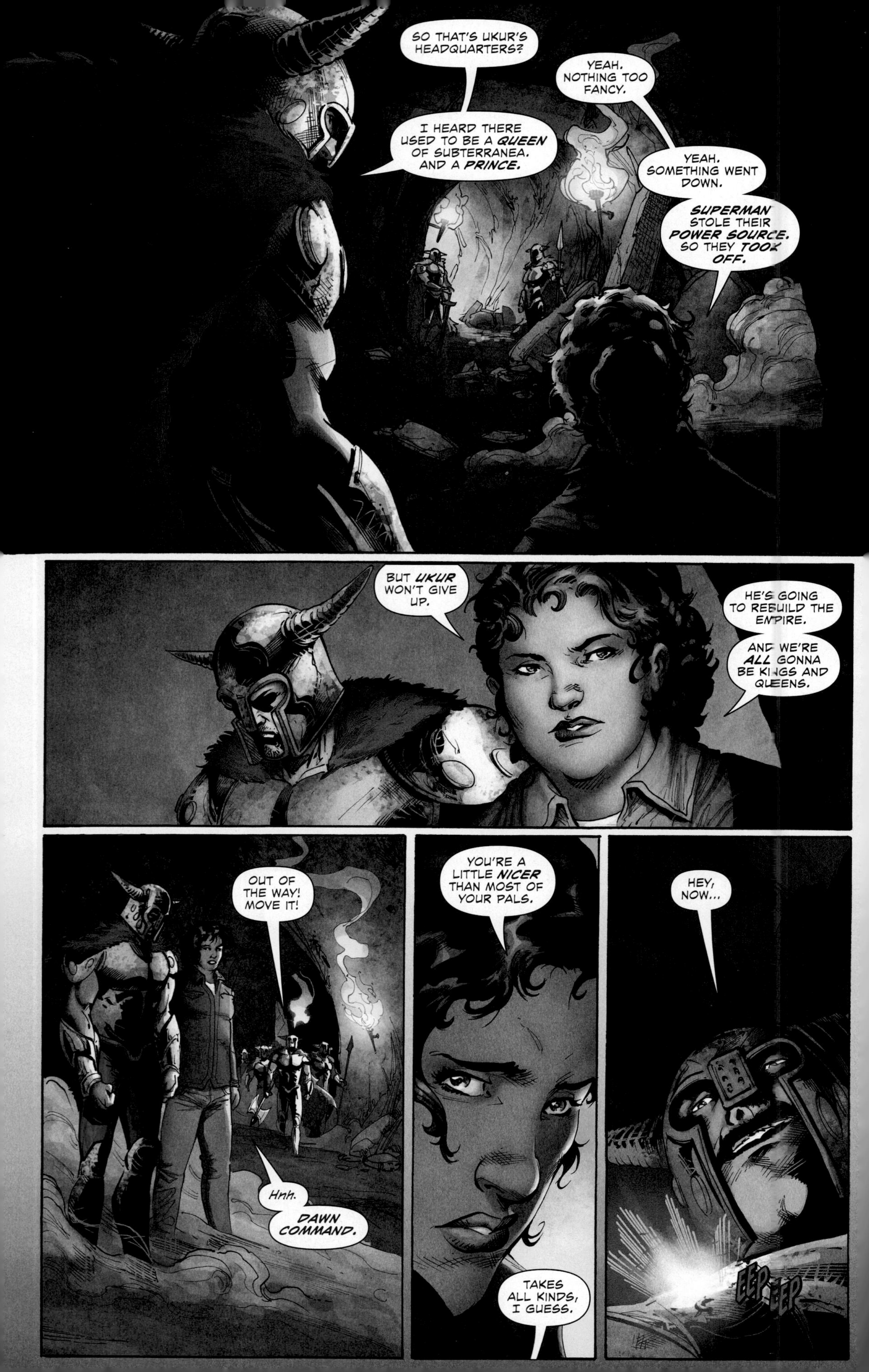
SO THAT'S UKUR'S HEADQUARTERS?
I HEARD THERE USED TO BE A *QUEEN* OF SUBTERRANEA. AND A *PRINCE.*
YEAH. NOTHING TOO FANCY.
YEAH. SOMETHING WENT DOWN.
SUPERMAN STOLE THEIR *POWER SOURCE.* SO THEY *TOOK OFF.*
BUT *UKUR* WON'T GIVE UP.
HE'S GOING TO REBUILD THE EMPIRE.
AND WE'RE *ALL* GONNA BE KINGS AND QUEENS.
OUT OF THE WAY! MOVE IT!
Hnh.
DAWN COMMAND.
YOU'RE A LITTLE *NICER* THAN MOST OF YOUR PALS.
TAKES ALL KINDS, I GUESS.
HEY, NOW...
EEP EEP

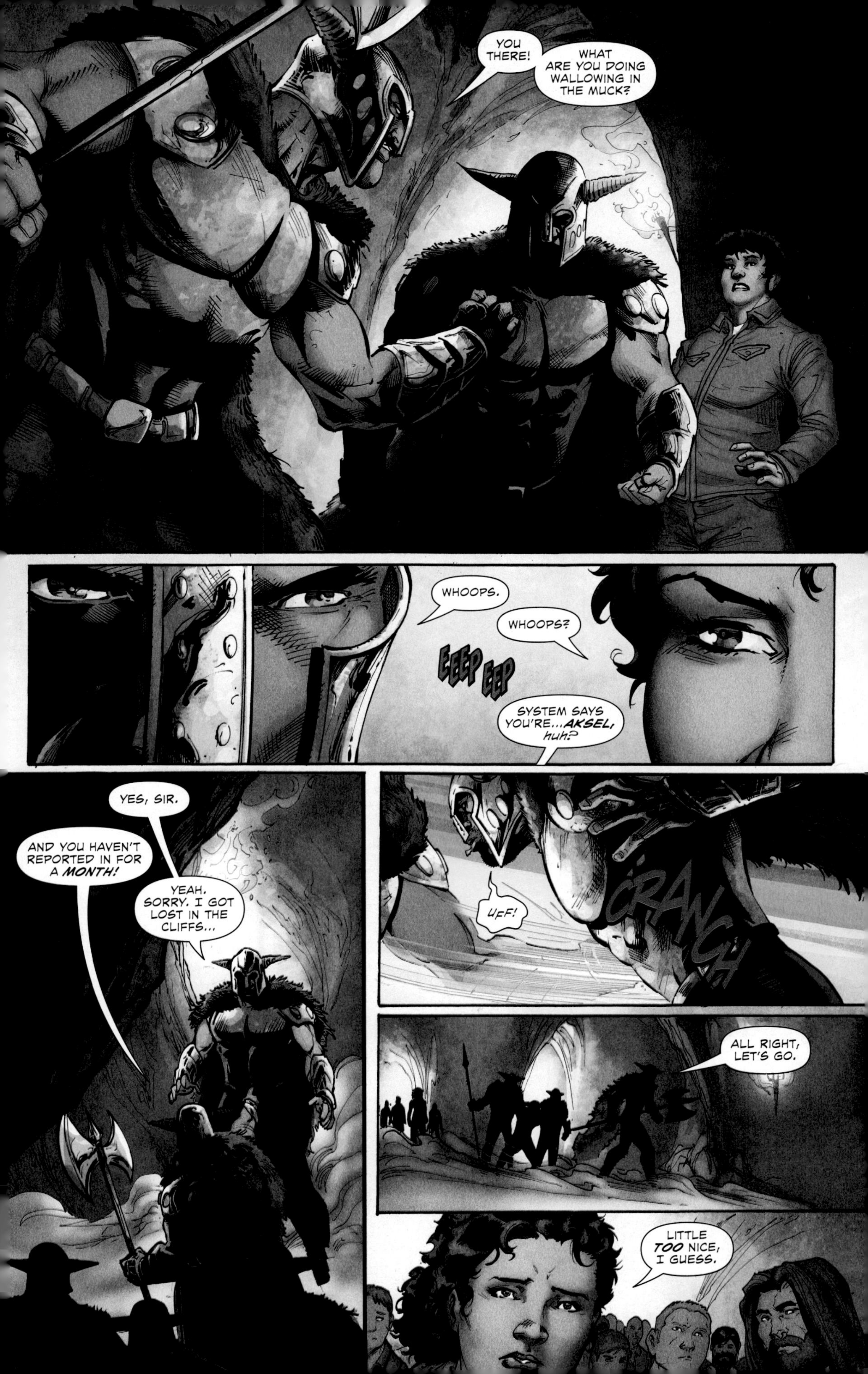
YOU THERE!
WHAT ARE YOU DOING WALLOWING IN THE MUCK?
WHOOPS.
WHOOPS?
EEEP EEP
SYSTEM SAYS YOU'RE... AKSEL, huh?
YES, SIR.
AND YOU HAVEN'T REPORTED IN FOR A MONTH!
YEAH. SORRY. I GOT LOST IN THE CLIFFS...
UFF!
CRANCH
ALL RIGHT, LET'S GO.
LITTLE TOO NICE, I GUESS.

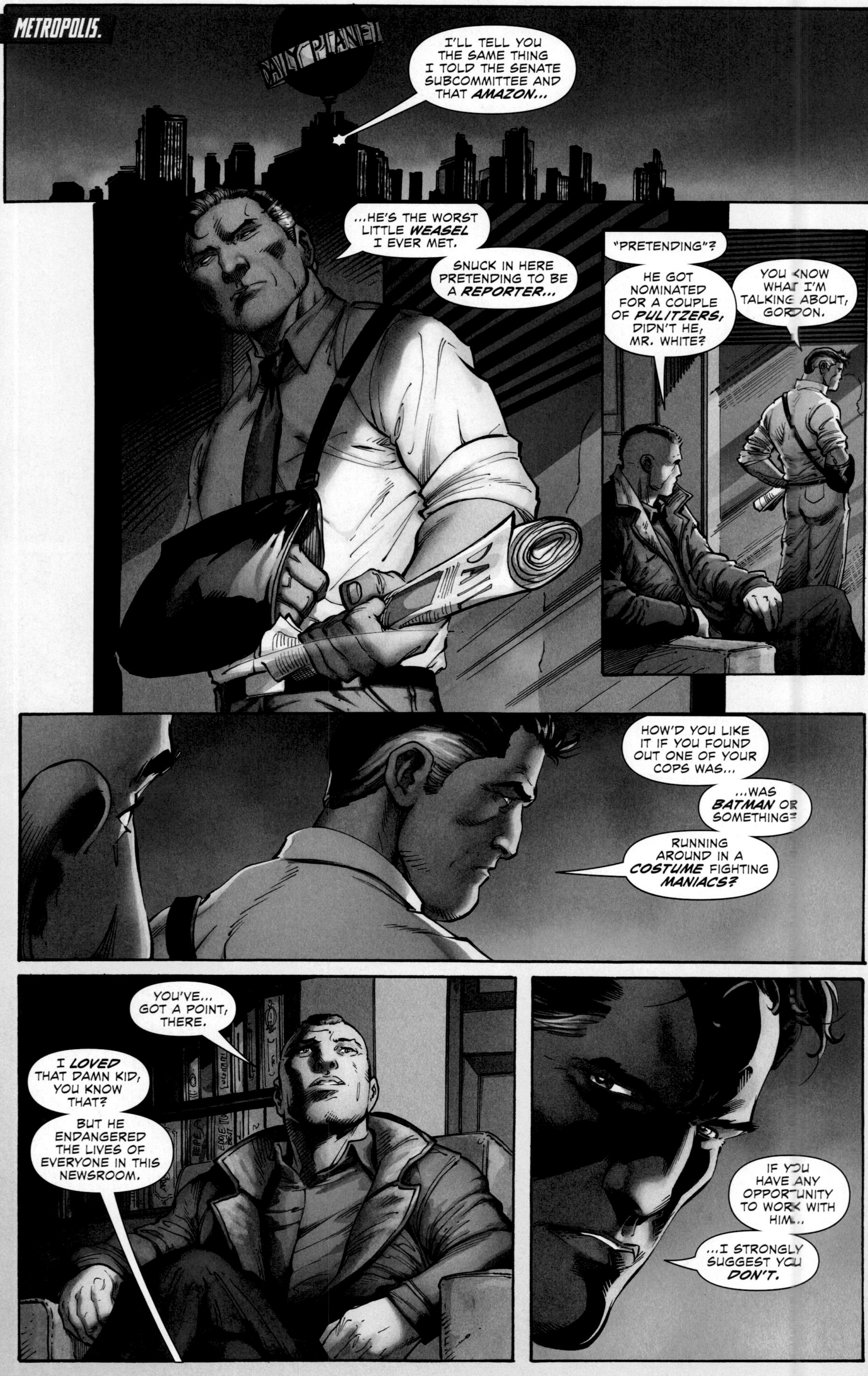
METROPOLIS.
DAILY PLANET
I'LL TELL YOU THE SAME THING I TOLD THE SENATE SUBCOMMITTEE AND THAT AMAZON...
...HE'S THE WORST LITTLE WEASEL I EVER MET.
SNUCK IN HERE PRETENDING TO BE A REPORTER...
"PRETENDING"?
HE GOT NOMINATED FOR A COUPLE OF PULITZERS, DIDN'T HE, MR. WHITE?
YOU KNOW WHAT I'M TALKING ABOUT, GORDON.
HOW'D YOU LIKE IT IF YOU FOUND OUT ONE OF YOUR COPS WAS...
...WAS BATMAN OR SOMETHING?
RUNNING AROUND IN A COSTUME FIGHTING MANIACS?
YOU'VE... GOT A POINT, THERE.
I LOVED THAT DAMN KID, YOU KNOW THAT?
BUT HE ENDANGERED THE LIVES OF EVERYONE IN THIS NEWSROOM.
IF YOU HAVE ANY OPPORTUNITY TO WORK WITH HIM...
...I STRONGLY SUGGEST YOU DON'T.

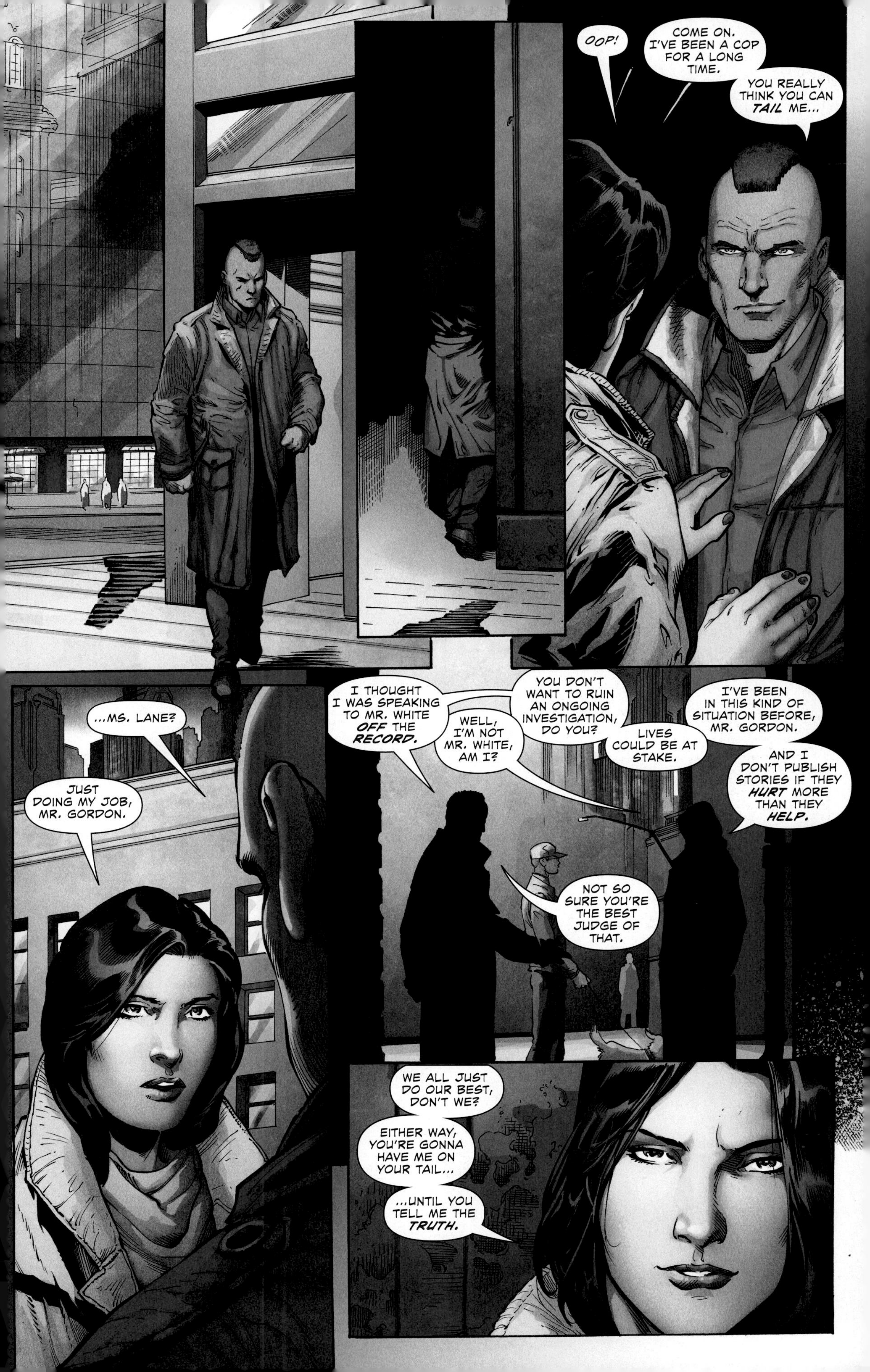
OOP!
COME ON. I'VE BEEN A COP FOR A LONG TIME.
YOU REALLY THINK YOU CAN TAIL ME...
...MS. LANE?
JUST DOING MY JOB, MR. GORDON.
I THOUGHT I WAS SPEAKING TO MR. WHITE OFF THE RECORD.
WELL, I'M NOT MR. WHITE, AM I?
YOU DON'T WANT TO RUIN AN ONGOING INVESTIGATION, DO YOU?
LIVES COULD BE AT STAKE.
I'VE BEEN IN THIS KIND OF SITUATION BEFORE, MR. GORDON.
AND I DON'T PUBLISH STORIES IF THEY HURT MORE THAN THEY HELP.
NOT SO SURE YOU'RE THE BEST JUDGE OF THAT.
WE ALL JUST DO OUR BEST, DON'T WE?
EITHER WAY, YOU'RE GONNA HAVE ME ON YOUR TAIL...
...UNTIL YOU TELL ME THE TRUTH.

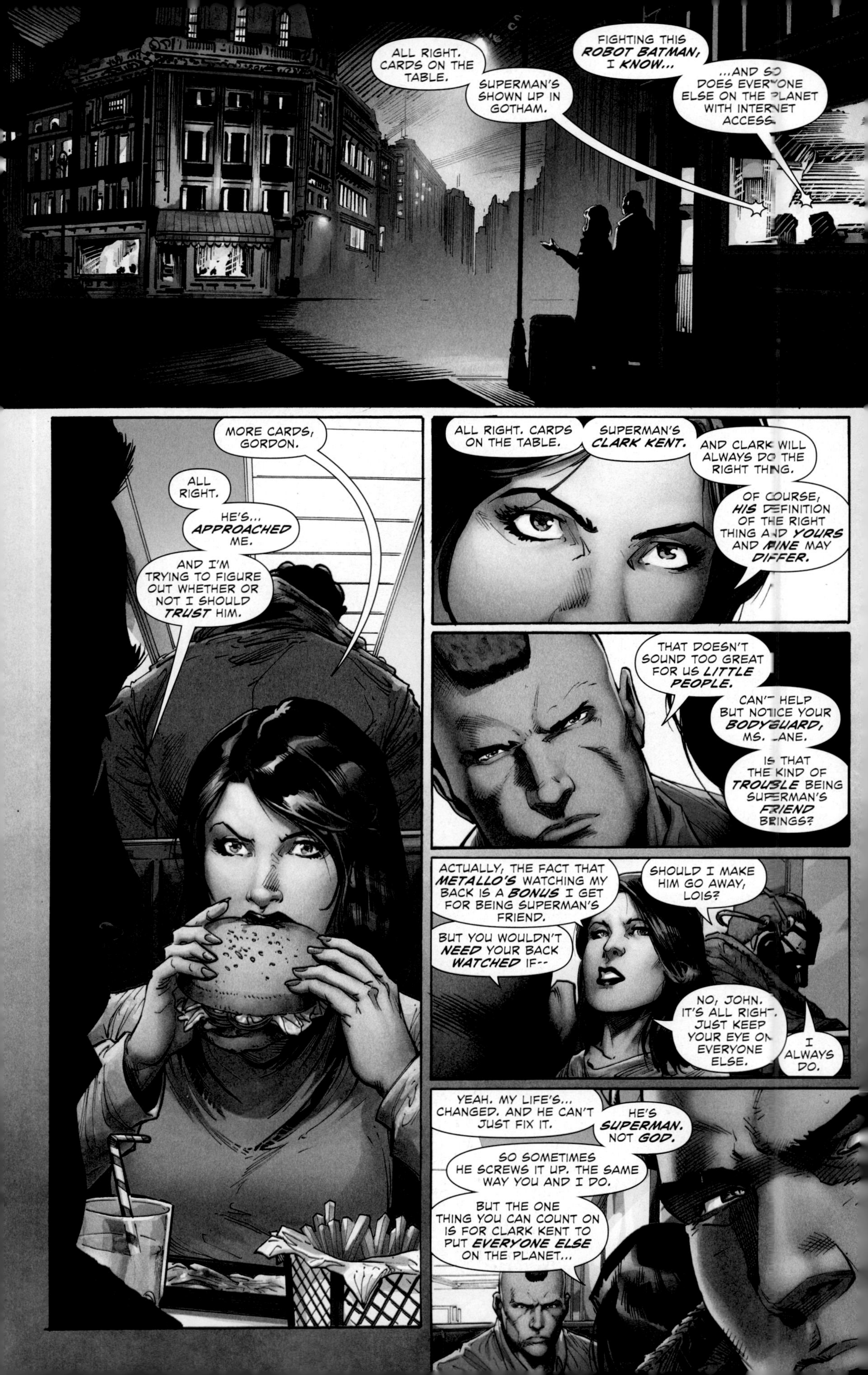
ALL RIGHT. CARDS ON THE TABLE.
SUPERMAN'S SHOWN UP IN GOTHAM.
FIGHTING THIS ROBOT BATMAN, I KNOW...
...AND SO DOES EVERYONE ELSE ON THE PLANET WITH INTERNET ACCESS.
MORE CARDS, GORDON.
ALL RIGHT.
HE'S... APPROACHED ME.
AND I'M TRYING TO FIGURE OUT WHETHER OR NOT I SHOULD TRUST HIM.
ALL RIGHT. CARDS ON THE TABLE.
SUPERMAN'S CLARK KENT.
AND CLARK WILL ALWAYS DO THE RIGHT THING.
OF COURSE, HIS DEFINITION OF THE RIGHT THING AND YOURS AND MINE MAY DIFFER.
THAT DOESN'T SOUND TOO GREAT FOR US LITTLE PEOPLE.
CAN'T HELP BUT NOTICE YOUR BODYGUARD, MS. LANE.
IS THAT THE KIND OF TROUBLE BEING SUPERMAN'S FRIEND BRINGS?
ACTUALLY, THE FACT THAT METALLO'S WATCHING MY BACK IS A BONUS I GET FOR BEING SUPERMAN'S FRIEND.
BUT YOU WOULDN'T NEED YOUR BACK WATCHED IF--
SHOULD I MAKE HIM GO AWAY, LOIS?
NO, JOHN. IT'S ALL RIGHT. JUST KEEP YOUR EYE ON EVERYONE ELSE.
I ALWAYS DO.
YEAH. MY LIFE'S... CHANGED. AND HE CAN'T JUST FIX IT.
HE'S SUPERMAN. NOT GOD.
SO SOMETIMES HE SCREWS IT UP. THE SAME WAY YOU AND I DO.
BUT THE ONE THING YOU CAN COUNT ON IS FOR CLARK KENT TO PUT EVERYONE ELSE ON THE PLANET...

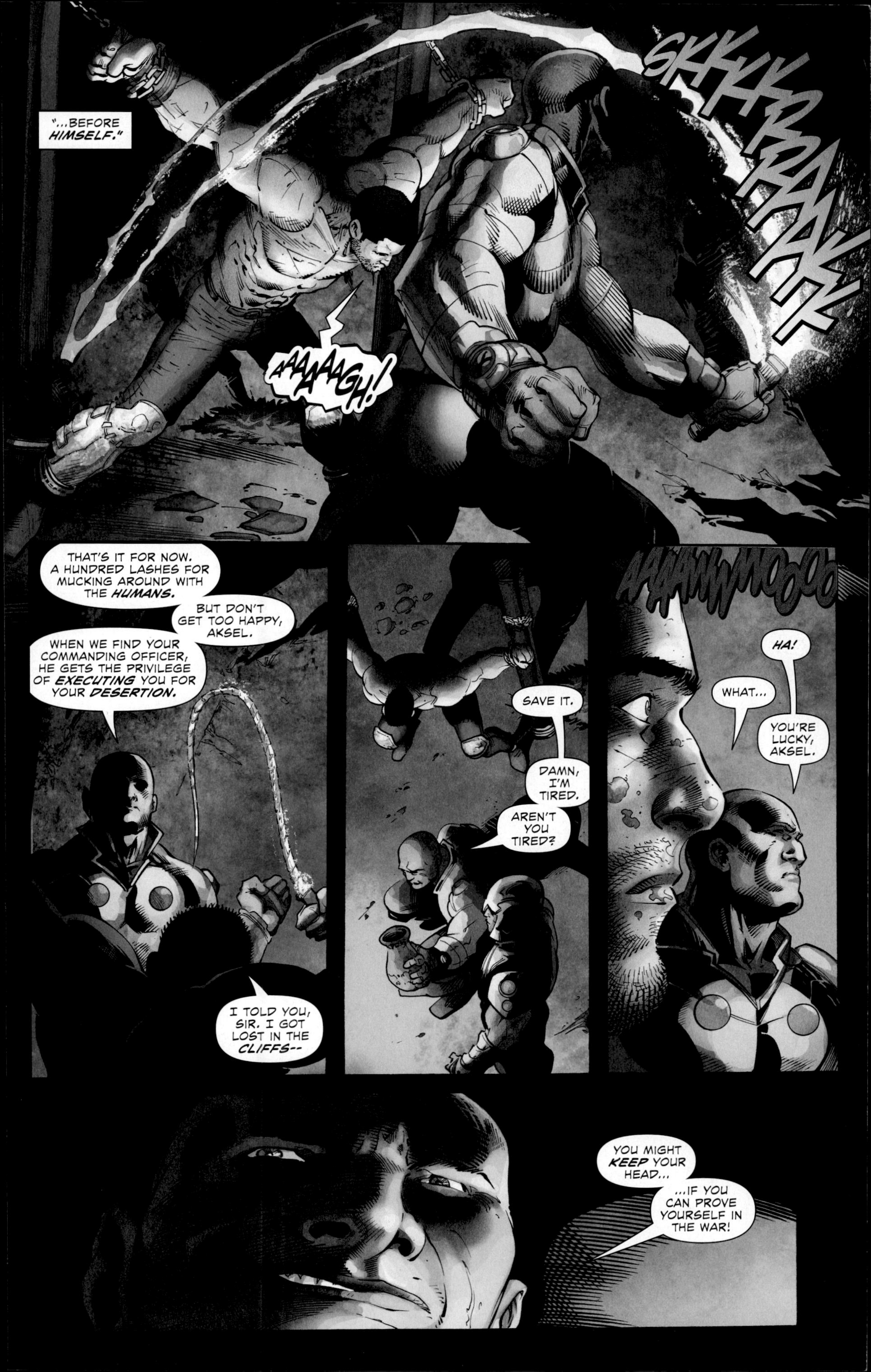
"...BEFORE HIMSELF."
SKKKRAKK
AAAAAAGH!
THAT'S IT FOR NOW. A HUNDRED LASHES FOR MUCKING AROUND WITH THE HUMANS.
BUT DON'T GET TOO HAPPY, AKSEL.
WHEN WE FIND YOUR COMMANDING OFFICER, HE GETS THE PRIVILEGE OF EXECUTING YOU FOR YOUR DESERTION.
I TOLD YOU, SIR. I GOT LOST IN THE CLIFFS--
SAVE IT.
DAMN, I'M TIRED.
AREN'T YOU TIRED?
AAAAWWOOOO
HA!
WHAT...
YOU'RE LUCKY, AKSEL.
YOU MIGHT KEEP YOUR HEAD...
...IF YOU CAN PROVE YOURSELF IN THE WAR!

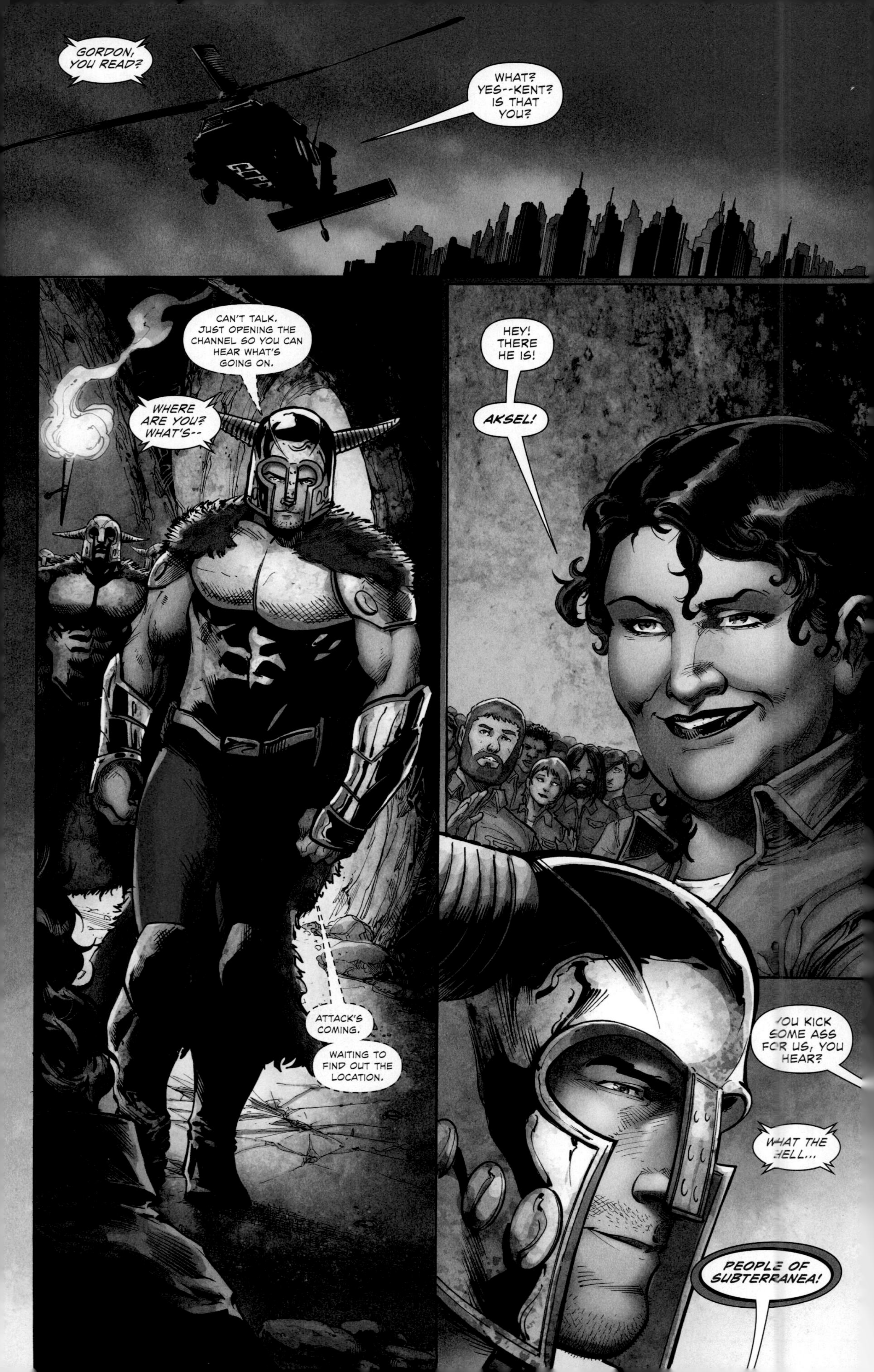
GORDON, YOU READ?
WHAT? YES--KENT? IS THAT YOU?
CAN'T TALK. JUST OPENING THE CHANNEL SO YOU CAN HEAR WHAT'S GOING ON.
WHERE ARE YOU? WHAT'S--
ATTACK'S COMING.
WAITING TO FIND OUT THE LOCATION.
HEY! THERE HE IS!
AKSEL!
YOU KICK SOME ASS FOR US, YOU HEAR?
WHAT THE HELL...
PEOPLE OF SUBTERRANEA!

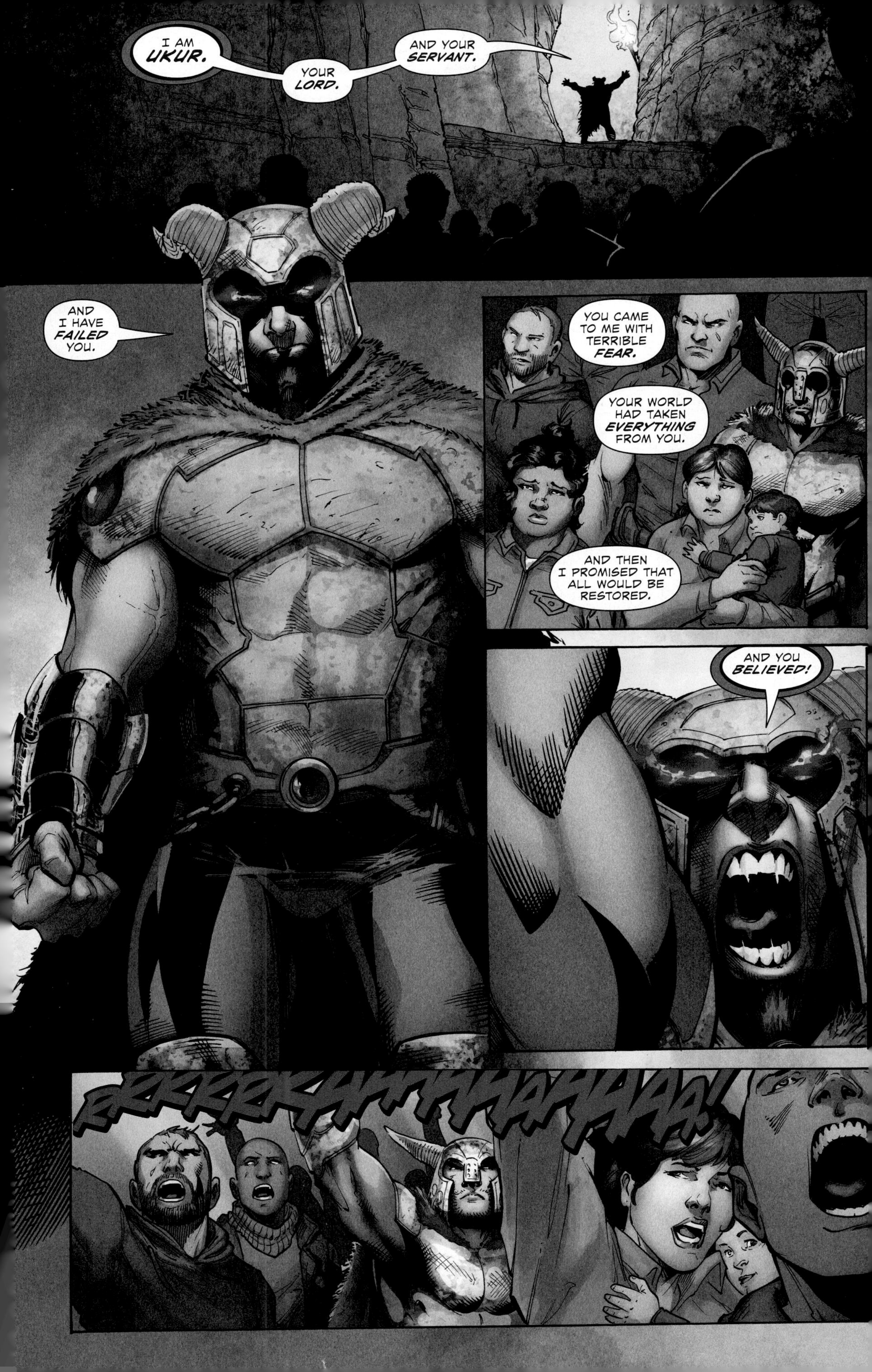

I AM *UKUR.*
YOUR *LORD.*
AND YOUR *SERVANT.*
AND I HAVE *FAILED* YOU.
YOU CAME TO ME WITH TERRIBLE *FEAR.*
YOUR WORLD HAD TAKEN *EVERYTHING* FROM YOU.
AND THEN I PROMISED THAT ALL WOULD BE RESTORED.
AND YOU *BELIEVED!*

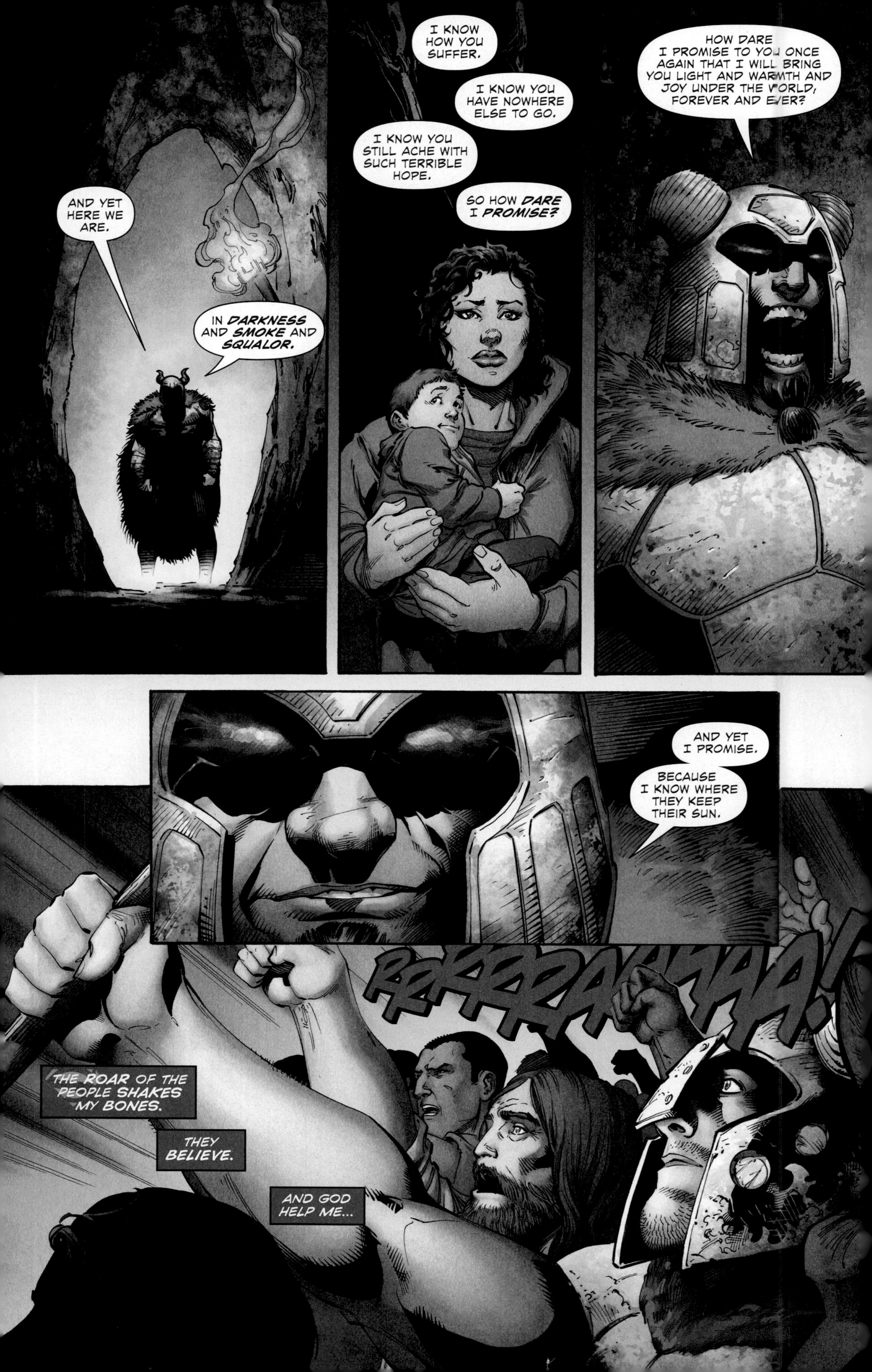
AND YET HERE WE ARE.
IN DARKNESS AND SMOKE AND SQUALOR.
I KNOW HOW YOU SUFFER.
I KNOW YOU HAVE NOWHERE ELSE TO GO.
I KNOW YOU STILL ACHE WITH SUCH TERRIBLE HOPE.
SO HOW DARE I PROMISE?
HOW DARE I PROMISE TO YOU ONCE AGAIN THAT I WILL BRING YOU LIGHT AND WARMTH AND JOY UNDER THE WORLD, FOREVER AND EVER?
AND YET I PROMISE.
BECAUSE I KNOW WHERE THEY KEEP THEIR SUN.
RRRRAAAAHHH!!
THE ROAR OF THE PEOPLE SHAKES MY BONES.
THEY BELIEVE.
AND GOD HELP ME...

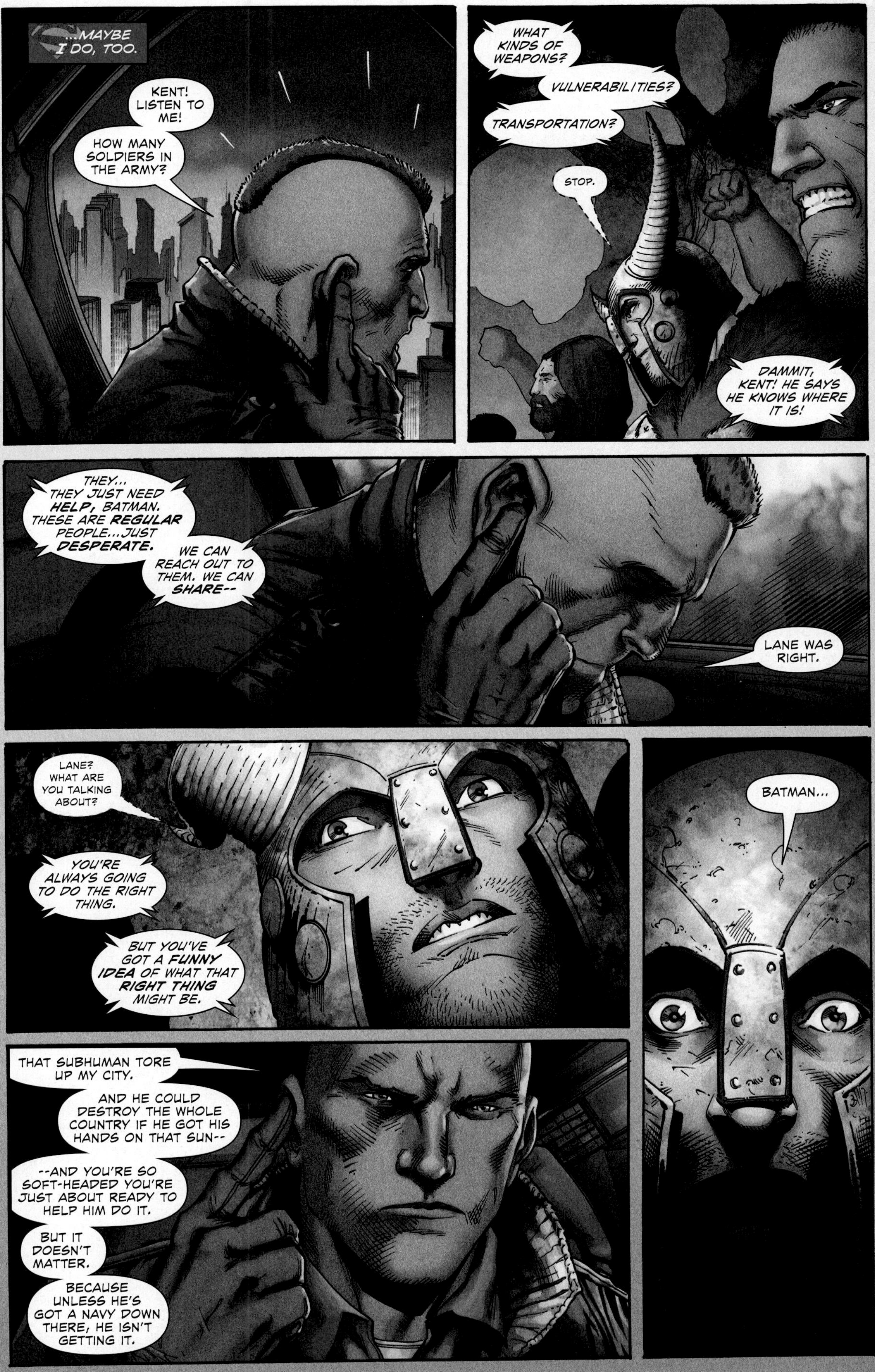
...MAYBE I DO, TOO.
KENT! LISTEN TO ME!
HOW MANY SOLDIERS IN THE ARMY?
WHAT KINDS OF WEAPONS?
VULNERABILITIES?
TRANSPORTATION?
STOP.
DAMMIT, KENT! HE SAYS HE KNOWS WHERE IT IS!
THEY... THEY JUST NEED HELP, BATMAN. THESE ARE REGULAR PEOPLE...JUST DESPERATE.
WE CAN REACH OUT TO THEM. WE CAN SHARE--
LANE WAS RIGHT.
LANE? WHAT ARE YOU TALKING ABOUT?
YOU'RE ALWAYS GOING TO DO THE RIGHT THING.
BUT YOU'VE GOT A FUNNY IDEA OF WHAT THAT RIGHT THING MIGHT BE.
BATMAN...
THAT SUBHUMAN TORE UP MY CITY.
AND HE COULD DESTROY THE WHOLE COUNTRY IF HE GOT HIS HANDS ON THAT SUN--
--AND YOU'RE SO SOFT-HEADED YOU'RE JUST ABOUT READY TO HELP HIM DO IT.
BUT IT DOESN'T MATTER.
BECAUSE UNLESS HE'S GOT A NAVY DOWN THERE, HE ISN'T GETTING IT.

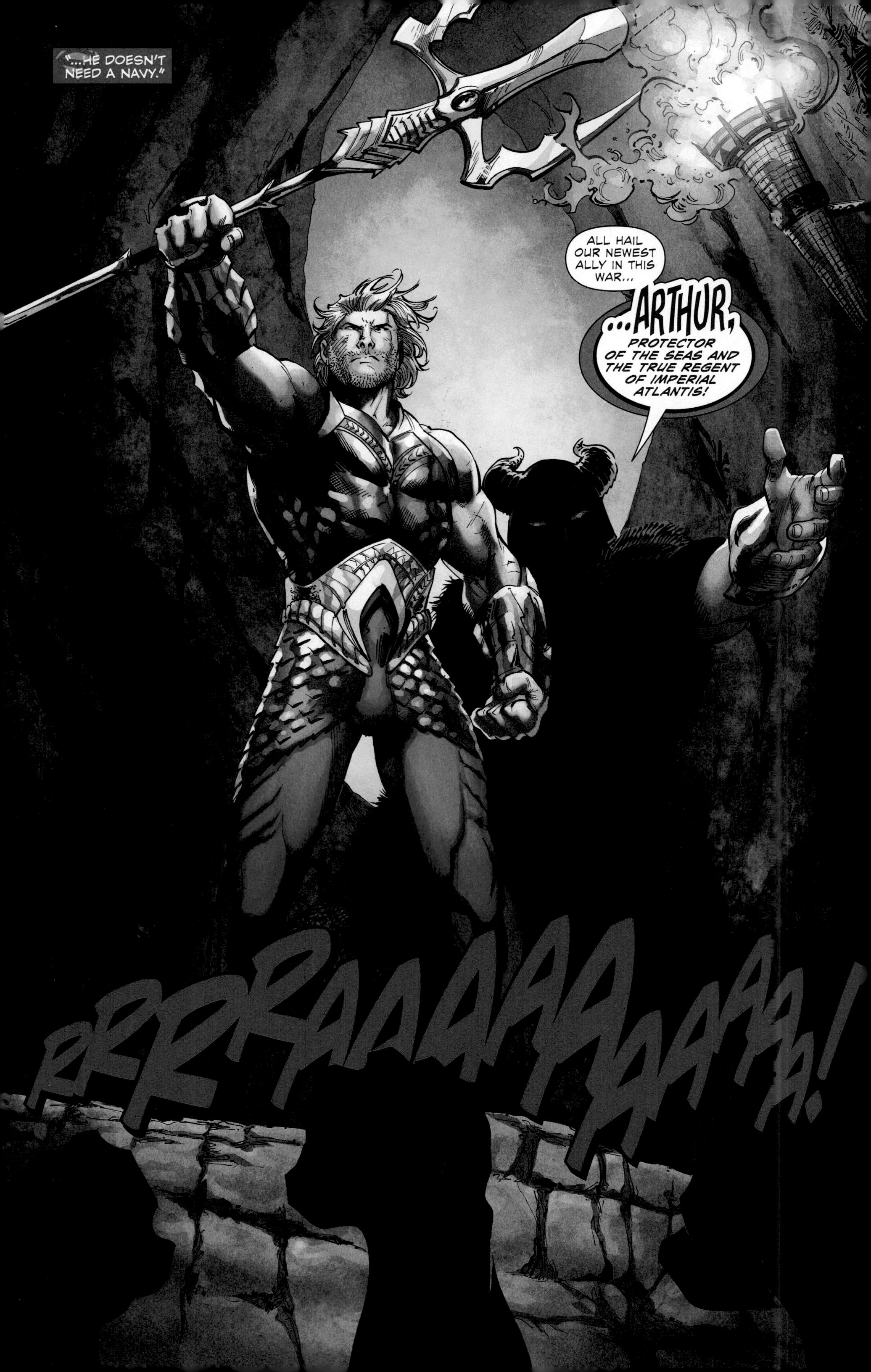
"...HE DOESN'T NEED A NAVY."
ALL HAIL OUR NEWEST ALLY IN THIS WAR...
...ARTHUR, PROTECTOR OF THE SEAS AND THE TRUE REGENT OF IMPERIAL ATLANTIS!
RRRRAAAAAAAAAAAA!

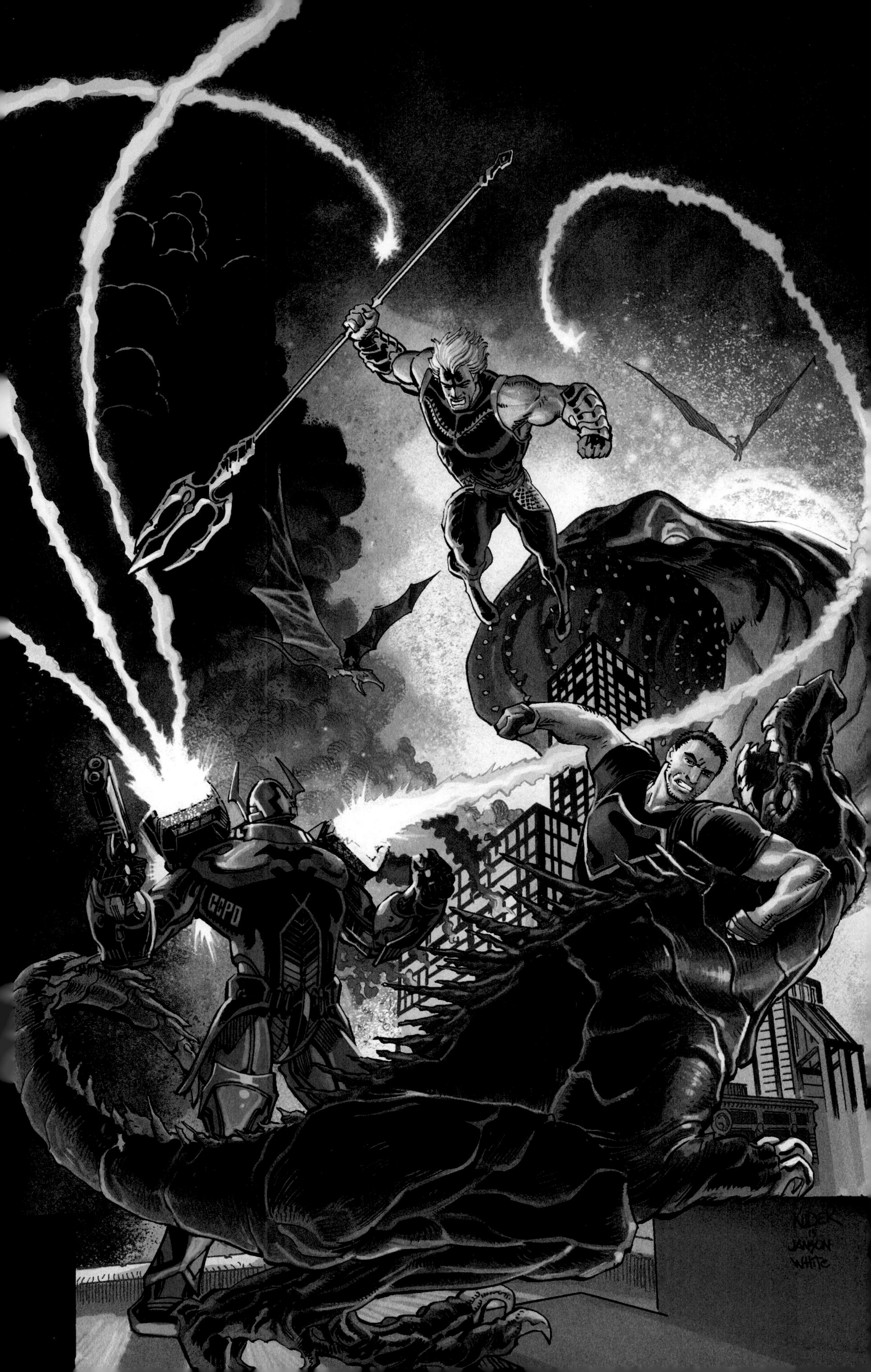
CCPD

TRUTH HURTS PART FOUR

GREG PAK writer ARDIAN SYAF YILDIRAY CINAR HOWARD PORTER pencillers VICENTE CIFUENTES YILDIRAY CINAR HOWARD PORTER inkers DEAN WHITE BETH SOTELO colorists ROB LEIGH letterer AARON KUDER KLAUS JANSON DEAN WHITE cover

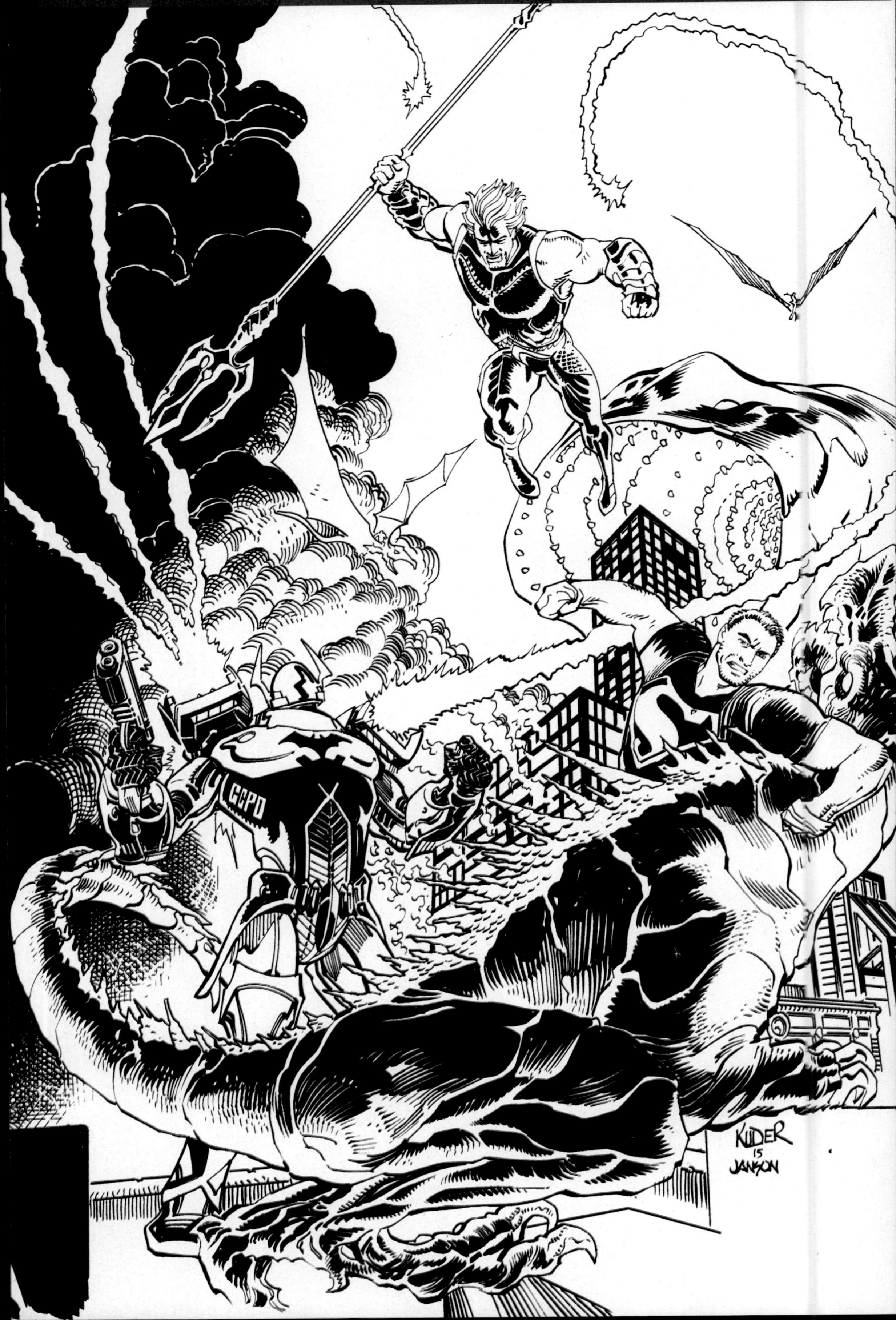

GCPD
KUDER 15 JANSON

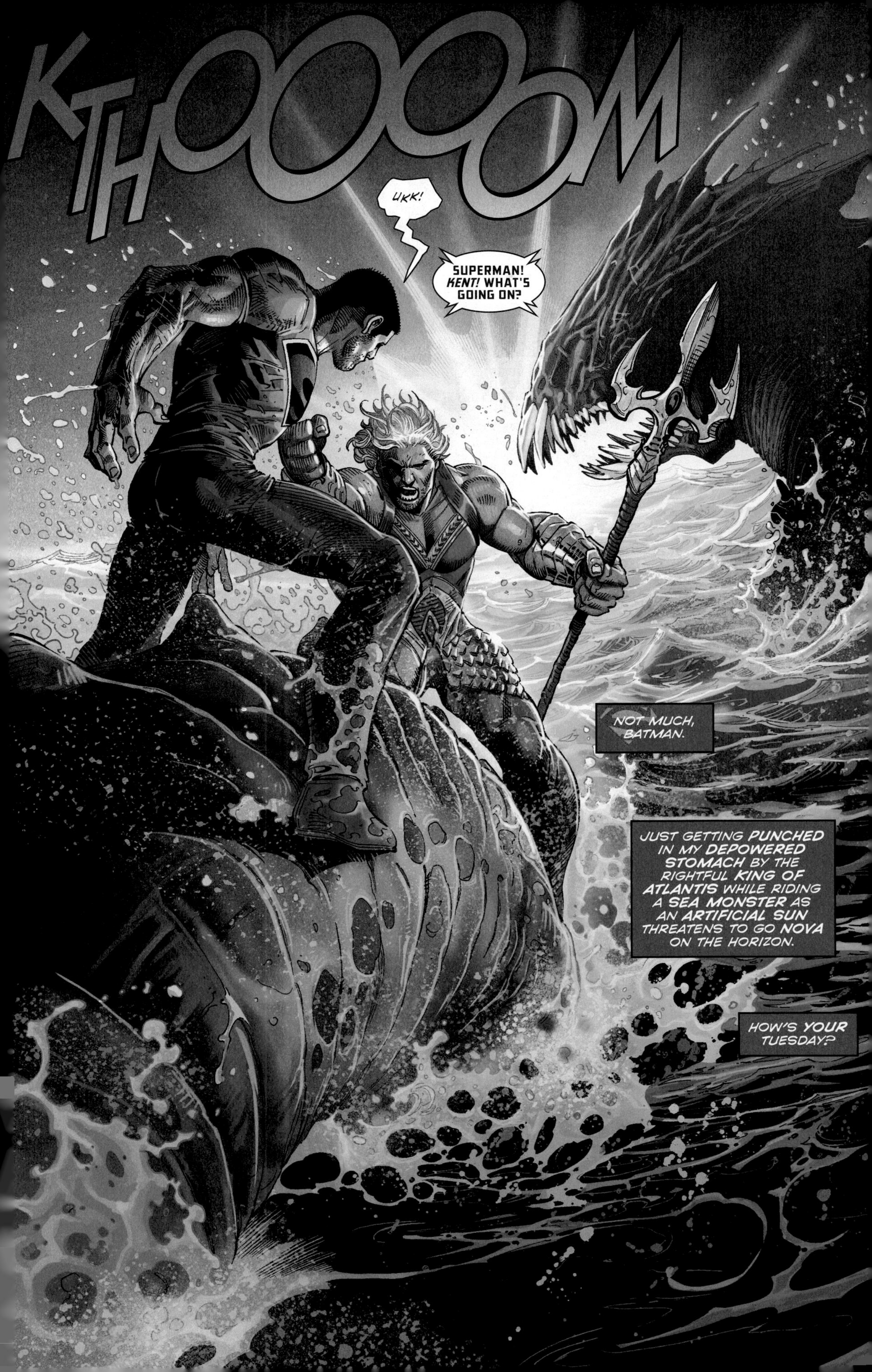
KTHOOOOOM
UKK!
SUPERMAN! KENT! WHAT'S GOING ON?
NOT MUCH, BATMAN.
JUST GETTING PUNCHED IN MY DEPOWERED STOMACH BY THE RIGHTFUL KING OF ATLANTIS WHILE RIDING A SEA MONSTER AS AN ARTIFICIAL SUN THREATENS TO GO NOVA ON THE HORIZON.
HOW'S YOUR TUESDAY?

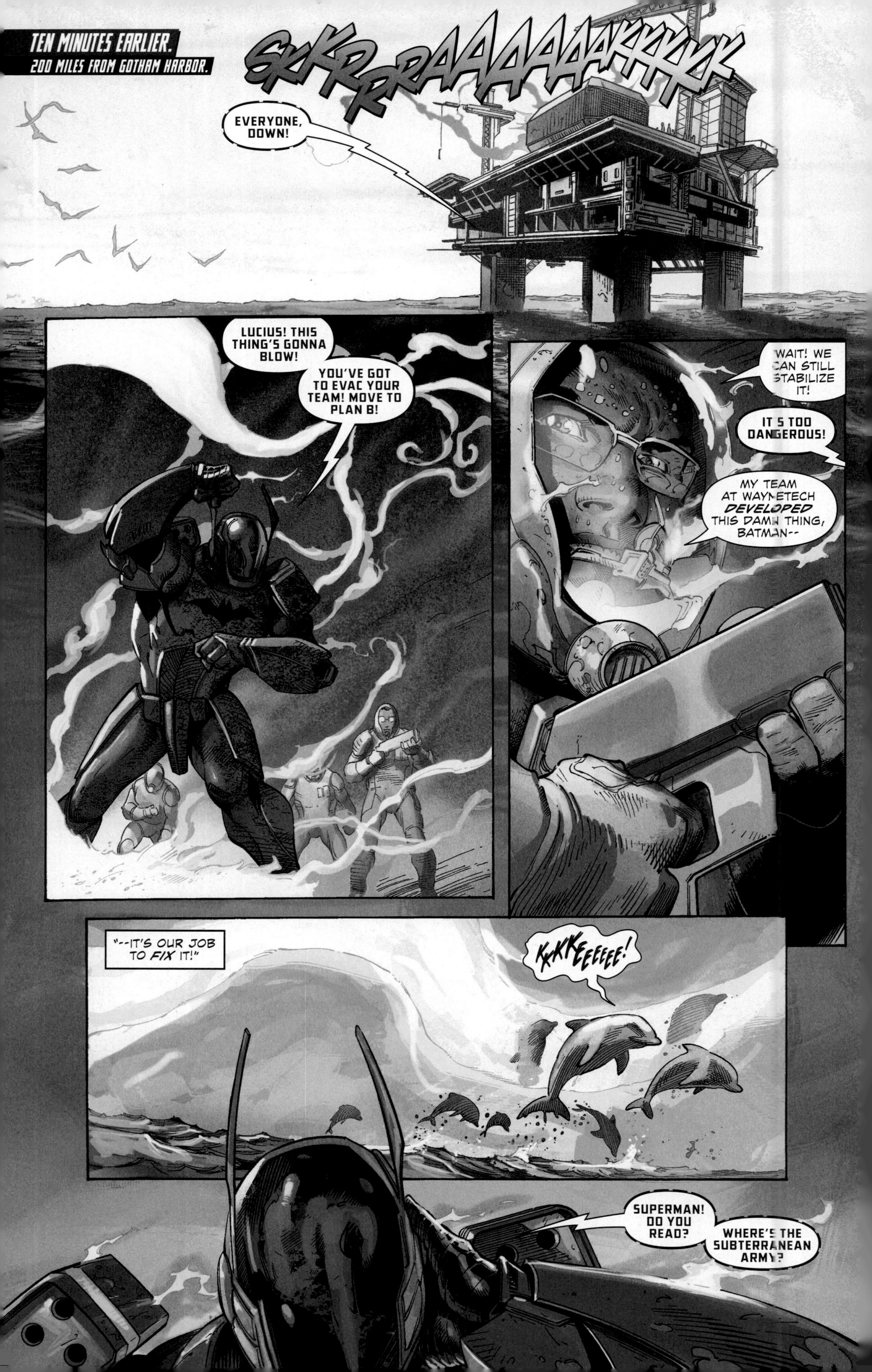TEN MINUTES EARLIER.
200 MILES FROM GOTHAM HARBOR.
SKKRRRAAAAAAAKKKKK
EVERYONE, DOWN!
LUCIUS! THIS THING'S GONNA BLOW!
YOU'VE GOT TO EVAC YOUR TEAM! MOVE TO PLAN B!
WAIT! WE CAN STILL STABILIZE IT!
IT'S TOO DANGEROUS!
MY TEAM AT WAYNETECH DEVELOPED THIS DAMN THING, BATMAN--
"--IT'S OUR JOB TO FIX IT!"
KKKKEEEEEE!
SUPERMAN! DO YOU READ?
WHERE'S THE SUBTERRANEAN ARMY?

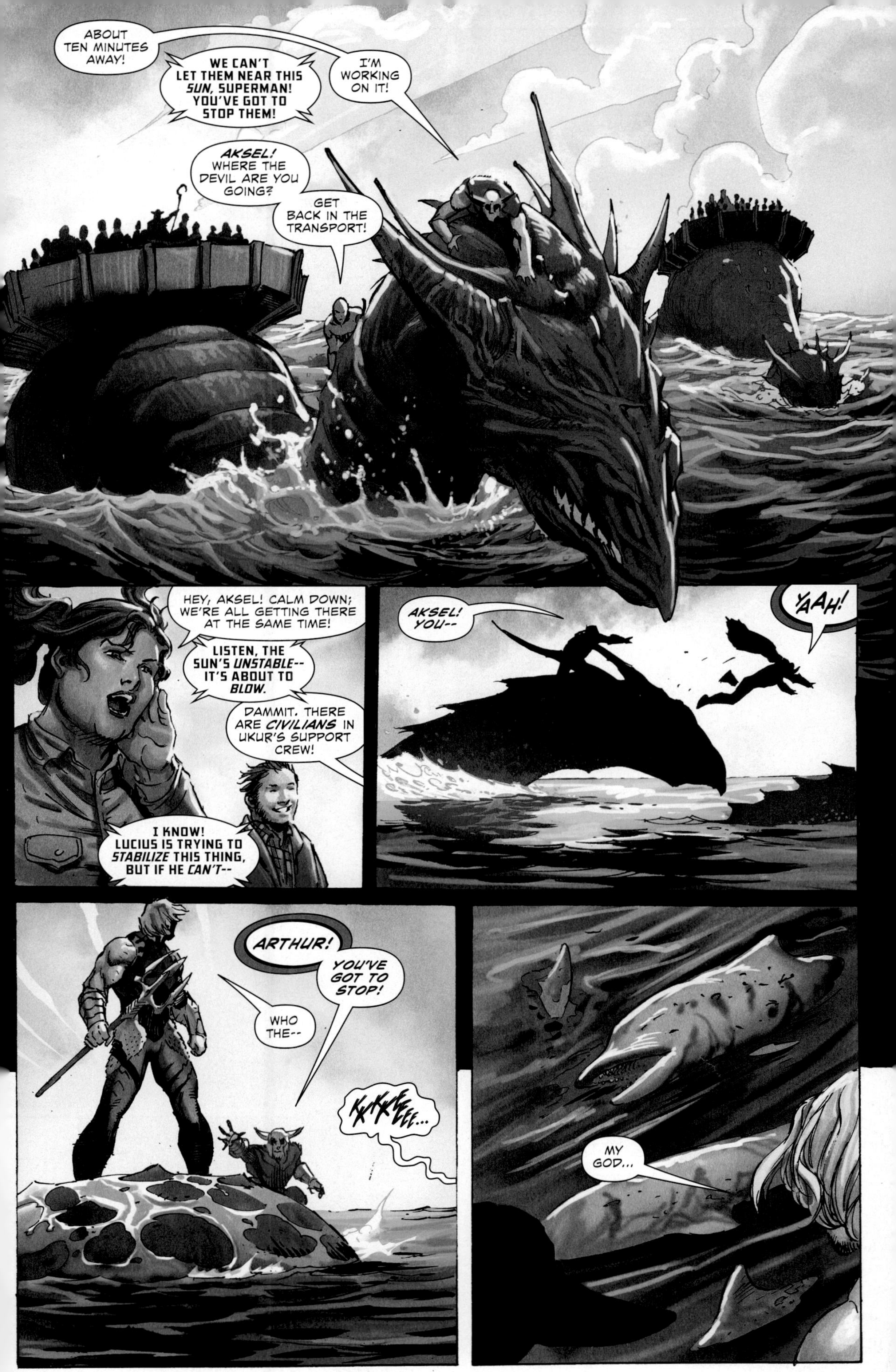

ABOUT TEN MINUTES AWAY!
WE CAN'T LET THEM NEAR THIS SUN, SUPERMAN! YOU'VE GOT TO STOP THEM!
I'M WORKING ON IT!
AKSEL! WHERE THE DEVIL ARE YOU GOING?
GET BACK IN THE TRANSPORT!
HEY, AKSEL! CALM DOWN; WE'RE ALL GETTING THERE AT THE SAME TIME!
LISTEN, THE SUN'S UNSTABLE-- IT'S ABOUT TO BLOW.
DAMMIT. THERE ARE CIVILIANS IN UKUR'S SUPPORT CREW!
I KNOW! LUCIUS IS TRYING TO STABILIZE THIS THING, BUT IF HE CAN'T--
AKSEL! YOU--
YAAH!
ARTHUR!
YOU'VE GOT TO STOP!
WHO THE--
KKKKEEEE...
MY GOD...

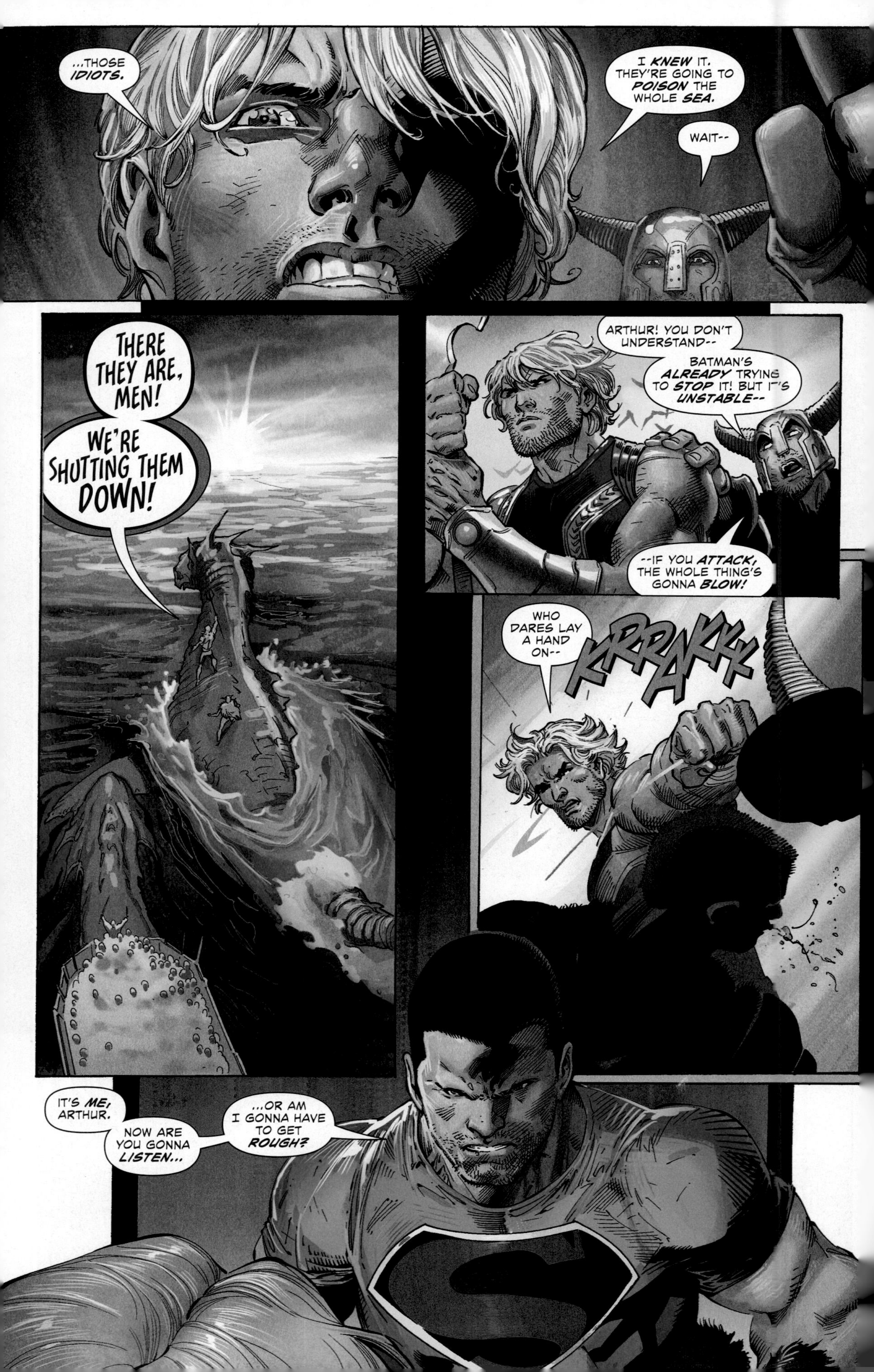
...THOSE IDIOTS.
I KNEW IT. THEY'RE GOING TO POISON THE WHOLE SEA.
WAIT--
THERE THEY ARE, MEN!
WE'RE SHUTTING THEM DOWN!
ARTHUR! YOU DON'T UNDERSTAND--
BATMAN'S ALREADY TRYING TO STOP IT! BUT IT'S UNSTABLE--
--IF YOU ATTACK, THE WHOLE THING'S GONNA BLOW!
WHO DARES LAY A HAND ON--
KRRAKKK
IT'S ME, ARTHUR.
NOW ARE YOU GONNA LISTEN...
...OR AM I GONNA HAVE TO GET ROUGH?

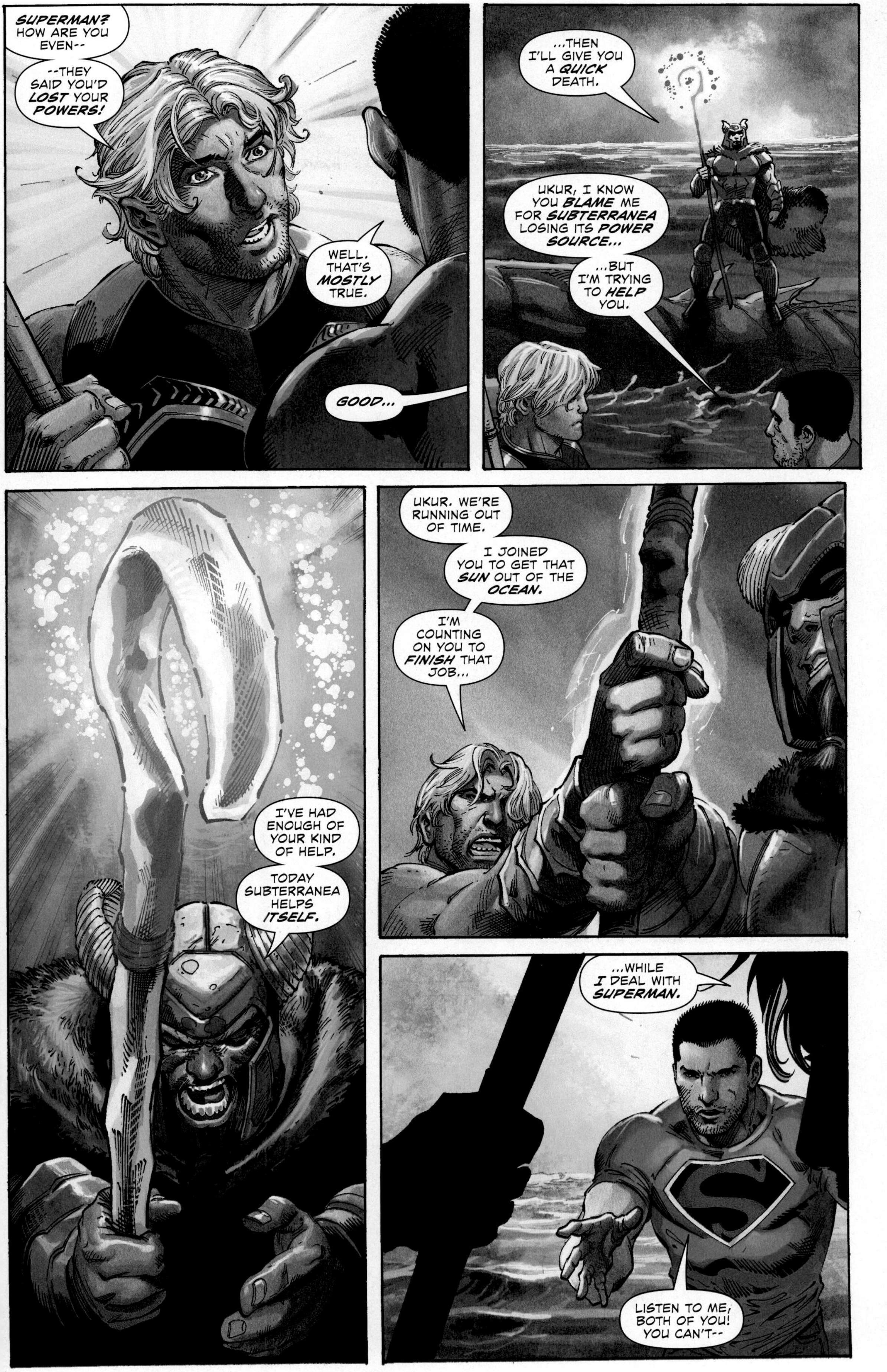
SUPERMAN? HOW ARE YOU EVEN--
--THEY SAID YOU'D LOST YOUR POWERS!
WELL. THAT'S MOSTLY TRUE.
GOOD...
...THEN I'LL GIVE YOU A QUICK DEATH.
UKUR, I KNOW YOU BLAME ME FOR SUBTERRANEA LOSING ITS POWER SOURCE...
...BUT I'M TRYING TO HELP YOU.
I'VE HAD ENOUGH OF YOUR KIND OF HELP.
TODAY SUBTERRANEA HELPS ITSELF.
UKUR. WE'RE RUNNING OUT OF TIME.
I JOINED YOU TO GET THAT SUN OUT OF THE OCEAN.
I'M COUNTING ON YOU TO FINISH THAT JOB...
...WHILE I DEAL WITH SUPERMAN.
LISTEN TO ME, BOTH OF YOU! YOU CAN'T--

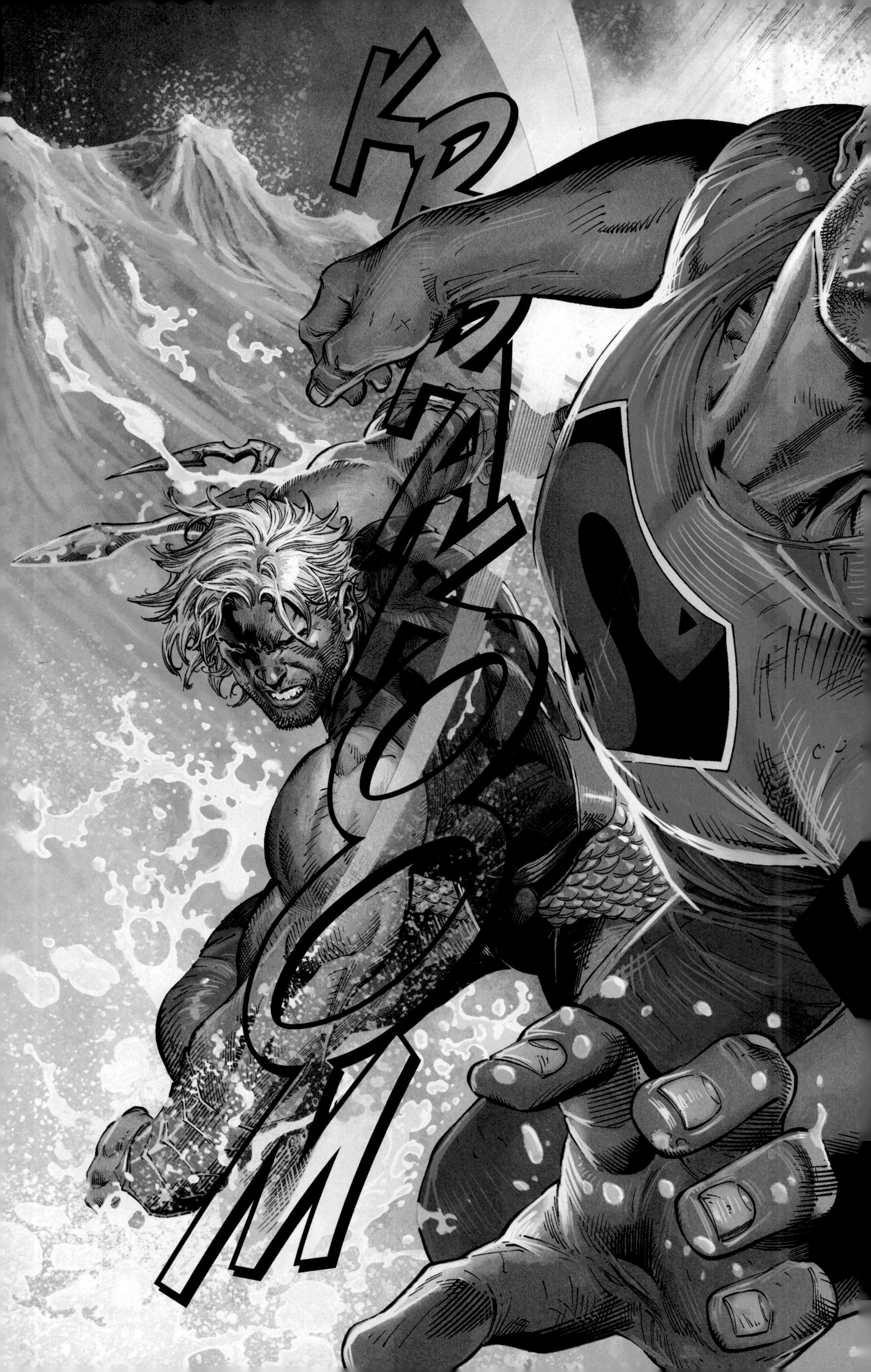

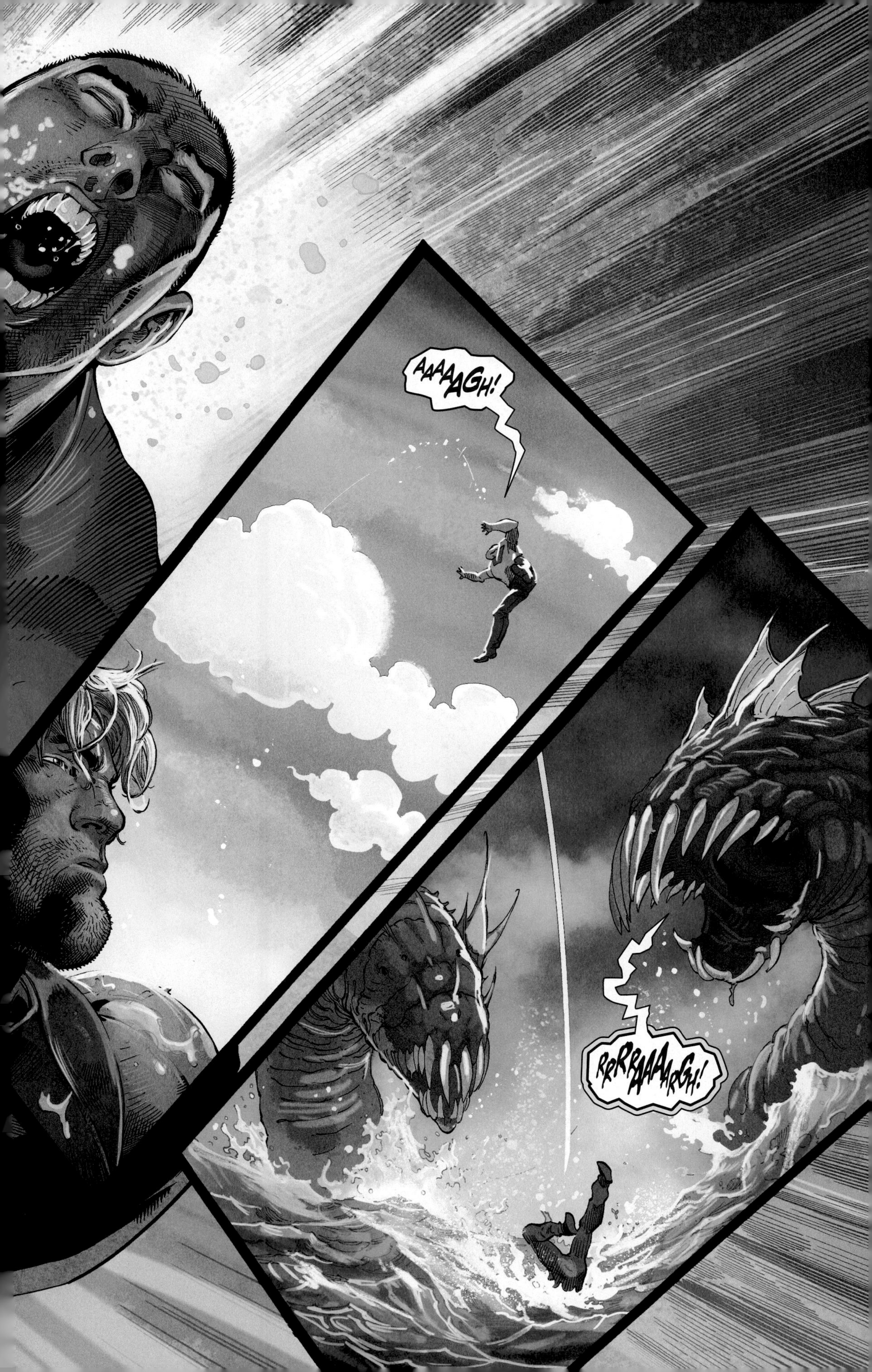
AAAAAGH!
RRRRAAAARGH!

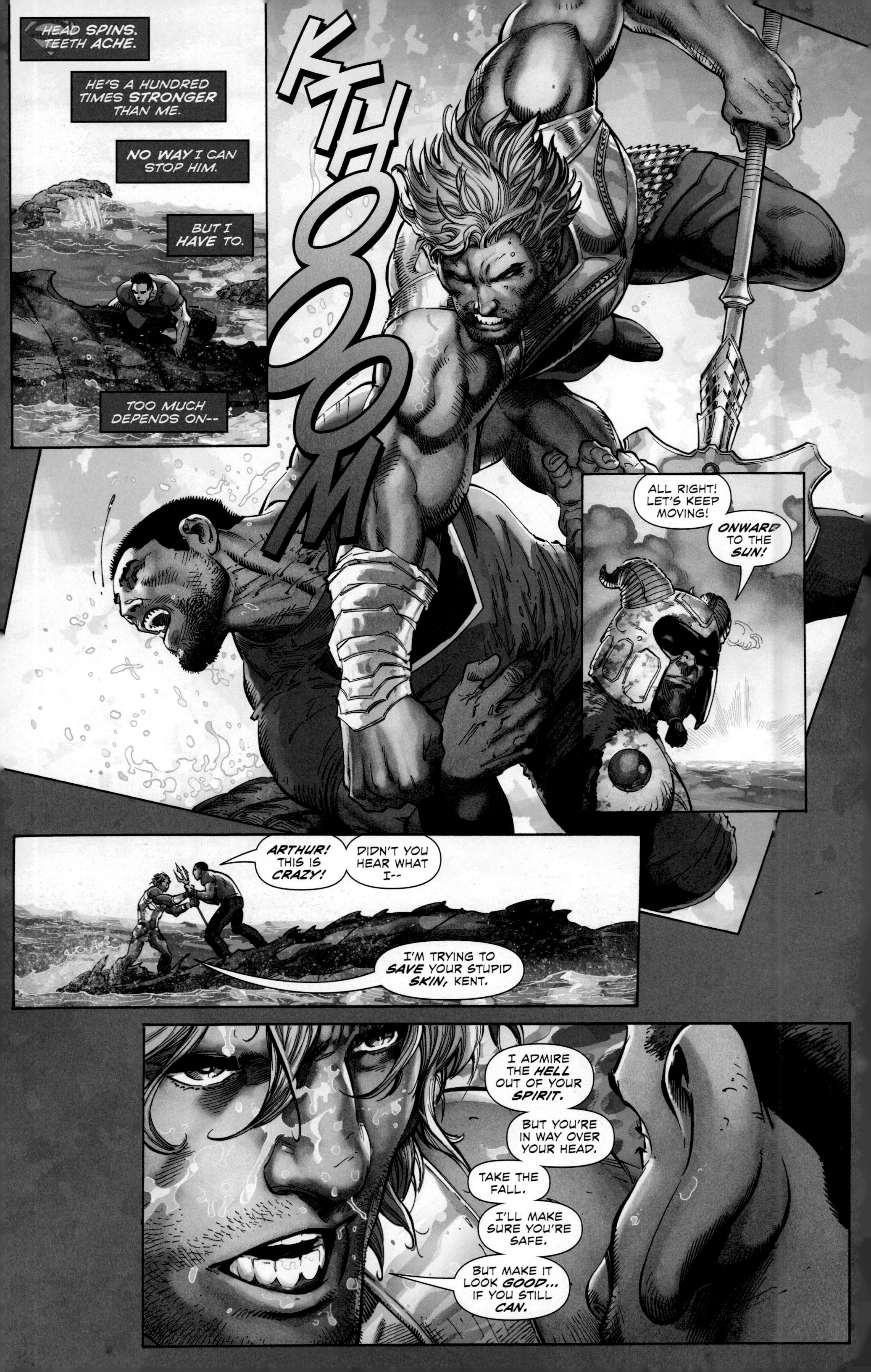
HEAD SPINS. TEETH ACHE.
HE'S A HUNDRED TIMES STRONGER THAN ME.
NO WAY I CAN STOP HIM.
BUT I HAVE TO.
TOO MUCH DEPENDS ON--
KTHOOOM
ALL RIGHT! LET'S KEEP MOVING!
ONWARD TO THE SUN!
ARTHUR! THIS IS CRAZY!
DIDN'T YOU HEAR WHAT I--
I'M TRYING TO SAVE YOUR STUPID SKIN, KENT.
I ADMIRE THE HELL OUT OF YOUR SPIRIT.
BUT YOU'RE IN WAY OVER YOUR HEAD.
TAKE THE FALL.
I'LL MAKE SURE YOU'RE SAFE.
BUT MAKE IT LOOK GOOD... IF YOU STILL CAN.

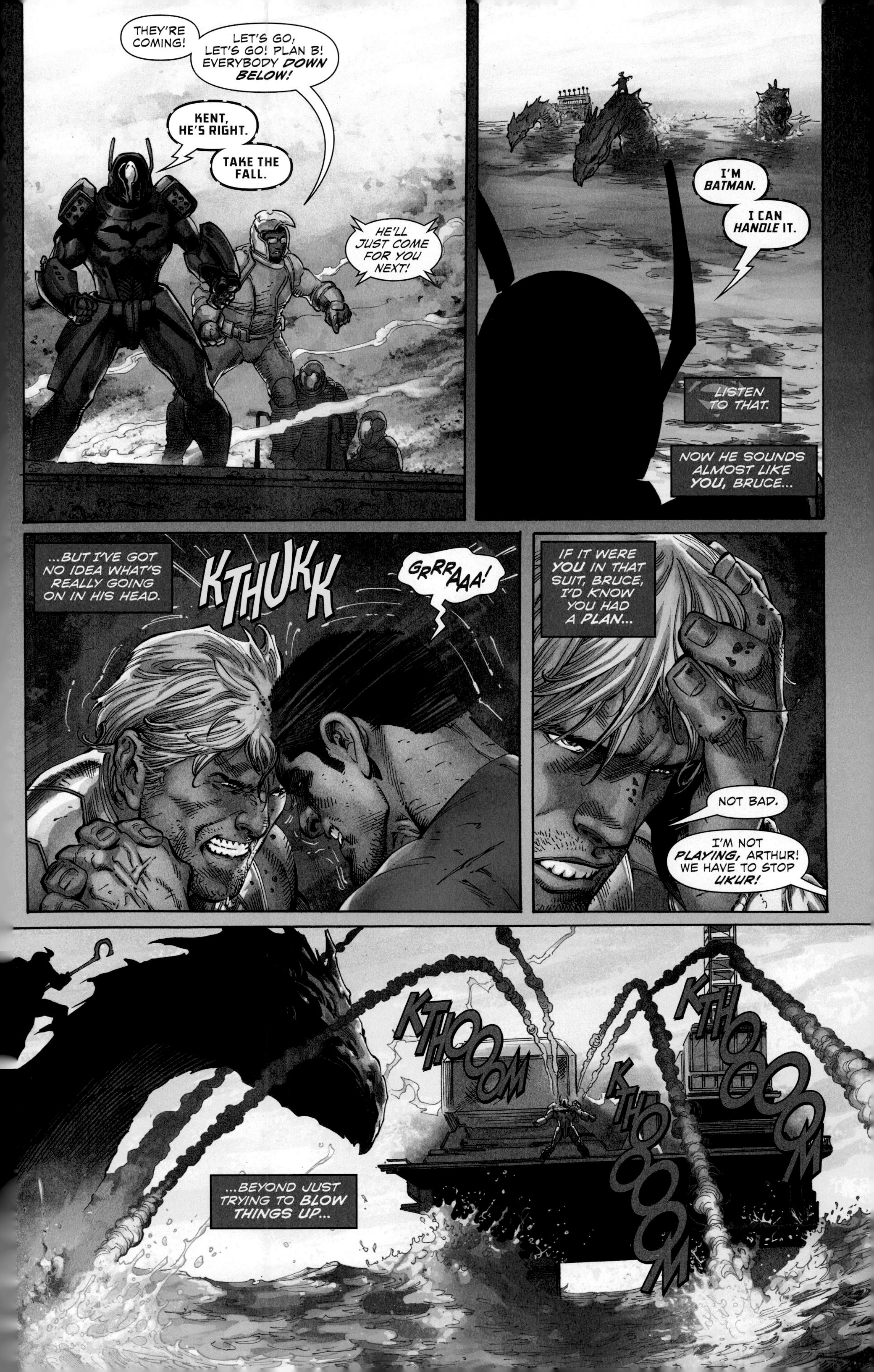

THEY'RE COMING!
LET'S GO, LET'S GO! PLAN B! EVERYBODY DOWN BELOW!
KENT, HE'S RIGHT.
TAKE THE FALL.
HE'LL JUST COME FOR YOU NEXT!
I'M BATMAN.
I CAN HANDLE IT.
LISTEN TO THAT.
NOW HE SOUNDS ALMOST LIKE YOU, BRUCE...
...BUT I'VE GOT NO IDEA WHAT'S REALLY GOING ON IN HIS HEAD.
KTHUKK
GRRRAAA!
IF IT WERE YOU IN THAT SUIT, BRUCE, I'D KNOW YOU HAD A PLAN...
NOT BAD.
I'M NOT PLAYING, ARTHUR! WE HAVE TO STOP UKUR!
KTHOOOOM
KTHOOOOM
KTHOOOOM
...BEYOND JUST TRYING TO BLOW THINGS UP...

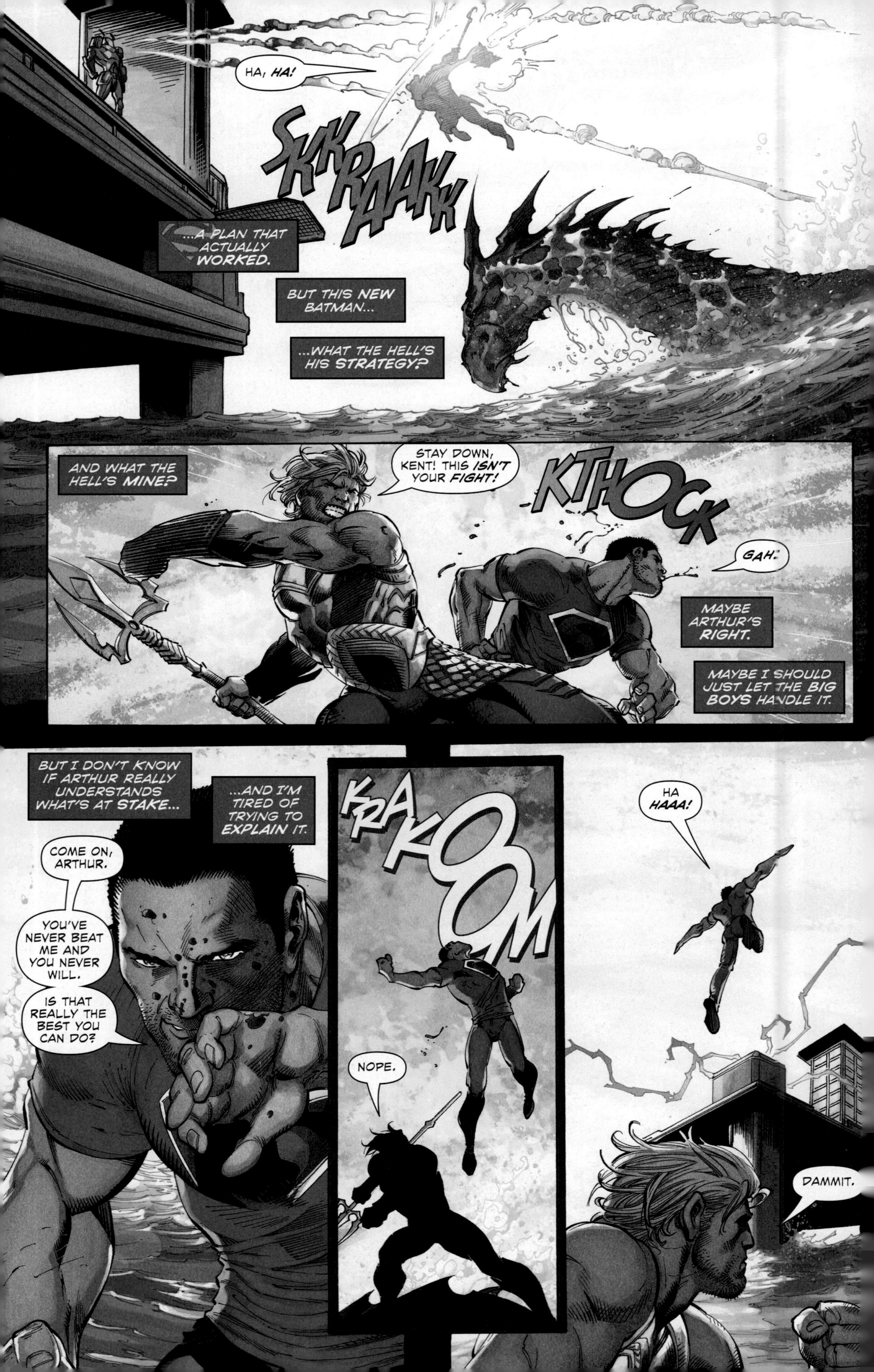
HA, HA!
SKKRAAKK
...A PLAN THAT ACTUALLY WORKED.
BUT THIS NEW BATMAN...
...WHAT THE HELL'S HIS STRATEGY?
AND WHAT THE HELL'S MINE?
STAY DOWN, KENT! THIS ISN'T YOUR FIGHT!
KTHOCK
GAH!
MAYBE ARTHUR'S RIGHT.
MAYBE I SHOULD JUST LET THE BIG BOYS HANDLE IT.
BUT I DON'T KNOW IF ARTHUR REALLY UNDERSTANDS WHAT'S AT STAKE...
...AND I'M TIRED OF TRYING TO EXPLAIN IT.
COME ON, ARTHUR.
YOU'VE NEVER BEAT ME AND YOU NEVER WILL.
IS THAT REALLY THE BEST YOU CAN DO?
KRAKOOM
NOPE.
HA HAAA!
DAMMIT.

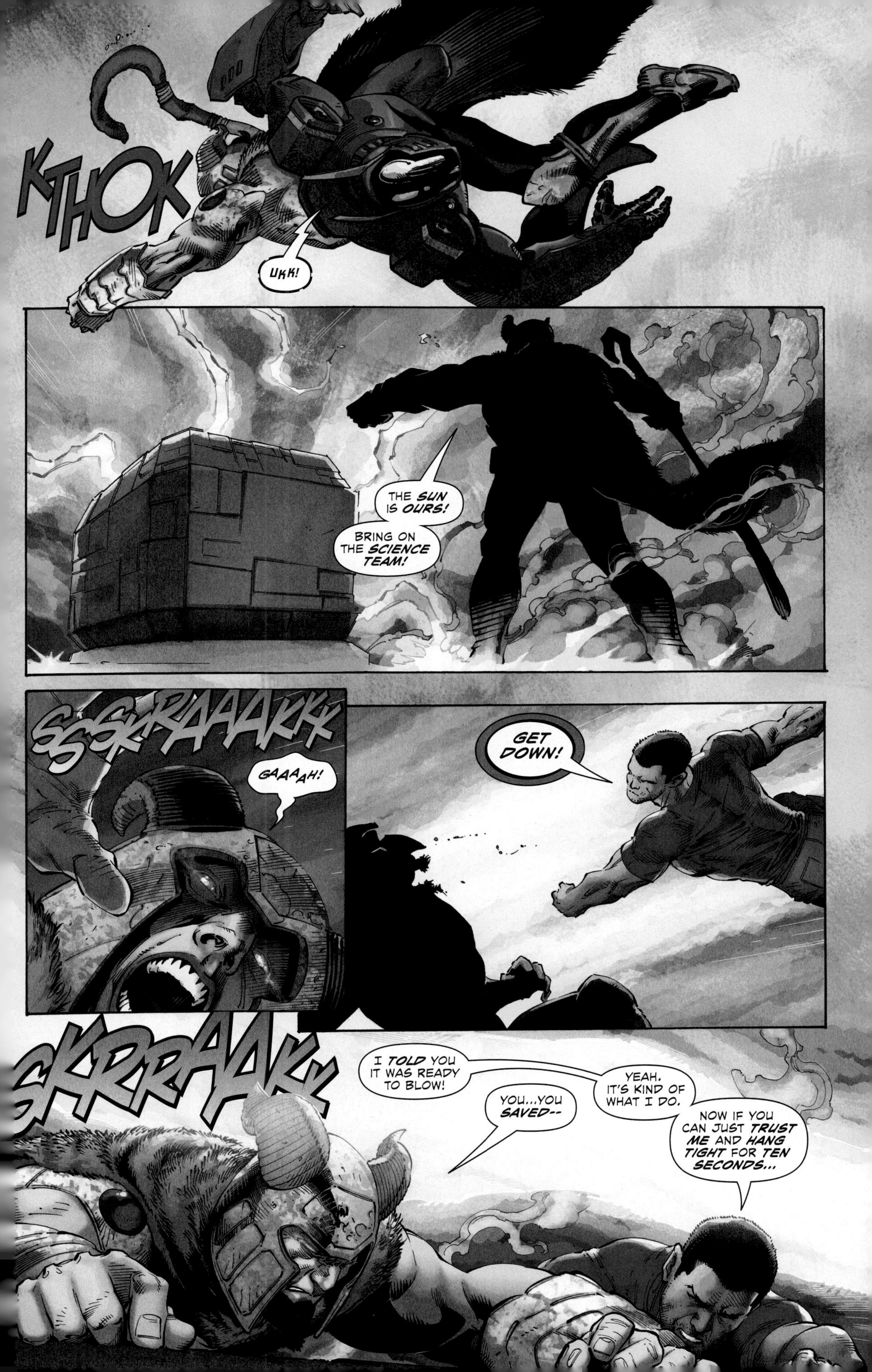
KTHOK
UKK!
THE SUN IS OURS!
BRING ON THE SCIENCE TEAM!
SSSKRAAAAKK
GAAAAH!
GET DOWN!
SKRRAAKK
I TOLD YOU IT WAS READY TO BLOW!
YEAH. IT'S KIND OF WHAT I DO.
YOU...YOU SAVED--
NOW IF YOU CAN JUST TRUST ME AND HANG TIGHT FOR TEN SECONDS...

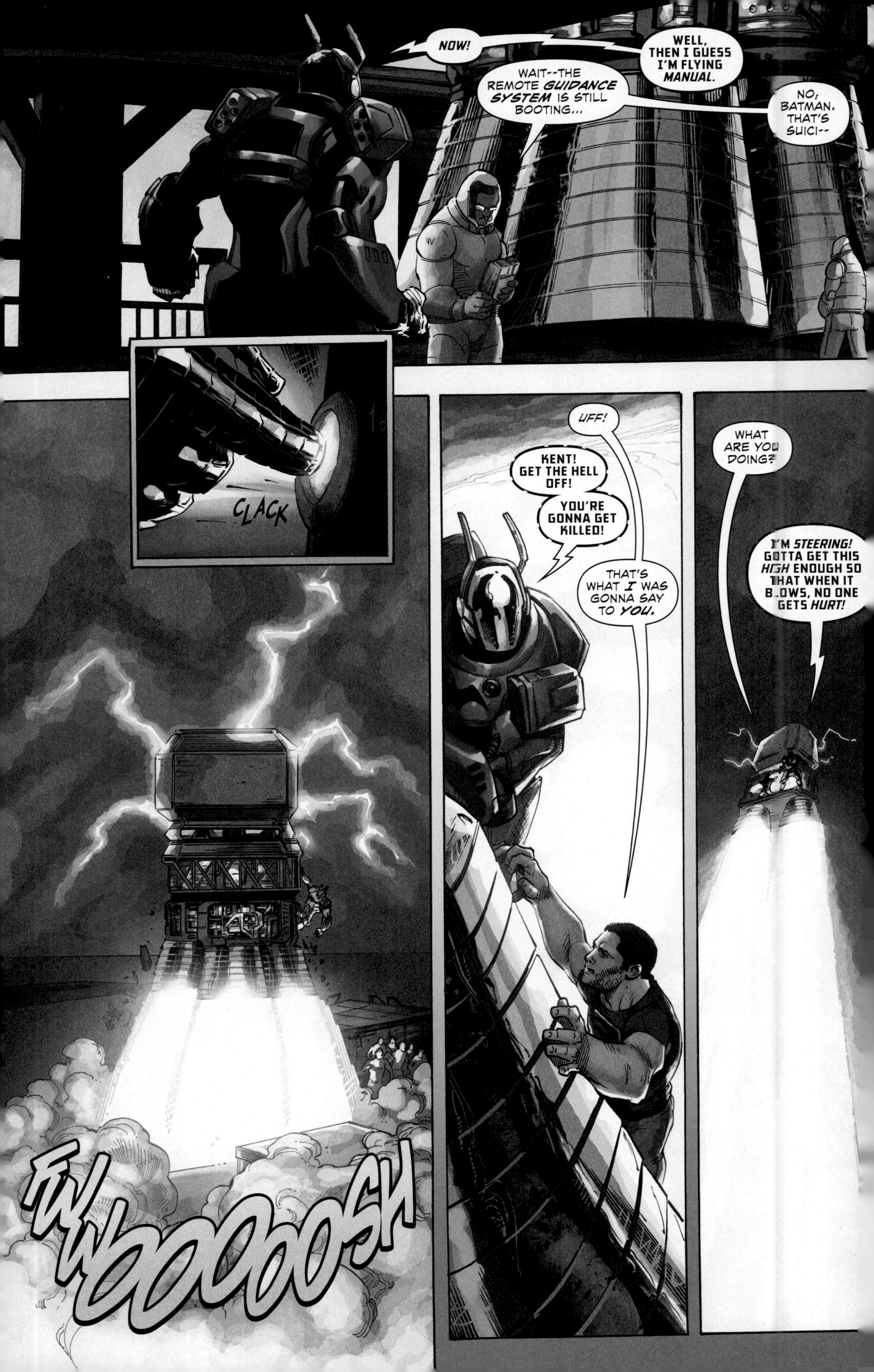
NOW!
WAIT--THE REMOTE GUIDANCE SYSTEM IS STILL BOOTING...
WELL, THEN I GUESS I'M FLYING MANUAL.
NO, BATMAN. THAT'S SUICI--
CLACK
FWOOOOSH
UFF!
KENT! GET THE HELL OFF!
YOU'RE GONNA GET KILLED!
THAT'S WHAT I WAS GONNA SAY TO YOU.
WHAT ARE YOU DOING?
I'M STEERING! GOTTA GET THIS HIGH ENOUGH SO THAT WHEN IT BLOWS, NO ONE GETS HURT!

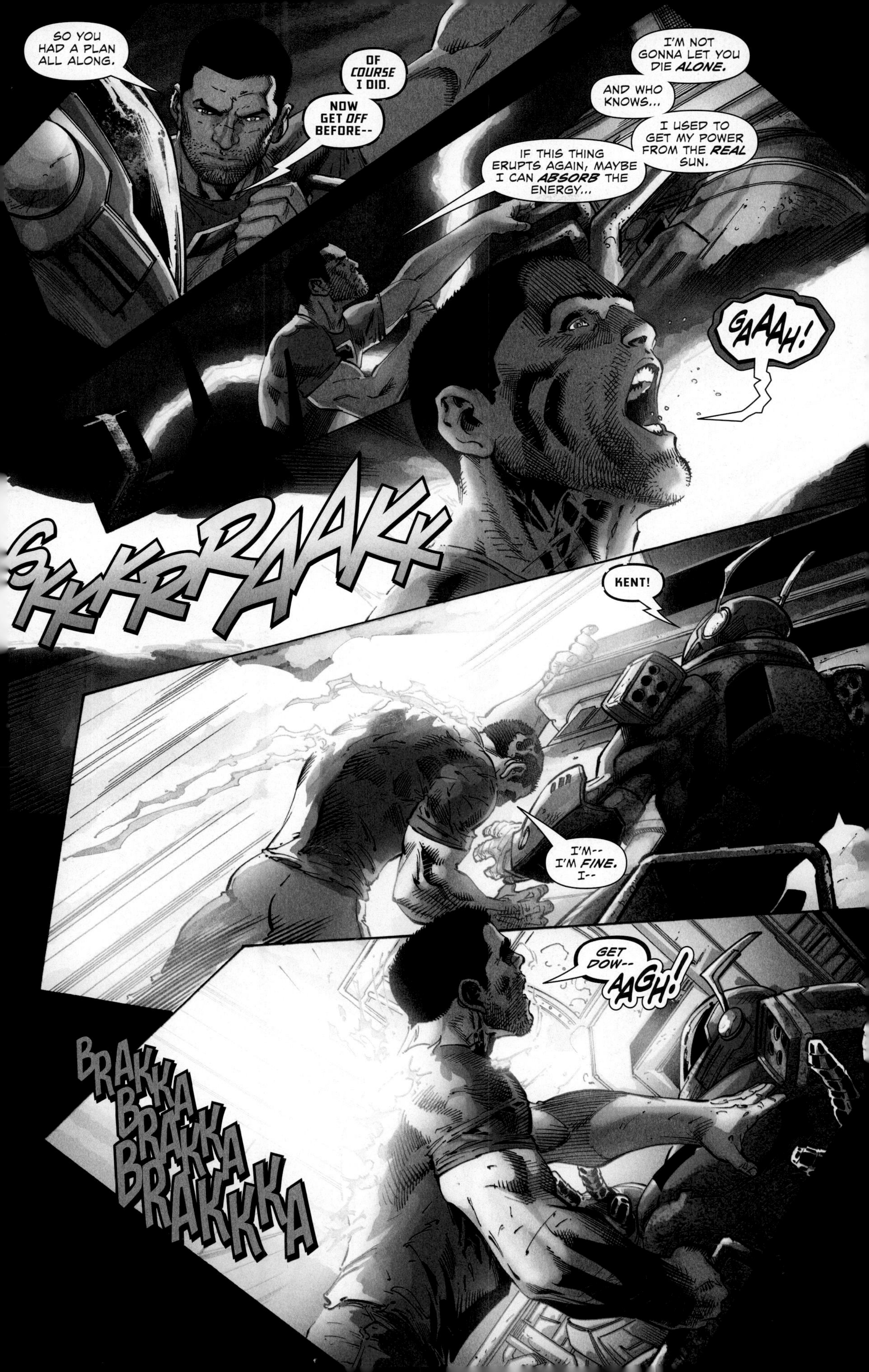
SO YOU HAD A PLAN ALL ALONG.
OF COURSE I DID.
NOW GET OFF BEFORE--
I'M NOT GONNA LET YOU DIE ALONE.
AND WHO KNOWS...
I USED TO GET MY POWER FROM THE REAL SUN.
IF THIS THING ERUPTS AGAIN, MAYBE I CAN ABSORB THE ENERGY...
GAAAH!
SKKRRAAKK
KENT!
I'M-- I'M FINE. I--
GET DOW-- AAGH!
BRAKKA BRAKKA BRAKKA BRAKKA

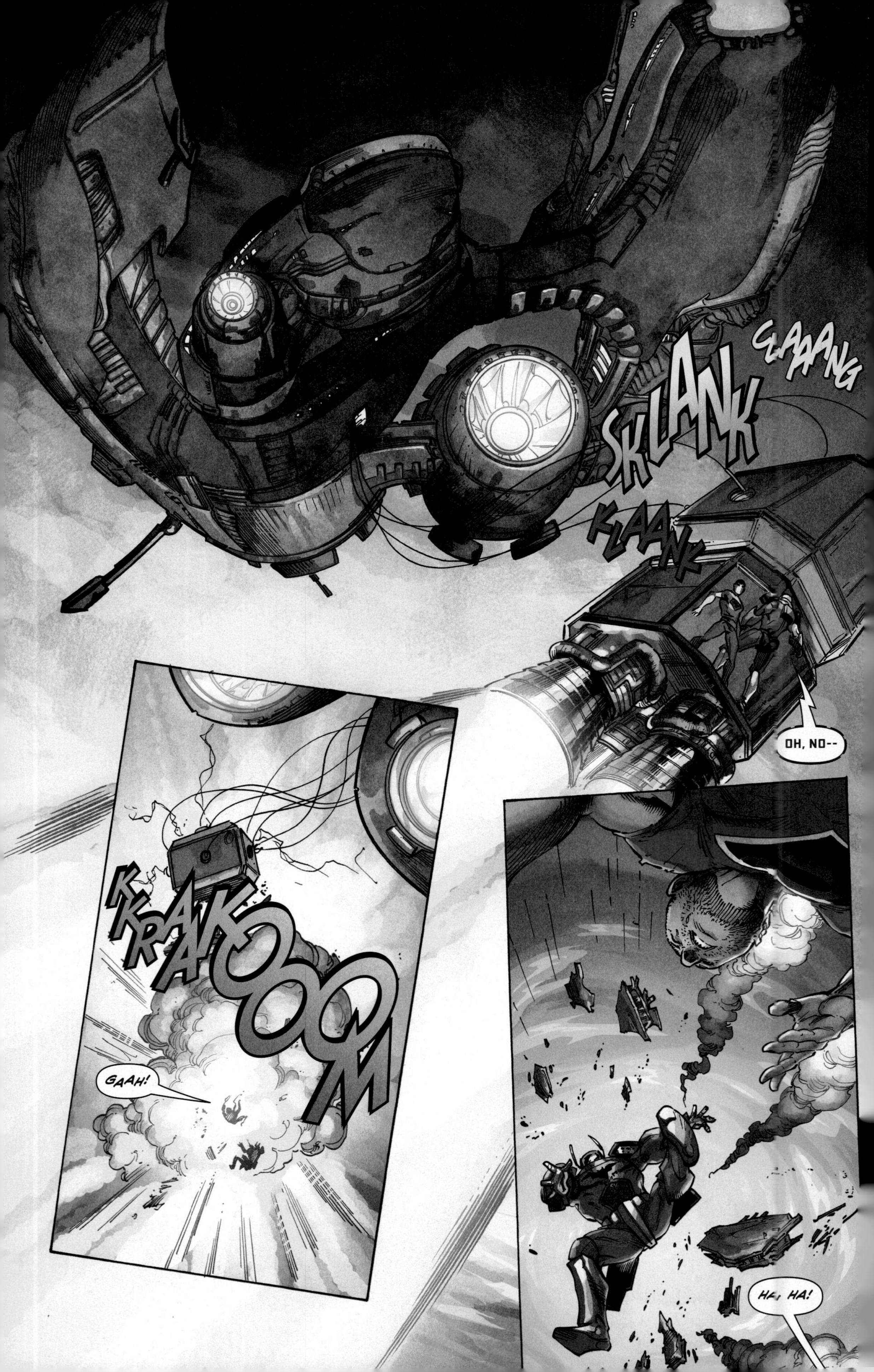
SKLANK
CLAAANG
KLAAANK
OH, NO--
KKRAKAKOOOM
GAAH!
HA! HA!

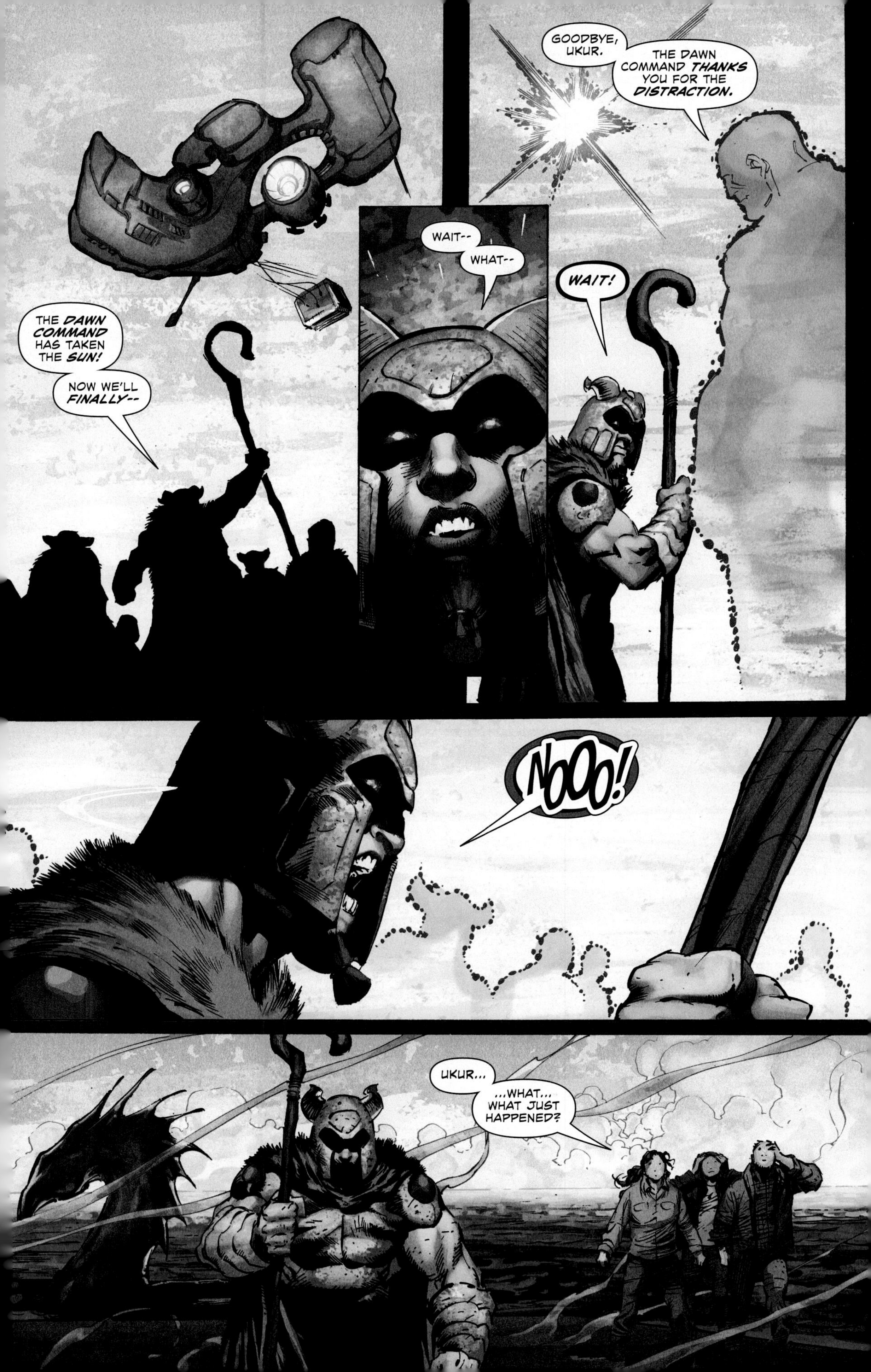
THE DAWN COMMAND HAS TAKEN THE SUN!
NOW WE'LL FINALLY--
GOODBYE, UKUR.
THE DAWN COMMAND THANKS YOU FOR THE DISTRACTION.
WAIT--
WHAT--
WAIT!
NOOO!
UKUR...
...WHAT... WHAT JUST HAPPENED?

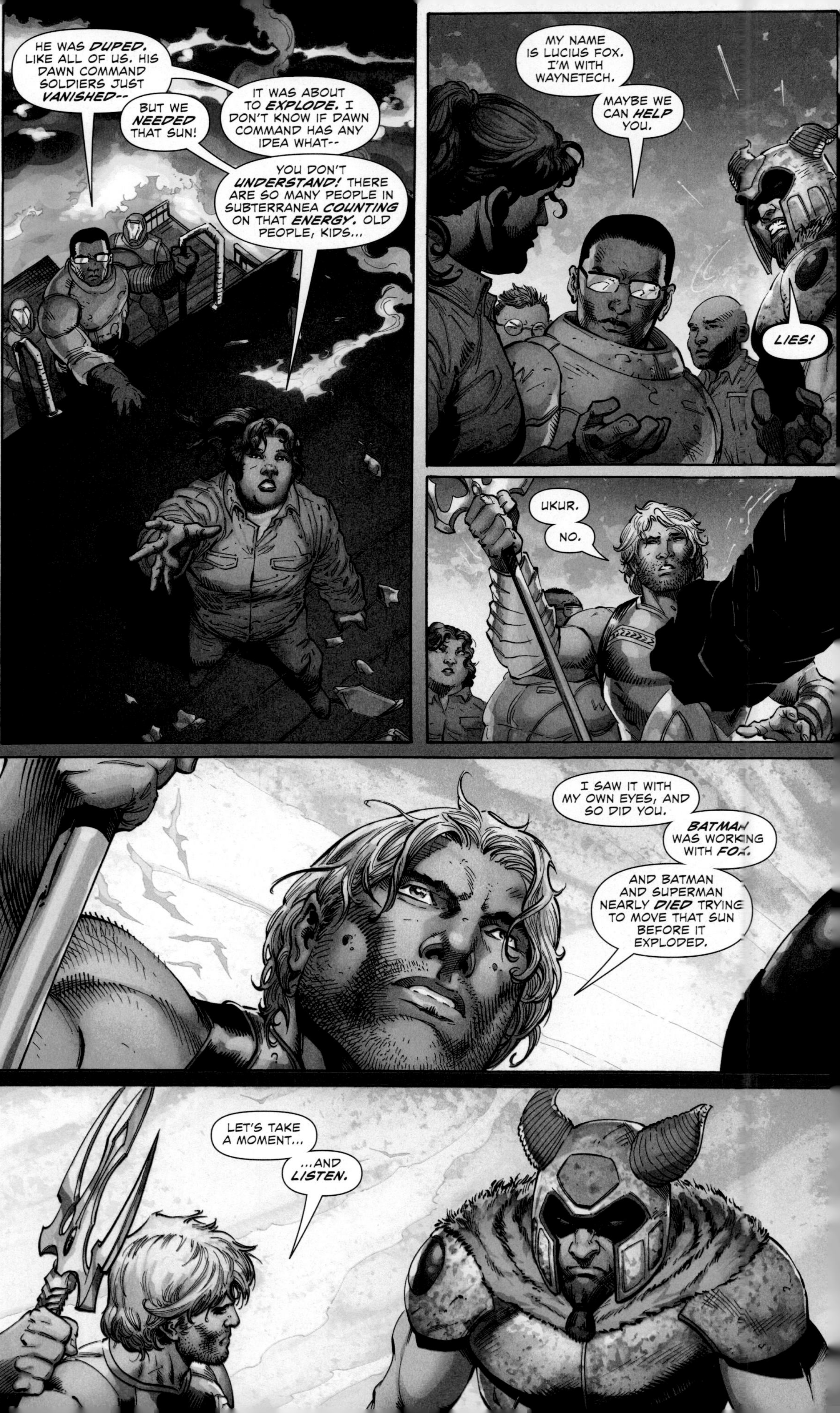
HE WAS DUPED. LIKE ALL OF US. HIS DAWN COMMAND SOLDIERS JUST VANISHED--
IT WAS ABOUT TO EXPLODE. I DON'T KNOW IF DAWN COMMAND HAS ANY IDEA WHAT--
BUT WE NEEDED THAT SUN!
YOU DON'T UNDERSTAND! THERE ARE SO MANY PEOPLE IN SUBTERRANEA COUNTING ON THAT ENERGY. OLD PEOPLE, KIDS...
MY NAME IS LUCIUS FOX. I'M WITH WAYNETECH.
MAYBE WE CAN HELP YOU.
LIES!
UKUR.
NO.
I SAW IT WITH MY OWN EYES, AND SO DID YOU.
BATMAN WAS WORKING WITH FOX.
AND BATMAN AND SUPERMAN NEARLY DIED TRYING TO MOVE THAT SUN BEFORE IT EXPLODED.
LET'S TAKE A MOMENT...
...AND LISTEN.

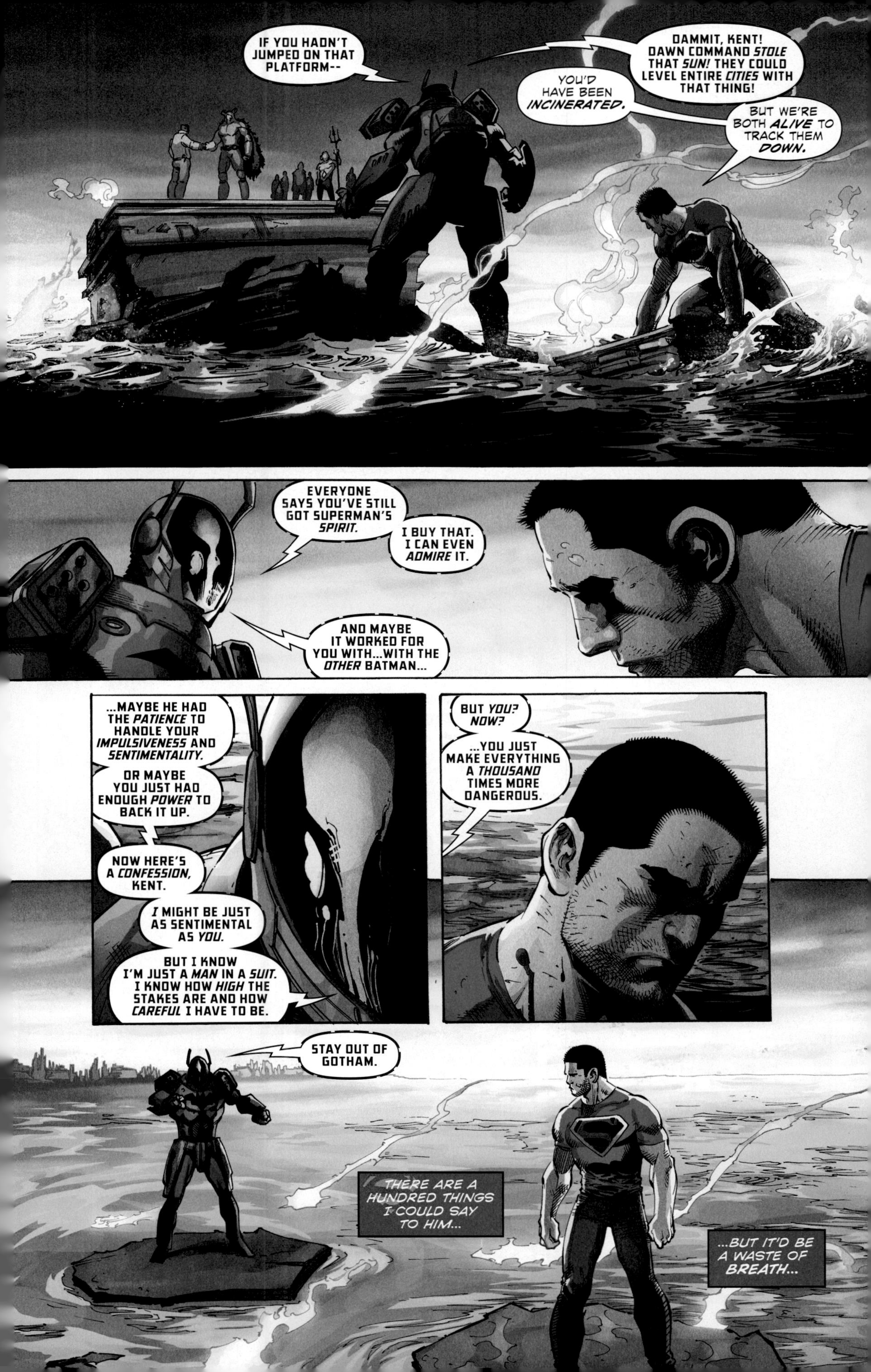
IF YOU HADN'T JUMPED ON THAT PLATFORM--
DAMMIT, KENT! DAWN COMMAND *STOLE* THAT *SUN!* THEY COULD LEVEL ENTIRE *CITIES* WITH THAT THING!
YOU'D HAVE BEEN *INCINERATED.*
BUT WE'RE BOTH *ALIVE* TO TRACK THEM *DOWN.*
EVERYONE SAYS YOU'VE STILL GOT SUPERMAN'S *SPIRIT.*
I BUY THAT. I CAN EVEN *ADMIRE* IT.
AND MAYBE IT WORKED FOR YOU WITH...WITH THE *OTHER* BATMAN...
...MAYBE HE HAD THE *PATIENCE* TO HANDLE YOUR *IMPULSIVENESS* AND *SENTIMENTALITY.*
OR MAYBE YOU JUST HAD ENOUGH *POWER* TO BACK IT UP.
NOW HERE'S A *CONFESSION,* KENT.
I MIGHT BE JUST AS SENTIMENTAL AS *YOU.*
BUT I KNOW I'M JUST A *MAN* IN A *SUIT.* I KNOW HOW *HIGH* THE STAKES ARE AND HOW *CAREFUL* I HAVE TO BE.
BUT *YOU?* *NOW?*
...YOU JUST MAKE EVERYTHING A *THOUSAND* TIMES MORE DANGEROUS.
STAY OUT OF GOTHAM.
THERE ARE A HUNDRED THINGS I COULD SAY TO HIM...
...BUT IT'D BE A WASTE OF *BREATH...*

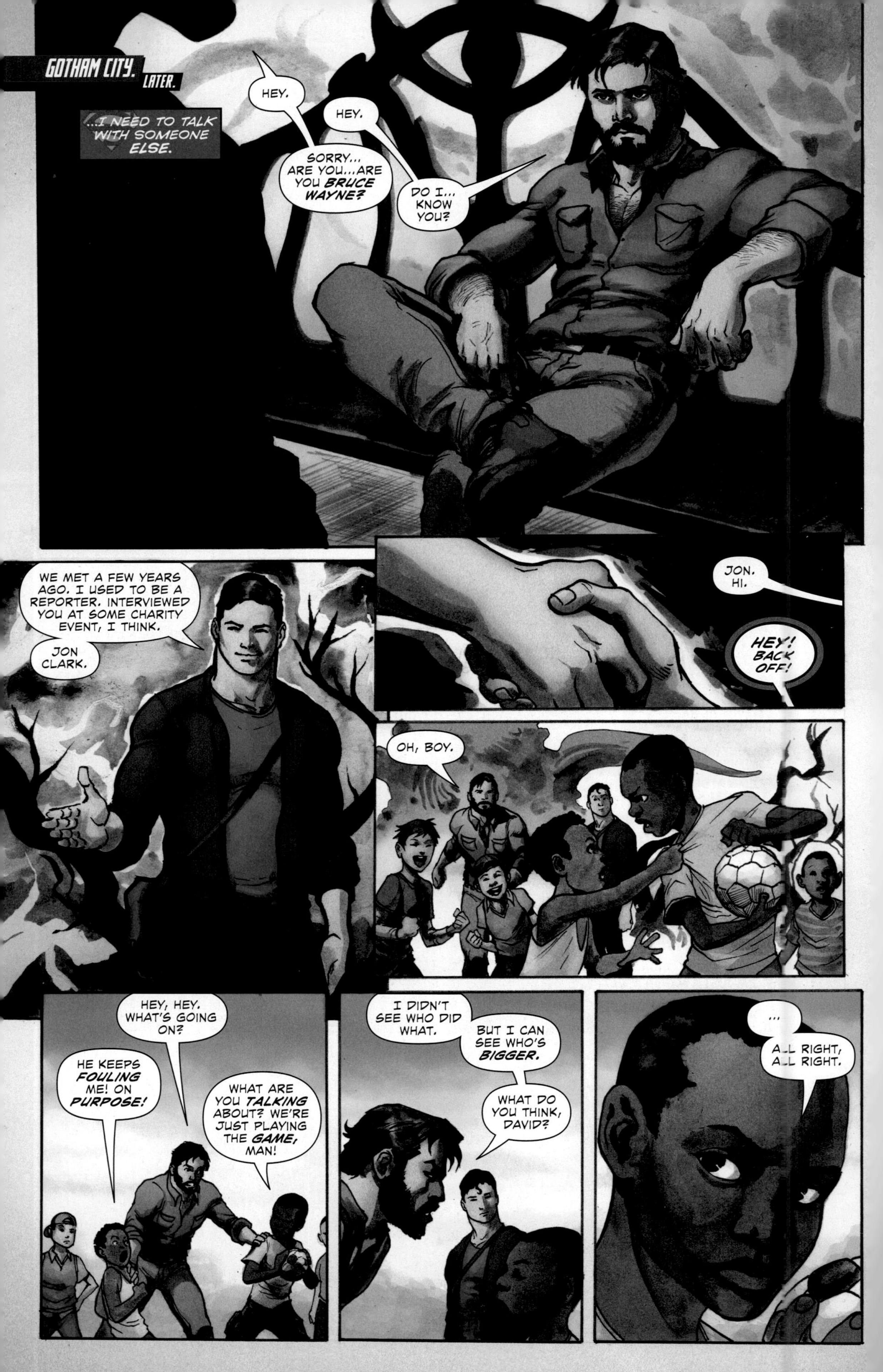
GOTHAM CITY.
LATER.
...I NEED TO TALK WITH SOMEONE ELSE.
HEY.
HEY.
SORRY... ARE YOU...ARE YOU BRUCE WAYNE?
DO I... KNOW YOU?
WE MET A FEW YEARS AGO. I USED TO BE A REPORTER. INTERVIEWED YOU AT SOME CHARITY EVENT, I THINK.
JON CLARK.
JON. HI.
HEY! BACK OFF!
OH, BOY.
HEY, HEY. WHAT'S GOING ON?
HE KEEPS FOULING ME! ON PURPOSE!
WHAT ARE YOU TALKING ABOUT? WE'RE JUST PLAYING THE GAME, MAN!
I DIDN'T SEE WHO DID WHAT.
BUT I CAN SEE WHO'S BIGGER.
WHAT DO YOU THINK, DAVID?
...
ALL RIGHT, ALL RIGHT.

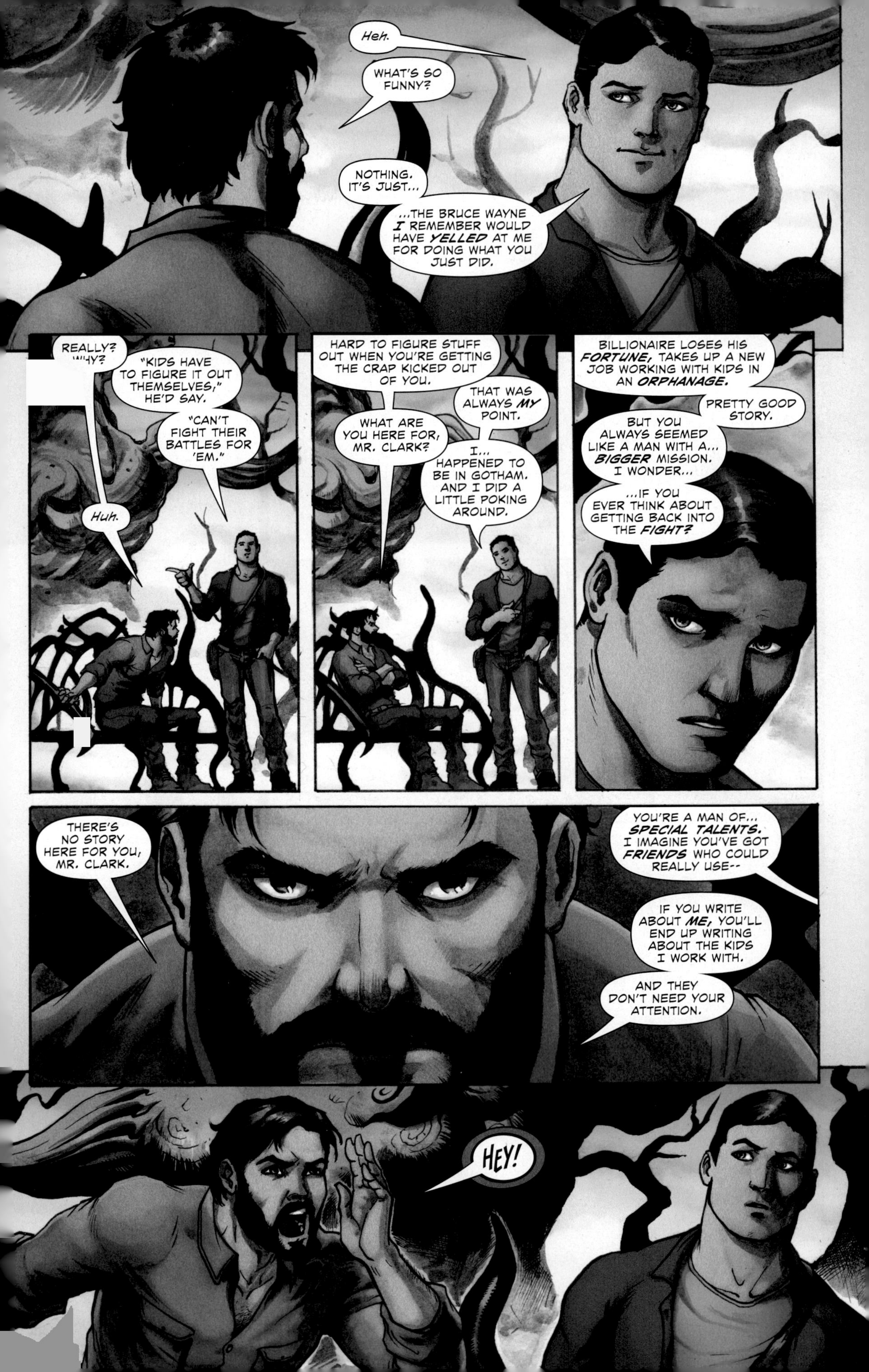
Heh.
WHAT'S SO FUNNY?
NOTHING. IT'S JUST...
...THE BRUCE WAYNE *I* REMEMBER WOULD HAVE *YELLED* AT ME FOR DOING WHAT YOU JUST DID.
REALLY? WHY?
"KIDS HAVE TO FIGURE IT OUT THEMSELVES," HE'D SAY.
"CAN'T FIGHT THEIR BATTLES FOR 'EM."
Huh.
HARD TO FIGURE STUFF OUT WHEN YOU'RE GETTING THE CRAP KICKED OUT OF YOU.
THAT WAS ALWAYS *MY* POINT.
WHAT ARE YOU HERE FOR, MR. CLARK?
I... HAPPENED TO BE IN GOTHAM. AND I DID A LITTLE POKING AROUND.
BILLIONAIRE LOSES HIS *FORTUNE,* TAKES UP A NEW JOB WORKING WITH KIDS IN AN *ORPHANAGE.*
PRETTY GOOD STORY.
BUT YOU ALWAYS SEEMED LIKE A MAN WITH A... *BIGGER* MISSION. I WONDER...
...IF YOU EVER THINK ABOUT GETTING BACK INTO THE *FIGHT?*
THERE'S NO STORY HERE FOR YOU, MR. CLARK.
YOU'RE A MAN OF... *SPECIAL TALENTS.* I IMAGINE YOU'VE GOT *FRIENDS* WHO COULD REALLY USE--
IF YOU WRITE ABOUT *ME,* YOU'LL END UP WRITING ABOUT THE KIDS I WORK WITH.
AND THEY DON'T NEED YOUR ATTENTION.
HEY!

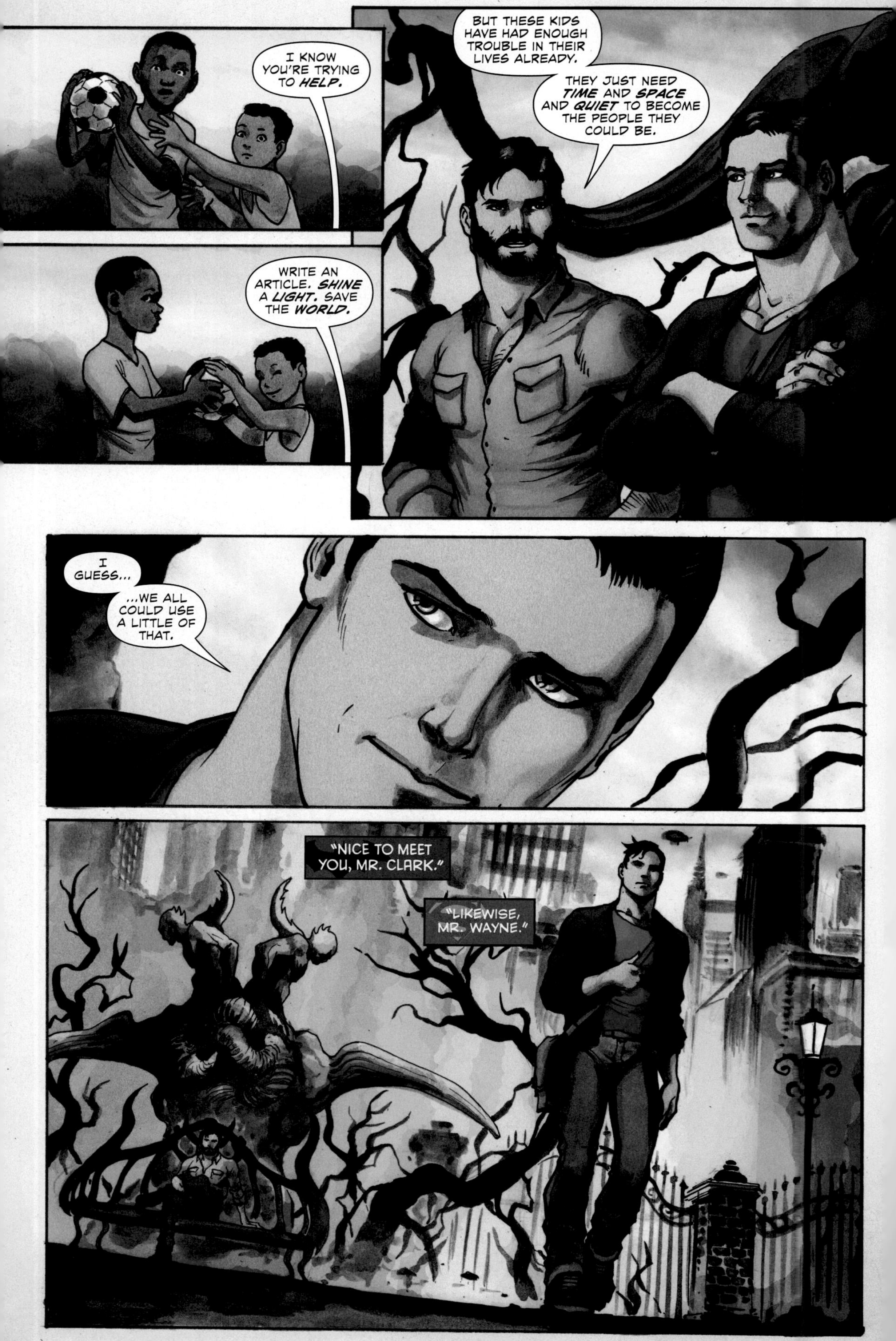
I KNOW YOU'RE TRYING TO *HELP.*
BUT THESE KIDS HAVE HAD ENOUGH TROUBLE IN THEIR LIVES ALREADY.
THEY JUST NEED *TIME* AND *SPACE* AND *QUIET* TO BECOME THE PEOPLE THEY COULD BE.
WRITE AN ARTICLE. *SHINE* A *LIGHT.* SAVE THE *WORLD.*
I GUESS...
...WE ALL COULD USE A LITTLE OF THAT.
"NICE TO MEET YOU, MR. CLARK."
"LIKEWISE, MR. WAYNE."

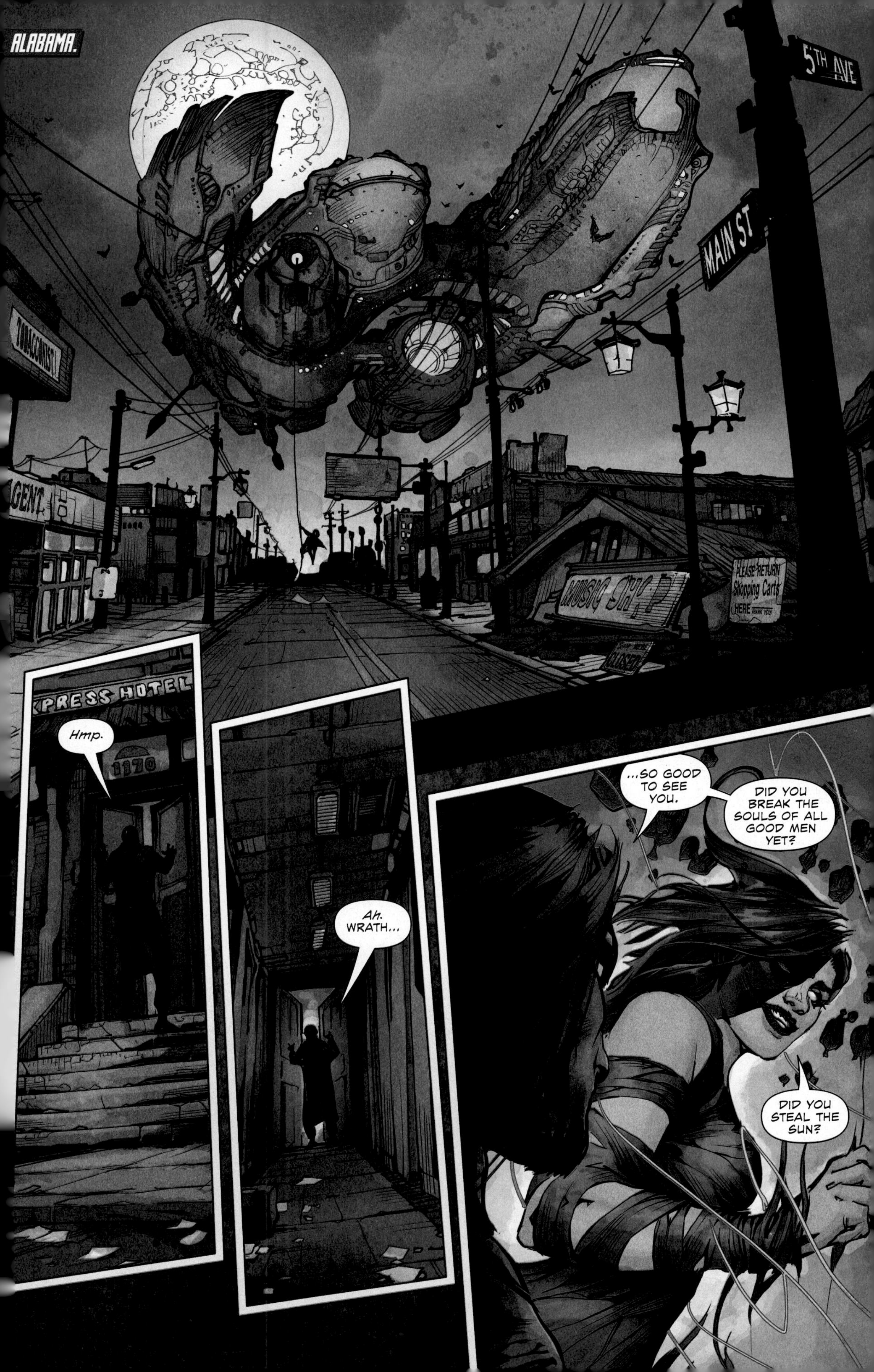

ALABAMA.
5TH AVE
MAIN ST
TOBACCONIST
AGENT
MUSIC SH P
PLEASE RETURN Shopping Carts HERE THANK YOU
CLOSED
XPRESS HOTEL
1170
Hmp.
Ah. WRATH...
...SO GOOD TO SEE YOU.
DID YOU BREAK THE SOULS OF ALL GOOD MEN YET?
DID YOU STEAL THE SUN?

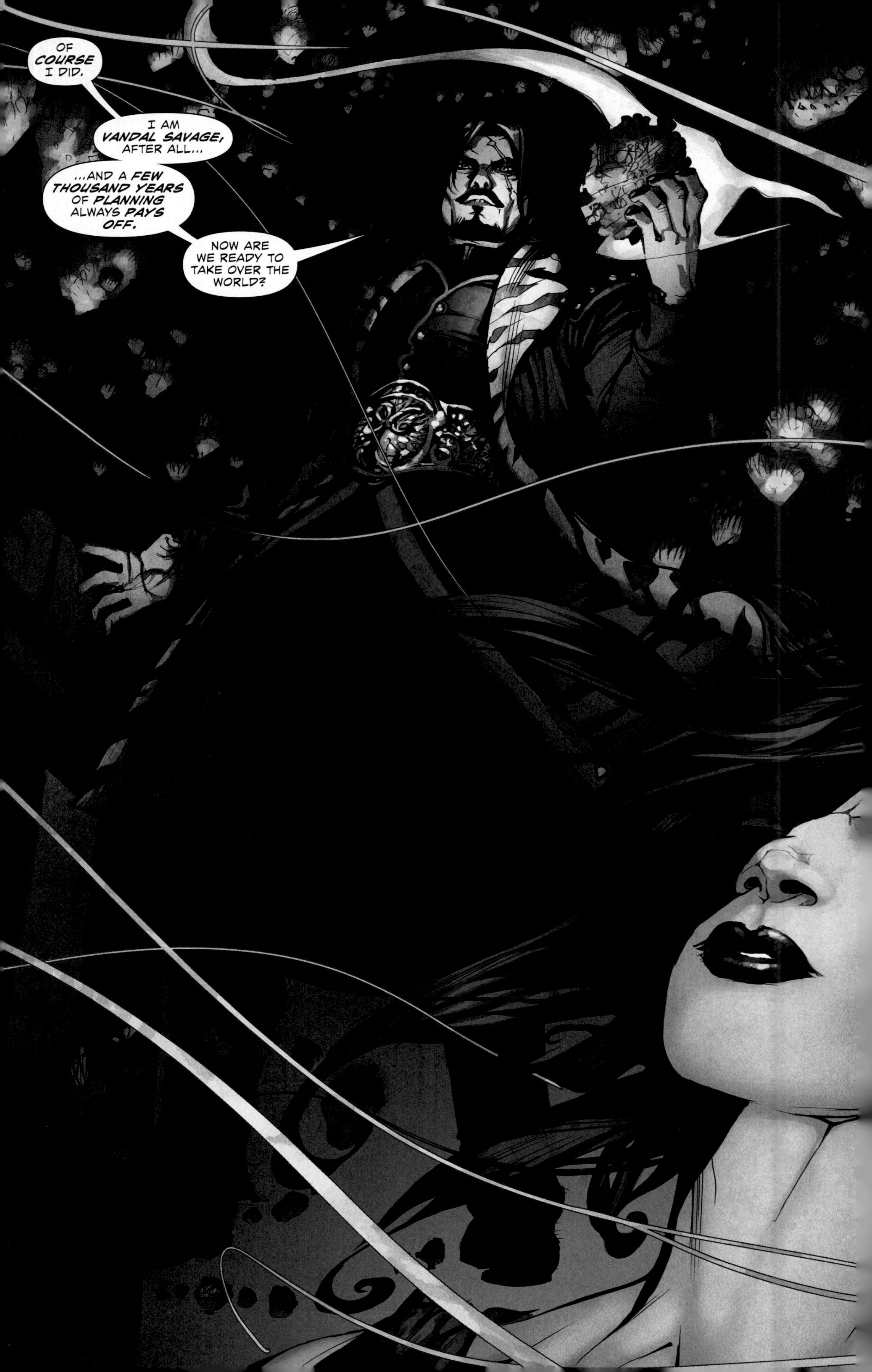

OF COURSE I DID.
I AM VANDAL SAVAGE, AFTER ALL...
...AND A FEW THOUSAND YEARS OF PLANNING ALWAYS PAYS OFF.
NOW ARE WE READY TO TAKE OVER THE WORLD?

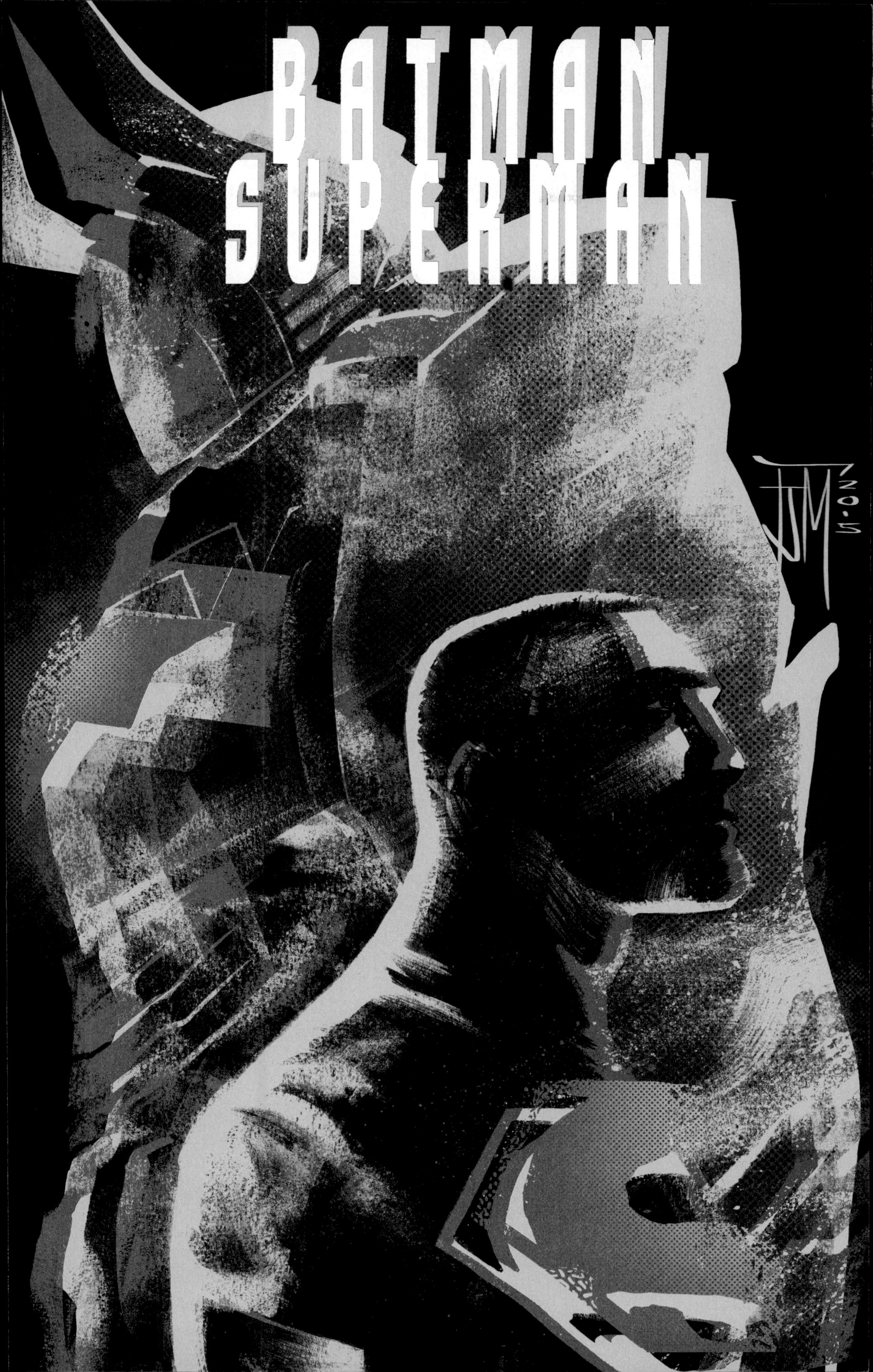
BATMAN
SUPERMAN

SAVAGE HUNT

GREG PAK writer **CLIFF RICHARDS** artist **BETH SOTELO** colorist **ROB LEIGH** letterer **FRANCIS MANAPUL** cover

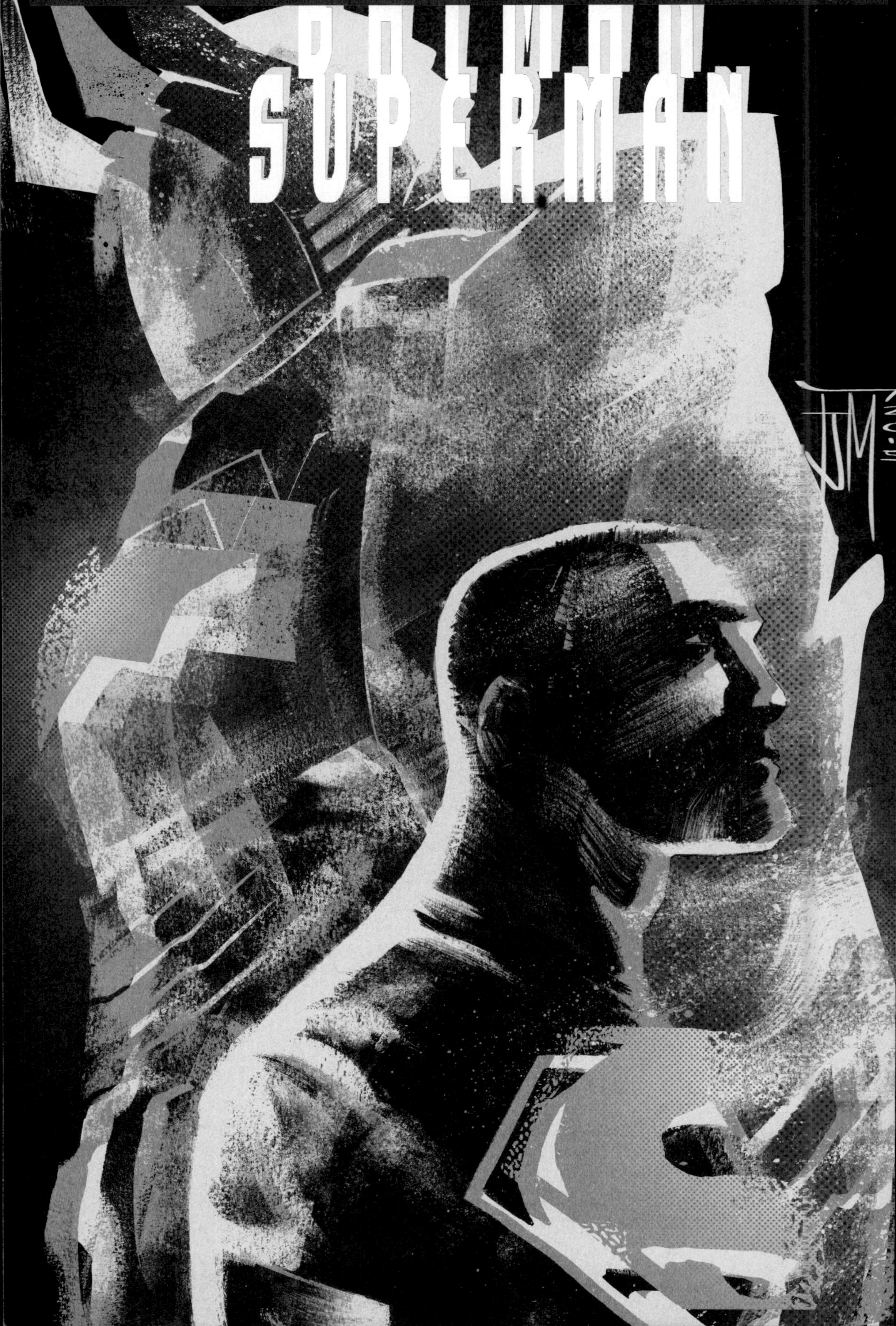
SUPERMAN

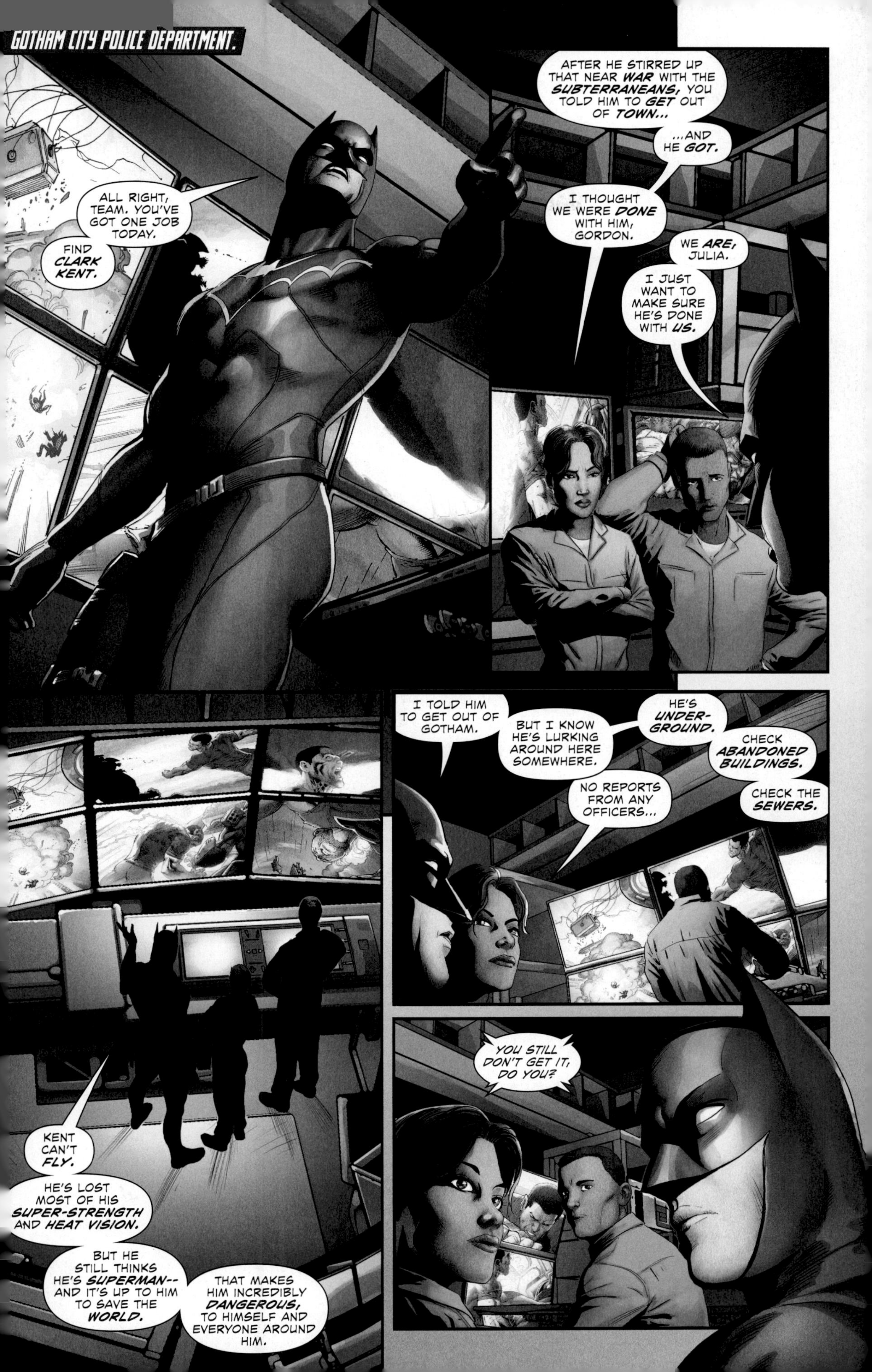
GOTHAM CITY POLICE DEPARTMENT.
ALL RIGHT, TEAM. YOU'VE GOT ONE JOB TODAY.
FIND CLARK KENT.
AFTER HE STIRRED UP THAT NEAR WAR WITH THE SUBTERRANEANS, YOU TOLD HIM TO GET OUT OF TOWN...
...AND HE GOT.
I THOUGHT WE WERE DONE WITH HIM, GORDON.
WE ARE, JULIA.
I JUST WANT TO MAKE SURE HE'S DONE WITH US.
KENT CAN'T FLY.
HE'S LOST MOST OF HIS SUPER-STRENGTH AND HEAT VISION.
BUT HE STILL THINKS HE'S SUPERMAN-- AND IT'S UP TO HIM TO SAVE THE WORLD.
THAT MAKES HIM INCREDIBLY DANGEROUS, TO HIMSELF AND EVERYONE AROUND HIM.
I TOLD HIM TO GET OUT OF GOTHAM.
BUT I KNOW HE'S LURKING AROUND HERE SOMEWHERE.
HE'S UNDER-GROUND.
CHECK ABANDONED BUILDINGS.
CHECK THE SEWERS.
NO REPORTS FROM ANY OFFICERS...
YOU STILL DON'T GET IT, DO YOU?

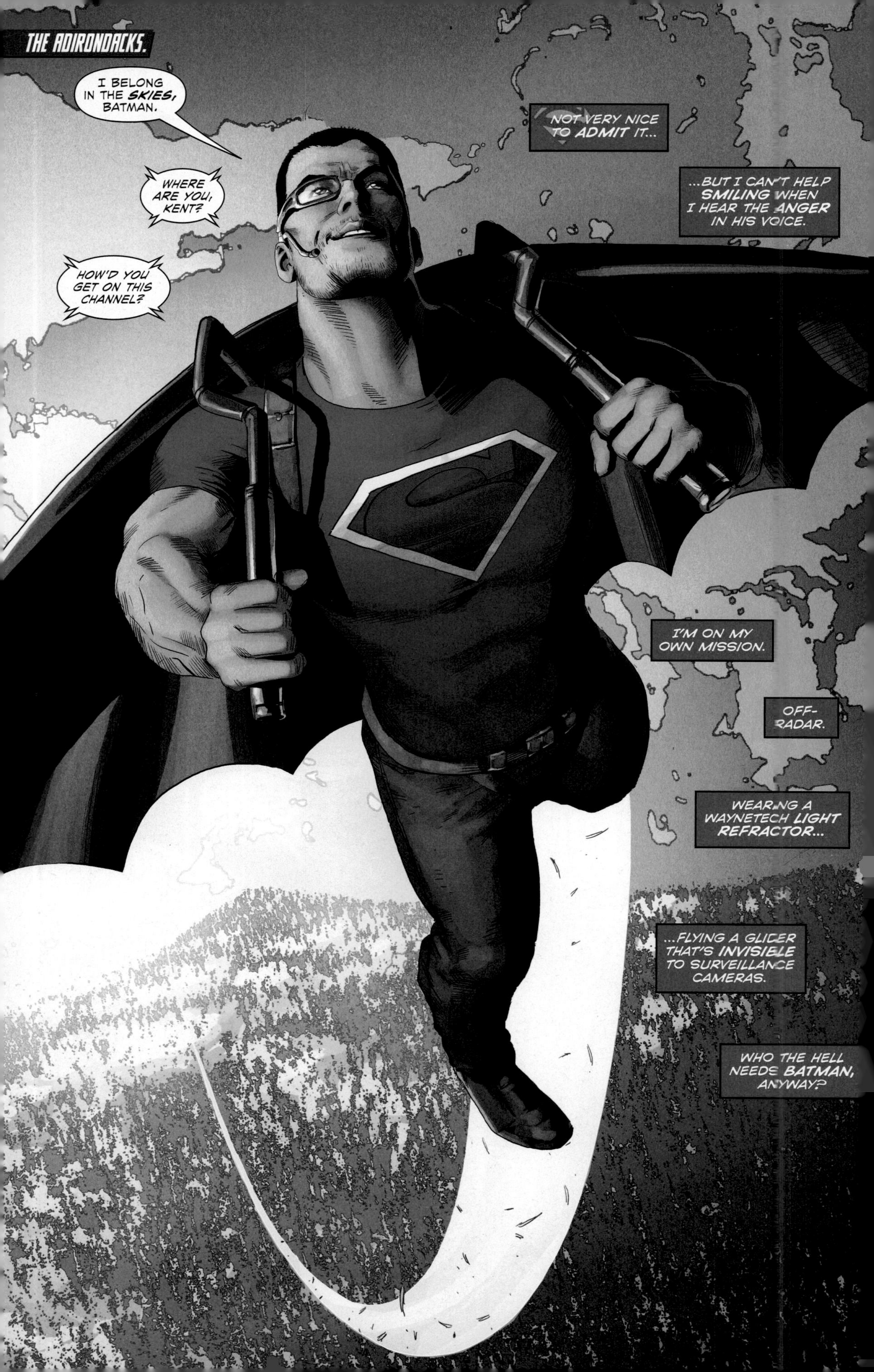
THE ADIRONDACKS.
I BELONG IN THE SKIES, BATMAN.
WHERE ARE YOU, KENT?
HOW'D YOU GET ON THIS CHANNEL?
NOT VERY NICE TO ADMIT IT...
...BUT I CAN'T HELP SMILING WHEN I HEAR THE ANGER IN HIS VOICE.
I'M ON MY OWN MISSION.
OFF-RADAR.
WEARING A WAYNETECH LIGHT REFRACTOR...
...FLYING A GLIDER THAT'S INVISIBLE TO SURVEILLANCE CAMERAS.
WHO THE HELL NEEDS BATMAN, ANYWAY?

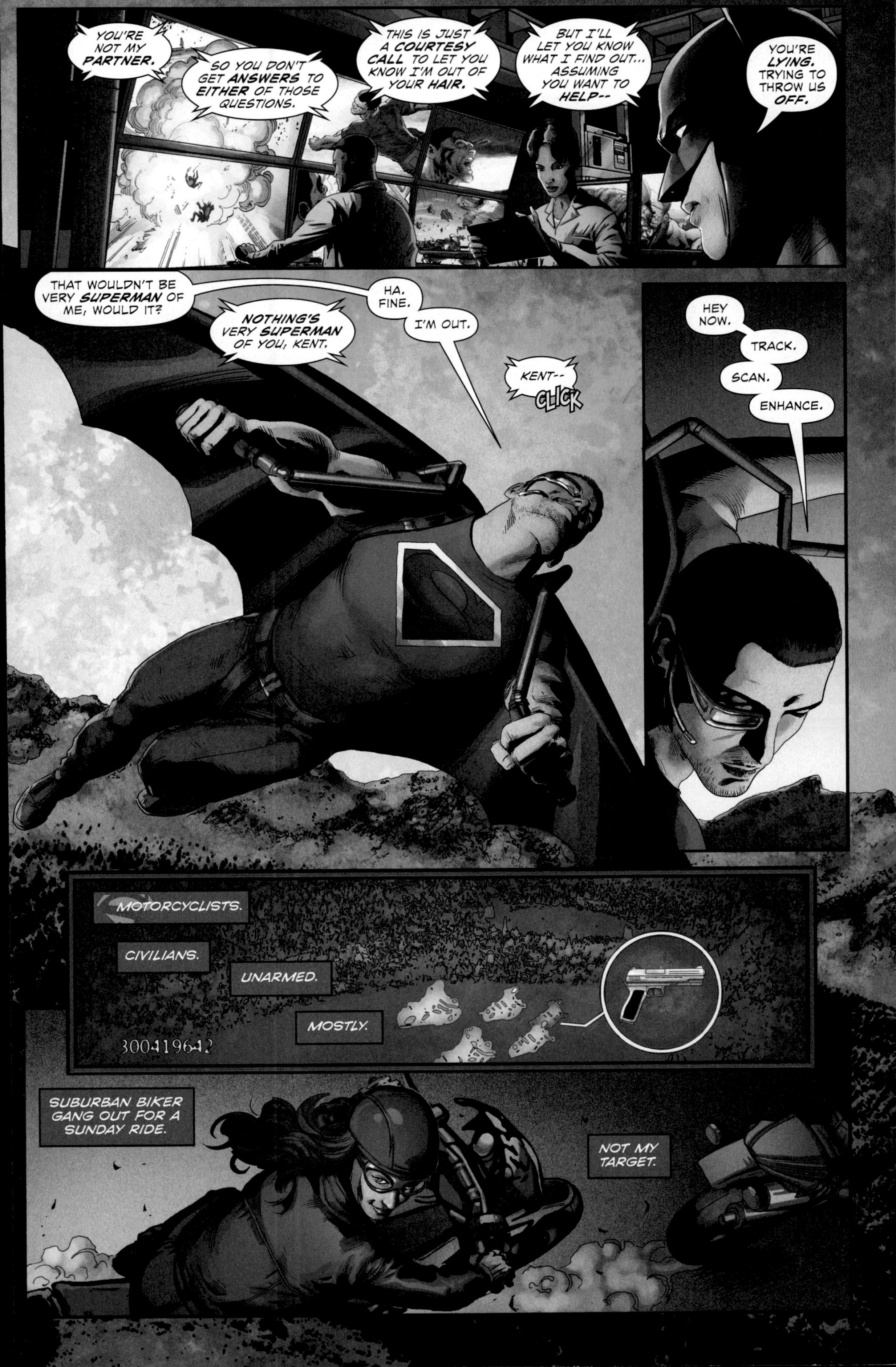

YOU'RE NOT MY PARTNER.
SO YOU DON'T GET ANSWERS TO EITHER OF THOSE QUESTIONS.
THIS IS JUST A COURTESY CALL TO LET YOU KNOW I'M OUT OF YOUR HAIR.
BUT I'LL LET YOU KNOW WHAT I FIND OUT... ASSUMING YOU WANT TO HELP--
YOU'RE LYING. TRYING TO THROW US OFF.
THAT WOULDN'T BE VERY SUPERMAN OF ME, WOULD IT?
NOTHING'S VERY SUPERMAN OF YOU, KENT.
HA. FINE.
I'M OUT.
KENT--
CLICK
HEY NOW.
TRACK.
SCAN.
ENHANCE.
MOTORCYCLISTS.
CIVILIANS.
UNARMED.
MOSTLY.
300419642
SUBURBAN BIKER GANG OUT FOR A SUNDAY RIDE.
NOT MY TARGET.

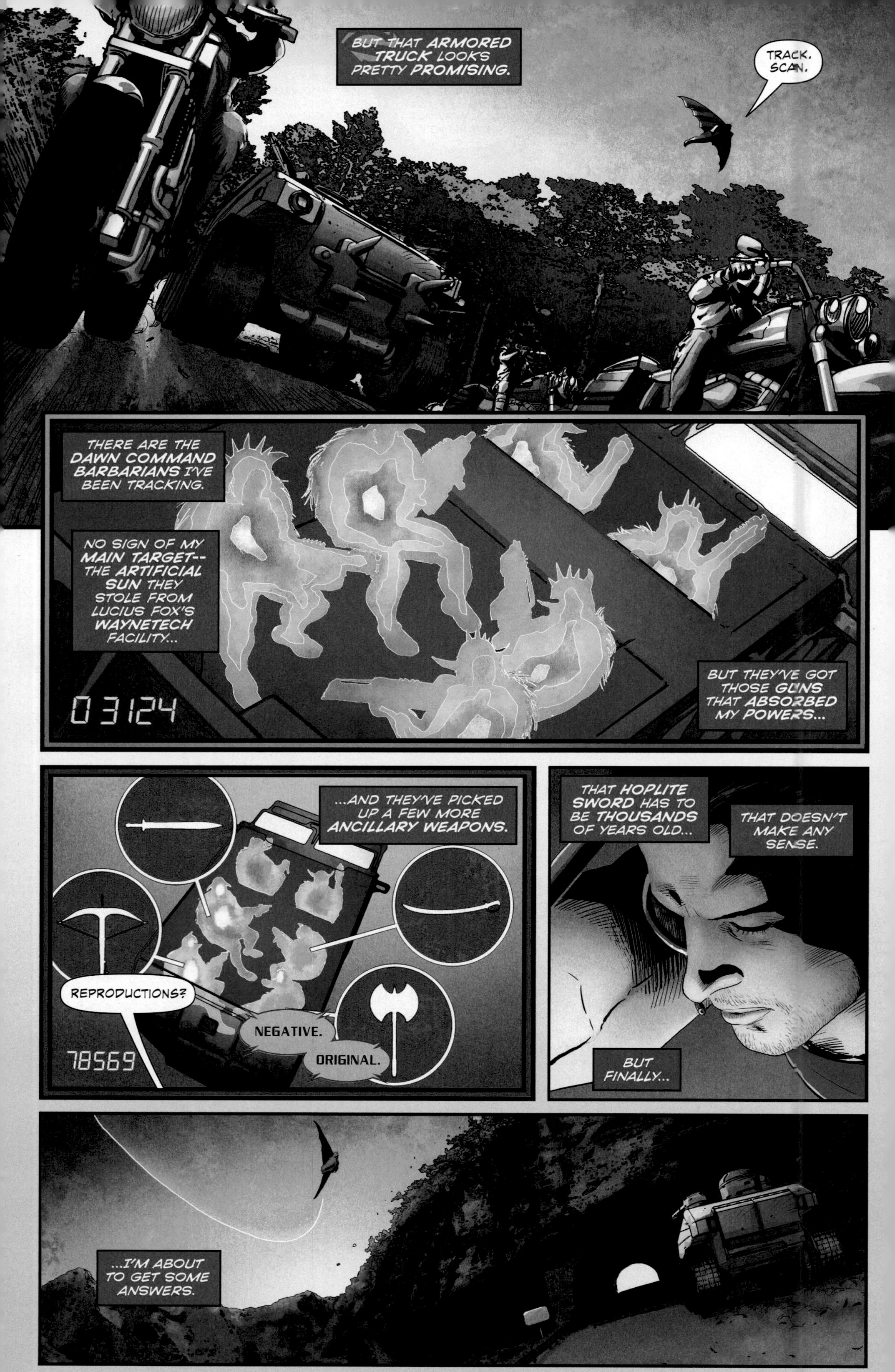
BUT THAT ARMORED TRUCK LOOKS PRETTY PROMISING.
TRACK. SCAN.
THERE ARE THE DAWN COMMAND BARBARIANS I'VE BEEN TRACKING.
NO SIGN OF MY MAIN TARGET-- THE ARTIFICIAL SUN THEY STOLE FROM LUCIUS FOX'S WAYNETECH FACILITY...
03124
BUT THEY'VE GOT THOSE GUNS THAT ABSORBED MY POWERS...
...AND THEY'VE PICKED UP A FEW MORE ANCILLARY WEAPONS.
REPRODUCTIONS?
NEGATIVE.
ORIGINAL.
78569
THAT HOPLITE SWORD HAS TO BE THOUSANDS OF YEARS OLD...
THAT DOESN'T MAKE ANY SENSE.
BUT FINALLY...
...I'M ABOUT TO GET SOME ANSWERS.

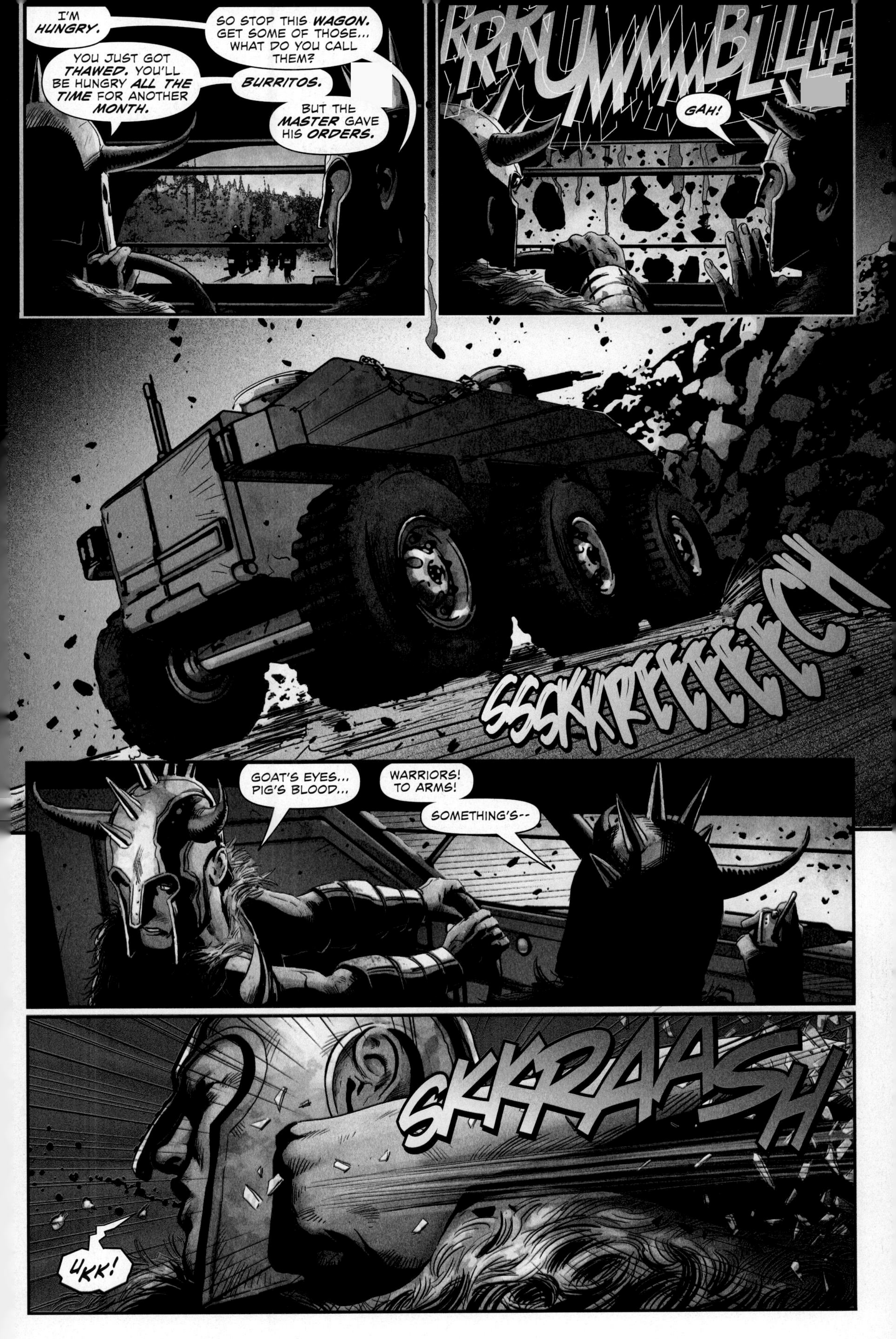
I'M HUNGRY.
SO STOP THIS WAGON. GET SOME OF THOSE... WHAT DO YOU CALL THEM?
YOU JUST GOT THAWED. YOU'LL BE HUNGRY ALL THE TIME FOR ANOTHER MONTH.
BURRITOS.
BUT THE MASTER GAVE HIS ORDERS.
KRKUMMBLLE
GAH!
SSSKKREEEEECH
GOAT'S EYES... PIG'S BLOOD...
WARRIORS! TO ARMS!
SOMETHING'S--
SKKRAASH
UKK!

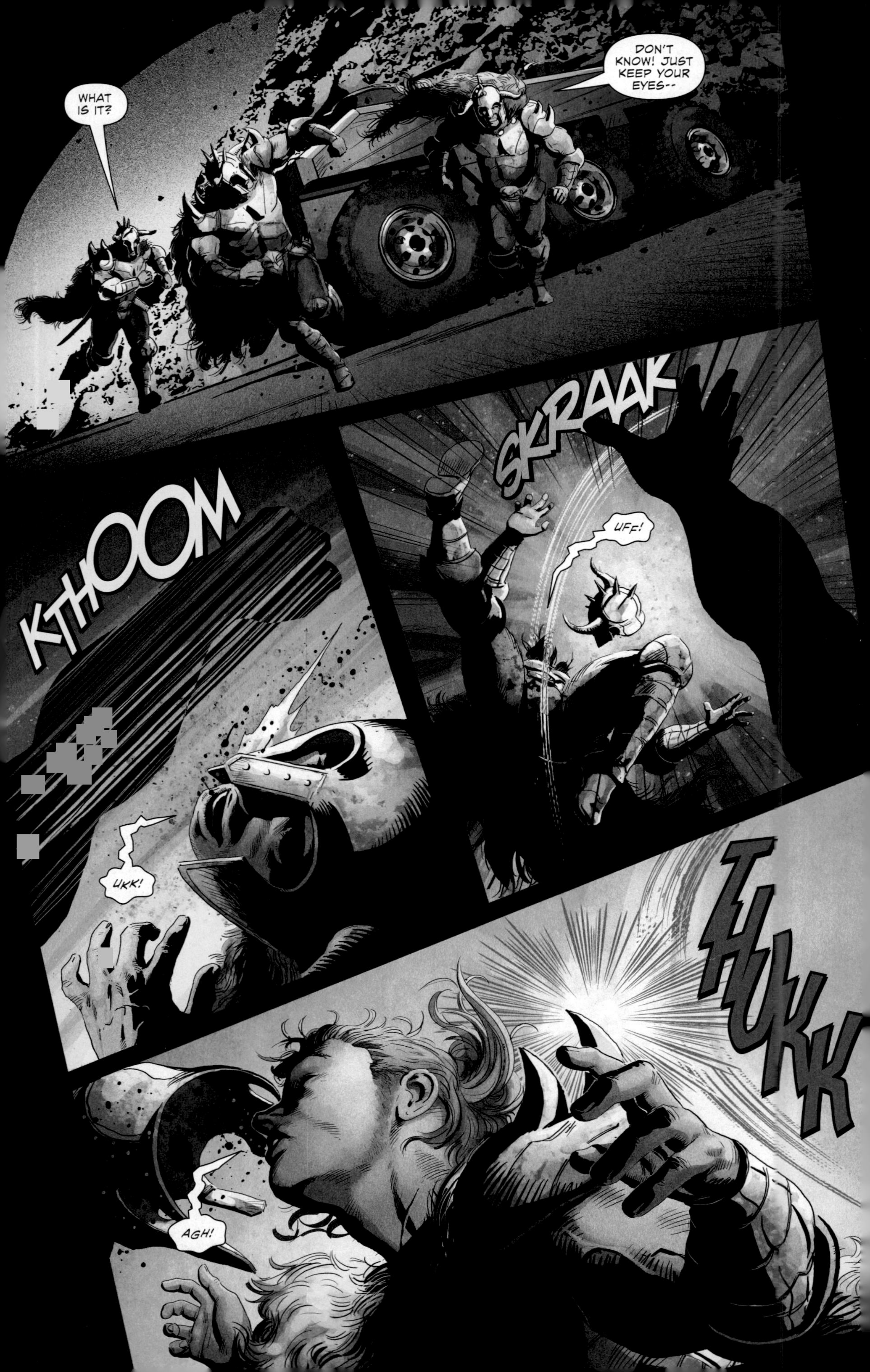
WHAT IS IT?
DON'T KNOW! JUST KEEP YOUR EYES--
SKRAAK
UFF!
KTHOOM
UKK!
THUKK
AGH!

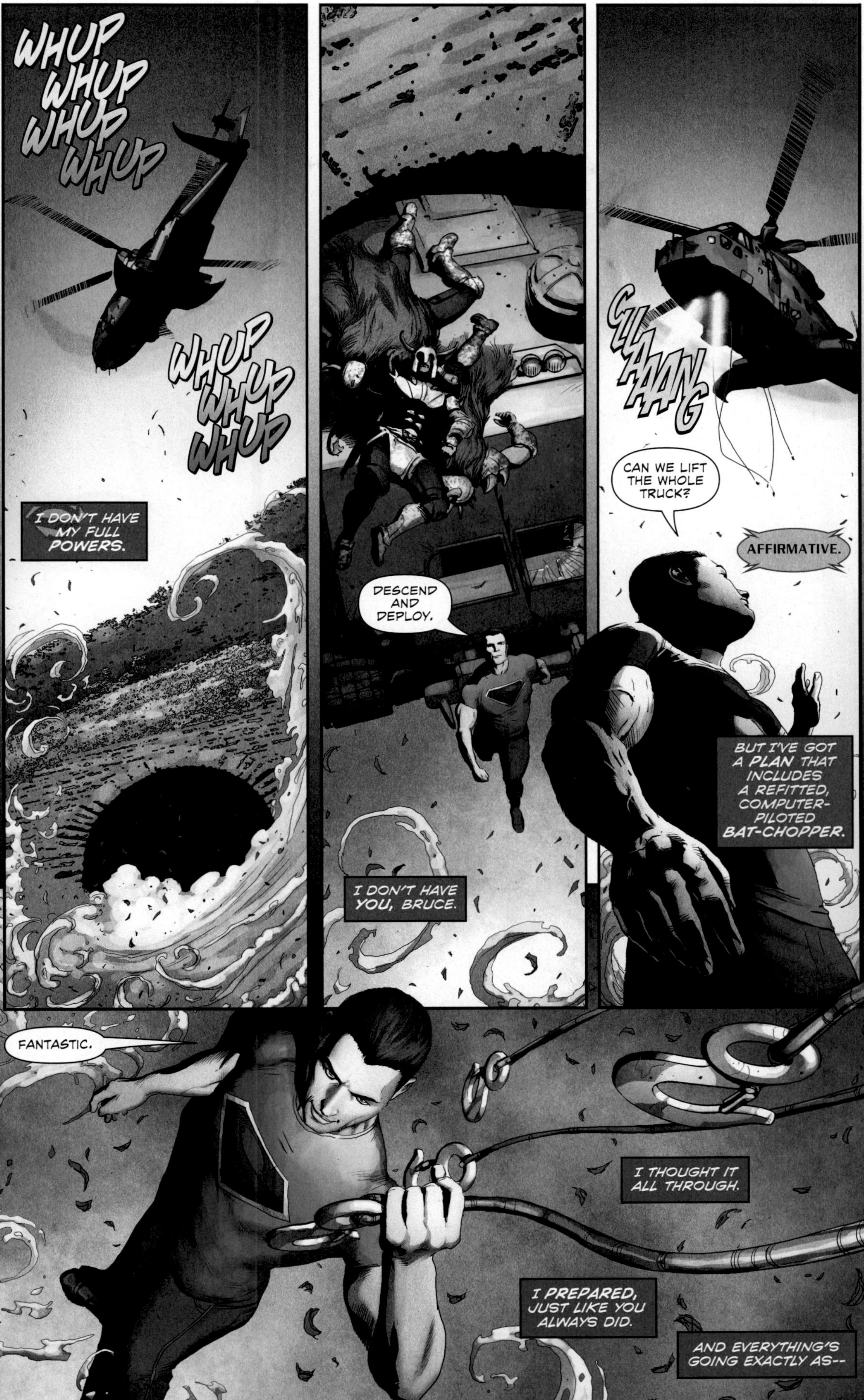
WHUP WHUP WHUP WHUP
WHUP WHUP WHUP
I DON'T HAVE MY FULL POWERS.
DESCEND AND DEPLOY.
I DON'T HAVE YOU, BRUCE.
CLLAAANG
CAN WE LIFT THE WHOLE TRUCK?
AFFIRMATIVE.
BUT I'VE GOT A PLAN THAT INCLUDES A REFITTED, COMPUTER-PILOTED BAT-CHOPPER.
FANTASTIC.
I THOUGHT IT ALL THROUGH.
I PREPARED, JUST LIKE YOU ALWAYS DID.
AND EVERYTHING'S GOING EXACTLY AS--

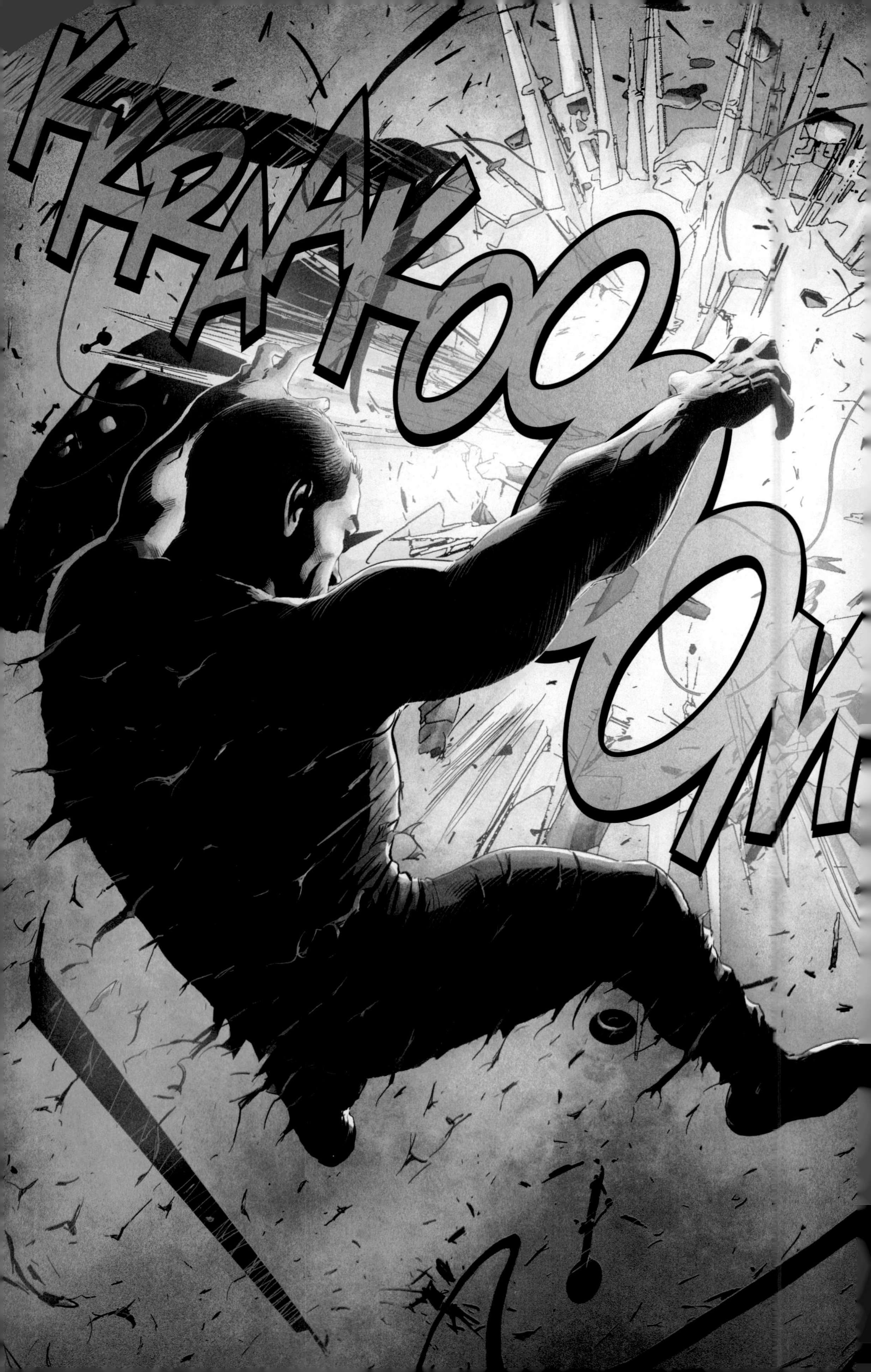

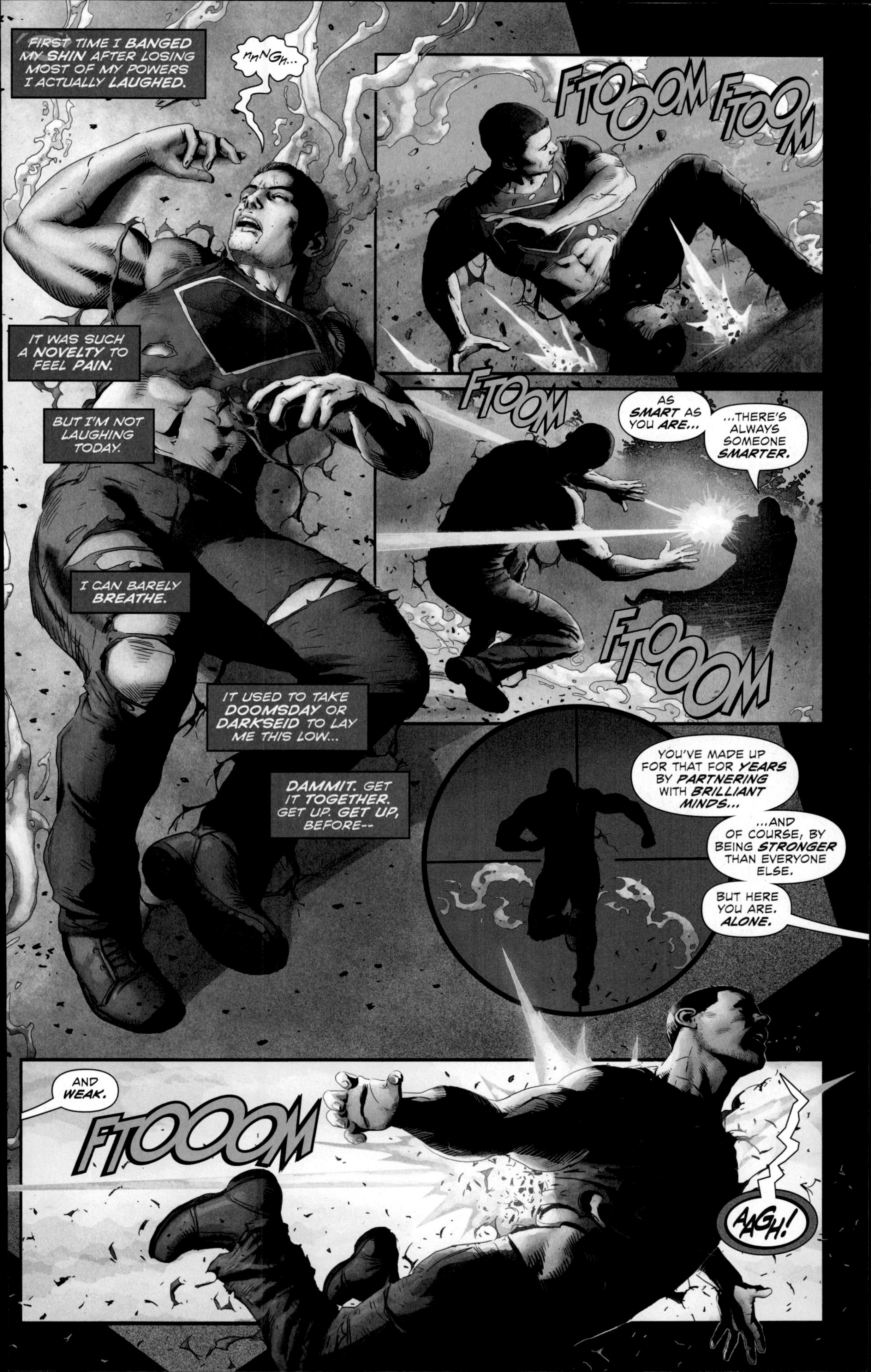

FIRST TIME I BANGED MY SHIN AFTER LOSING MOST OF MY POWERS I ACTUALLY LAUGHED.
nnNGh...
IT WAS SUCH A NOVELTY TO FEEL PAIN.
BUT I'M NOT LAUGHING TODAY.
I CAN BARELY BREATHE.
IT USED TO TAKE DOOMSDAY OR DARKSEID TO LAY ME THIS LOW...
DAMMIT. GET IT TOGETHER. GET UP. GET UP, BEFORE--
FTOOOOM FTOOM
FTOOM
AS SMART AS YOU ARE...
...THERE'S ALWAYS SOMEONE SMARTER.
FTOOOOM
YOU'VE MADE UP FOR THAT FOR YEARS BY PARTNERING WITH BRILLIANT MINDS...
...AND OF COURSE, BY BEING STRONGER THAN EVERYONE ELSE.
BUT HERE YOU ARE. ALONE.
AND WEAK.
FTOOOM
AAGH!

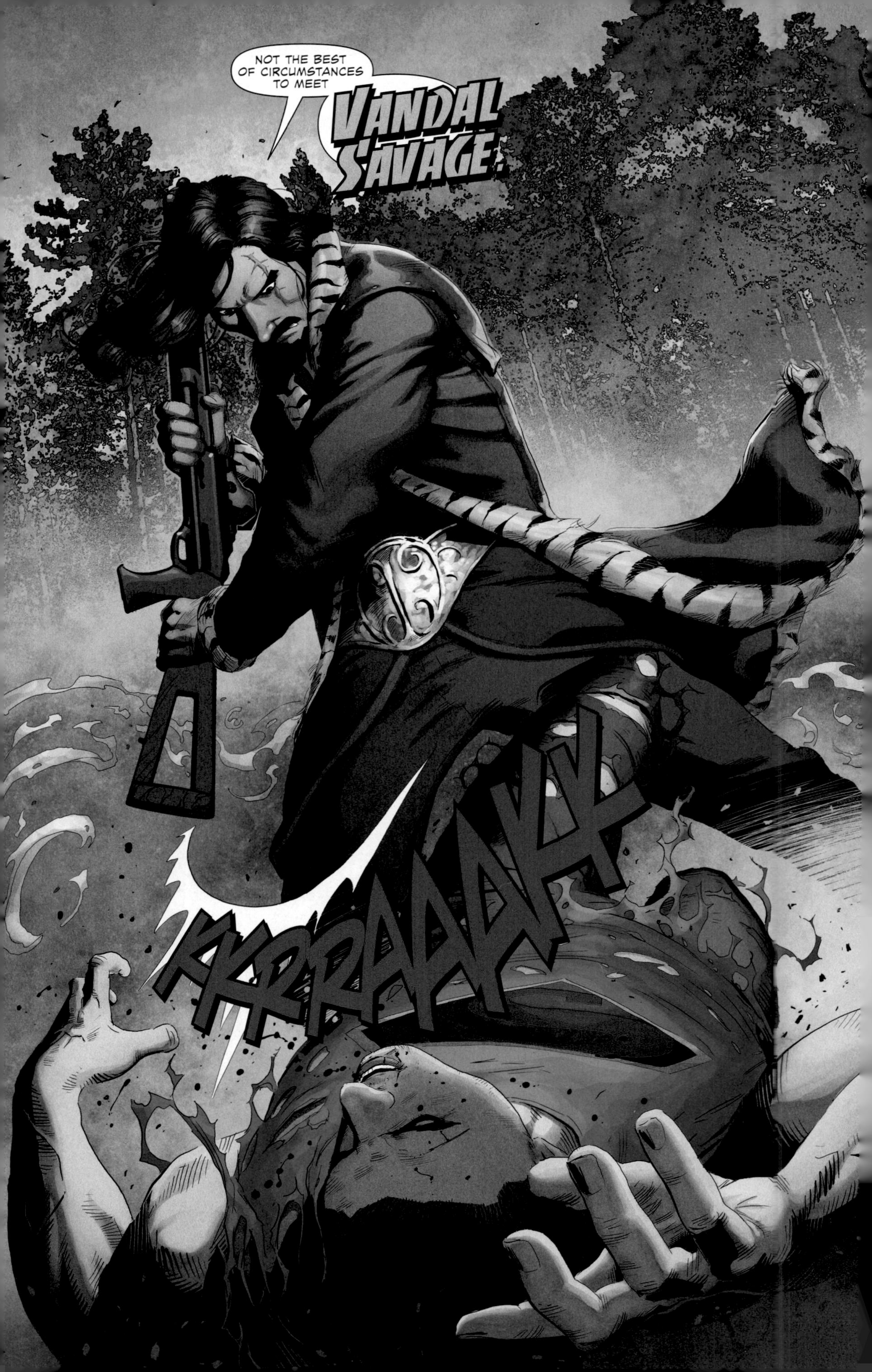
NOT THE BEST OF CIRCUMSTANCES TO MEET
VANDAL SAVAGE.
KKRRAAKK

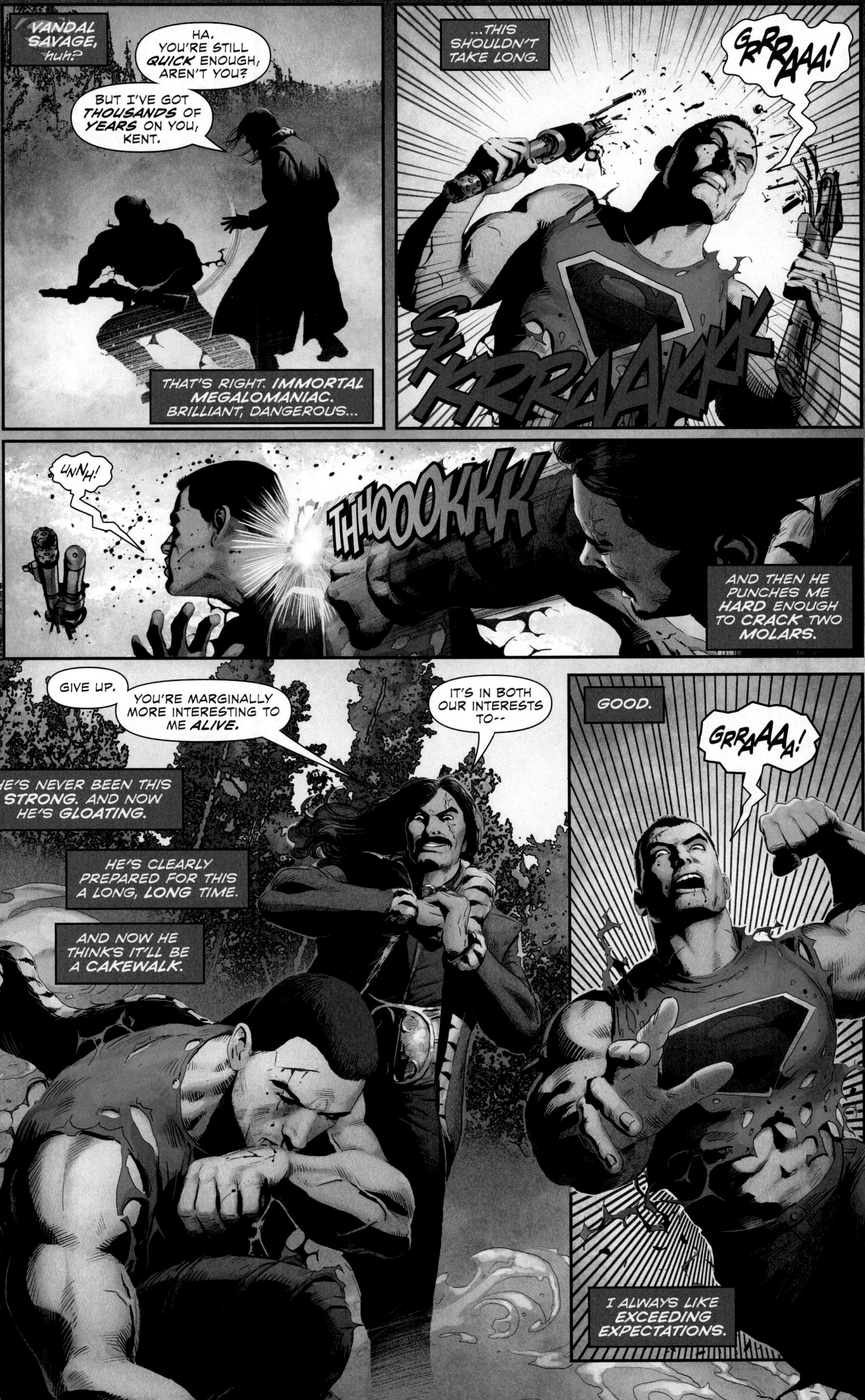
VANDAL SAVAGE, huh?
HA. YOU'RE STILL QUICK ENOUGH, AREN'T YOU?
BUT I'VE GOT THOUSANDS OF YEARS ON YOU, KENT.
THAT'S RIGHT. IMMORTAL MEGALOMANIAC. BRILLIANT, DANGEROUS...
...THIS SHOULDN'T TAKE LONG.
GRRRAAA!
SKKRRAAKK
UNNH!
THHOOOKKK
AND THEN HE PUNCHES ME HARD ENOUGH TO CRACK TWO MOLARS.
GIVE UP.
YOU'RE MARGINALLY MORE INTERESTING TO ME ALIVE.
IT'S IN BOTH OUR INTERESTS TO--
HE'S NEVER BEEN THIS STRONG. AND NOW HE'S GLOATING.
HE'S CLEARLY PREPARED FOR THIS A LONG, LONG TIME.
AND NOW HE THINKS IT'LL BE A CAKEWALK.
GOOD.
GRRAAAA!
I ALWAYS LIKE EXCEEDING EXPECTATIONS.

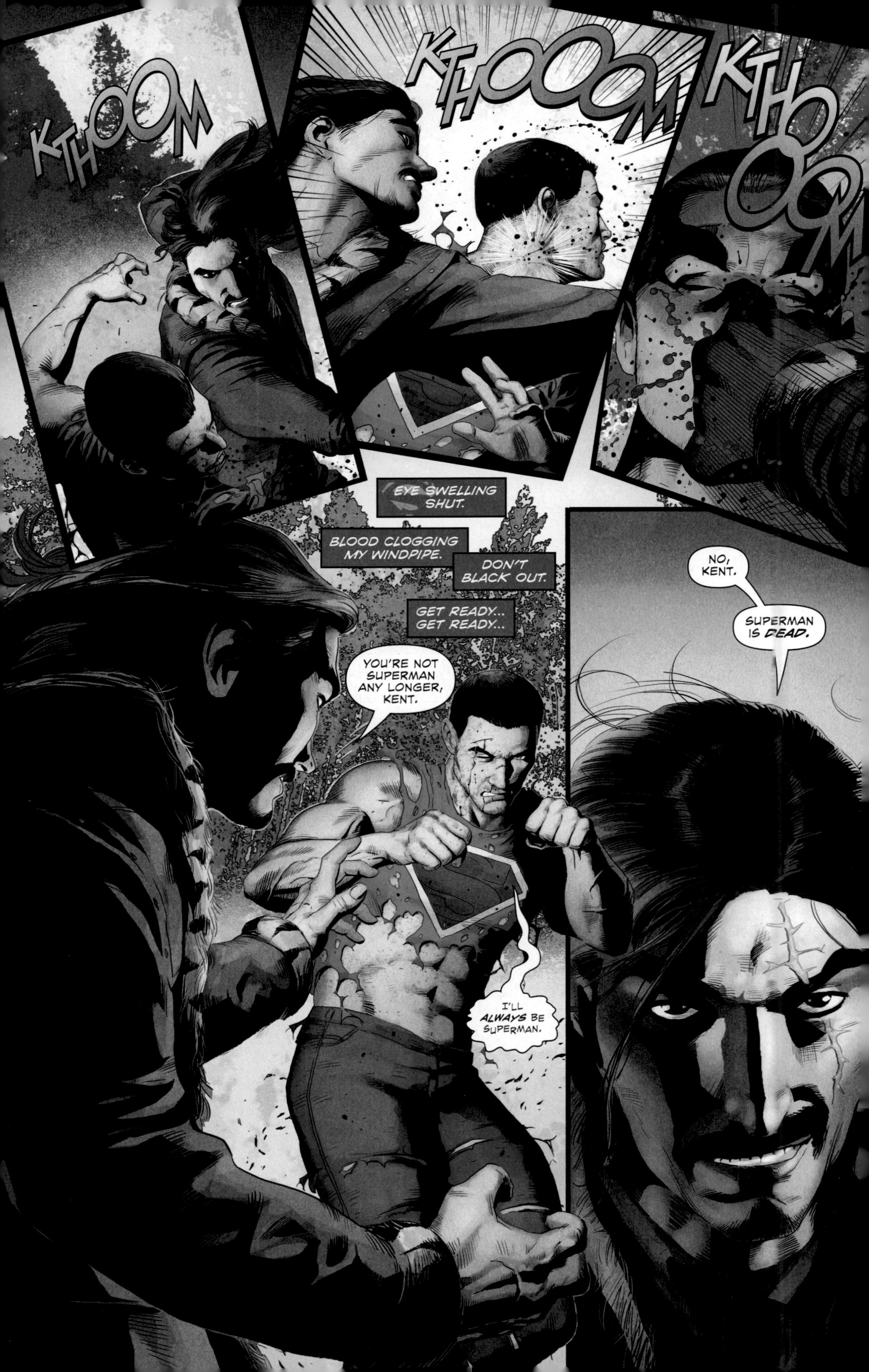
KTHOOM
KTHOOOOM
KTHOOOM
EYE SWELLING SHUT.
BLOOD CLOGGING MY WINDPIPE.
DON'T BLACK OUT.
GET READY... GET READY...
YOU'RE NOT SUPERMAN ANY LONGER, KENT.
I'LL ALWAYS BE SUPERMAN.
NO, KENT.
SUPERMAN IS DEAD.

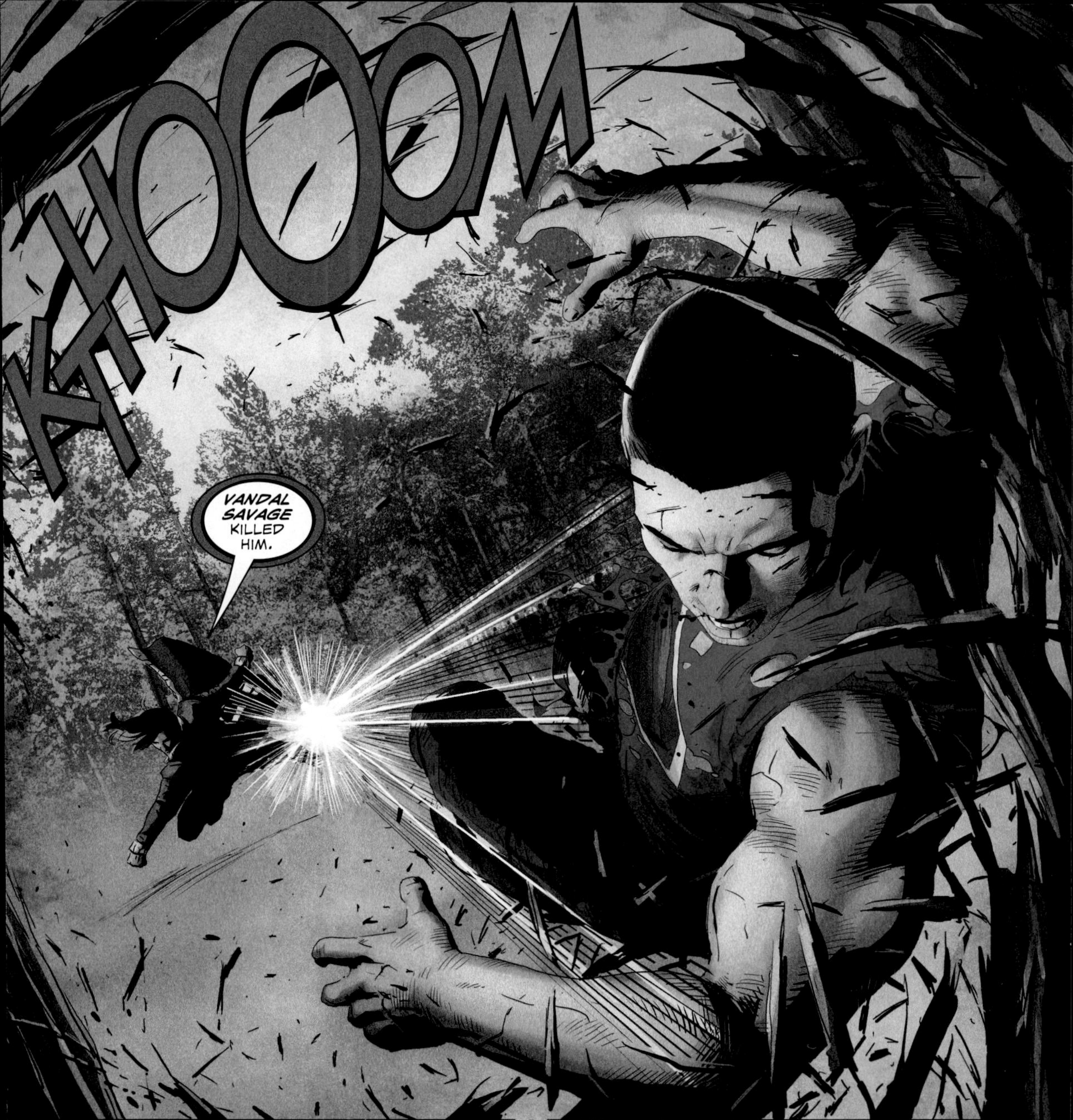
KTHOOOM
VANDAL SAVAGE KILLED HIM.

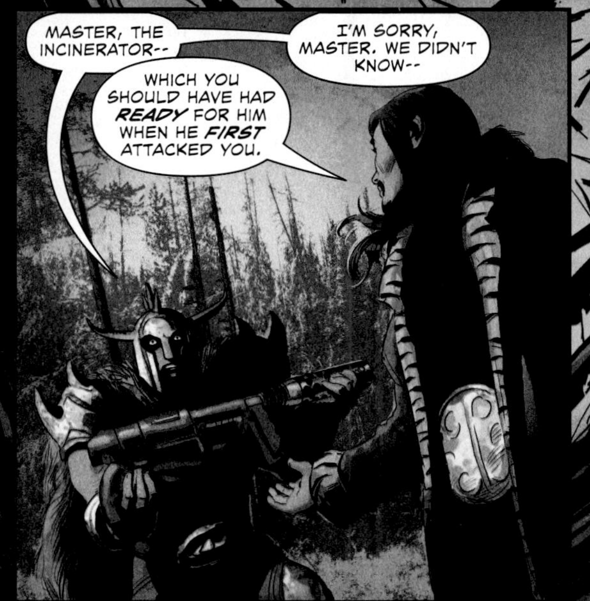
MASTER, THE INCINERATOR--
I'M SORRY, MASTER. WE DIDN'T KNOW--
WHICH YOU SHOULD HAVE HAD READY FOR HIM WHEN HE FIRST ATTACKED YOU.

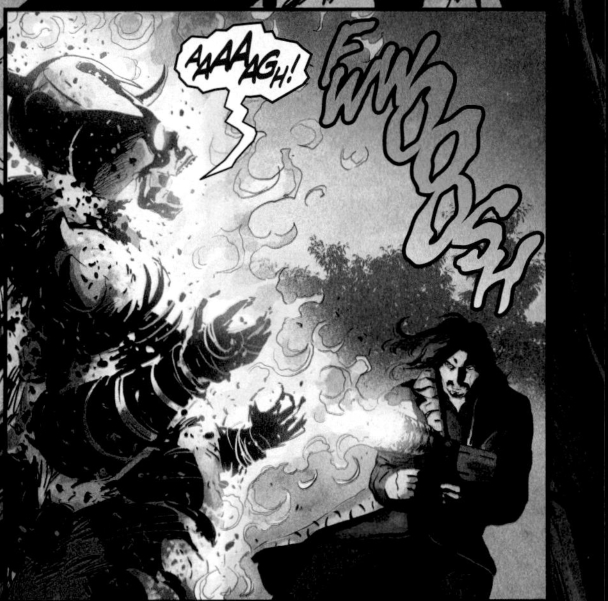
AAAAAGH!
FWOOOOSH

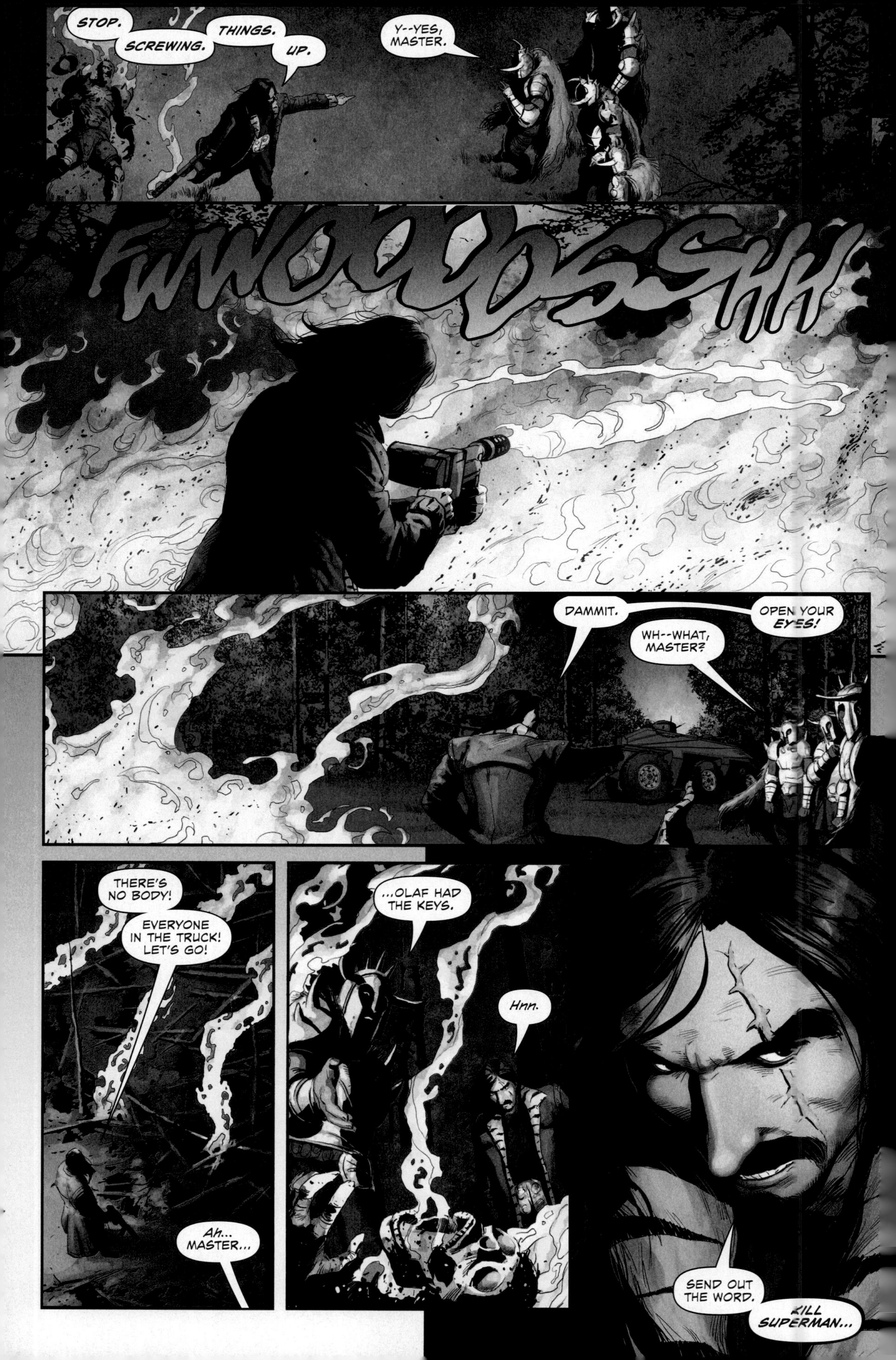
STOP.
SCREWING.
THINGS.
UP.
Y--YES, MASTER.
FWOOOOSHH
DAMMIT.
OPEN YOUR EYES!
WH--WHAT, MASTER?
THERE'S NO BODY!
EVERYONE IN THE TRUCK! LET'S GO!
Ah... MASTER...
...OLAF HAD THE KEYS.
Hnn.
SEND OUT THE WORD.
KILL SUPERMAN...

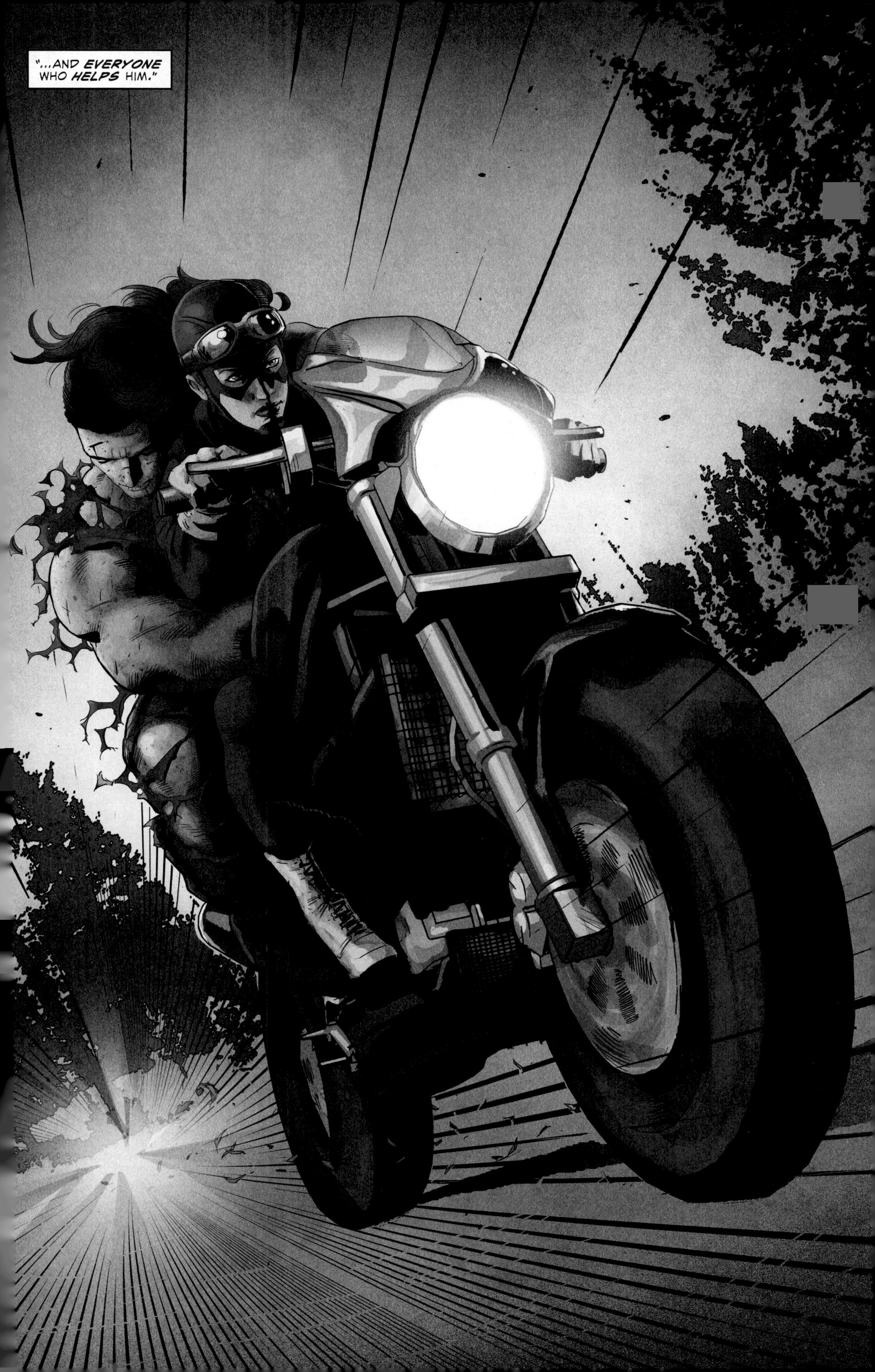
"...AND EVERYONE WHO HELPS HIM."

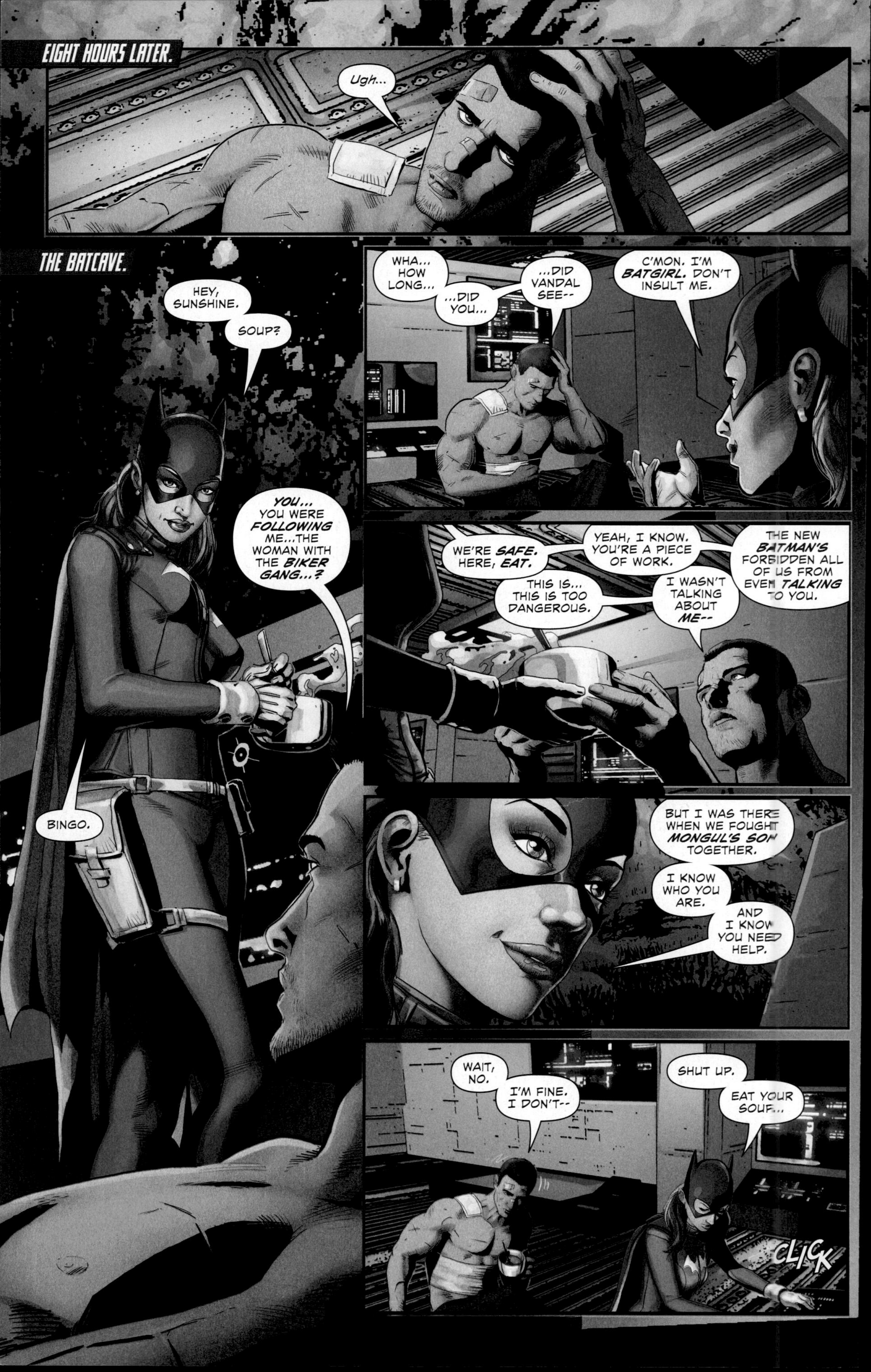
EIGHT HOURS LATER.
Ugh...
THE BATCAVE.
HEY, SUNSHINE.
SOUP?
YOU... YOU WERE FOLLOWING ME...THE WOMAN WITH THE BIKER GANG...?
BINGO.
WHA... HOW LONG...
...DID YOU...
...DID VANDAL SEE--
C'MON. I'M BATGIRL. DON'T INSULT ME.
WE'RE SAFE. HERE, EAT.
THIS IS... THIS IS TOO DANGEROUS.
YEAH, I KNOW. YOU'RE A PIECE OF WORK.
I WASN'T TALKING ABOUT ME--
THE NEW BATMAN'S FORBIDDEN ALL OF US FROM EVEN TALKING TO YOU.
BUT I WAS THERE WHEN WE FOUGHT MONGUL'S SON TOGETHER.
I KNOW WHO YOU ARE.
AND I KNOW YOU NEED HELP.
WAIT, NO.
I'M FINE. I DON'T--
SHUT UP.
EAT YOUR SOUP...
CLICK

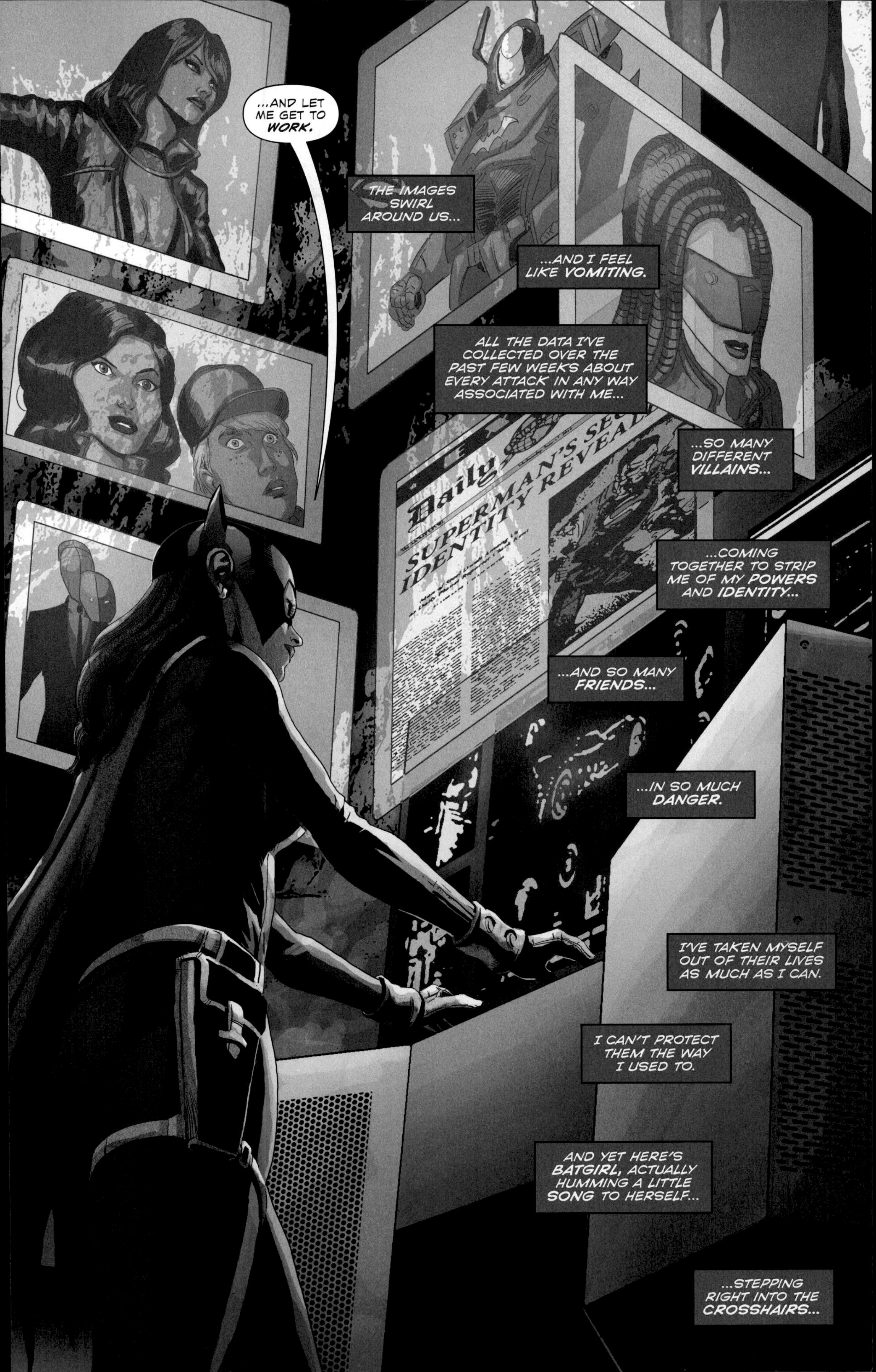

...AND LET ME GET TO WORK.
THE IMAGES SWIRL AROUND US...
...AND I FEEL LIKE VOMITING.
ALL THE DATA I'VE COLLECTED OVER THE PAST FEW WEEKS ABOUT EVERY ATTACK IN ANY WAY ASSOCIATED WITH ME...
...SO MANY DIFFERENT VILLAINS...
...COMING TOGETHER TO STRIP ME OF MY POWERS AND IDENTITY...
...AND SO MANY FRIENDS...
...IN SO MUCH DANGER.
I'VE TAKEN MYSELF OUT OF THEIR LIVES AS MUCH AS I CAN.
I CAN'T PROTECT THEM THE WAY I USED TO.
AND YET HERE'S BATGIRL, ACTUALLY HUMMING A LITTLE SONG TO HERSELF...
...STEPPING RIGHT INTO THE CROSSHAIRS...
Daily
SUPERMAN'S SECRET IDENTITY REVEALED

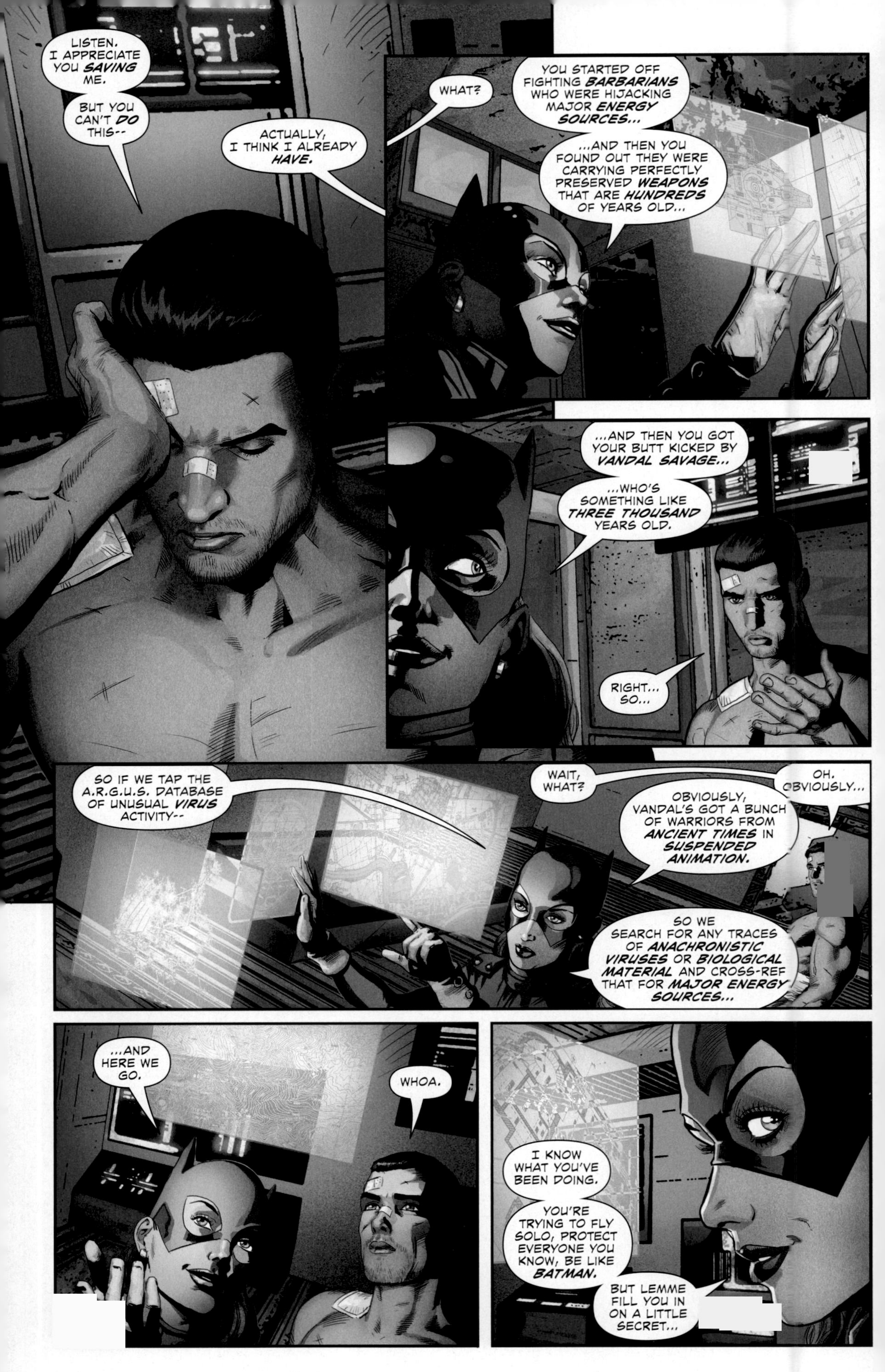
LISTEN. I APPRECIATE YOU SAVING ME.
BUT YOU CAN'T DO THIS--
ACTUALLY, I THINK I ALREADY HAVE.
WHAT?
YOU STARTED OFF FIGHTING BARBARIANS WHO WERE HIJACKING MAJOR ENERGY SOURCES...
...AND THEN YOU FOUND OUT THEY WERE CARRYING PERFECTLY PRESERVED WEAPONS THAT ARE HUNDREDS OF YEARS OLD...
...AND THEN YOU GOT YOUR BUTT KICKED BY VANDAL SAVAGE...
...WHO'S SOMETHING LIKE THREE THOUSAND YEARS OLD.
RIGHT... SO...
SO IF WE TAP THE A.R.G.U.S. DATABASE OF UNUSUAL VIRUS ACTIVITY--
WAIT, WHAT?
OH. OBVIOUSLY...
OBVIOUSLY, VANDAL'S GOT A BUNCH OF WARRIORS FROM ANCIENT TIMES IN SUSPENDED ANIMATION.
SO WE SEARCH FOR ANY TRACES OF ANACHRONISTIC VIRUSES OR BIOLOGICAL MATERIAL AND CROSS-REF THAT FOR MAJOR ENERGY SOURCES...
...AND HERE WE GO.
WHOA.
I KNOW WHAT YOU'VE BEEN DOING.
YOU'RE TRYING TO FLY SOLO, PROTECT EVERYONE YOU KNOW, BE LIKE BATMAN.
BUT LEMME FILL YOU IN ON A LITTLE SECRET...

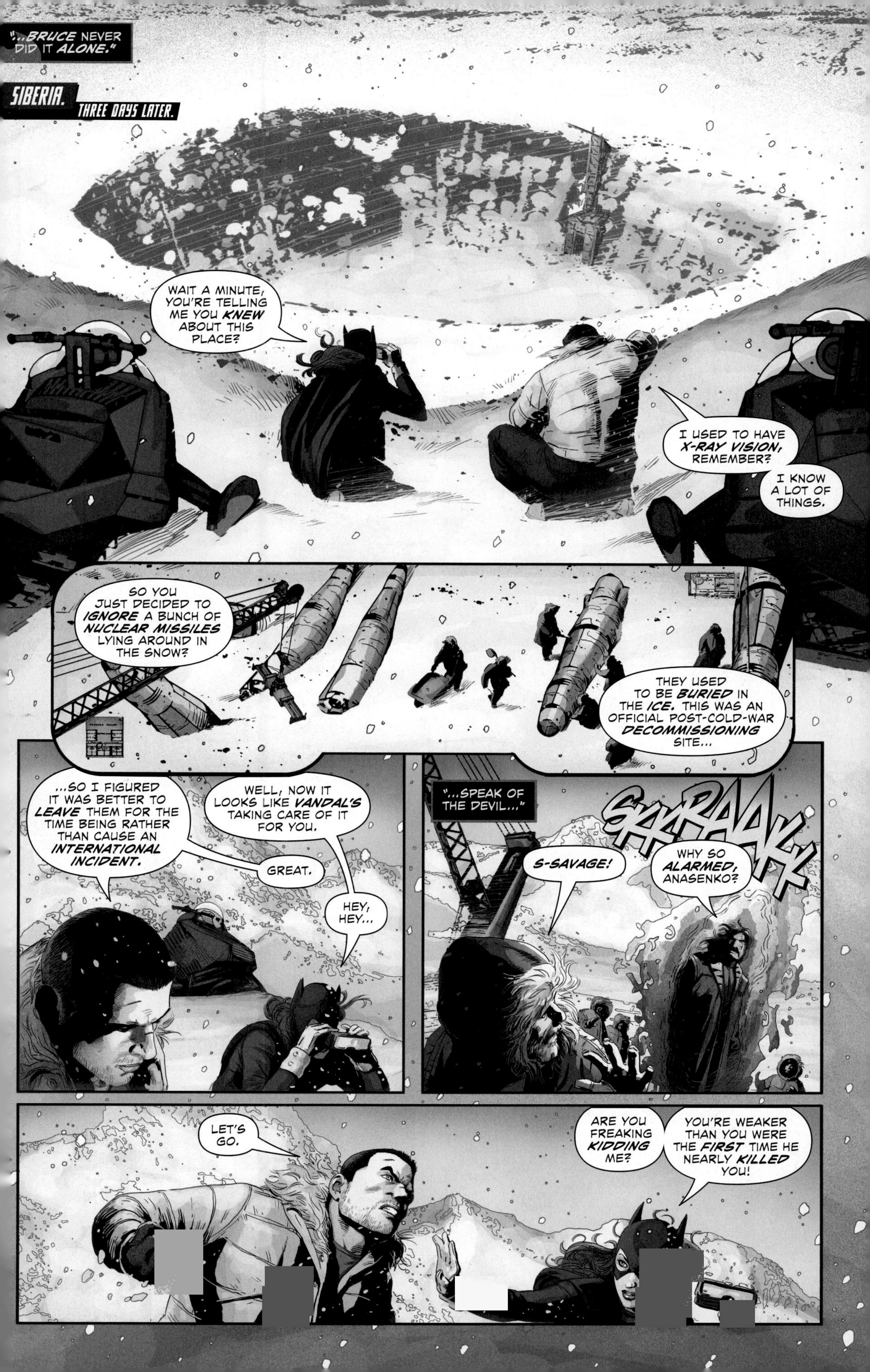
"...BRUCE NEVER DID IT ALONE."
SIBERIA.
THREE DAYS LATER.
WAIT A MINUTE, YOU'RE TELLING ME YOU KNEW ABOUT THIS PLACE?
I USED TO HAVE X-RAY VISION, REMEMBER?
I KNOW A LOT OF THINGS.
SO YOU JUST DECIDED TO IGNORE A BUNCH OF NUCLEAR MISSILES LYING AROUND IN THE SNOW?
THEY USED TO BE BURIED IN THE ICE. THIS WAS AN OFFICIAL POST-COLD-WAR DECOMMISSIONING SITE...
...SO I FIGURED IT WAS BETTER TO LEAVE THEM FOR THE TIME BEING RATHER THAN CAUSE AN INTERNATIONAL INCIDENT.
WELL, NOW IT LOOKS LIKE VANDAL'S TAKING CARE OF IT FOR YOU.
GREAT.
HEY, HEY...
"...SPEAK OF THE DEVIL..."
SKKRAAKK
S-SAVAGE!
WHY SO ALARMED, ANASENKO?
LET'S GO.
ARE YOU FREAKING KIDDING ME?
YOU'RE WEAKER THAN YOU WERE THE FIRST TIME HE NEARLY KILLED YOU!

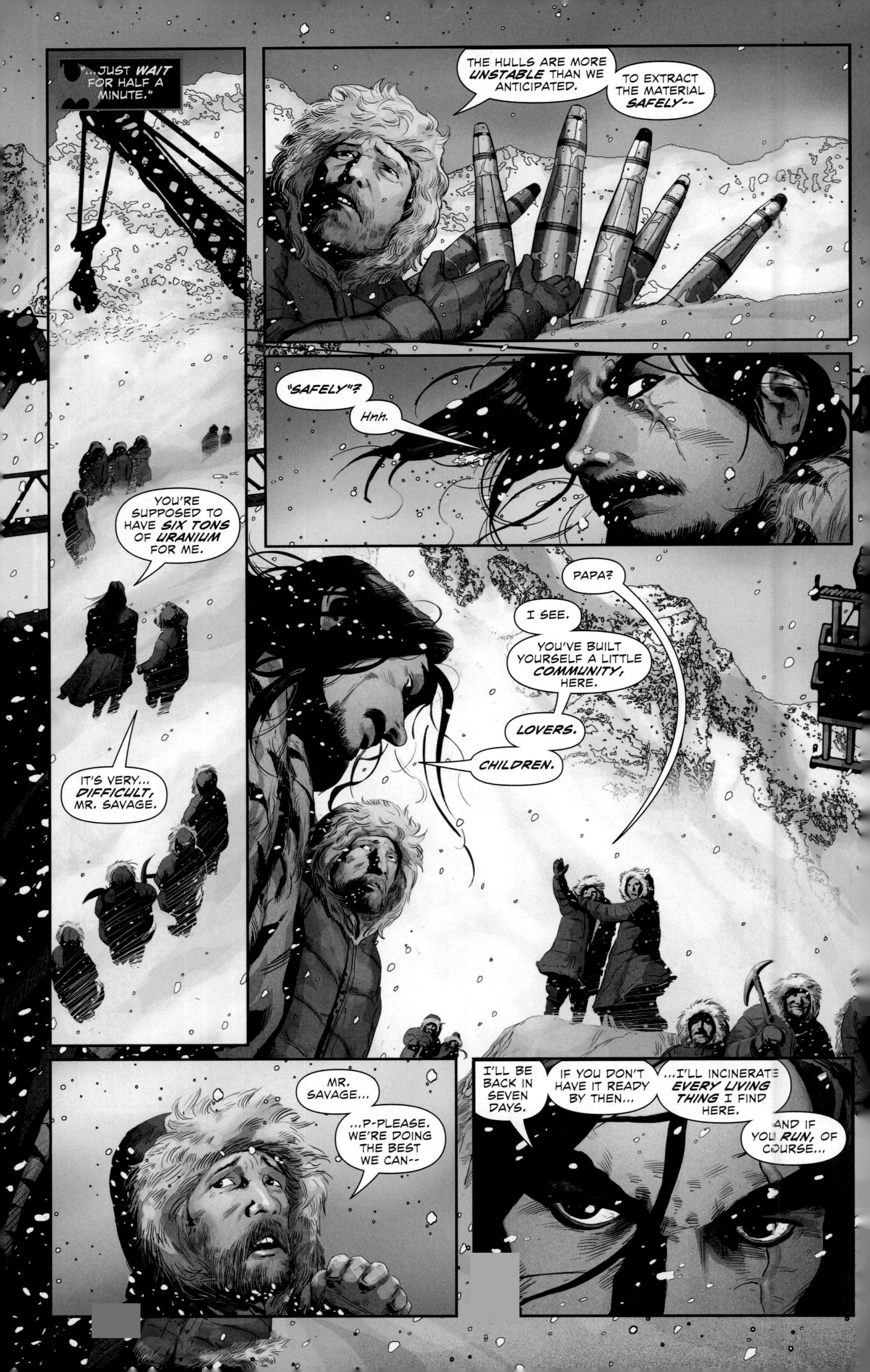
"...JUST WAIT FOR HALF A MINUTE."
THE HULLS ARE MORE UNSTABLE THAN WE ANTICIPATED.
TO EXTRACT THE MATERIAL SAFELY--
"SAFELY"?
Hnh.
YOU'RE SUPPOSED TO HAVE SIX TONS OF URANIUM FOR ME.
IT'S VERY... DIFFICULT, MR. SAVAGE.
PAPA?
I SEE.
YOU'VE BUILT YOURSELF A LITTLE COMMUNITY, HERE.
LOVERS.
CHILDREN.
MR. SAVAGE...
...P-PLEASE. WE'RE DOING THE BEST WE CAN--
I'LL BE BACK IN SEVEN DAYS.
IF YOU DON'T HAVE IT READY BY THEN...
...I'LL INCINERATE EVERY LIVING THING I FIND HERE.
AND IF YOU RUN, OF COURSE...

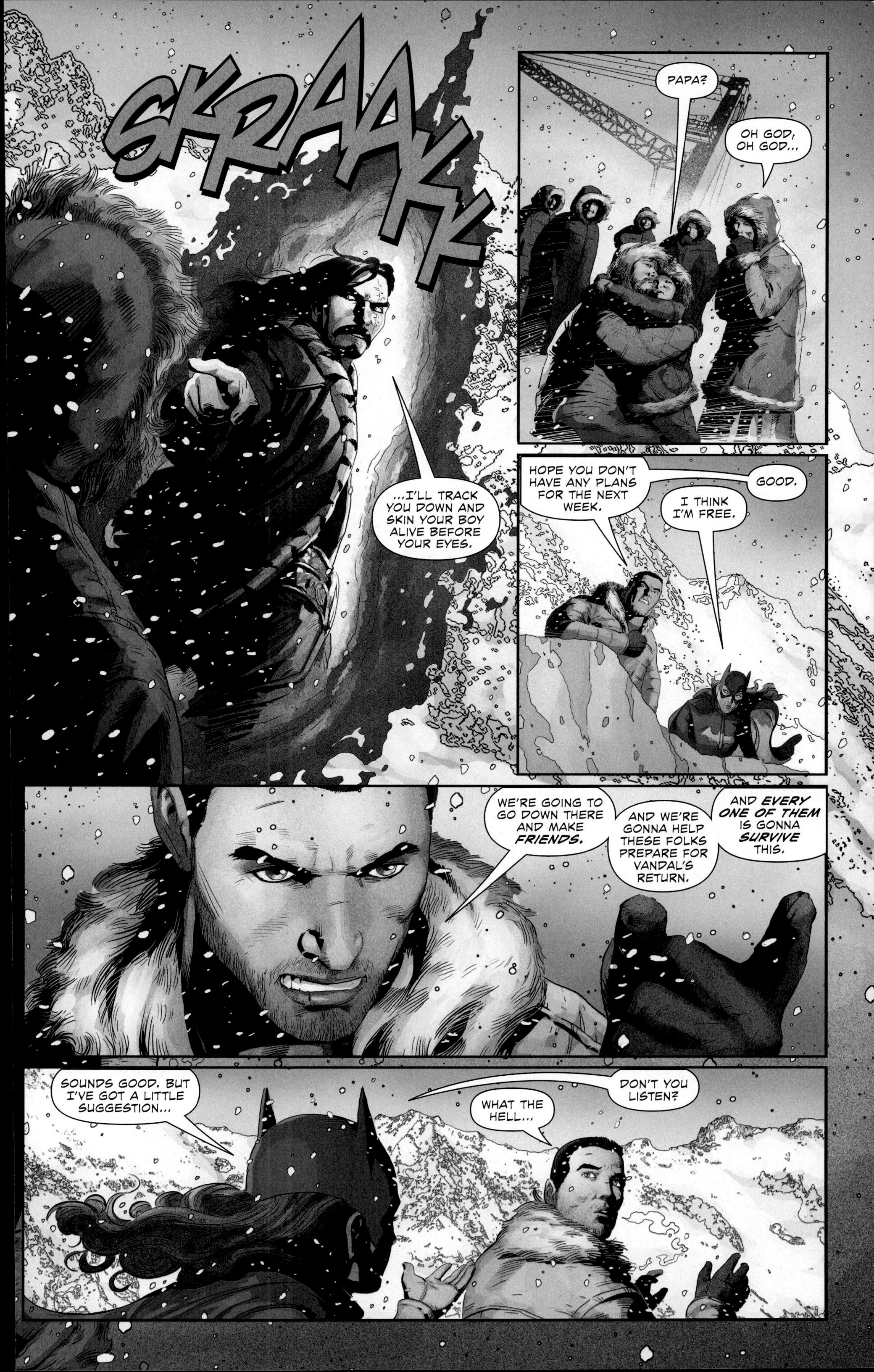
SKRAAKK
...I'LL TRACK YOU DOWN AND SKIN YOUR BOY ALIVE BEFORE YOUR EYES.
PAPA?
OH GOD, OH GOD...
HOPE YOU DON'T HAVE ANY PLANS FOR THE NEXT WEEK.
I THINK I'M FREE.
GOOD.
WE'RE GOING TO GO DOWN THERE AND MAKE FRIENDS.
AND WE'RE GONNA HELP THESE FOLKS PREPARE FOR VANDAL'S RETURN.
AND EVERY ONE OF THEM IS GONNA SURVIVE THIS.
SOUNDS GOOD. BUT I'VE GOT A LITTLE SUGGESTION...
WHAT THE HELL...
DON'T YOU LISTEN?

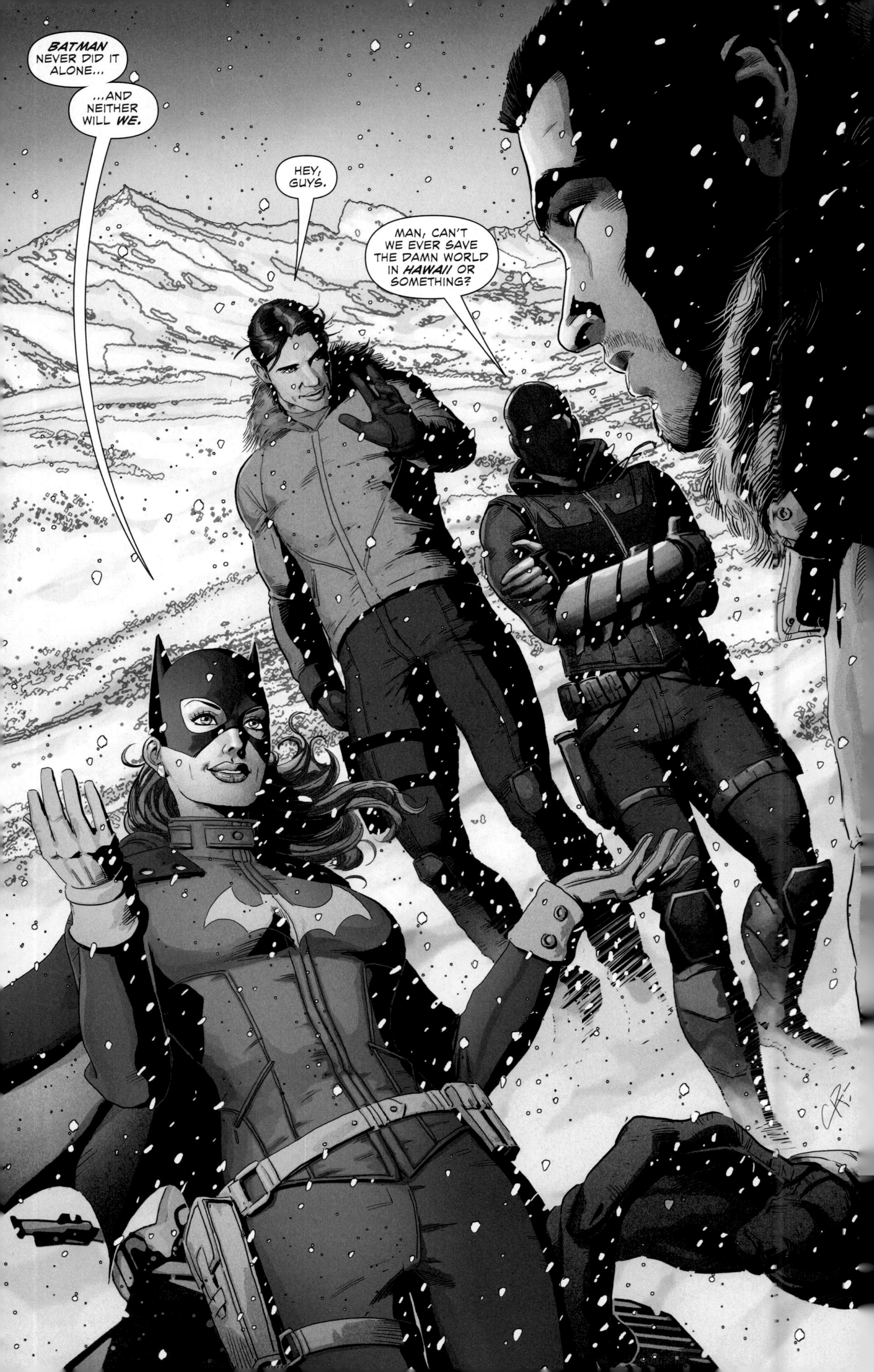
BATMAN NEVER DID IT ALONE...
...AND NEITHER WILL WE.
HEY, GUYS.
MAN, CAN'T WE EVER SAVE THE DAMN WORLD IN HAWAII OR SOMETHING?

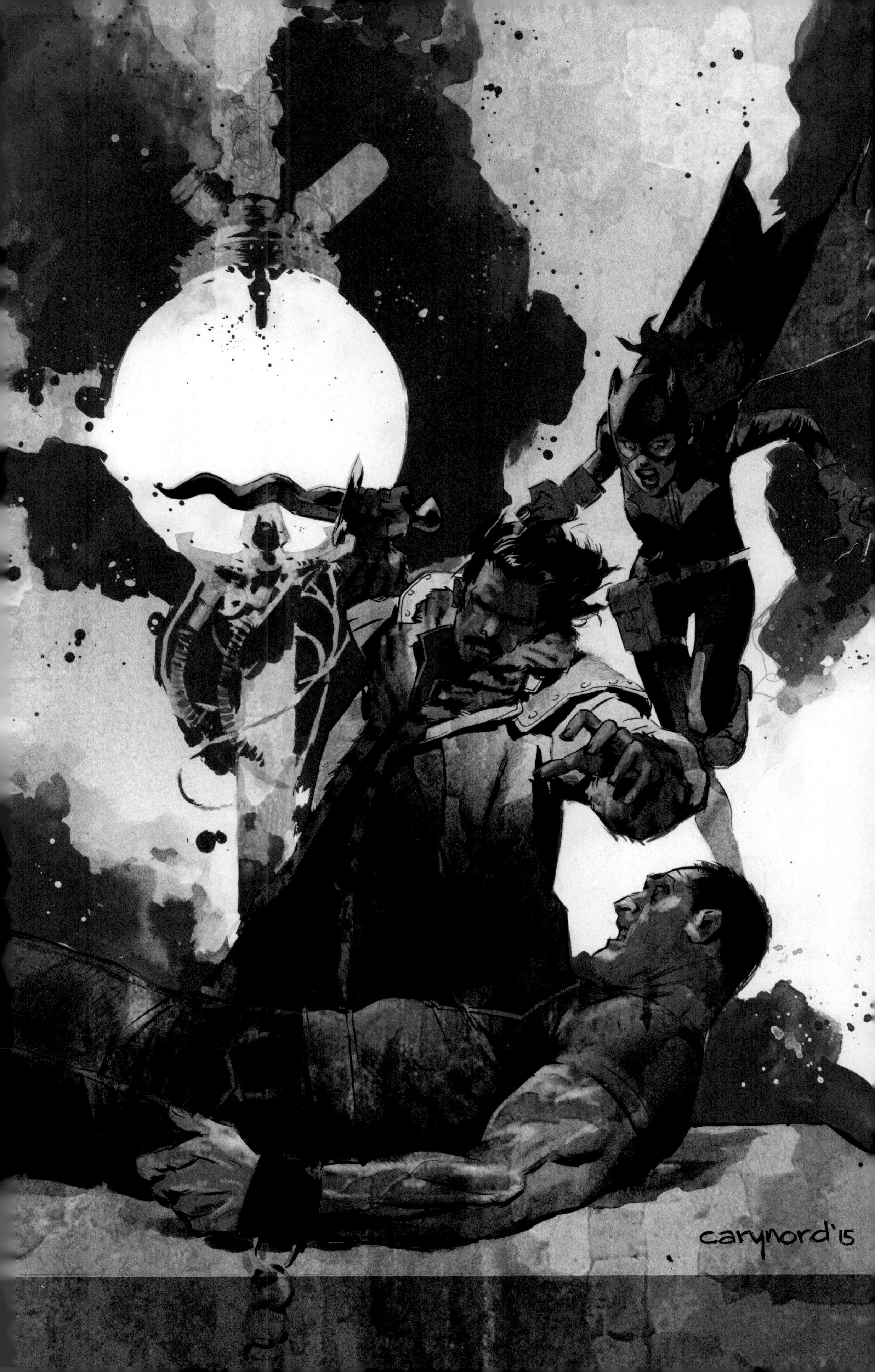
carynord'15

TEAMWORK

GREG PAK writer **ARDIAN SYAF CLIFF RICHARDS** pencillers **VICENTE CIFUENTES CLIFF RICHARDS** inkers **BETH SOTELO** colorist **ROB LEIGH** letterer **CARY NORD** cover

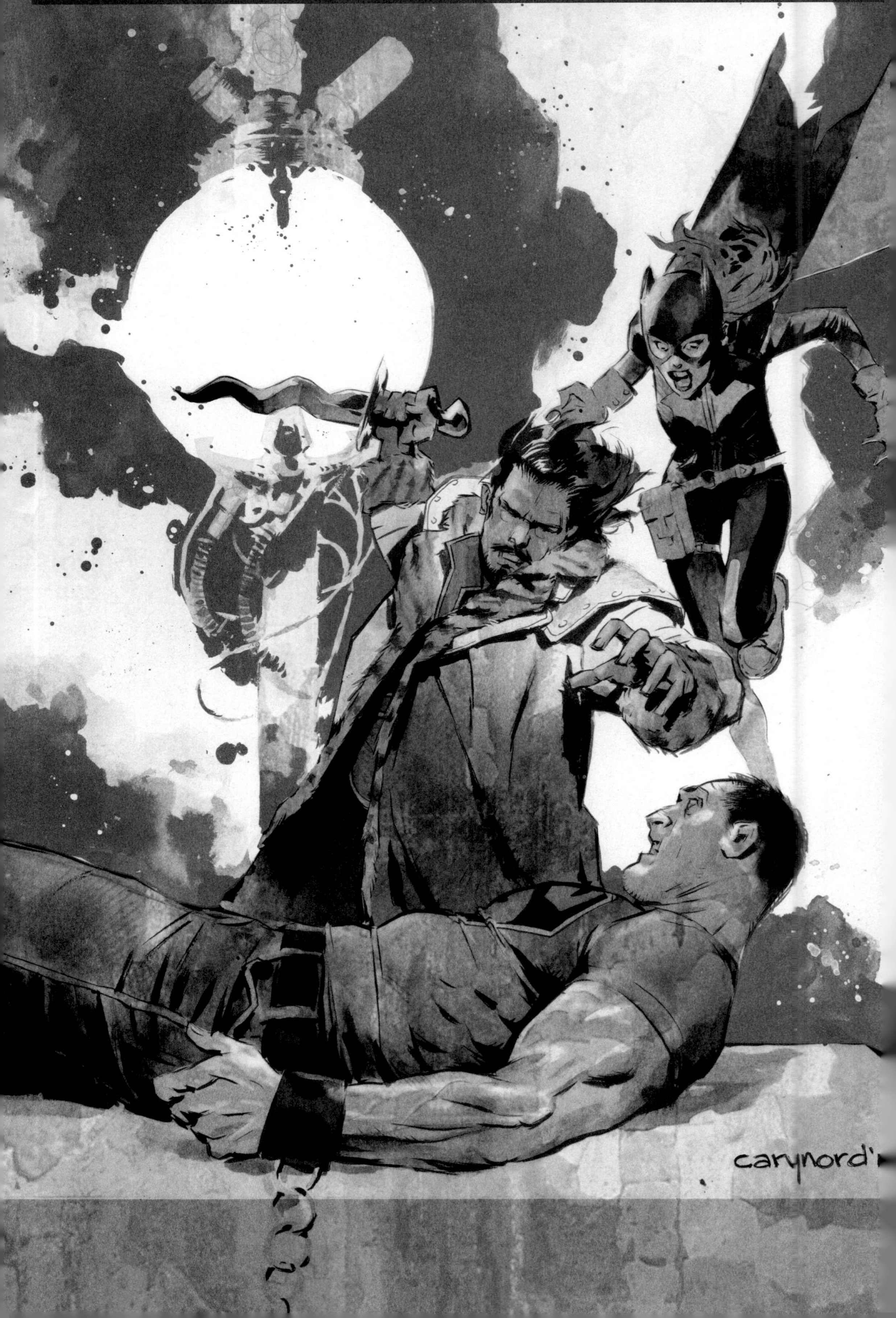
carynord

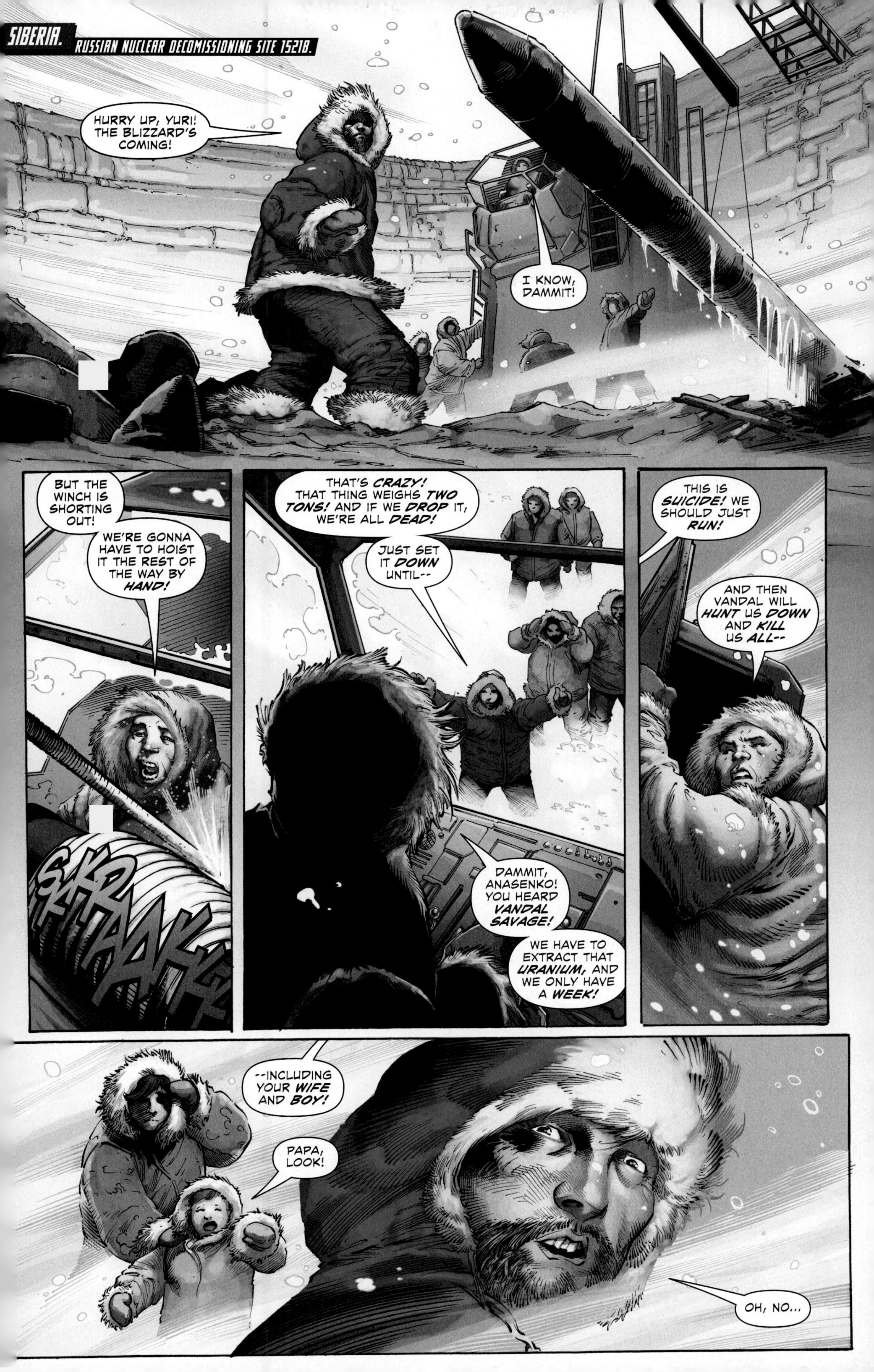
SIBERIA.
RUSSIAN NUCLEAR DECOMISSIONING SITE 15218.
HURRY UP, YURI! THE BLIZZARD'S COMING!
I KNOW, DAMMIT!
BUT THE WINCH IS SHORTING OUT!
WE'RE GONNA HAVE TO HOIST IT THE REST OF THE WAY BY HAND!
SKRTHAAKK
THAT'S CRAZY! THAT THING WEIGHS TWO TONS! AND IF WE DROP IT, WE'RE ALL DEAD!
JUST SET IT DOWN UNTIL--
DAMMIT, ANASENKO! YOU HEARD VANDAL SAVAGE!
WE HAVE TO EXTRACT THAT URANIUM, AND WE ONLY HAVE A WEEK!
THIS IS SUICIDE! WE SHOULD JUST RUN!
AND THEN VANDAL WILL HUNT US DOWN AND KILL US ALL--
--INCLUDING YOUR WIFE AND BOY!
PAPA, LOOK!
OH, NO...

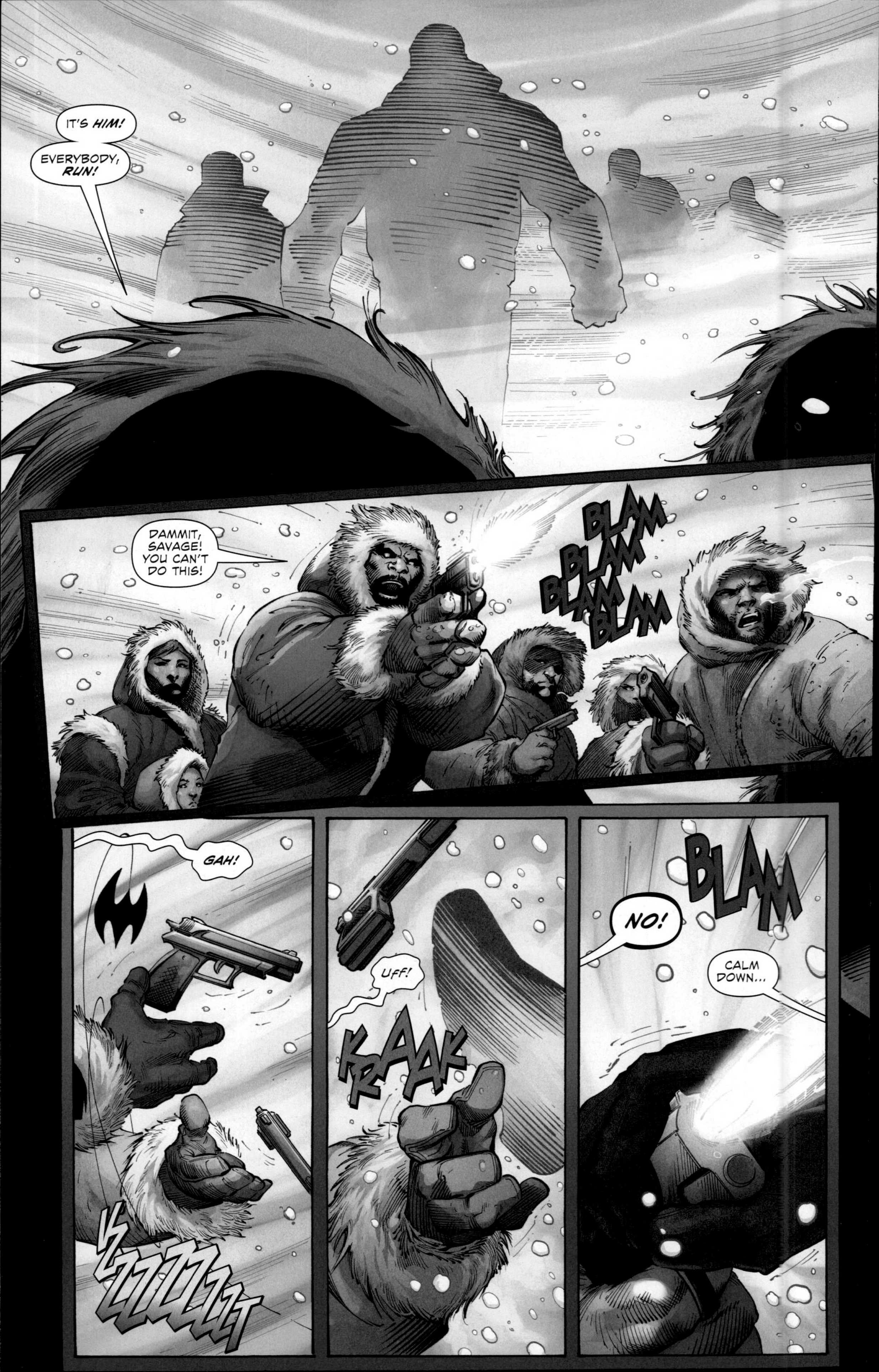
IT'S HIM!
EVERYBODY, RUN!
DAMMIT, SAVAGE! YOU CAN'T DO THIS!
BLAM BLAM BLAM BLAM
GAH!
VZZZZZZZT
Uff!
KRAAK
NO!
BLAM
CALM DOWN...

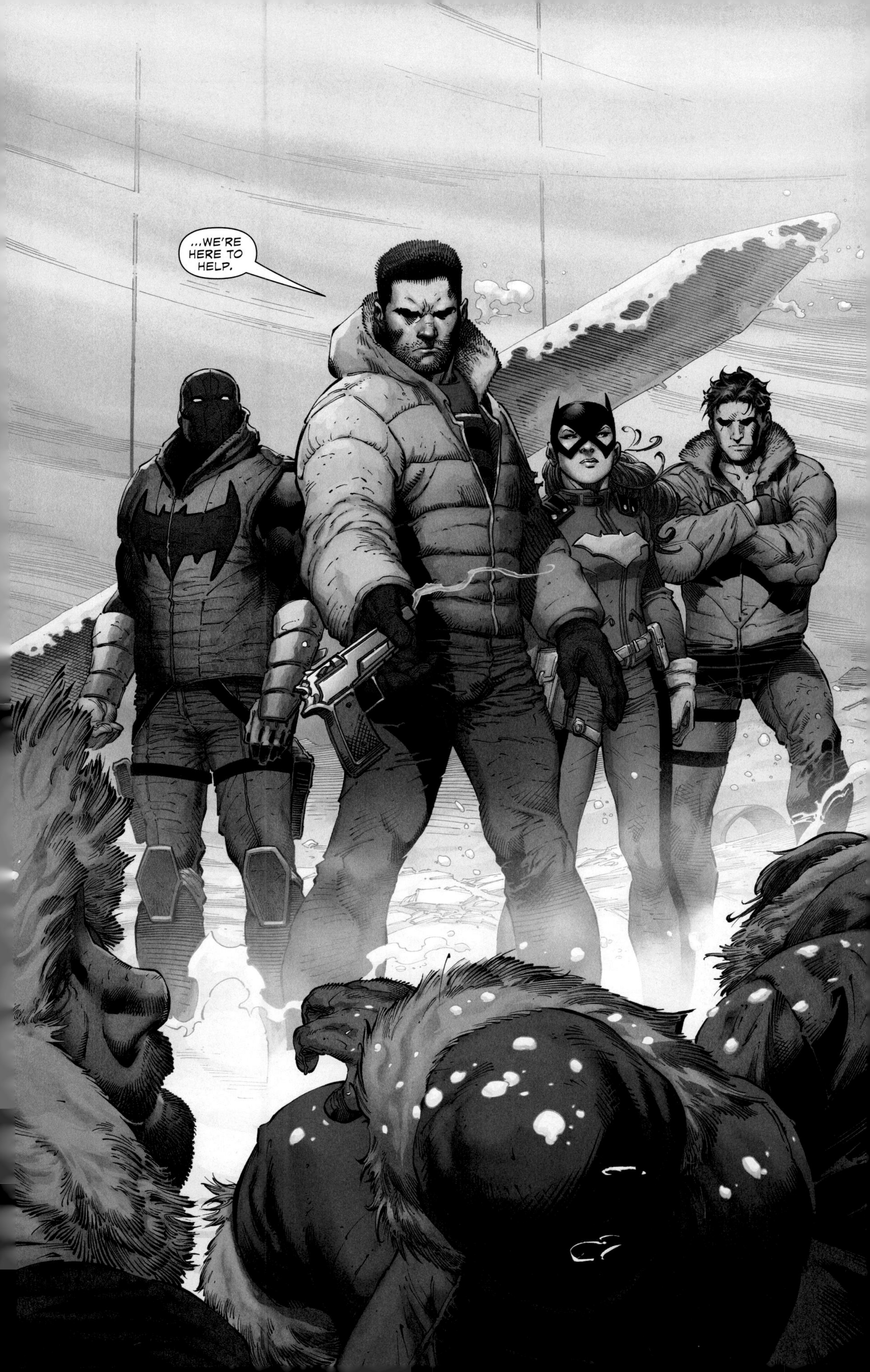
...WE'RE HERE TO HELP.

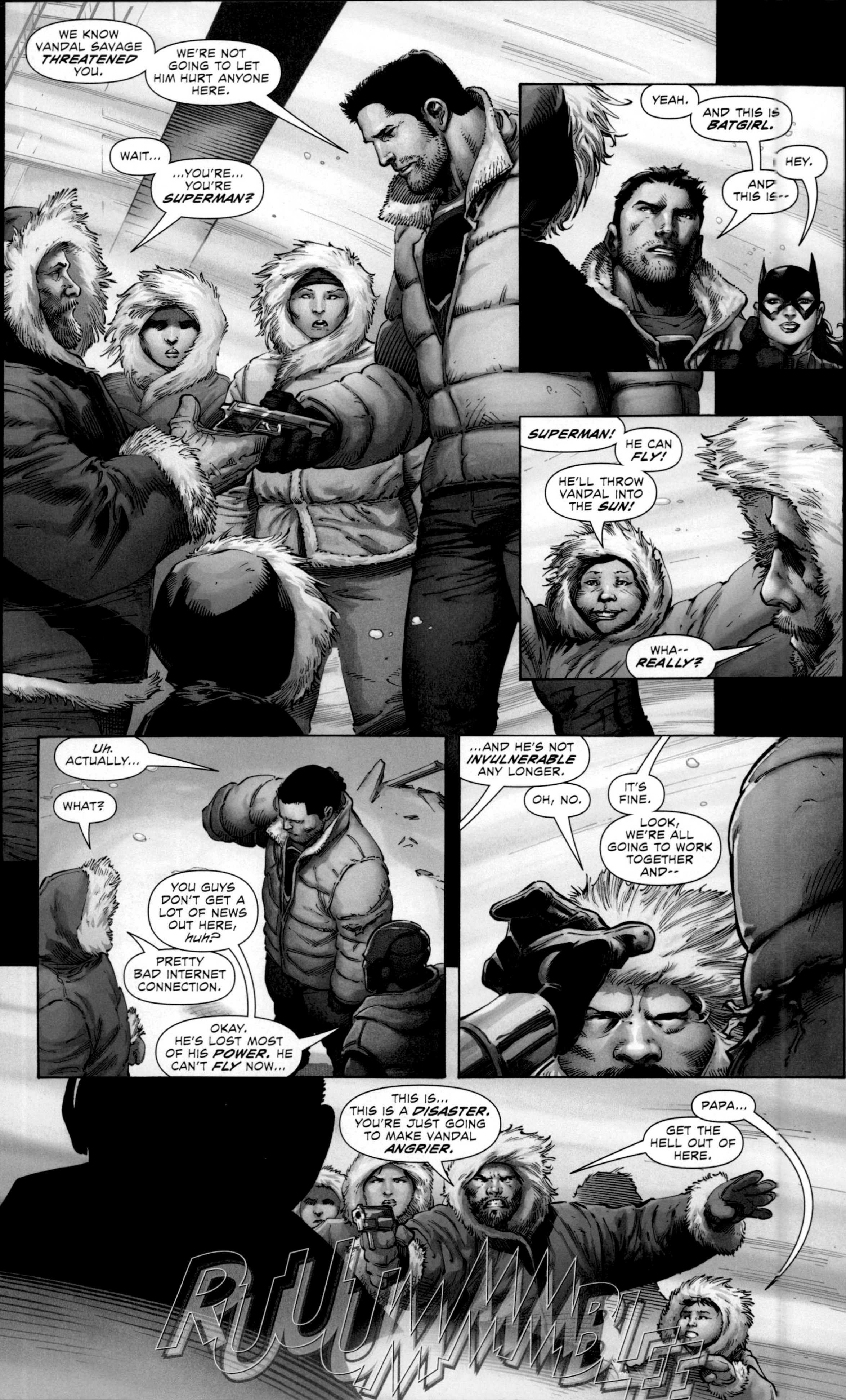
WE KNOW VANDAL SAVAGE THREATENED YOU.
WE'RE NOT GOING TO LET HIM HURT ANYONE HERE.
WAIT...
...YOU'RE... YOU'RE SUPERMAN?
YEAH.
AND THIS IS BATGIRL.
HEY.
AND THIS IS--
SUPERMAN!
HE CAN FLY!
HE'LL THROW VANDAL INTO THE SUN!
WHA-- REALLY?
Uh. ACTUALLY...
WHAT?
YOU GUYS DON'T GET A LOT OF NEWS OUT HERE, huh?
PRETTY BAD INTERNET CONNECTION.
OKAY. HE'S LOST MOST OF HIS POWER. HE CAN'T FLY NOW...
...AND HE'S NOT INVULNERABLE ANY LONGER.
OH, NO.
IT'S FINE.
LOOK, WE'RE ALL GOING TO WORK TOGETHER AND--
THIS IS... THIS IS A DISASTER. YOU'RE JUST GOING TO MAKE VANDAL ANGRIER.
PAPA...
GET THE HELL OUT OF HERE.
RUUMMMBLE

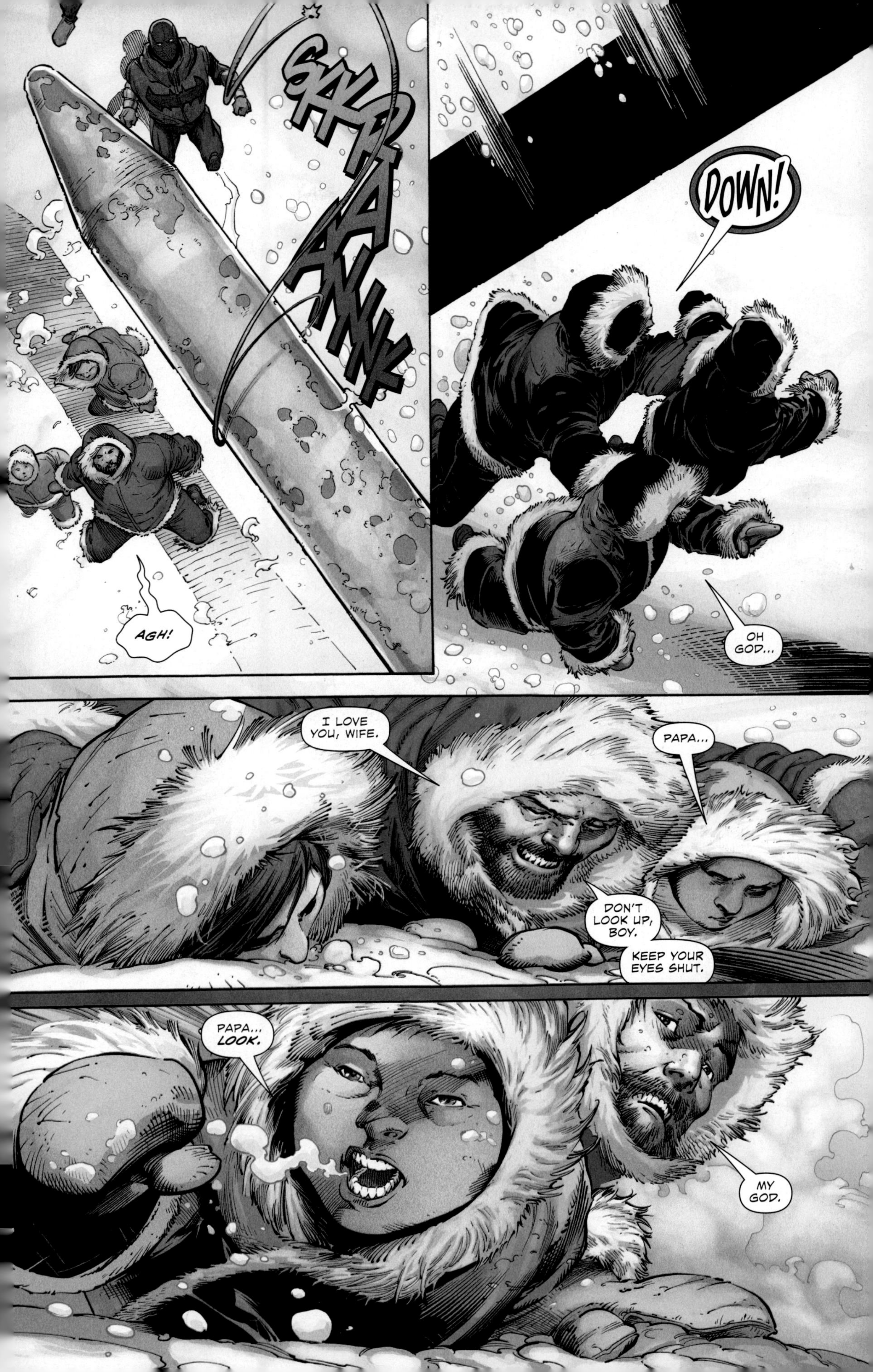
SKKRAAANNK
AGH!
DOWN!
OH GOD...
I LOVE YOU, WIFE.
PAPA...
DON'T LOOK UP, BOY.
KEEP YOUR EYES SHUT.
PAPA... LOOK.
MY GOD.

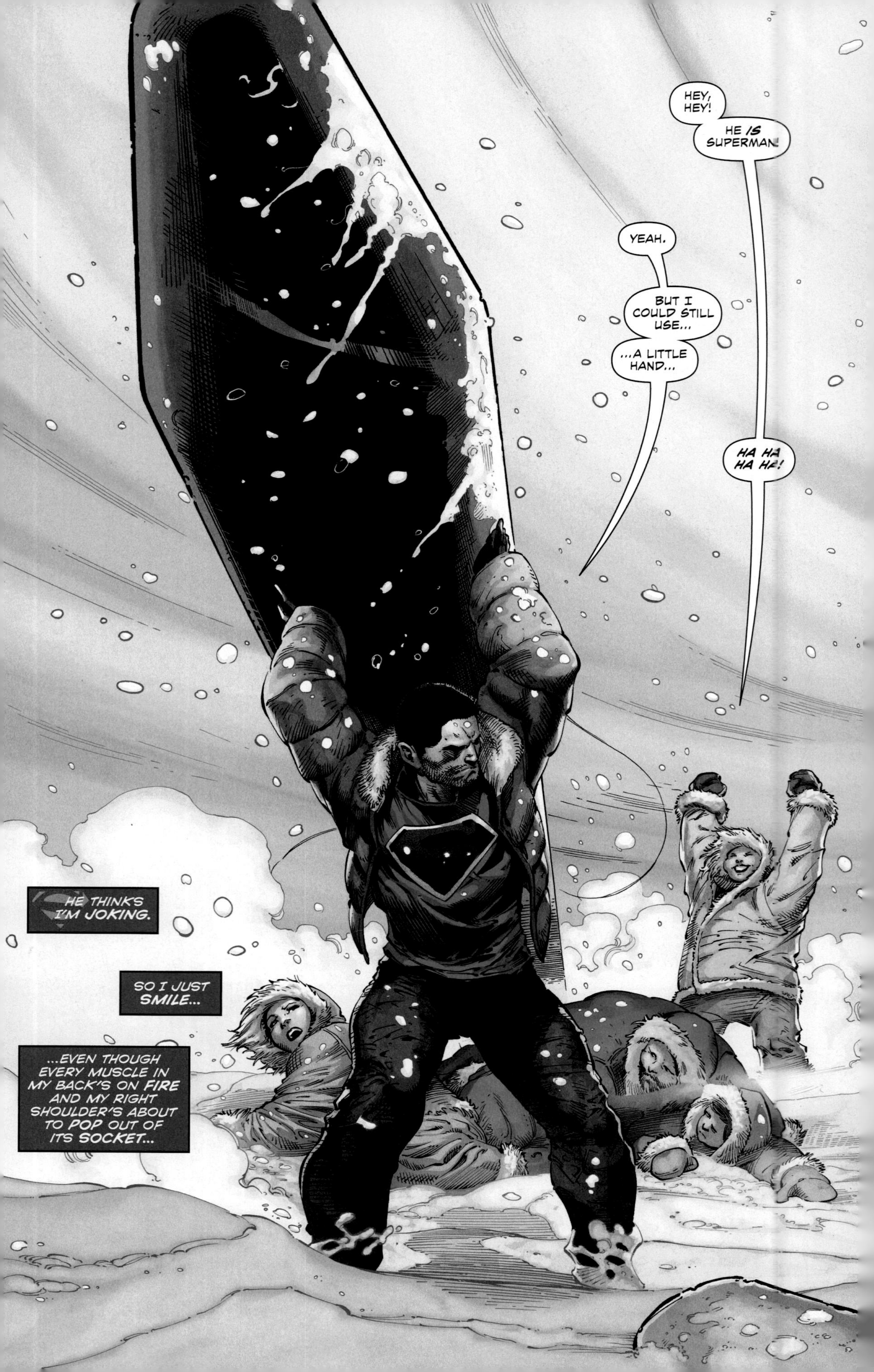
HEY, HEY!
HE IS SUPERMAN!
YEAH.
BUT I COULD STILL USE...
...A LITTLE HAND...
HA HA HA HA!
HE THINKS I'M JOKING.
SO I JUST SMILE...
...EVEN THOUGH EVERY MUSCLE IN MY BACK'S ON FIRE AND MY RIGHT SHOULDER'S ABOUT TO POP OUT OF ITS SOCKET...

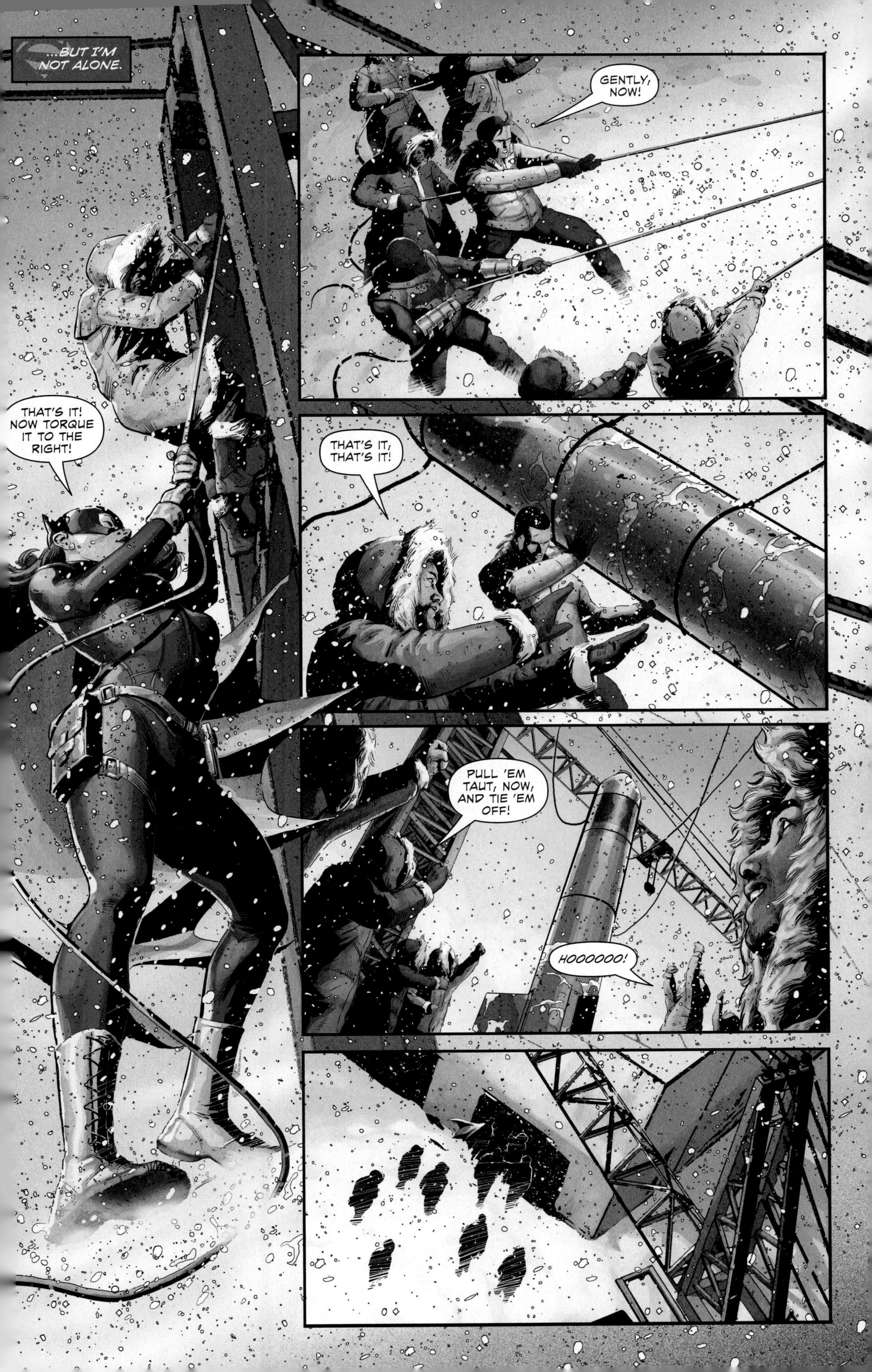
...BUT I'M NOT ALONE.
GENTLY, NOW!
THAT'S IT! NOW TORQUE IT TO THE RIGHT!
THAT'S IT, THAT'S IT!
PULL 'EM TAUT, NOW, AND TIE 'EM OFF!
HOOOOOO!

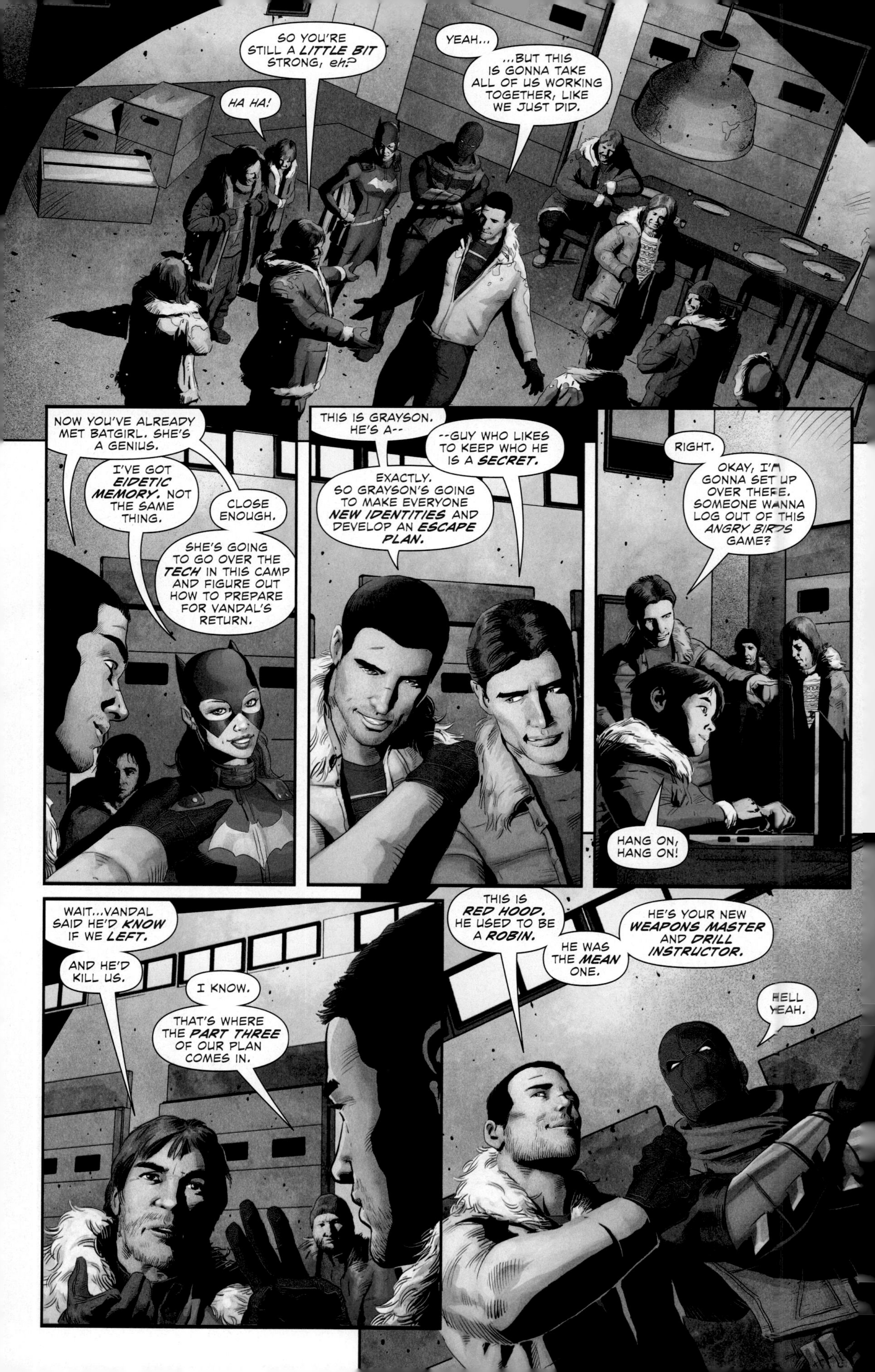
SO YOU'RE STILL A LITTLE BIT STRONG, eh?
HA HA!
YEAH...
...BUT THIS IS GONNA TAKE ALL OF US WORKING TOGETHER, LIKE WE JUST DID.
NOW YOU'VE ALREADY MET BATGIRL. SHE'S A GENIUS.
I'VE GOT EIDETIC MEMORY. NOT THE SAME THING.
CLOSE ENOUGH.
SHE'S GOING TO GO OVER THE TECH IN THIS CAMP AND FIGURE OUT HOW TO PREPARE FOR VANDAL'S RETURN.
THIS IS GRAYSON. HE'S A--
--GUY WHO LIKES TO KEEP WHO HE IS A SECRET.
EXACTLY. SO GRAYSON'S GOING TO MAKE EVERYONE NEW IDENTITIES AND DEVELOP AN ESCAPE PLAN.
RIGHT.
OKAY, I'M GONNA SET UP OVER THERE. SOMEONE WANNA LOG OUT OF THIS ANGRY BIRDS GAME?
HANG ON, HANG ON!
WAIT...VANDAL SAID HE'D KNOW IF WE LEFT.
AND HE'D KILL US.
I KNOW.
THAT'S WHERE THE PART THREE OF OUR PLAN COMES IN.
THIS IS RED HOOD. HE USED TO BE A ROBIN.
HE WAS THE MEAN ONE.
HE'S YOUR NEW WEAPONS MASTER AND DRILL INSTRUCTOR.
HELL YEAH.

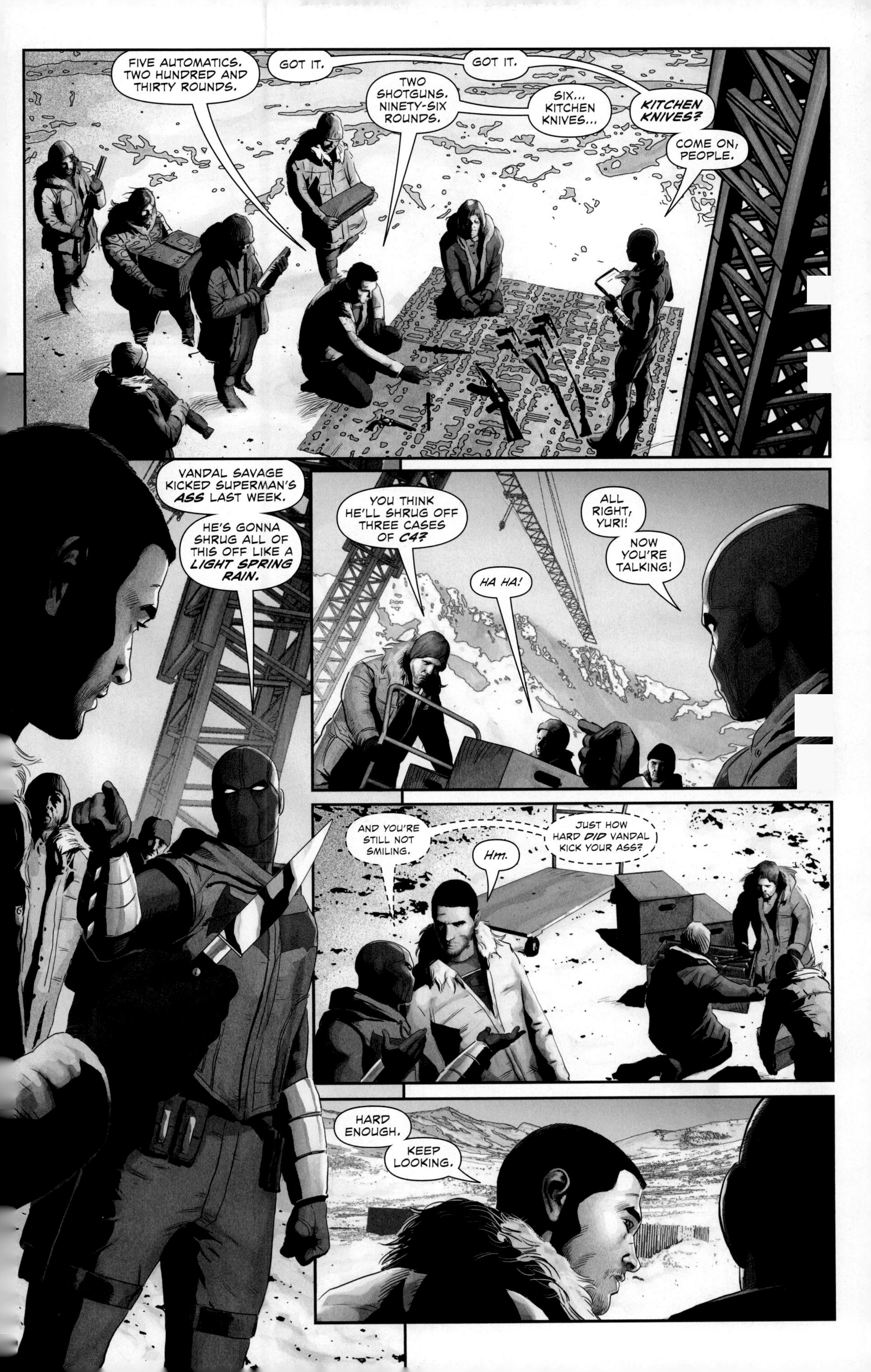
FIVE AUTOMATICS. TWO HUNDRED AND THIRTY ROUNDS.
GOT IT.
TWO SHOTGUNS. NINETY-SIX ROUNDS.
GOT IT.
SIX... KITCHEN KNIVES...
KITCHEN KNIVES?
COME ON, PEOPLE.
VANDAL SAVAGE KICKED SUPERMAN'S ASS LAST WEEK.
HE'S GONNA SHRUG ALL OF THIS OFF LIKE A LIGHT SPRING RAIN.
YOU THINK HE'LL SHRUG OFF THREE CASES OF C4?
HA HA!
ALL RIGHT, YURI!
NOW YOU'RE TALKING!
AND YOU'RE STILL NOT SMILING.
Hm.
JUST HOW HARD DID VANDAL KICK YOUR ASS?
HARD ENOUGH.
KEEP LOOKING.

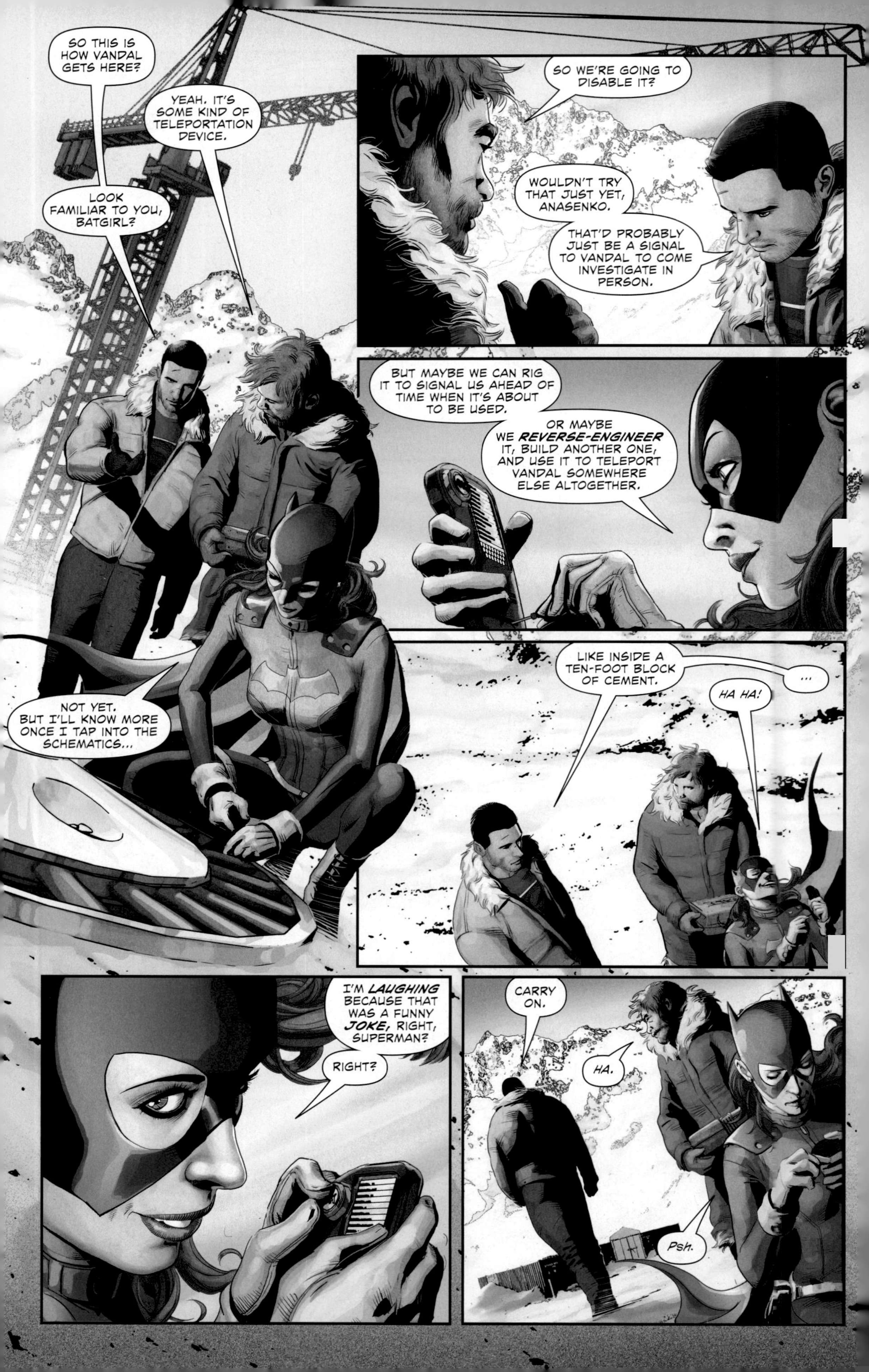
SO THIS IS HOW VANDAL GETS HERE?
YEAH. IT'S SOME KIND OF TELEPORTATION DEVICE.
LOOK FAMILIAR TO YOU, BATGIRL?
NOT YET. BUT I'LL KNOW MORE ONCE I TAP INTO THE SCHEMATICS...
SO WE'RE GOING TO DISABLE IT?
WOULDN'T TRY THAT JUST YET, ANASENKO.
THAT'D PROBABLY JUST BE A SIGNAL TO VANDAL TO COME INVESTIGATE IN PERSON.
BUT MAYBE WE CAN RIG IT TO SIGNAL US AHEAD OF TIME WHEN IT'S ABOUT TO BE USED.
OR MAYBE WE REVERSE-ENGINEER IT, BUILD ANOTHER ONE, AND USE IT TO TELEPORT VANDAL SOMEWHERE ELSE ALTOGETHER.
LIKE INSIDE A TEN-FOOT BLOCK OF CEMENT.
...
HA HA!
I'M LAUGHING BECAUSE THAT WAS A FUNNY JOKE, RIGHT, SUPERMAN?
RIGHT?
CARRY ON.
HA.
Psh.

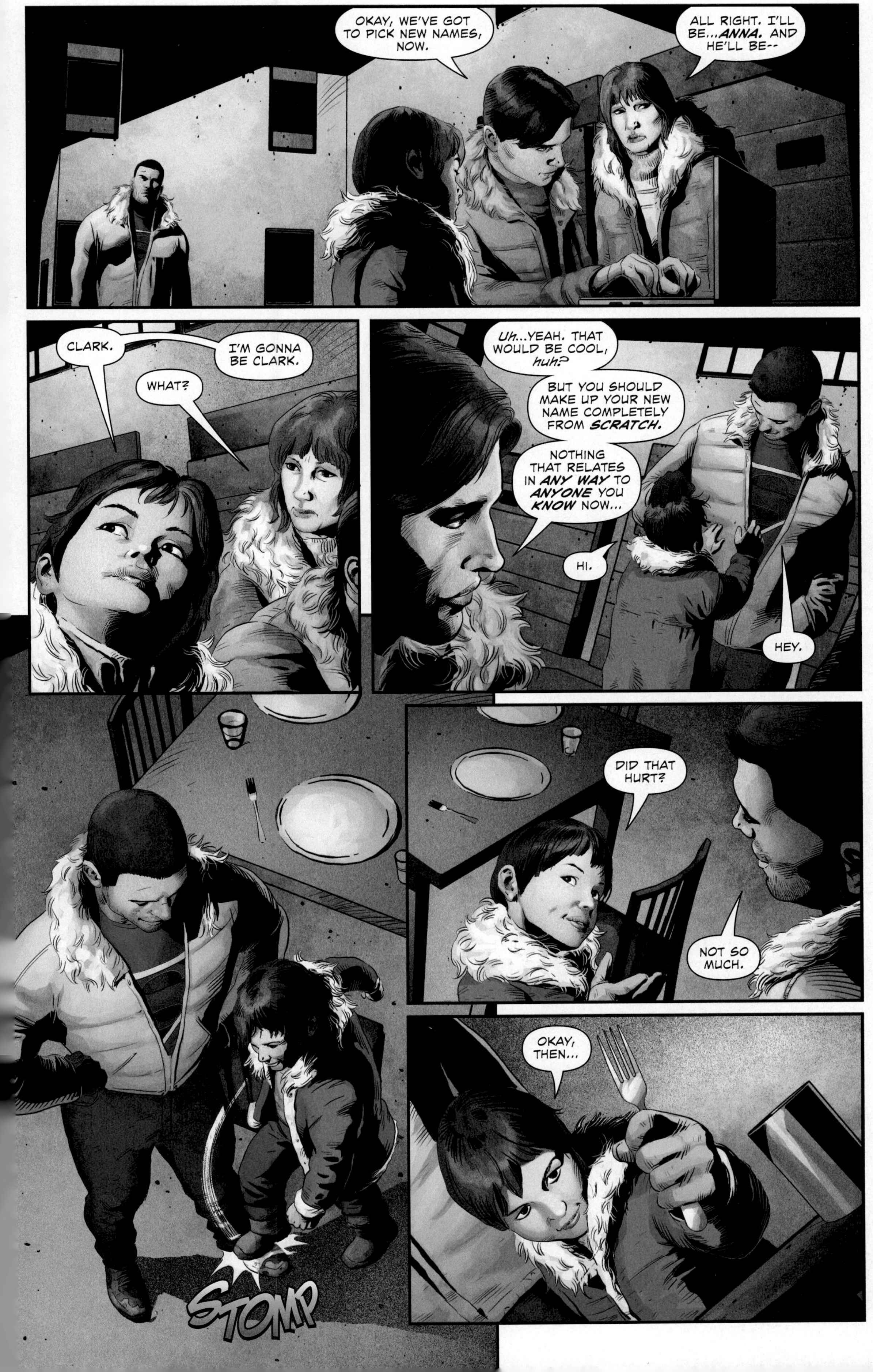
OKAY, WE'VE GOT TO PICK NEW NAMES, NOW.
ALL RIGHT. I'LL BE...ANNA. AND HE'LL BE--
CLARK.
I'M GONNA BE CLARK.
WHAT?
Uh...YEAH. THAT WOULD BE COOL, huh?
BUT YOU SHOULD MAKE UP YOUR NEW NAME COMPLETELY FROM SCRATCH.
NOTHING THAT RELATES IN ANY WAY TO ANYONE YOU KNOW NOW...
HI.
HEY.
STOMP
DID THAT HURT?
NOT SO MUCH.
OKAY, THEN...

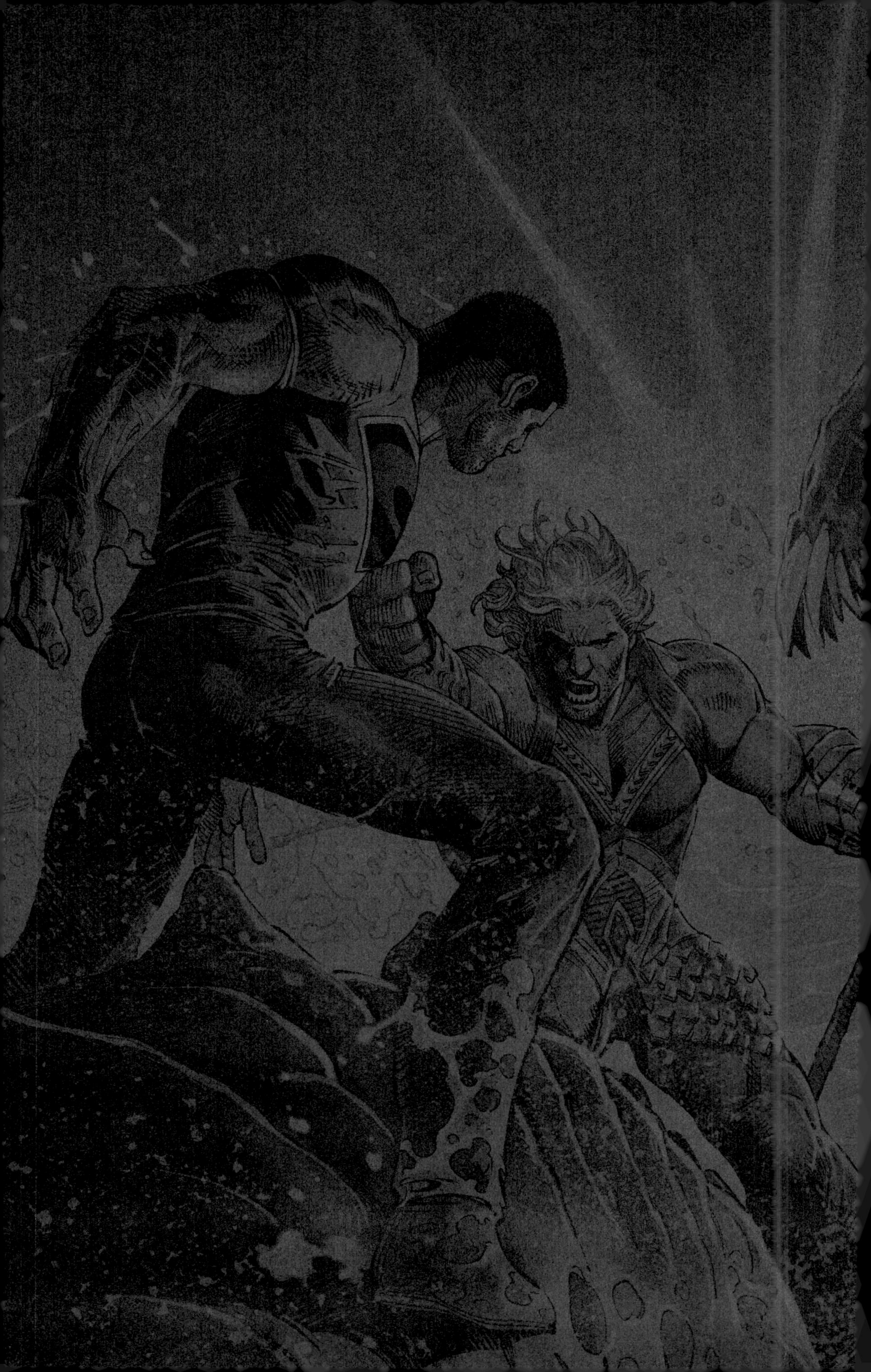

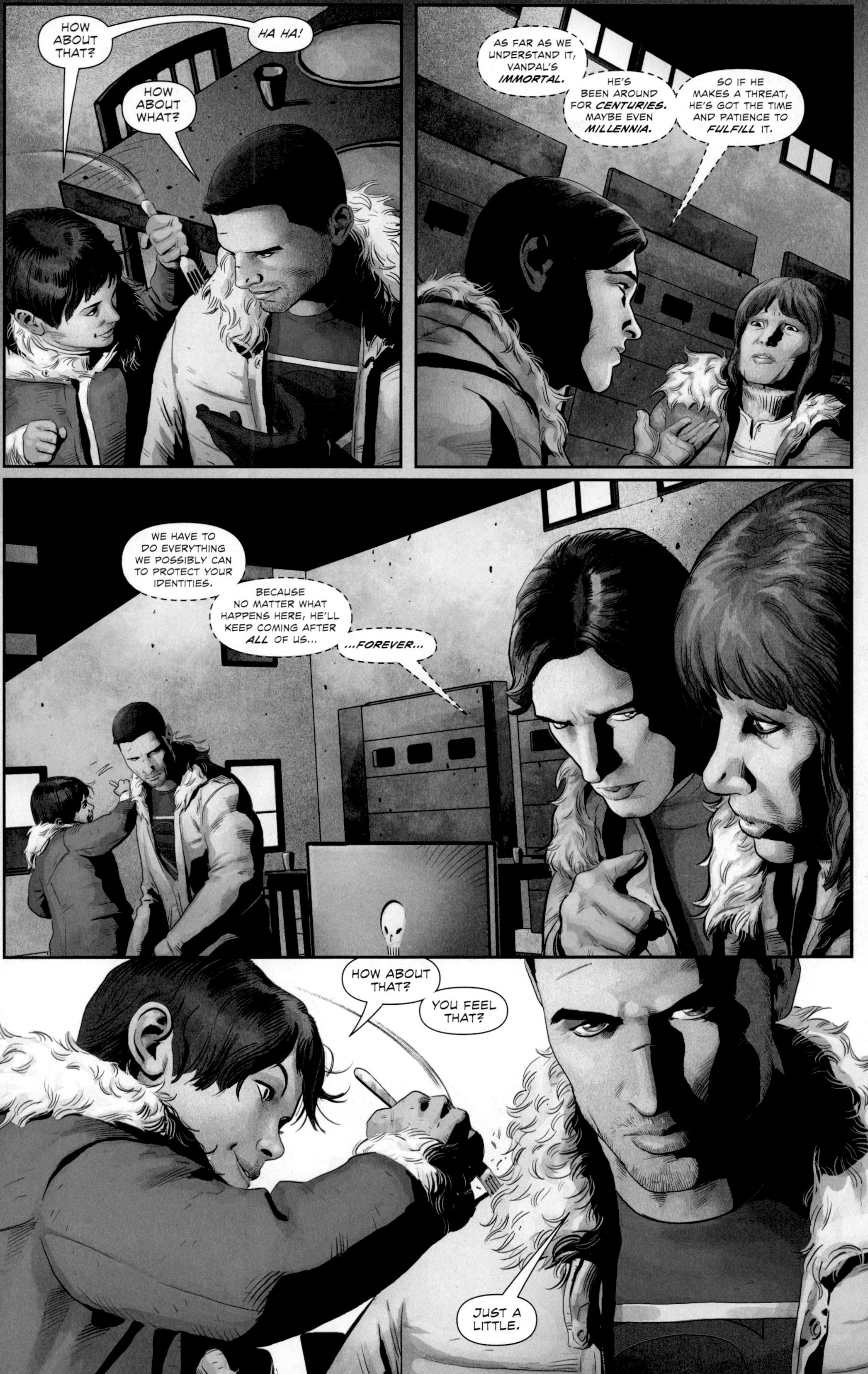

HOW ABOUT THAT?
HA HA!
HOW ABOUT WHAT?
AS FAR AS WE UNDERSTAND IT, VANDAL'S *IMMORTAL.*
HE'S BEEN AROUND FOR *CENTURIES.* MAYBE EVEN *MILLENNIA.*
SO IF HE MAKES A THREAT, HE'S GOT THE TIME AND PATIENCE TO *FULFILL* IT.
WE HAVE TO DO EVERYTHING WE POSSIBLY CAN TO PROTECT YOUR IDENTITIES.
BECAUSE NO MATTER WHAT HAPPENS HERE, HE'LL KEEP COMING AFTER *ALL* OF US...
...*FOREVER*...
HOW ABOUT THAT?
YOU FEEL THAT?
JUST A LITTLE.

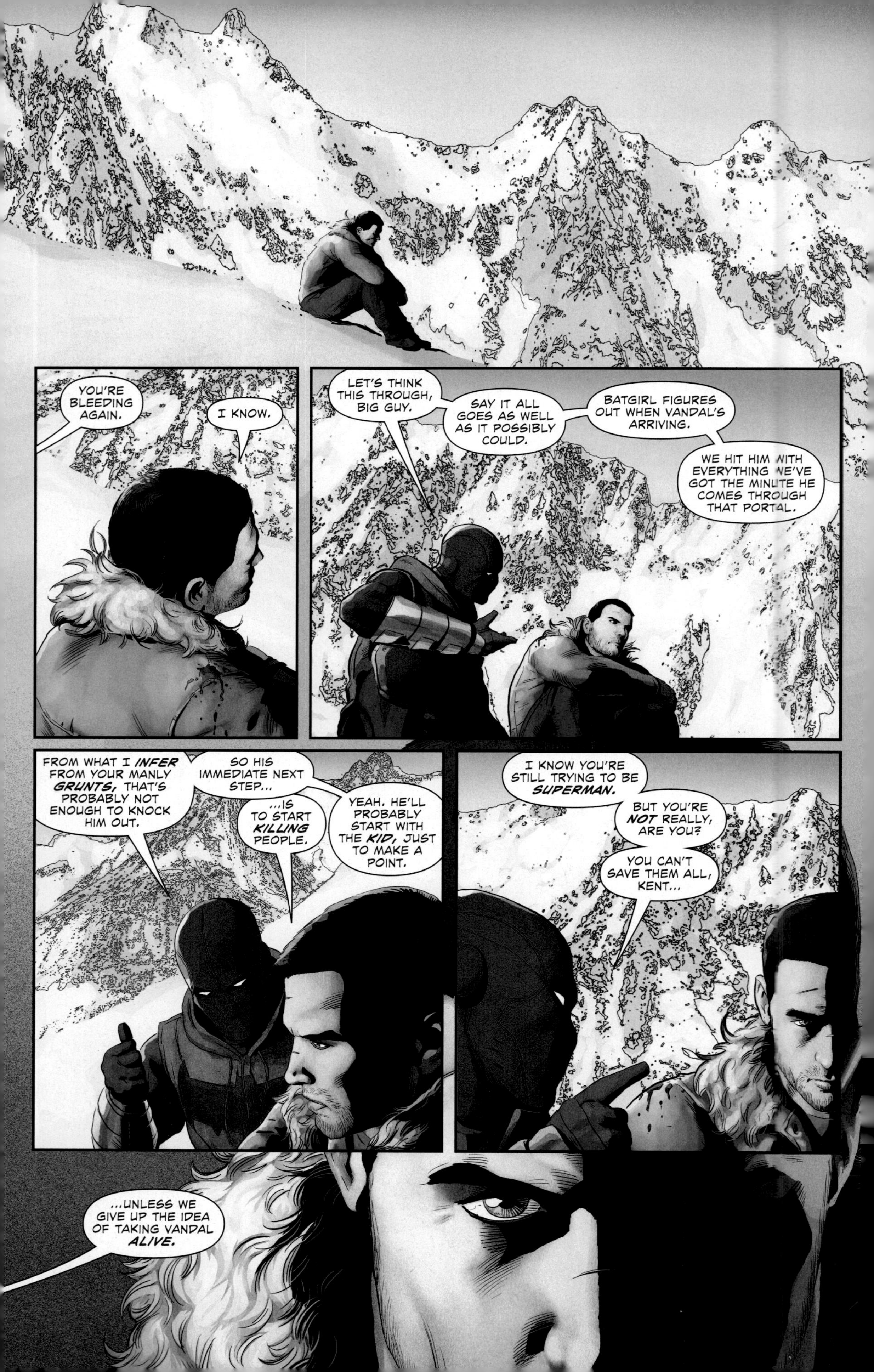
YOU'RE BLEEDING AGAIN.
I KNOW.
LET'S THINK THIS THROUGH, BIG GUY.
SAY IT ALL GOES AS WELL AS IT POSSIBLY COULD.
BATGIRL FIGURES OUT WHEN VANDAL'S ARRIVING.
WE HIT HIM WITH EVERYTHING WE'VE GOT THE MINUTE HE COMES THROUGH THAT PORTAL.
FROM WHAT I *INFER* FROM YOUR MANLY *GRUNTS,* THAT'S PROBABLY NOT ENOUGH TO KNOCK HIM OUT.
SO HIS IMMEDIATE NEXT STEP...
...IS TO START *KILLING* PEOPLE.
YEAH. HE'LL PROBABLY START WITH THE *KID,* JUST TO MAKE A POINT.
I KNOW YOU'RE STILL TRYING TO BE *SUPERMAN.*
BUT YOU'RE *NOT* REALLY, ARE YOU?
YOU CAN'T SAVE THEM ALL, KENT...
...UNLESS WE GIVE UP THE IDEA OF TAKING VANDAL *ALIVE.*

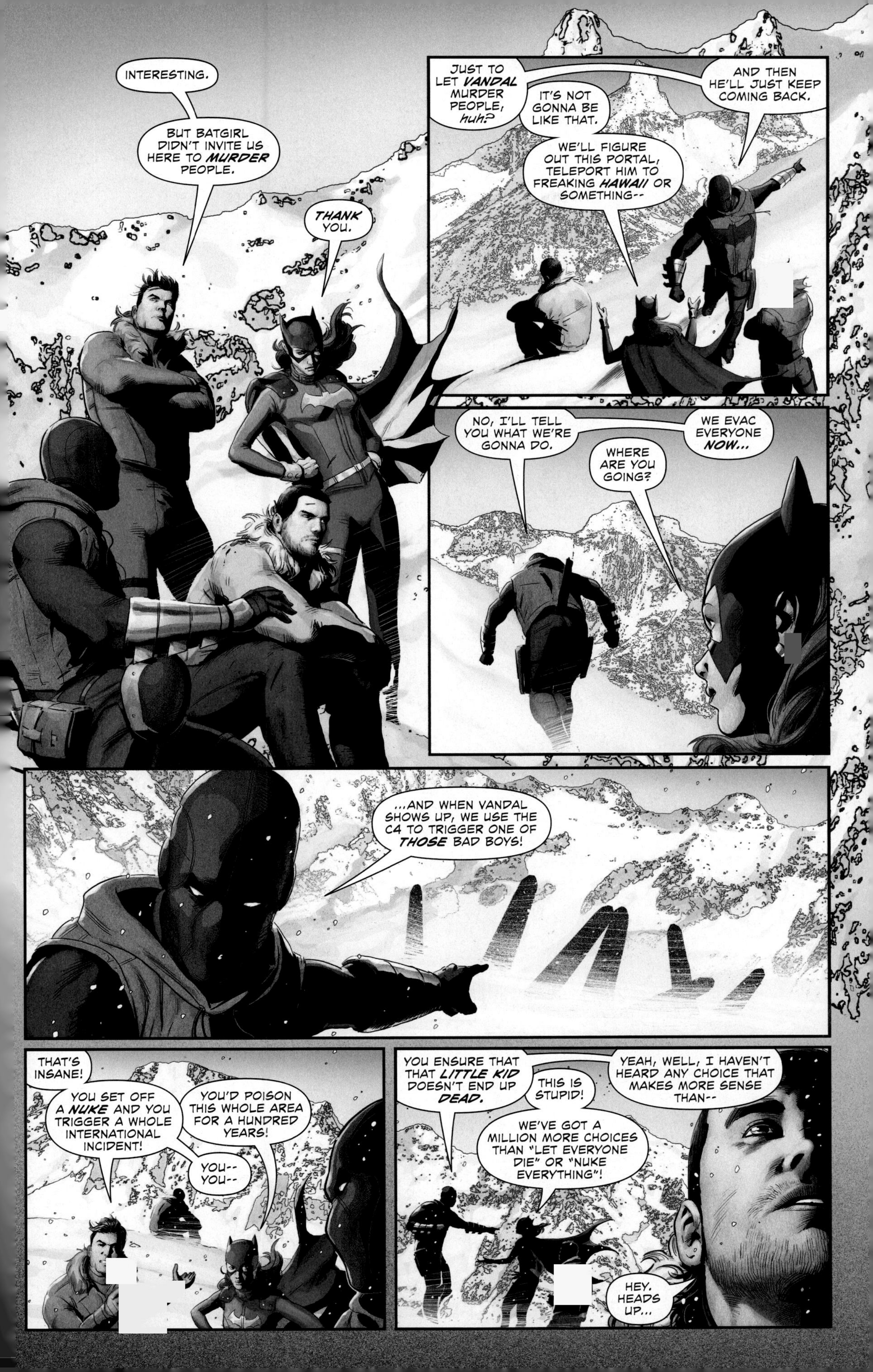

INTERESTING.
BUT BATGIRL DIDN'T INVITE US HERE TO MURDER PEOPLE.
THANK YOU.
JUST TO LET VANDAL MURDER PEOPLE, huh?
AND THEN HE'LL JUST KEEP COMING BACK.
IT'S NOT GONNA BE LIKE THAT.
WE'LL FIGURE OUT THIS PORTAL, TELEPORT HIM TO FREAKING HAWAII OR SOMETHING--
NO, I'LL TELL YOU WHAT WE'RE GONNA DO.
WE EVAC EVERYONE NOW...
WHERE ARE YOU GOING?
...AND WHEN VANDAL SHOWS UP, WE USE THE C4 TO TRIGGER ONE OF THOSE BAD BOYS!
THAT'S INSANE!
YOU SET OFF A NUKE AND YOU TRIGGER A WHOLE INTERNATIONAL INCIDENT!
YOU'D POISON THIS WHOLE AREA FOR A HUNDRED YEARS!
YOU-- YOU--
YOU ENSURE THAT THAT LITTLE KID DOESN'T END UP DEAD.
YEAH, WELL, I HAVEN'T HEARD ANY CHOICE THAT MAKES MORE SENSE THAN--
THIS IS STUPID!
WE'VE GOT A MILLION MORE CHOICES THAN "LET EVERYONE DIE" OR "NUKE EVERYTHING"!
HEY. HEADS UP...

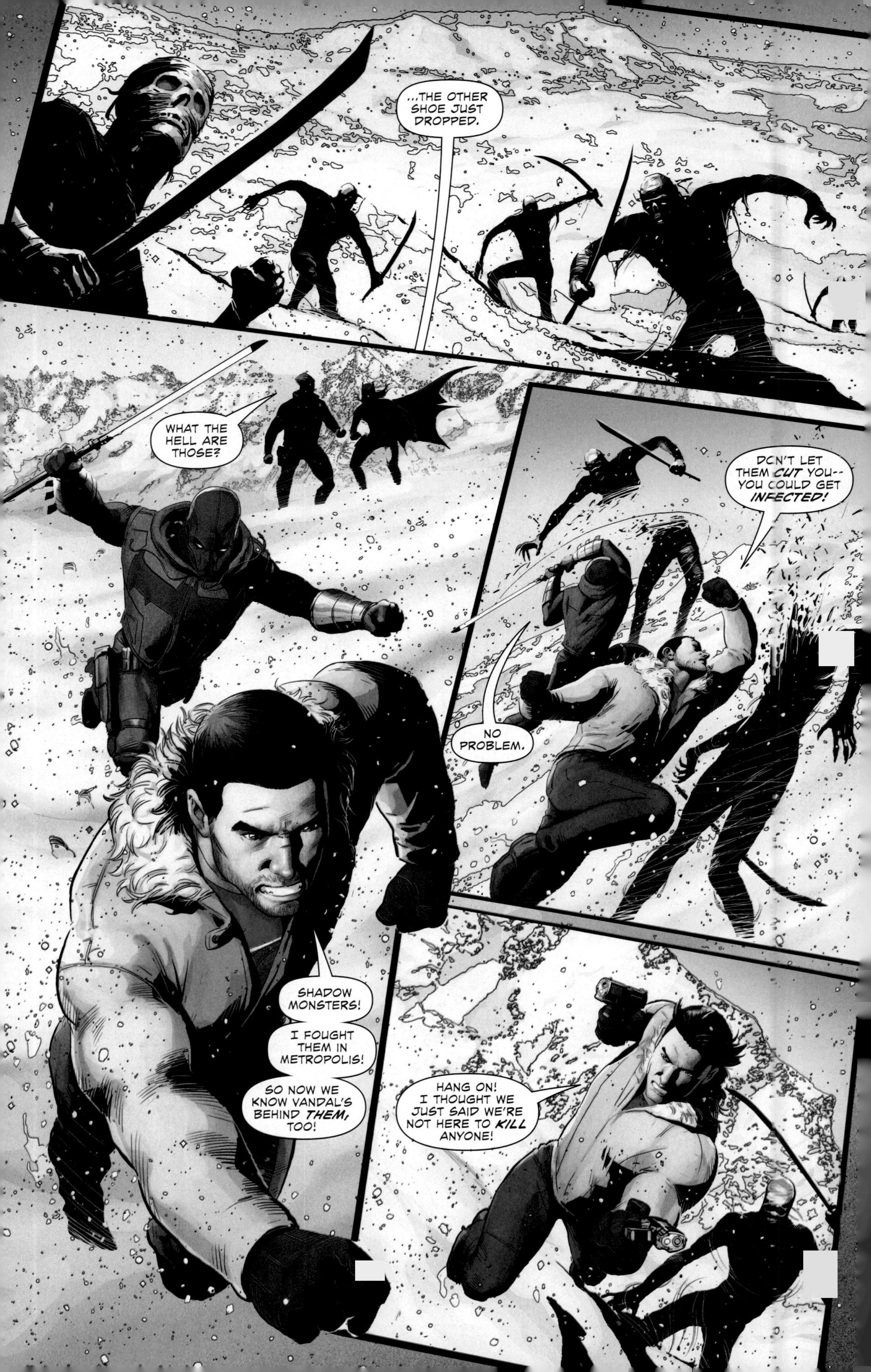

...THE OTHER SHOE JUST DROPPED.
WHAT THE HELL ARE THOSE?
SHADOW MONSTERS!
I FOUGHT THEM IN METROPOLIS!
SO NOW WE KNOW VANDAL'S BEHIND THEM, TOO!
DON'T LET THEM CUT YOU--YOU COULD GET INFECTED!
NO PROBLEM.
HANG ON! I THOUGHT WE JUST SAID WE'RE NOT HERE TO KILL ANYONE!

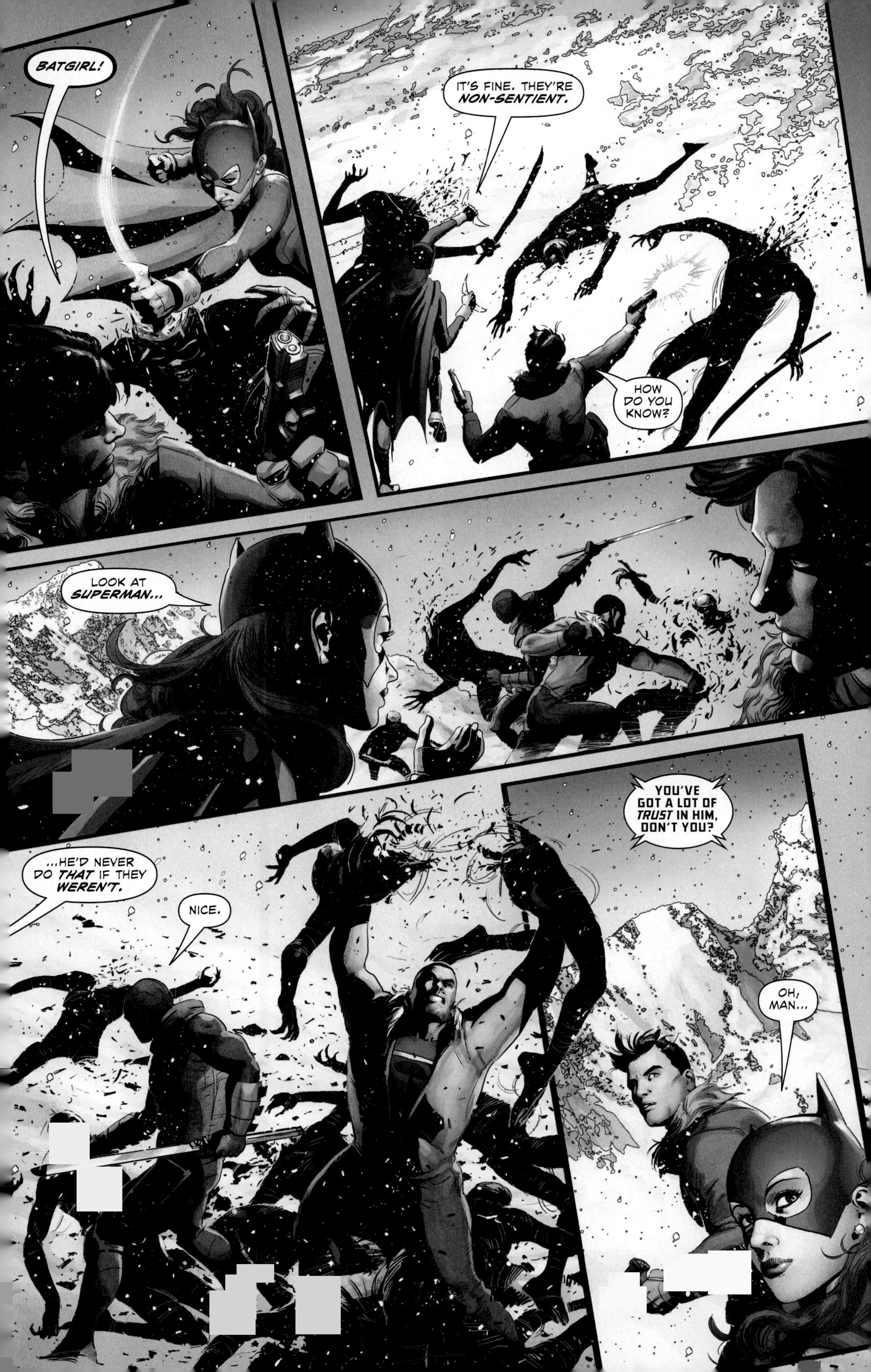
BATGIRL!
IT'S FINE. THEY'RE NON-SENTIENT.
HOW DO YOU KNOW?
LOOK AT SUPERMAN...
...HE'D NEVER DO THAT IF THEY WEREN'T.
NICE.
YOU'VE GOT A LOT OF TRUST IN HIM, DON'T YOU?
OH, MAN...

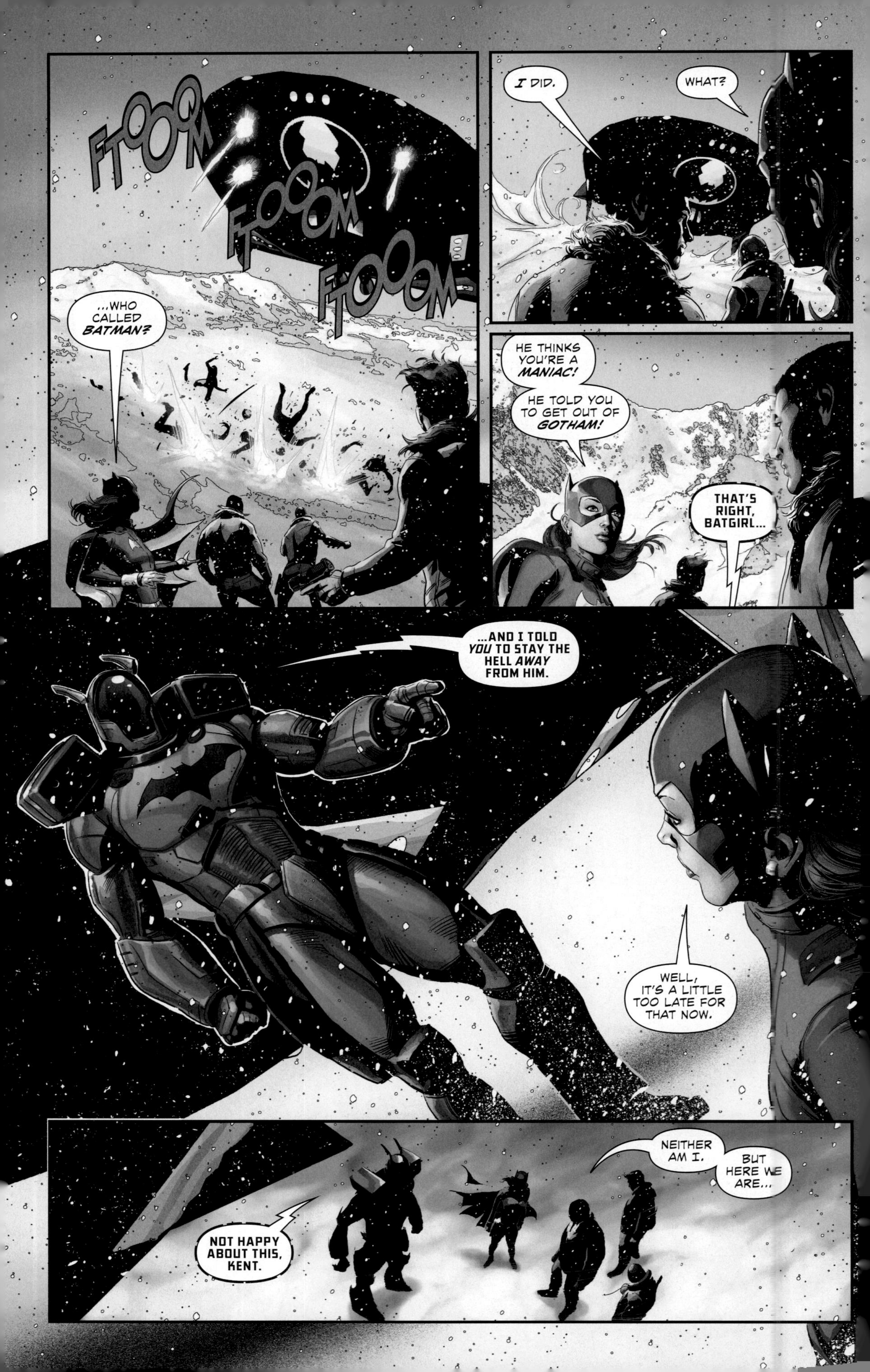

FTOOOM
FTOOOM
FTOOOM
...WHO CALLED BATMAN?
I DID.
WHAT?
HE THINKS YOU'RE A MANIAC!
HE TOLD YOU TO GET OUT OF GOTHAM!
THAT'S RIGHT, BATGIRL...
...AND I TOLD YOU TO STAY THE HELL AWAY FROM HIM.
WELL, IT'S A LITTLE TOO LATE FOR THAT NOW.
NOT HAPPY ABOUT THIS, KENT.
NEITHER AM I.
BUT HERE WE ARE...

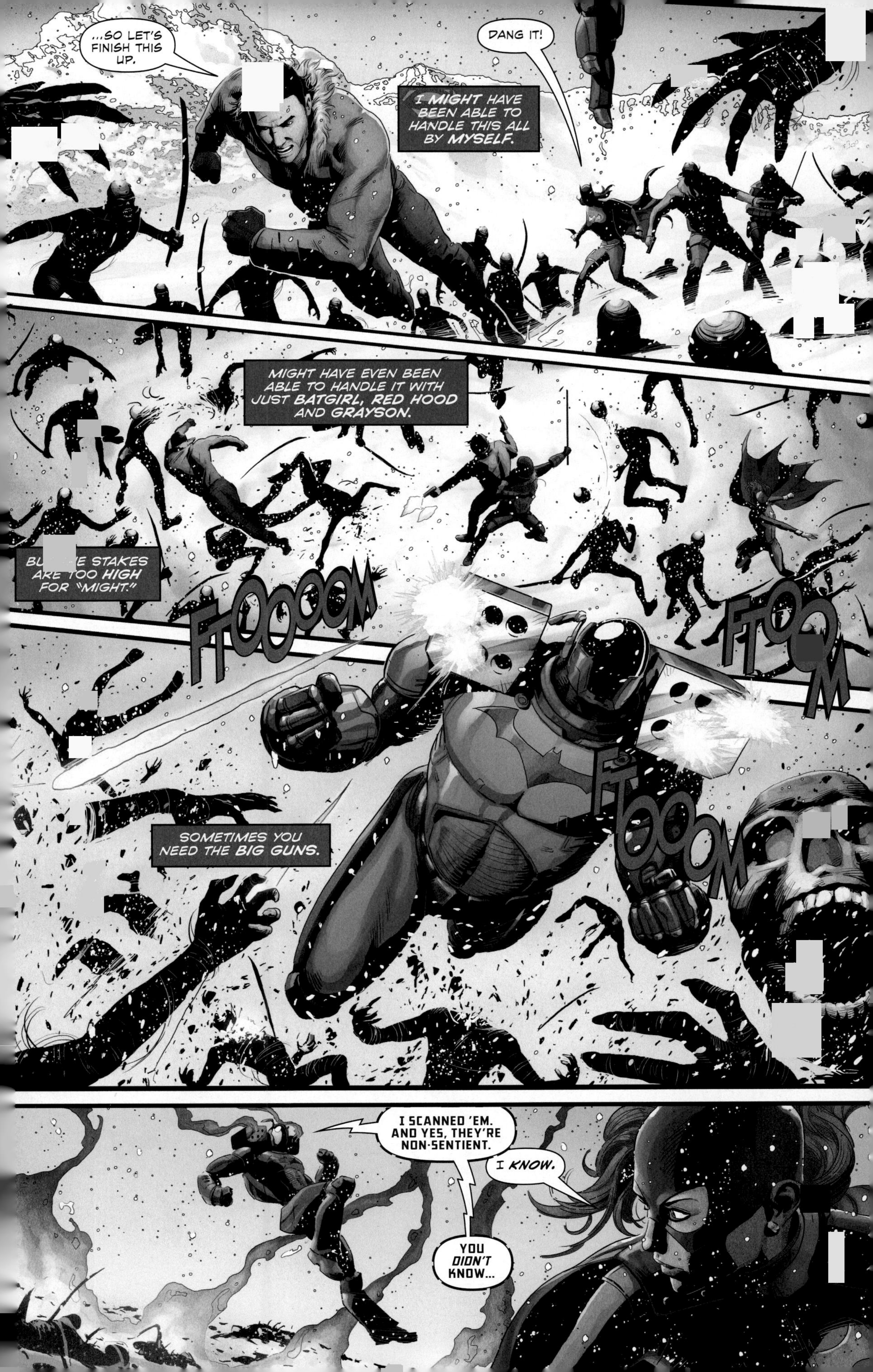
...SO LET'S FINISH THIS UP.
DANG IT!
I MIGHT HAVE BEEN ABLE TO HANDLE THIS ALL BY MYSELF.
MIGHT HAVE EVEN BEEN ABLE TO HANDLE IT WITH JUST BATGIRL, RED HOOD AND GRAYSON.
BU E STAKES ARE TOO HIGH FOR "MIGHT."
FTOOOOM
FTOO M
FTOOOM
SOMETIMES YOU NEED THE BIG GUNS.
I SCANNED 'EM. AND YES, THEY'RE NON-SENTIENT.
I KNOW.
YOU DIDN'T KNOW...

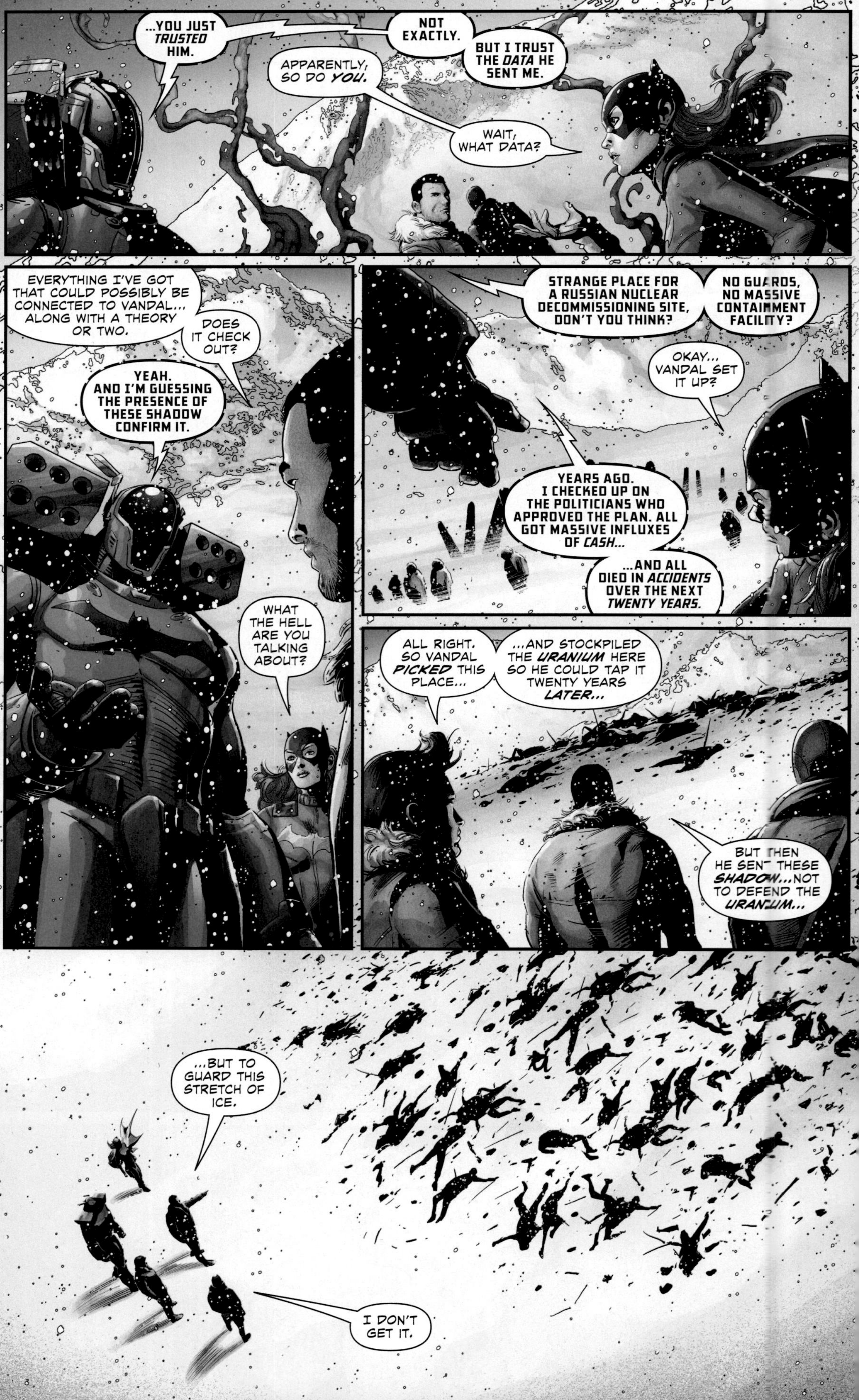
...YOU JUST TRUSTED HIM.
NOT EXACTLY.
BUT I TRUST THE DATA HE SENT ME.
APPARENTLY, SO DO YOU.
WAIT, WHAT DATA?
EVERYTHING I'VE GOT THAT COULD POSSIBLY BE CONNECTED TO VANDAL... ALONG WITH A THEORY OR TWO.
DOES IT CHECK OUT?
YEAH. AND I'M GUESSING THE PRESENCE OF THESE SHADOW CONFIRM IT.
WHAT THE HELL ARE YOU TALKING ABOUT?
STRANGE PLACE FOR A RUSSIAN NUCLEAR DECOMMISSIONING SITE, DON'T YOU THINK?
NO GUARDS, NO MASSIVE CONTAINMENT FACILITY?
OKAY... VANDAL SET IT UP?
YEARS AGO. I CHECKED UP ON THE POLITICIANS WHO APPROVED THE PLAN. ALL GOT MASSIVE INFLUXES OF CASH...
...AND ALL DIED IN ACCIDENTS OVER THE NEXT TWENTY YEARS.
ALL RIGHT. SO VANDAL PICKED THIS PLACE...
...AND STOCKPILED THE URANIUM HERE SO HE COULD TAP IT TWENTY YEARS LATER...
BUT THEN HE SENT THESE SHADOW...NOT TO DEFEND THE URANIUM...
...BUT TO GUARD THIS STRETCH OF ICE.
I DON'T GET IT.

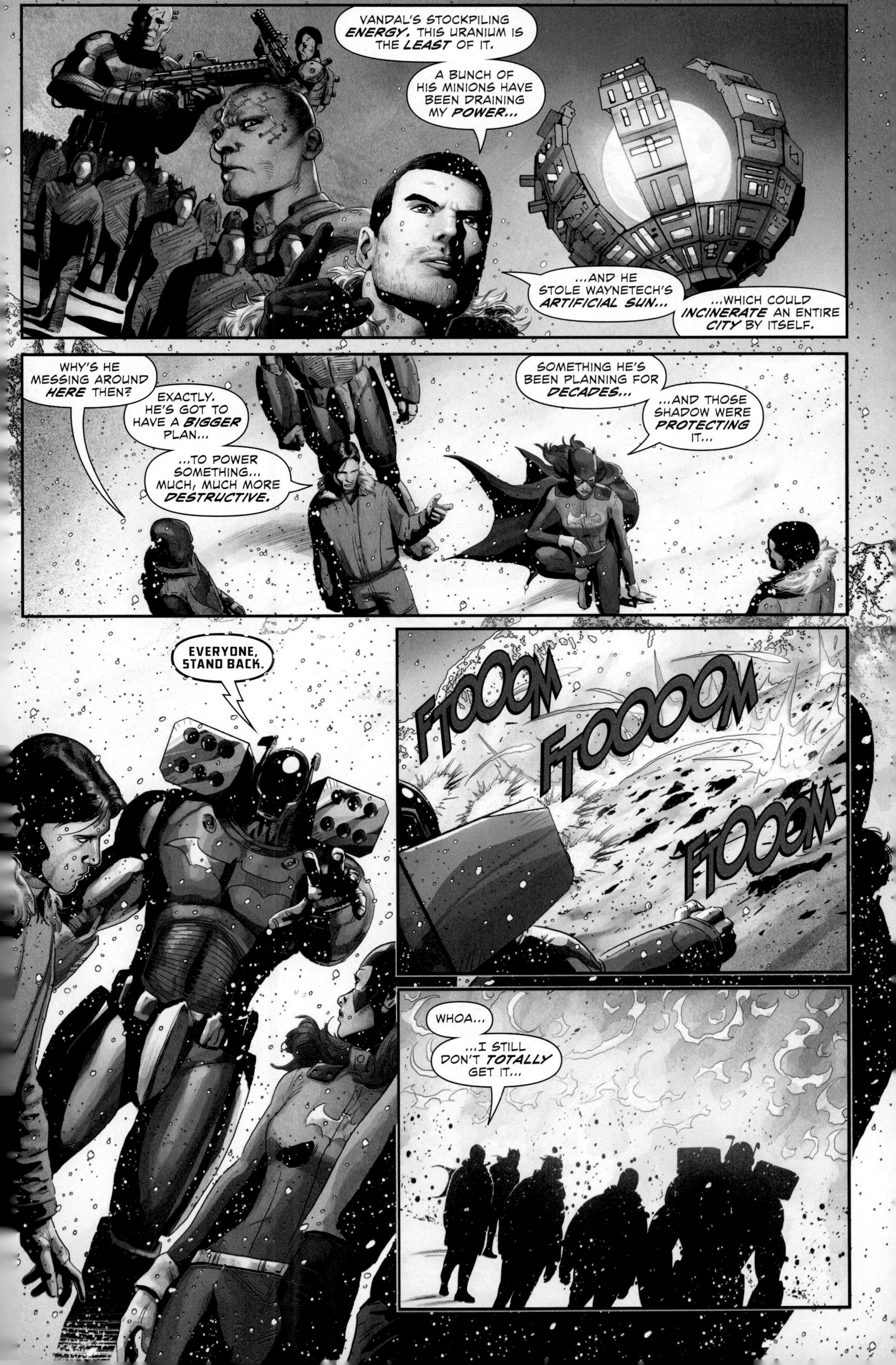
VANDAL'S STOCKPILING ENERGY. THIS URANIUM IS THE LEAST OF IT.
A BUNCH OF HIS MINIONS HAVE BEEN DRAINING MY POWER...
...AND HE STOLE WAYNETECH'S ARTIFICIAL SUN...
...WHICH COULD INCINERATE AN ENTIRE CITY BY ITSELF.
WHY'S HE MESSING AROUND HERE THEN?
EXACTLY. HE'S GOT TO HAVE A BIGGER PLAN...
...TO POWER SOMETHING... MUCH, MUCH MORE DESTRUCTIVE.
SOMETHING HE'S BEEN PLANNING FOR DECADES...
...AND THOSE SHADOW WERE PROTECTING IT...
EVERYONE, STAND BACK.
FTOOOM
FTOOOOOM
FTOOOM
WHOA...
...I STILL DON'T TOTALLY GET IT...

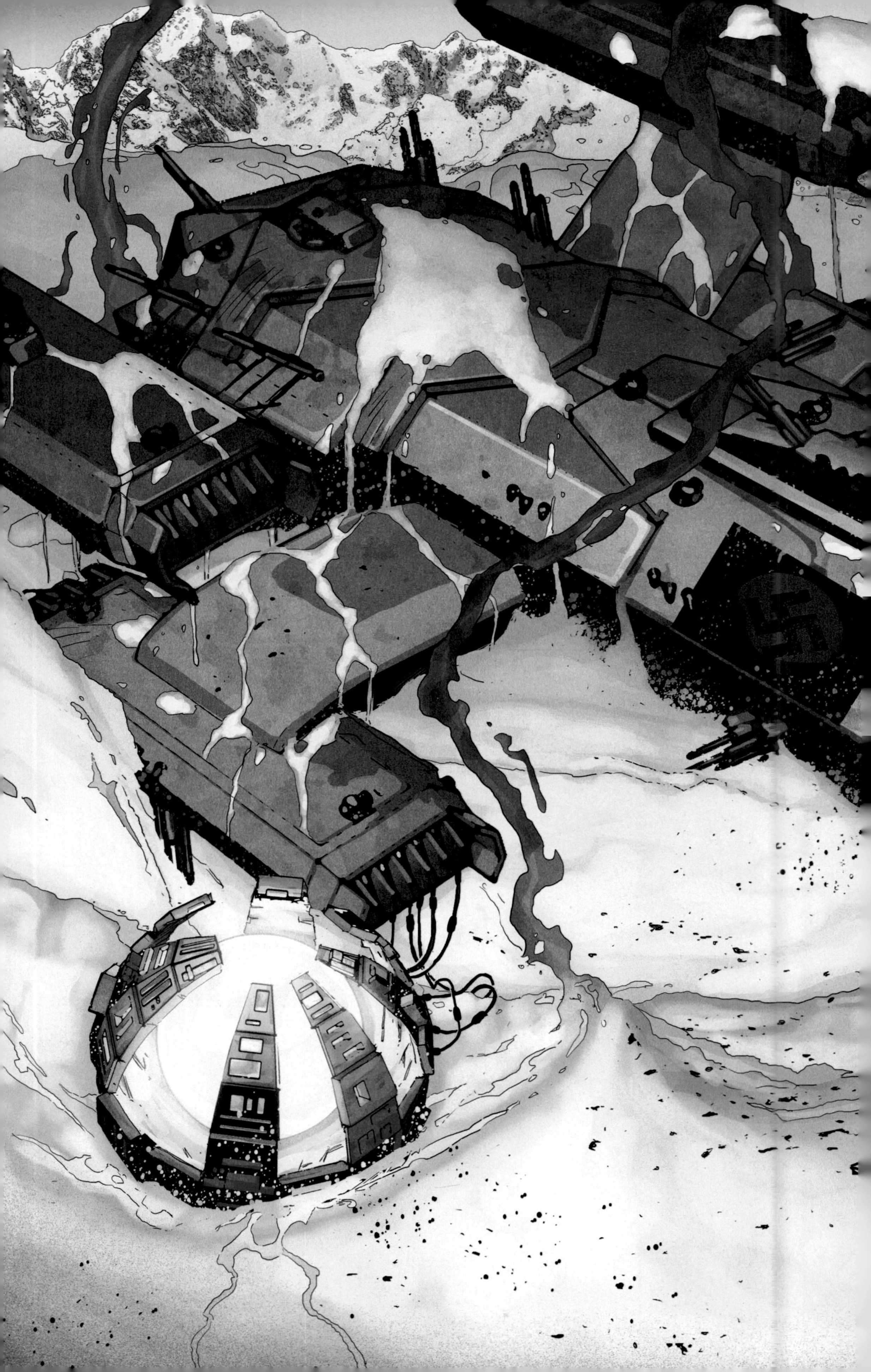

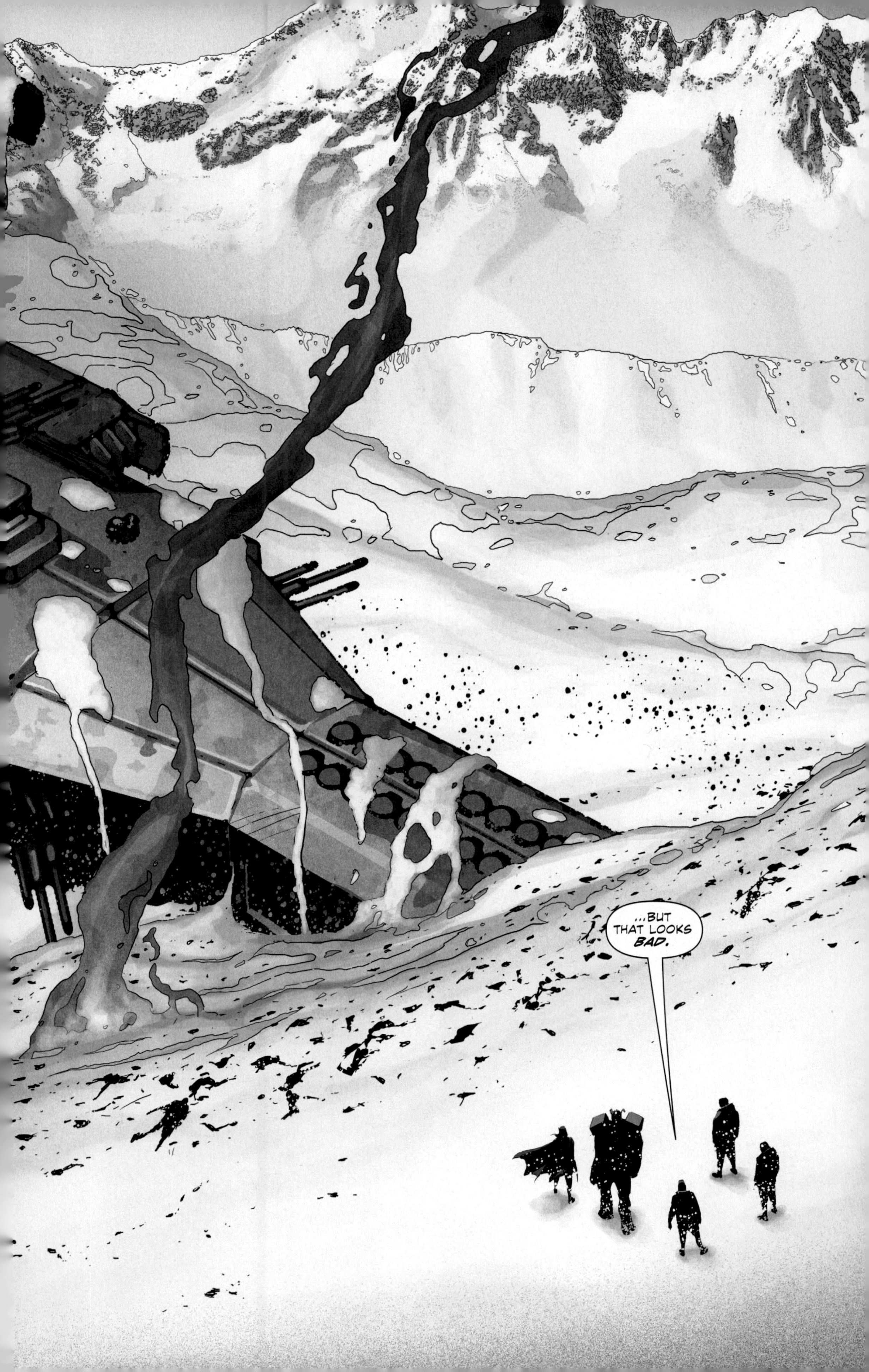
...BUT THAT LOOKS BAD.

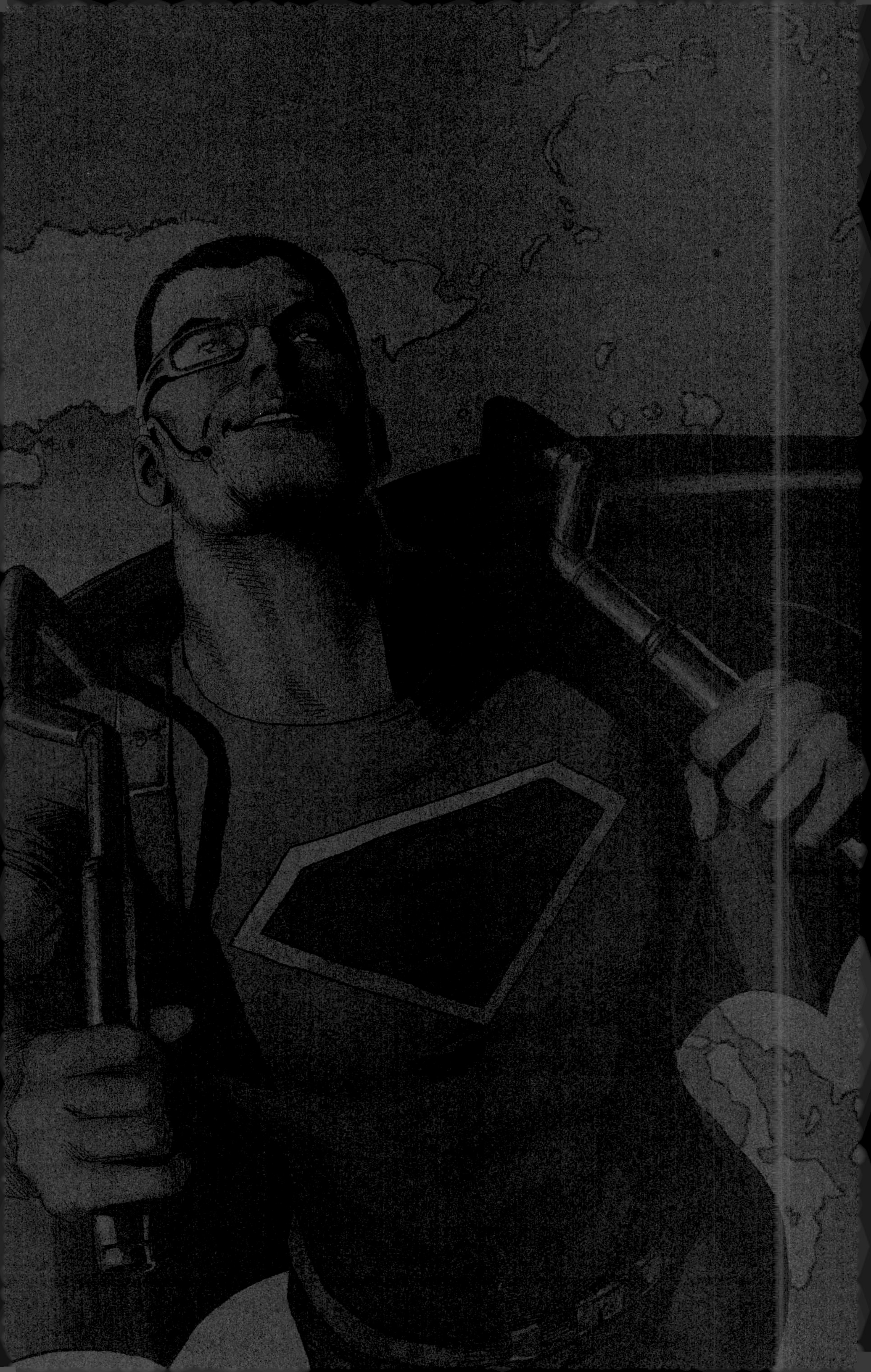

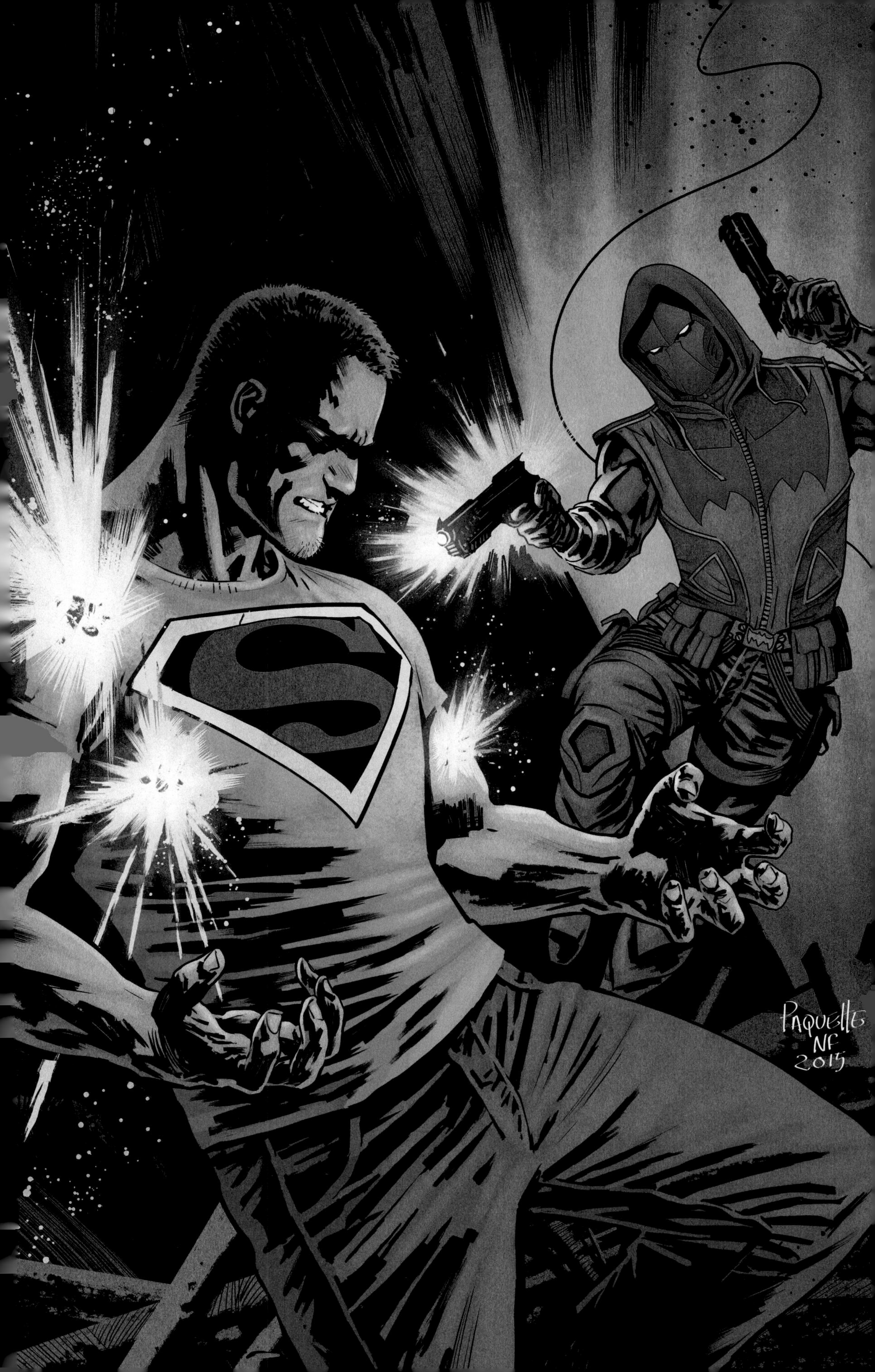
PAQUETTE
NF
2015

TRUST

GREG PAK writer **CLIFF RICHARDS** **JACK HERBERT** artists **BETH SOTELO** **WIL QUINTANA** colorists **ROB LEIGH** letterer **YANICK PAQUETTE** **NATHAN FAIRBAIRN** cover

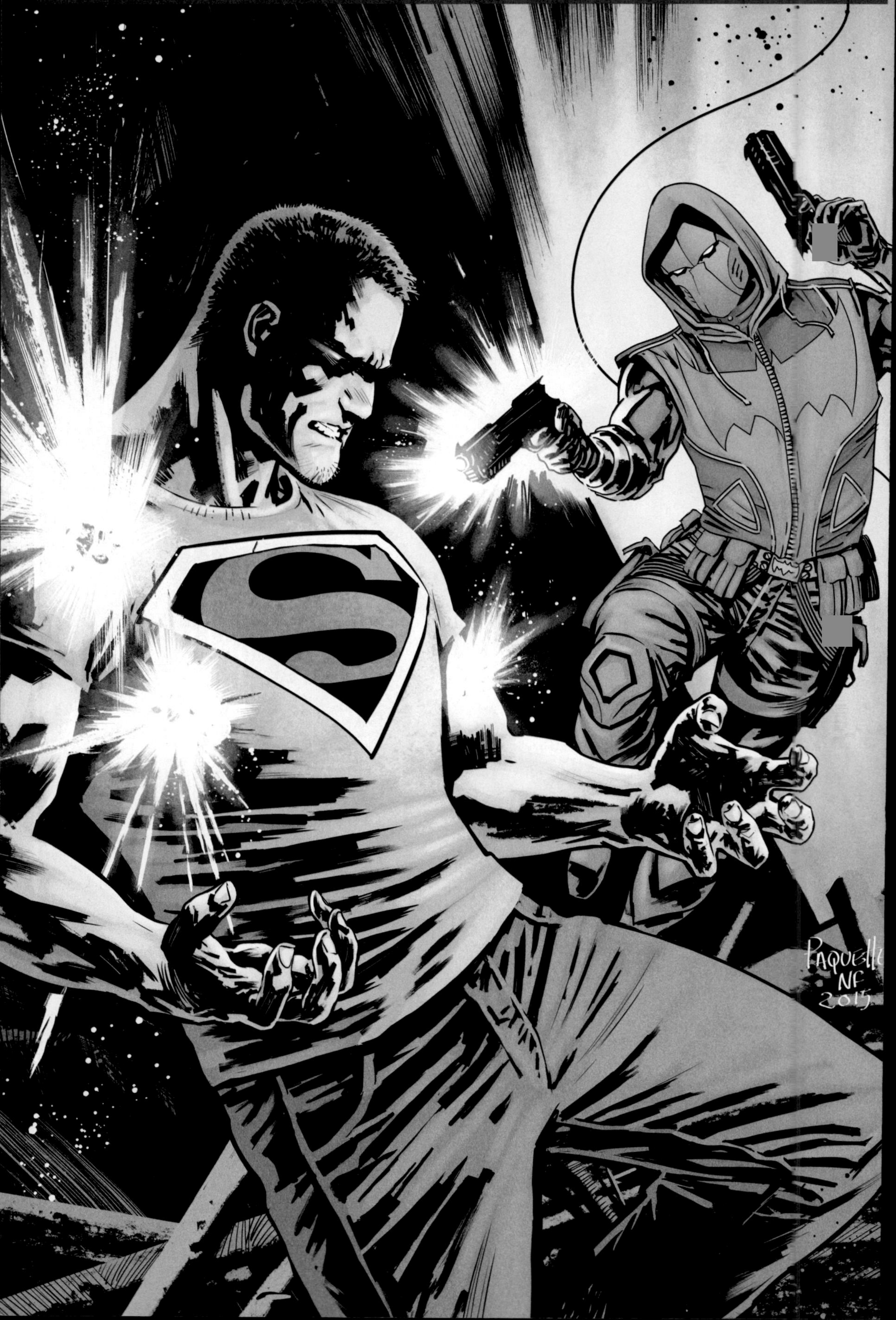
PAQUETTE
NF
2015

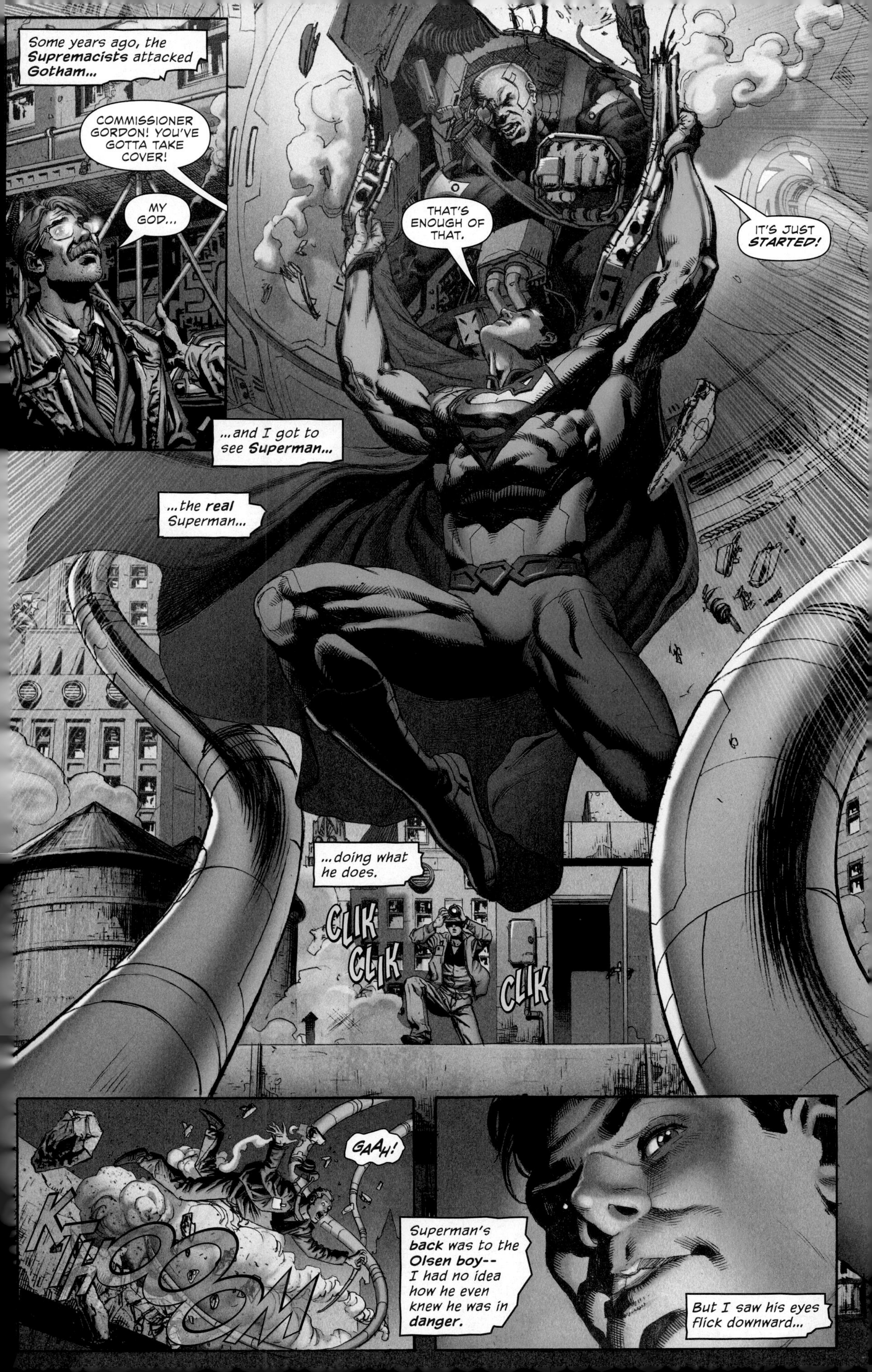
Some years ago, the Supremacists attacked Gotham...
COMMISSIONER GORDON! YOU'VE GOTTA TAKE COVER!
MY GOD...
THAT'S ENOUGH OF THAT.
IT'S JUST STARTED!
...and I got to see Superman...
...the real Superman...
...doing what he does.
CLIK
CLIK
CLIK
GAAH!
KTHOOOM
Superman's back was to the Olsen boy-- I had no idea how he even knew he was in danger.
But I saw his eyes flick downward...

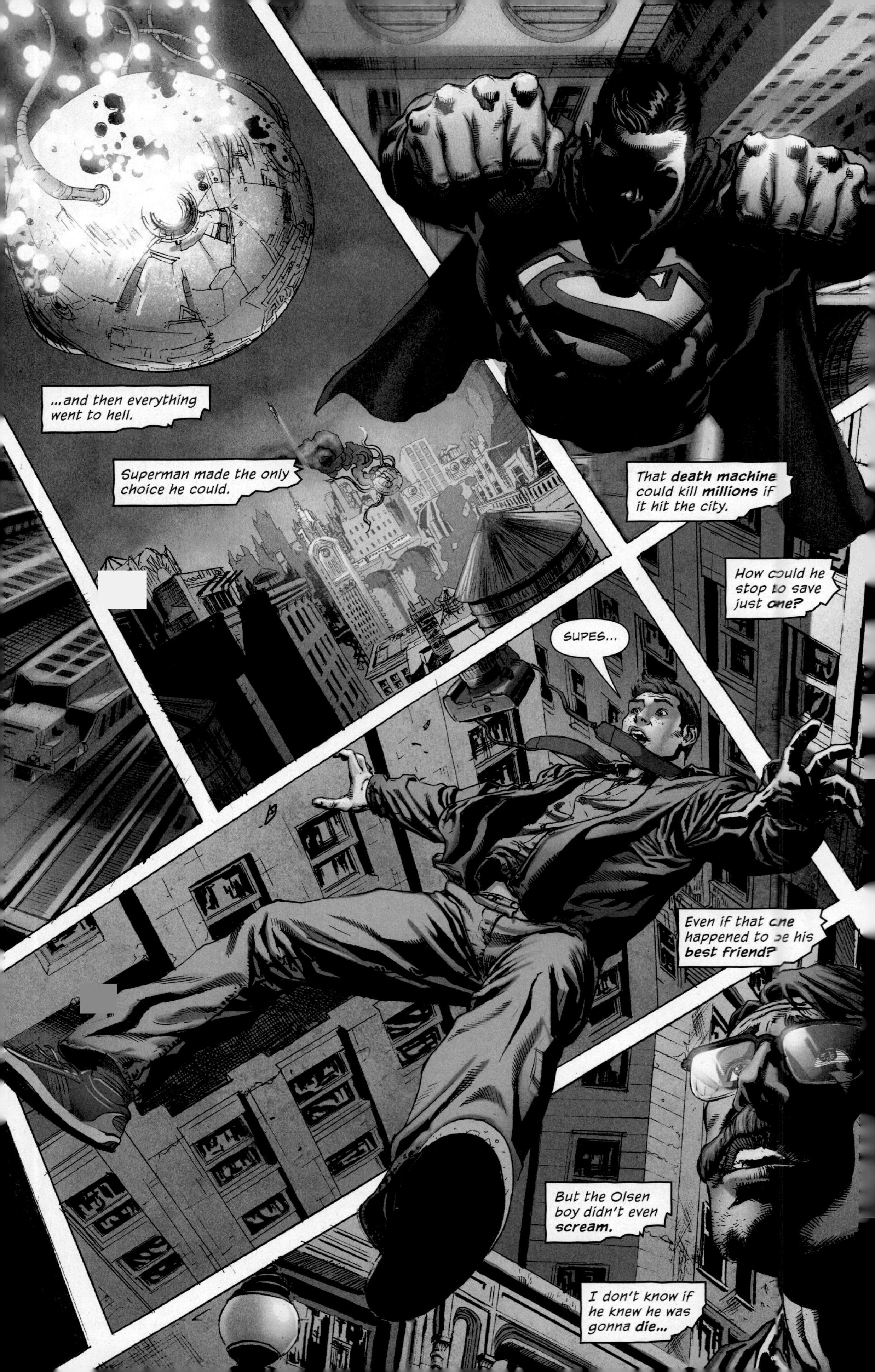
...and then everything went to hell.
Superman made the only choice he could.
That death machine could kill millions if it hit the city.
How could he stop to save just one?
SUPES...
Even if that one happened to be his best friend?
But the Olsen boy didn't even scream.
I don't know if he knew he was gonna die...

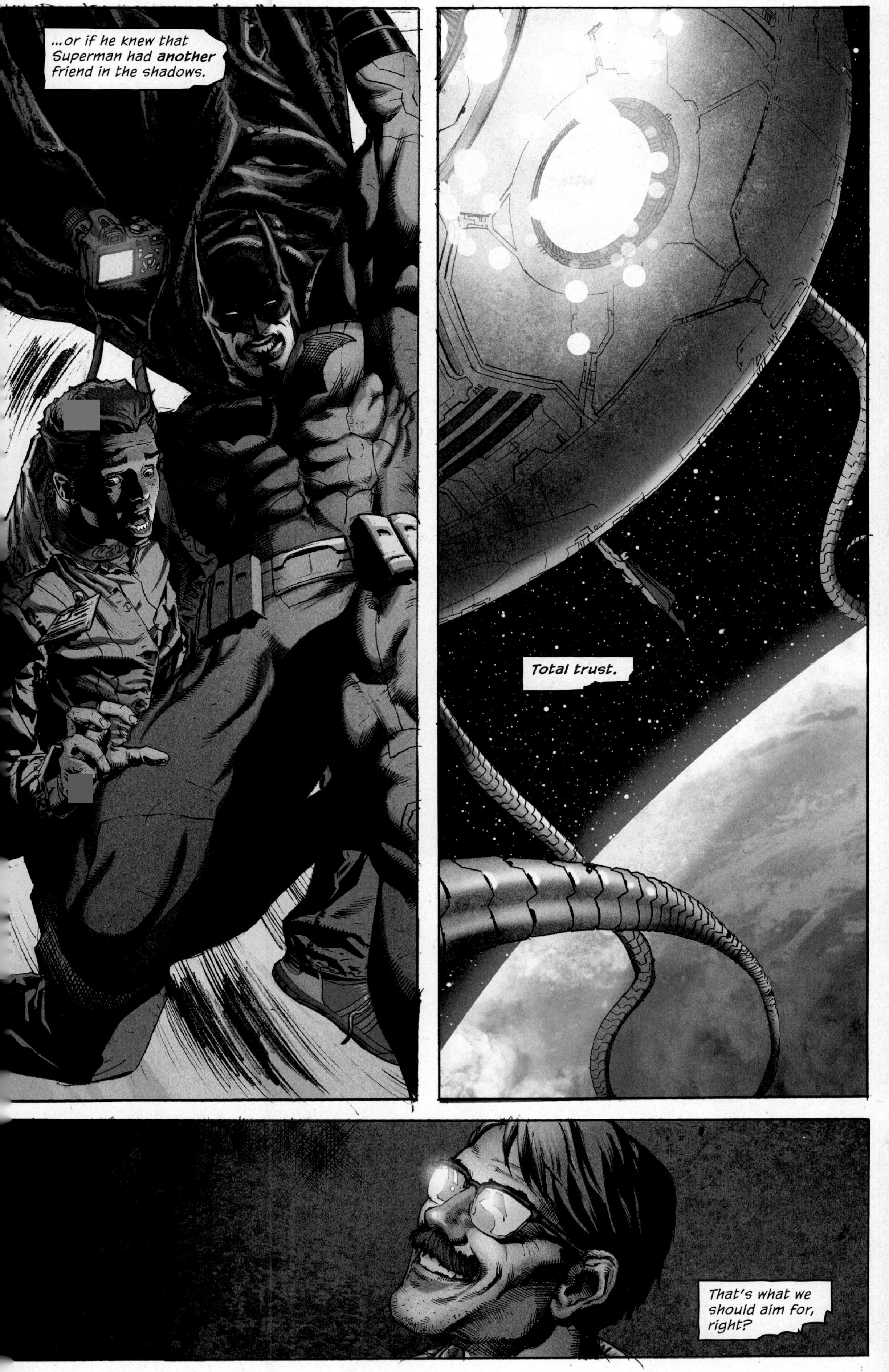
...or if he knew that Superman had **another** friend in the shadows.
Total trust.
That's what we should aim for, right?

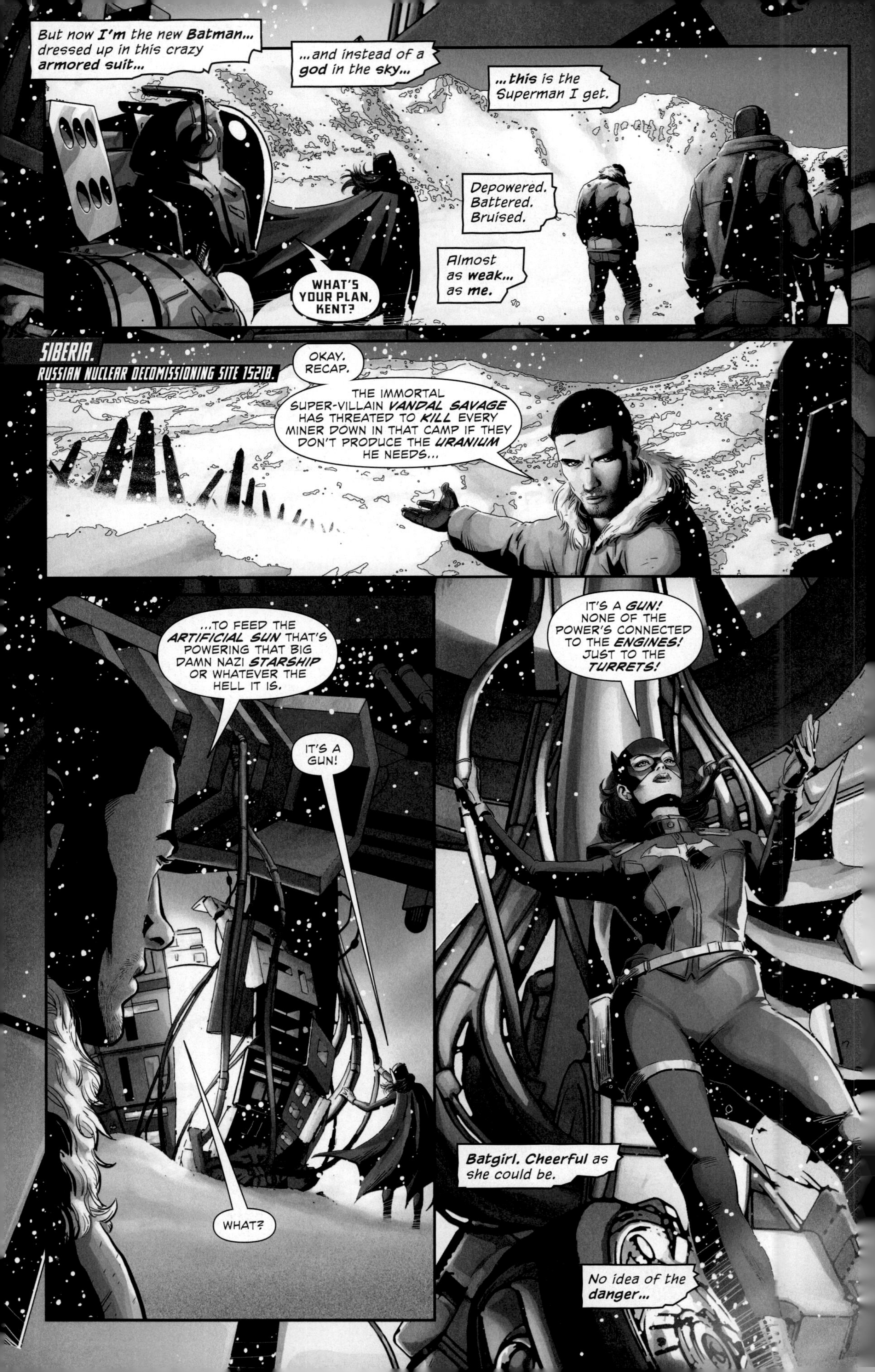
But now I'm the new Batman... dressed up in this crazy armored suit...
...and instead of a god in the sky...
...this is the Superman I get.
Depowered. Battered. Bruised.
Almost as weak... as me.
WHAT'S YOUR PLAN, KENT?
SIBERIA.
RUSSIAN NUCLEAR DECOMISSIONING SITE 15218.
OKAY. RECAP.
THE IMMORTAL SUPER-VILLAIN VANDAL SAVAGE HAS THREATED TO KILL EVERY MINER DOWN IN THAT CAMP IF THEY DON'T PRODUCE THE URANIUM HE NEEDS...
...TO FEED THE ARTIFICIAL SUN THAT'S POWERING THAT BIG DAMN NAZI STARSHIP OR WHATEVER THE HELL IT IS.
IT'S A GUN!
WHAT?
IT'S A GUN! NONE OF THE POWER'S CONNECTED TO THE ENGINES! JUST TO THE TURRETS!
Batgirl. Cheerful as she could be.
No idea of the danger...

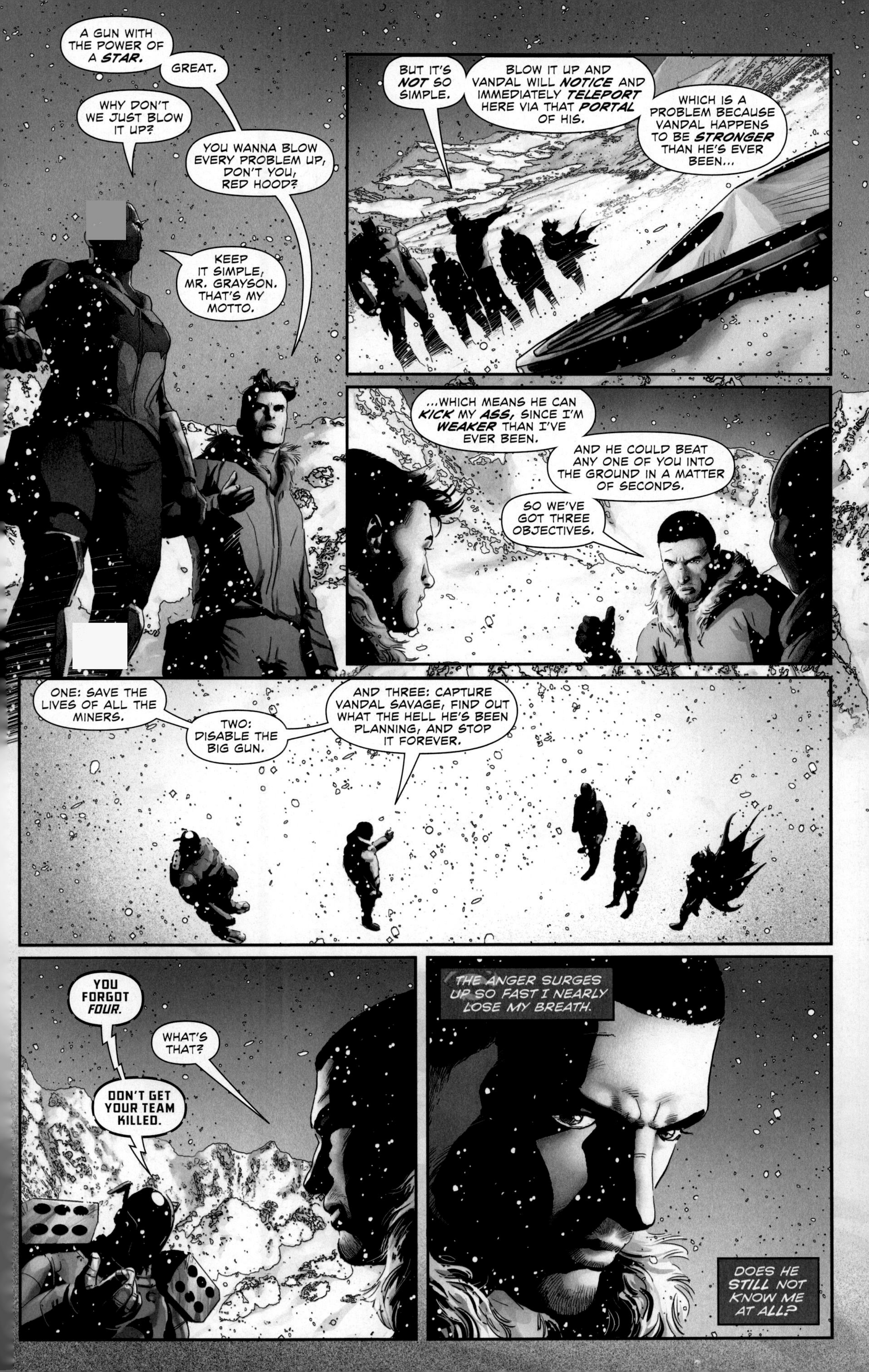
A GUN WITH THE POWER OF A STAR.
GREAT.
WHY DON'T WE JUST BLOW IT UP?
YOU WANNA BLOW EVERY PROBLEM UP, DON'T YOU, RED HOOD?
KEEP IT SIMPLE, MR. GRAYSON. THAT'S MY MOTTO.
BUT IT'S NOT SO SIMPLE.
BLOW IT UP AND VANDAL WILL NOTICE AND IMMEDIATELY TELEPORT HERE VIA THAT PORTAL OF HIS.
WHICH IS A PROBLEM BECAUSE VANDAL HAPPENS TO BE STRONGER THAN HE'S EVER BEEN...
...WHICH MEANS HE CAN KICK MY ASS, SINCE I'M WEAKER THAN I'VE EVER BEEN.
AND HE COULD BEAT ANY ONE OF YOU INTO THE GROUND IN A MATTER OF SECONDS.
SO WE'VE GOT THREE OBJECTIVES.
ONE: SAVE THE LIVES OF ALL THE MINERS.
TWO: DISABLE THE BIG GUN.
AND THREE: CAPTURE VANDAL SAVAGE, FIND OUT WHAT THE HELL HE'S BEEN PLANNING, AND STOP IT FOREVER.
YOU FORGOT FOUR.
WHAT'S THAT?
DON'T GET YOUR TEAM KILLED.
THE ANGER SURGES UP SO FAST I NEARLY LOSE MY BREATH.
DOES HE STILL NOT KNOW ME AT ALL?

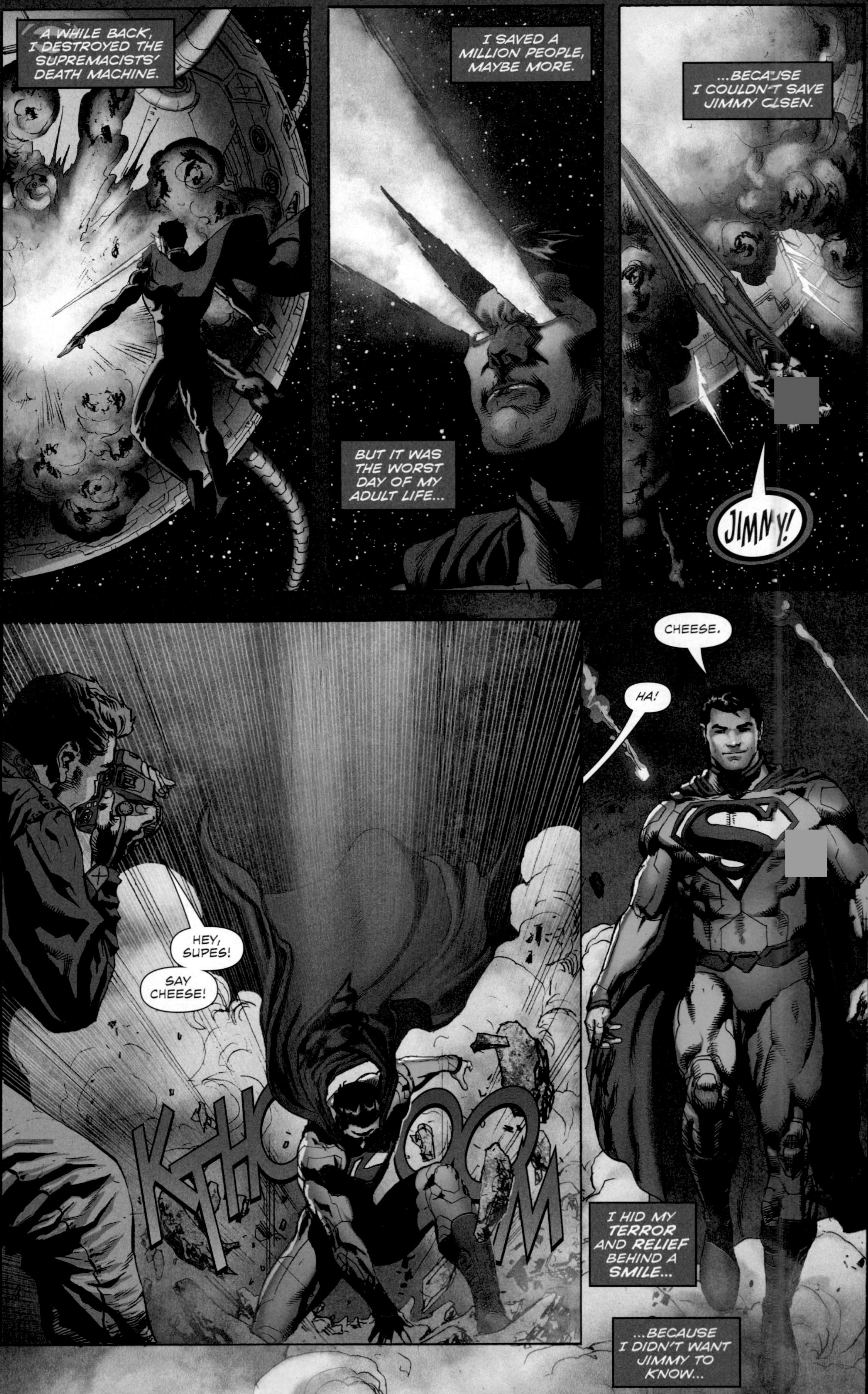
A WHILE BACK, I DESTROYED THE SUPREMACISTS' DEATH MACHINE.
I SAVED A MILLION PEOPLE, MAYBE MORE.
BUT IT WAS THE WORST DAY OF MY ADULT LIFE...
...BECAUSE I COULDN'T SAVE JIMMY OLSEN.
JIMMY!
HEY, SUPES!
SAY CHEESE!
KTHOOOOM
HA!
CHEESE.
I HID MY TERROR AND RELIEF BEHIND A SMILE...
...BECAUSE I DIDN'T WANT JIMMY TO KNOW...

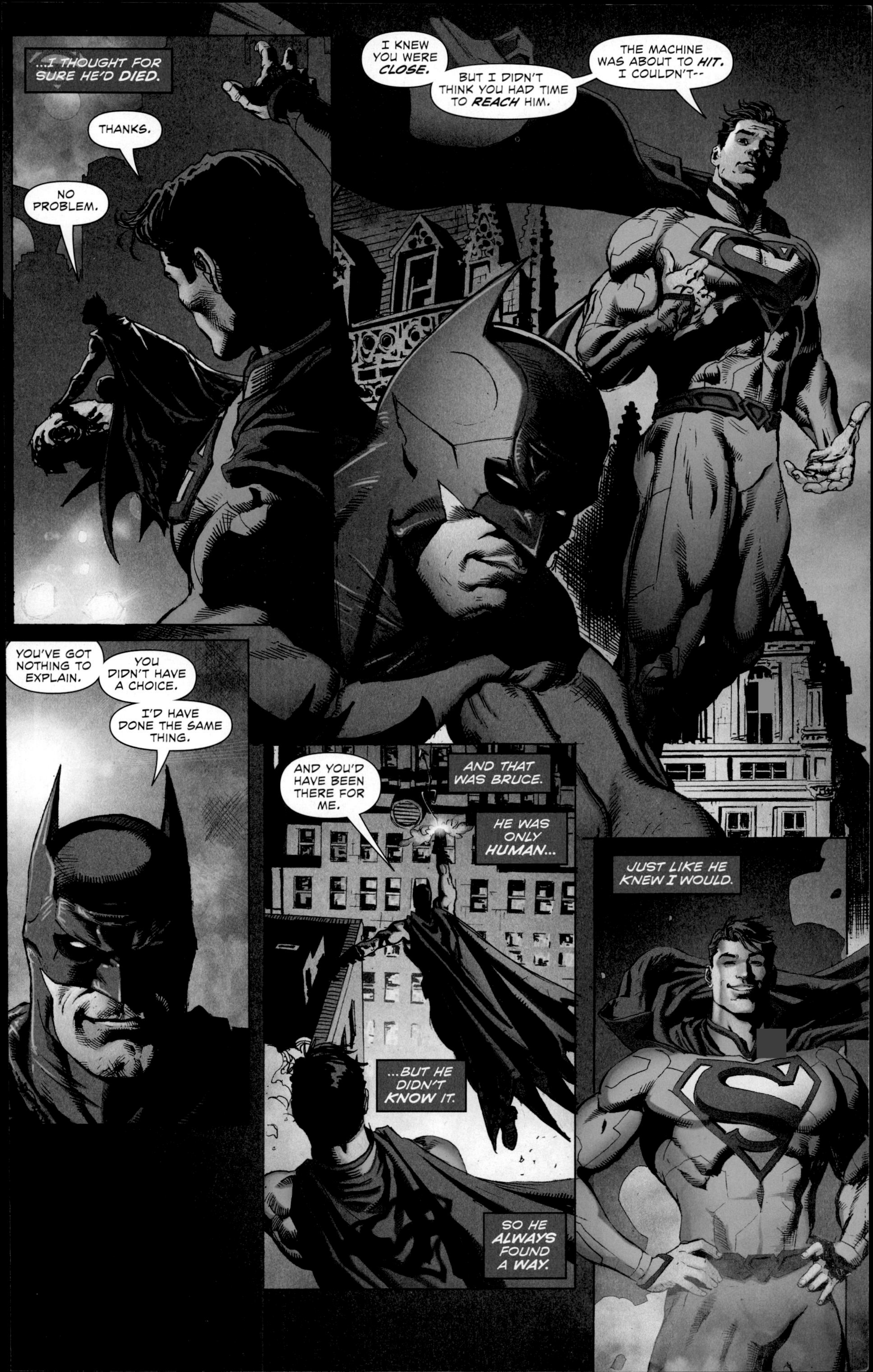

...I THOUGHT FOR SURE HE'D DIED.
THANKS.
NO PROBLEM.
I KNEW YOU WERE CLOSE.
BUT I DIDN'T THINK YOU HAD TIME TO REACH HIM.
THE MACHINE WAS ABOUT TO HIT. I COULDN'T--
YOU'VE GOT NOTHING TO EXPLAIN.
YOU DIDN'T HAVE A CHOICE.
I'D HAVE DONE THE SAME THING.
AND YOU'D HAVE BEEN THERE FOR ME.
AND THAT WAS BRUCE.
HE WAS ONLY HUMAN...
...BUT HE DIDN'T KNOW IT.
SO HE ALWAYS FOUND A WAY.
JUST LIKE HE KNEW I WOULD.

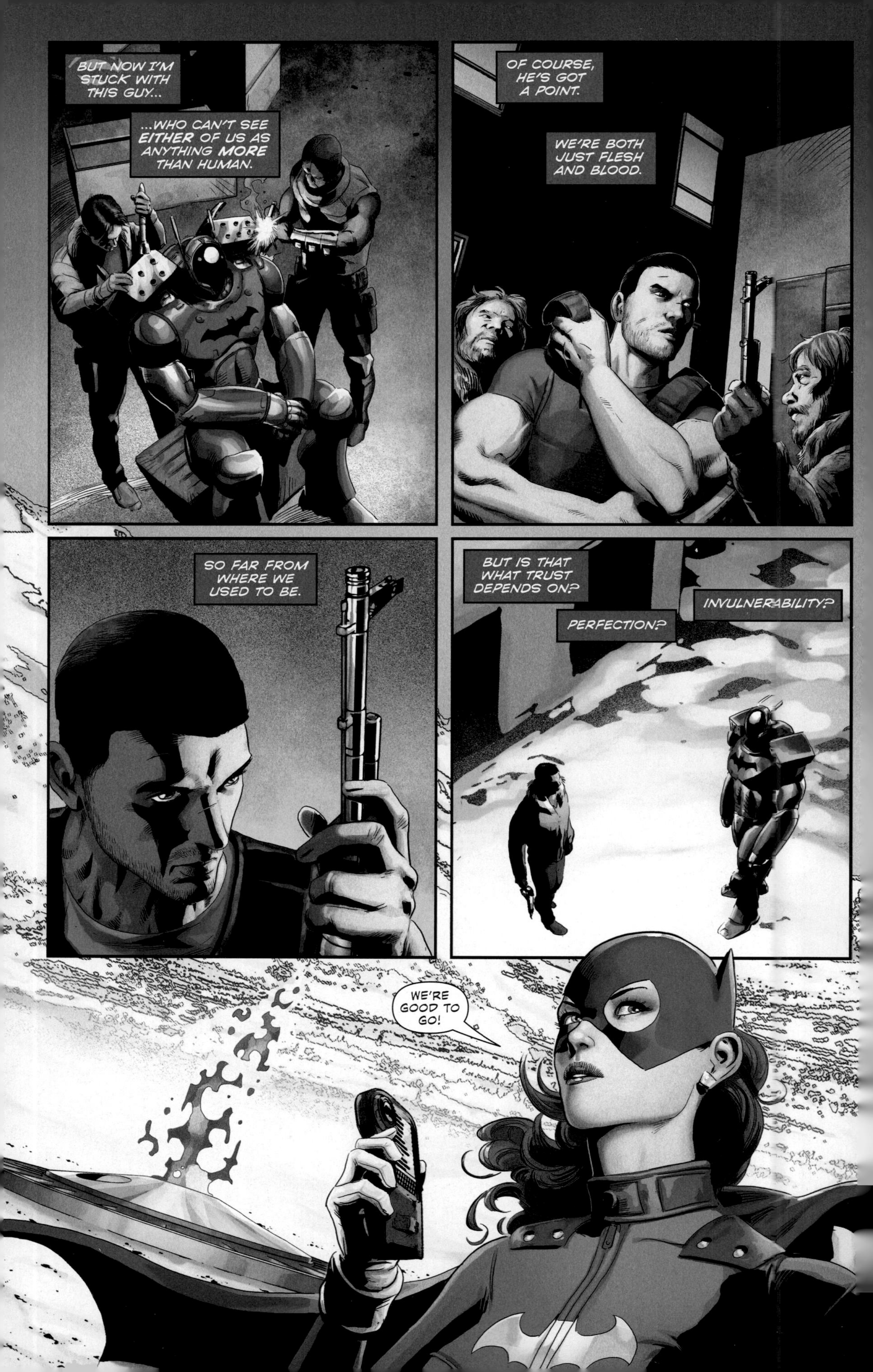
BUT NOW I'M STUCK WITH THIS GUY...
...WHO CAN'T SEE EITHER OF US AS ANYTHING MORE THAN HUMAN.
OF COURSE, HE'S GOT A POINT.
WE'RE BOTH JUST FLESH AND BLOOD.
SO FAR FROM WHERE WE USED TO BE.
BUT IS THAT WHAT TRUST DEPENDS ON?
PERFECTION?
INVULNERABILITY?
WE'RE GOOD TO GO!

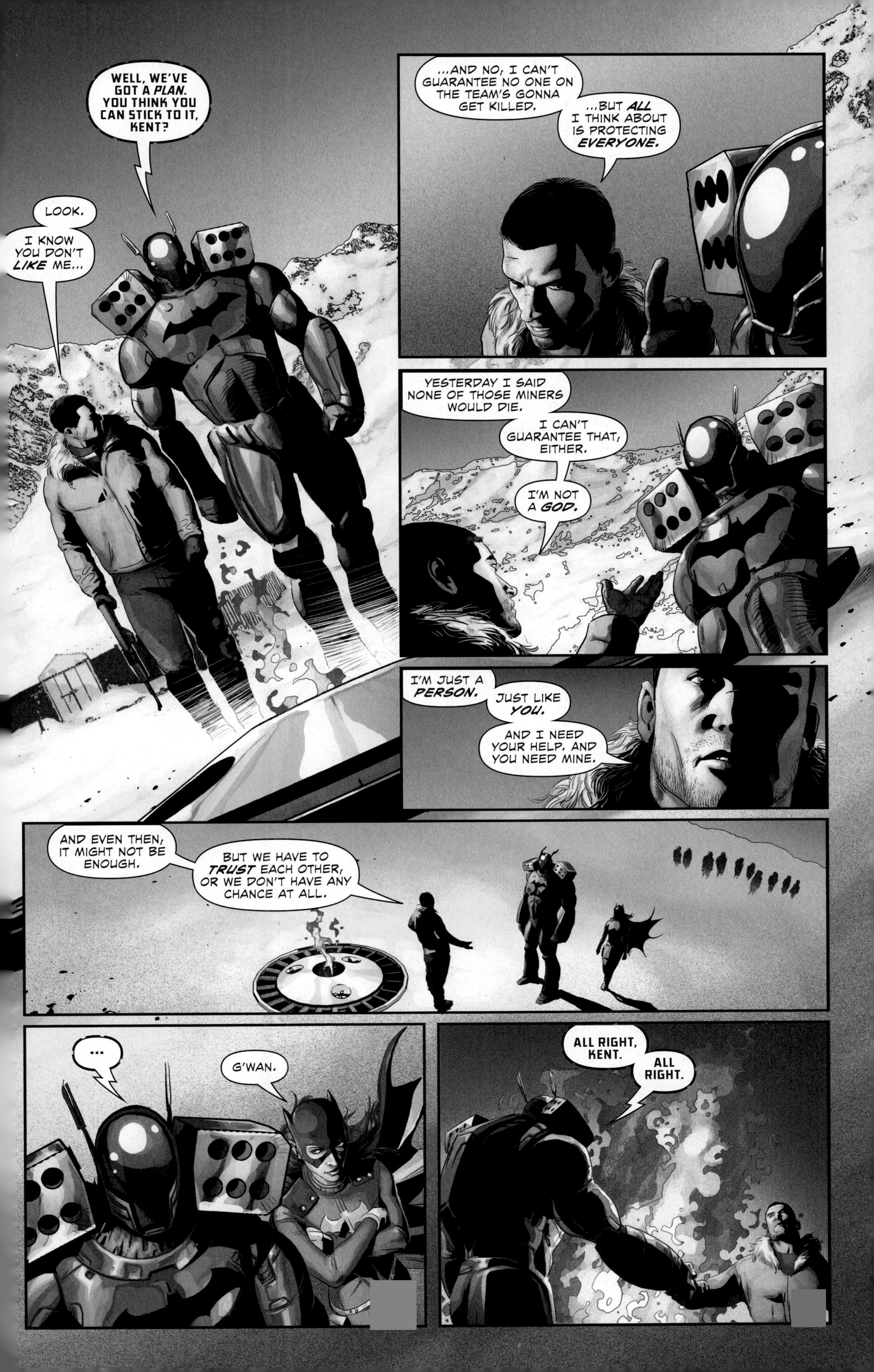
WELL, WE'VE GOT A *PLAN.* YOU THINK YOU CAN STICK TO IT, KENT?
LOOK.
I KNOW YOU DON'T *LIKE* ME...
...AND NO, I CAN'T GUARANTEE NO ONE ON THE TEAM'S GONNA GET KILLED.
...BUT *ALL* I THINK ABOUT IS PROTECTING *EVERYONE.*
YESTERDAY I SAID NONE OF THOSE MINERS WOULD DIE.
I CAN'T GUARANTEE THAT, EITHER.
I'M NOT A *GOD.*
I'M JUST A *PERSON.*
JUST LIKE *YOU.*
AND I NEED YOUR HELP. AND YOU NEED MINE.
AND EVEN THEN, IT MIGHT NOT BE ENOUGH.
BUT WE HAVE TO *TRUST* EACH OTHER, OR WE DON'T HAVE ANY CHANCE AT ALL.
...
G'WAN.
ALL RIGHT, KENT.
ALL RIGHT.

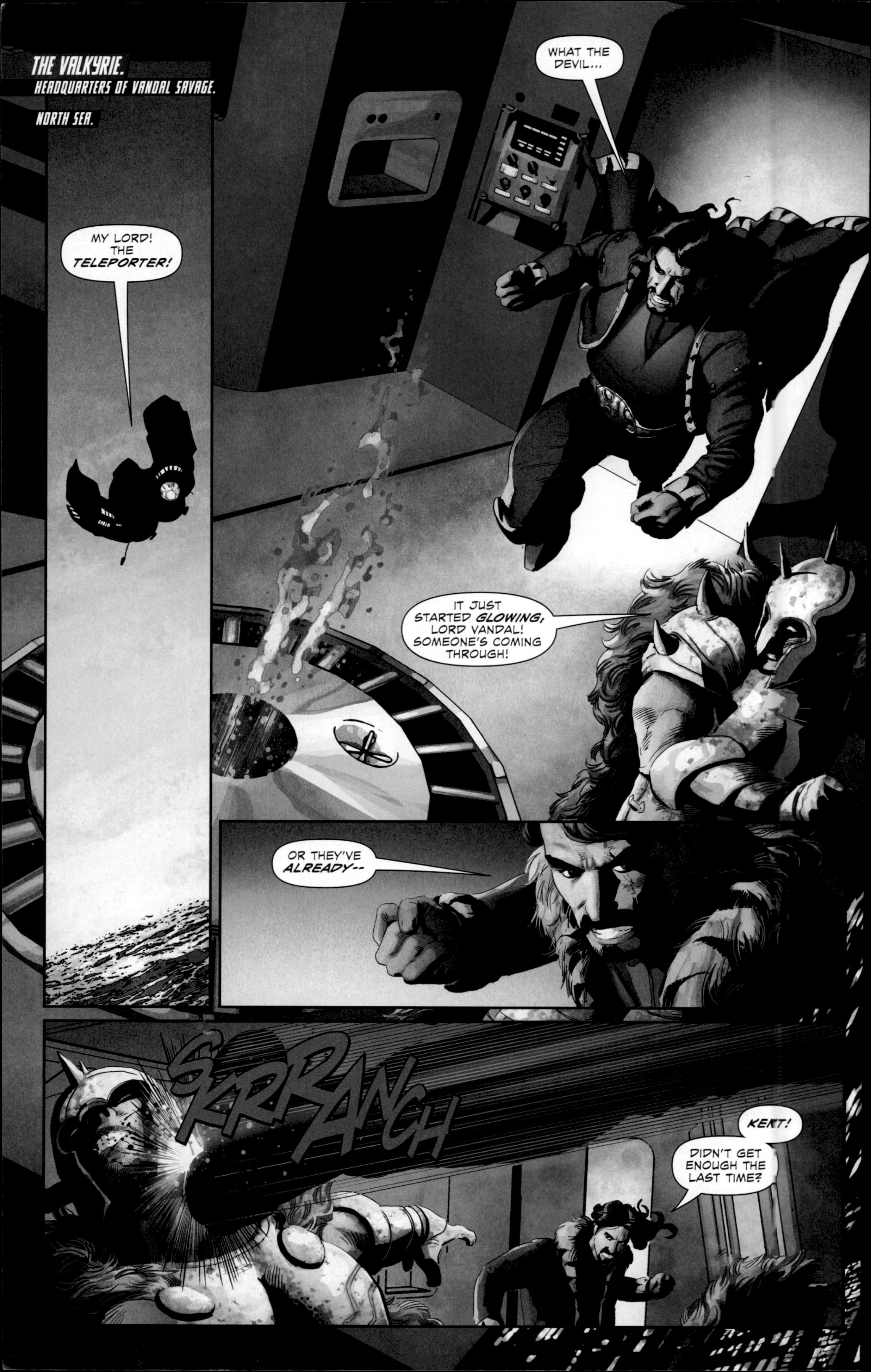

THE VALKYRIE.
HEADQUARTERS OF VANDAL SAVAGE.
NORTH SEA.
MY LORD! THE TELEPORTER!
WHAT THE DEVIL...
IT JUST STARTED GLOWING, LORD VANDAL! SOMEONE'S COMING THROUGH!
OR THEY'VE ALREADY--
SKRRANCH
KENT!
DIDN'T GET ENOUGH THE LAST TIME?

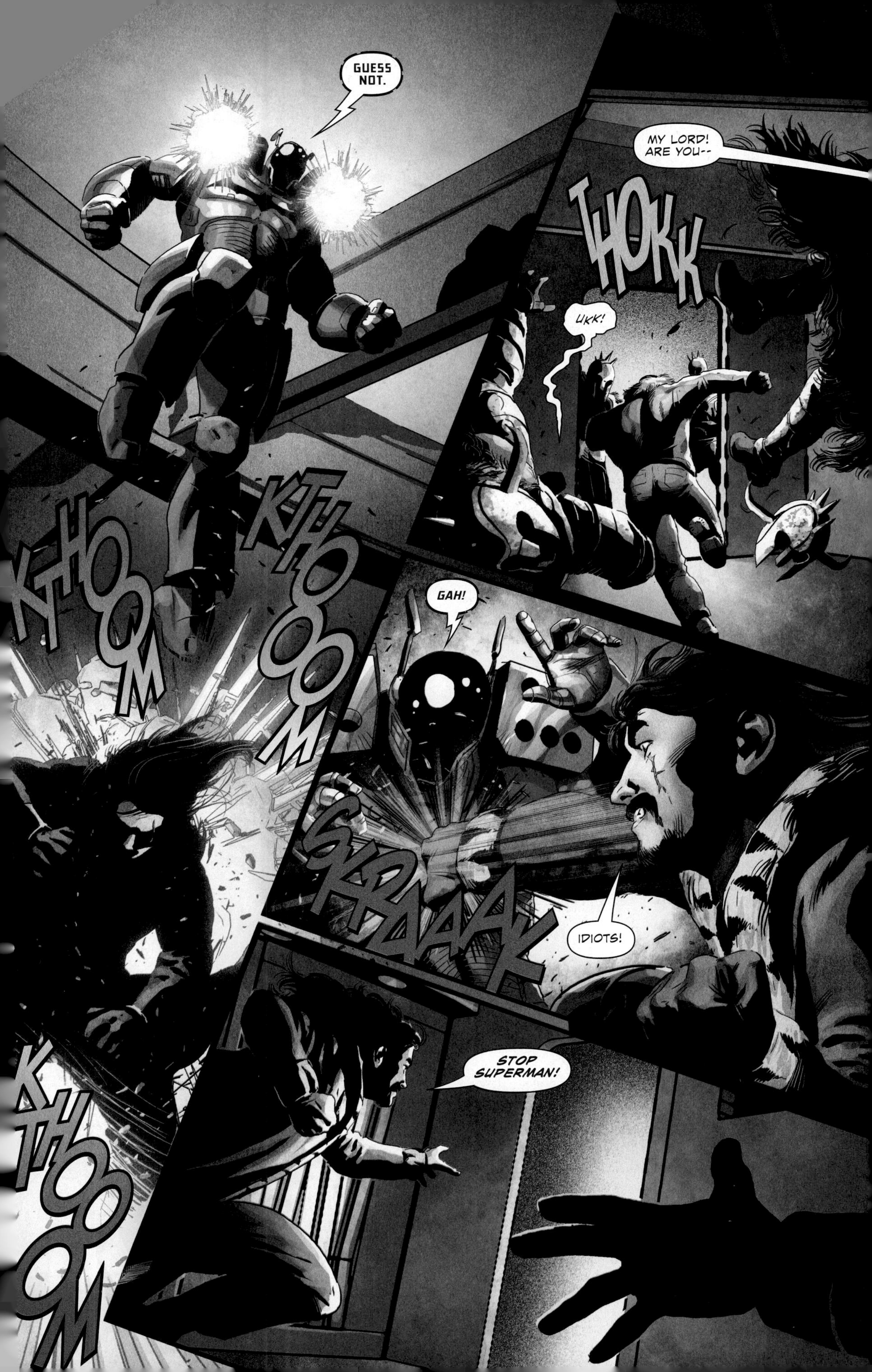
GUESS NOT.
MY LORD! ARE YOU--
THOKK
UKK!
KTHOOOM
KTHOOOOM
GAH!
SKRAAAK
IDIOTS!
STOP SUPERMAN!
KTHOOOOM

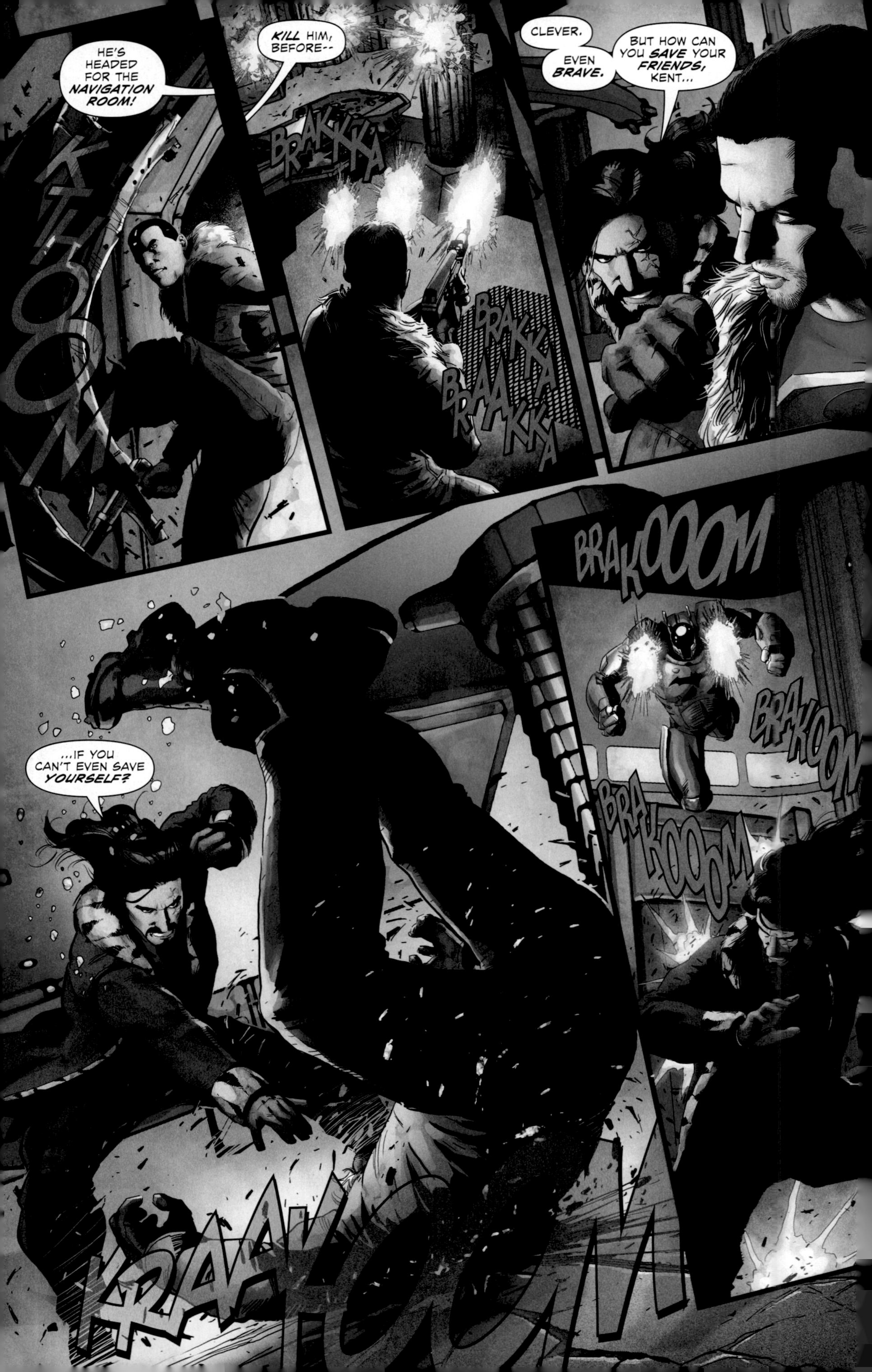

HE'S HEADED FOR THE NAVIGATION ROOM!
KATHOOOM
KILL HIM, BEFORE--
BRAKKKA
BRAKKKA
BRAAKKKA
CLEVER.
EVEN BRAVE.
BUT HOW CAN YOU SAVE YOUR FRIENDS, KENT...
BRAKOOOM
BRAKOOM
BRAKOOOM
...IF YOU CAN'T EVEN SAVE YOURSELF?

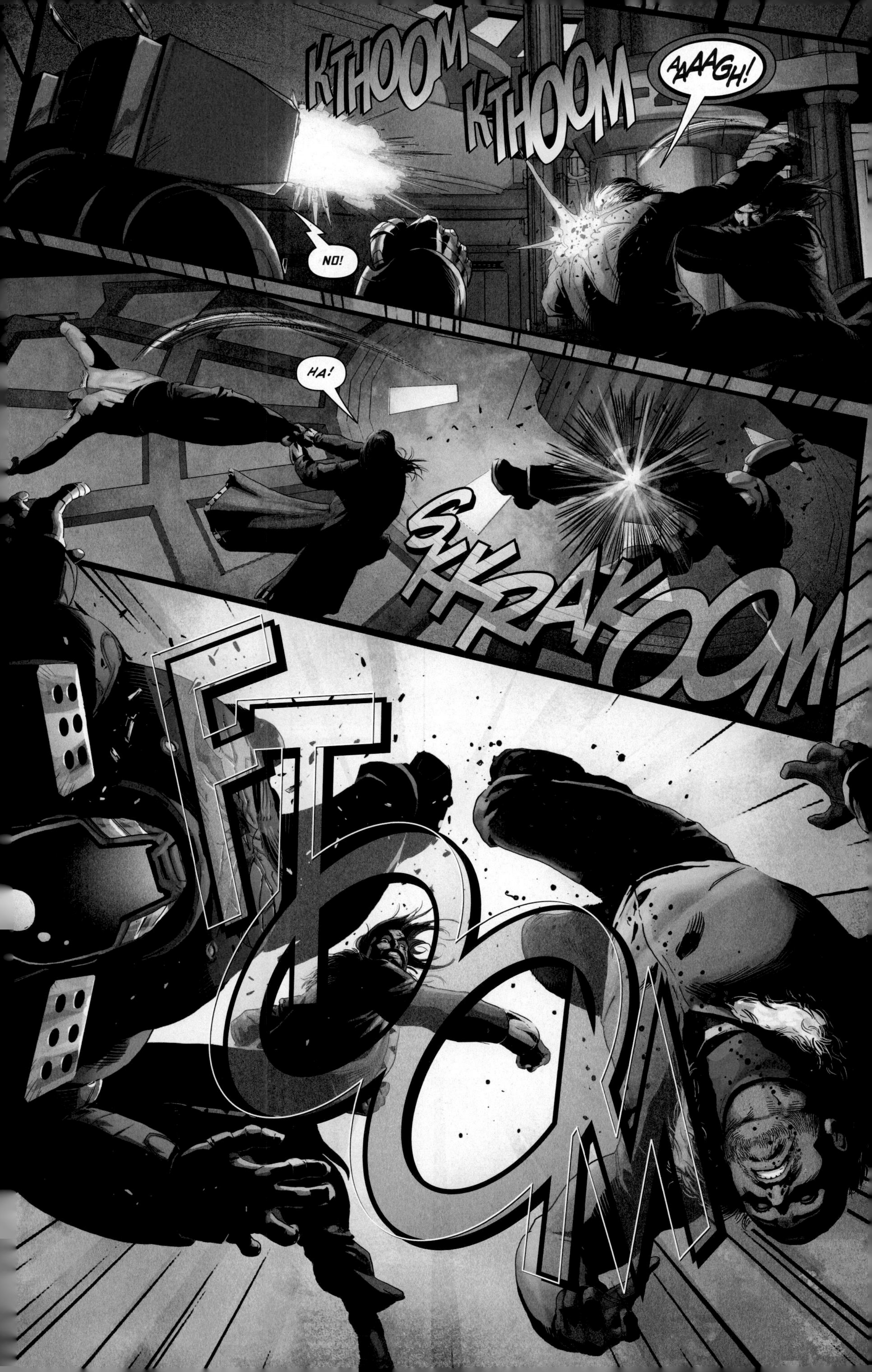
KTHOOM
KTHOOM
AAAAGH!
NO!
HA!
SKKRAKOOM
FTOOM

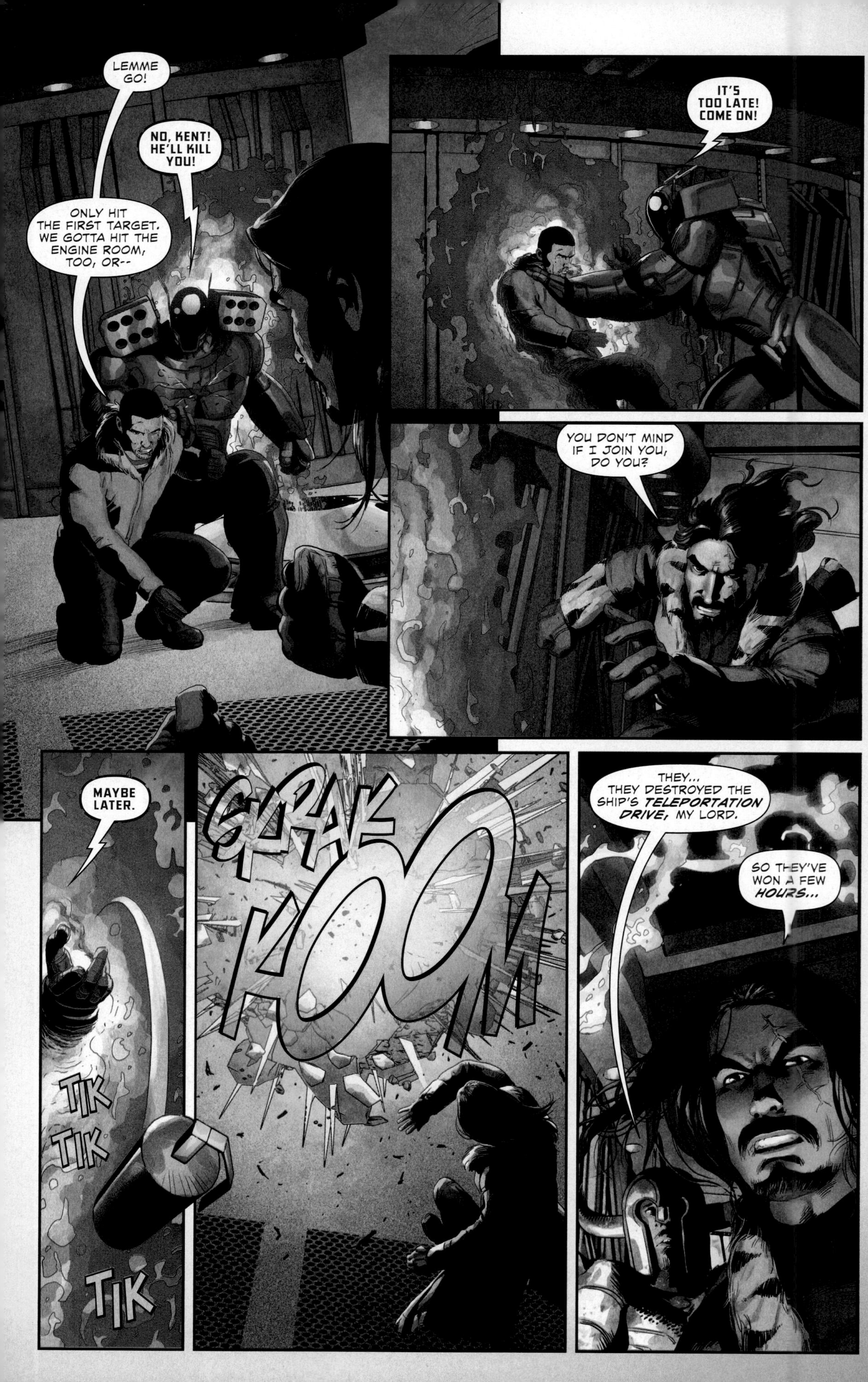
LEMME GO!
NO, KENT! HE'LL KILL YOU!
ONLY HIT THE FIRST TARGET. WE GOTTA HIT THE ENGINE ROOM, TOO, OR--
IT'S TOO LATE! COME ON!
YOU DON'T MIND IF I JOIN YOU, DO YOU?
MAYBE LATER.
TIK
TIK
TIK
SKRAK
KOOM
THEY... THEY DESTROYED THE SHIP'S *TELEPORTATION DRIVE,* MY LORD.
SO THEY'VE WON A FEW *HOURS...*

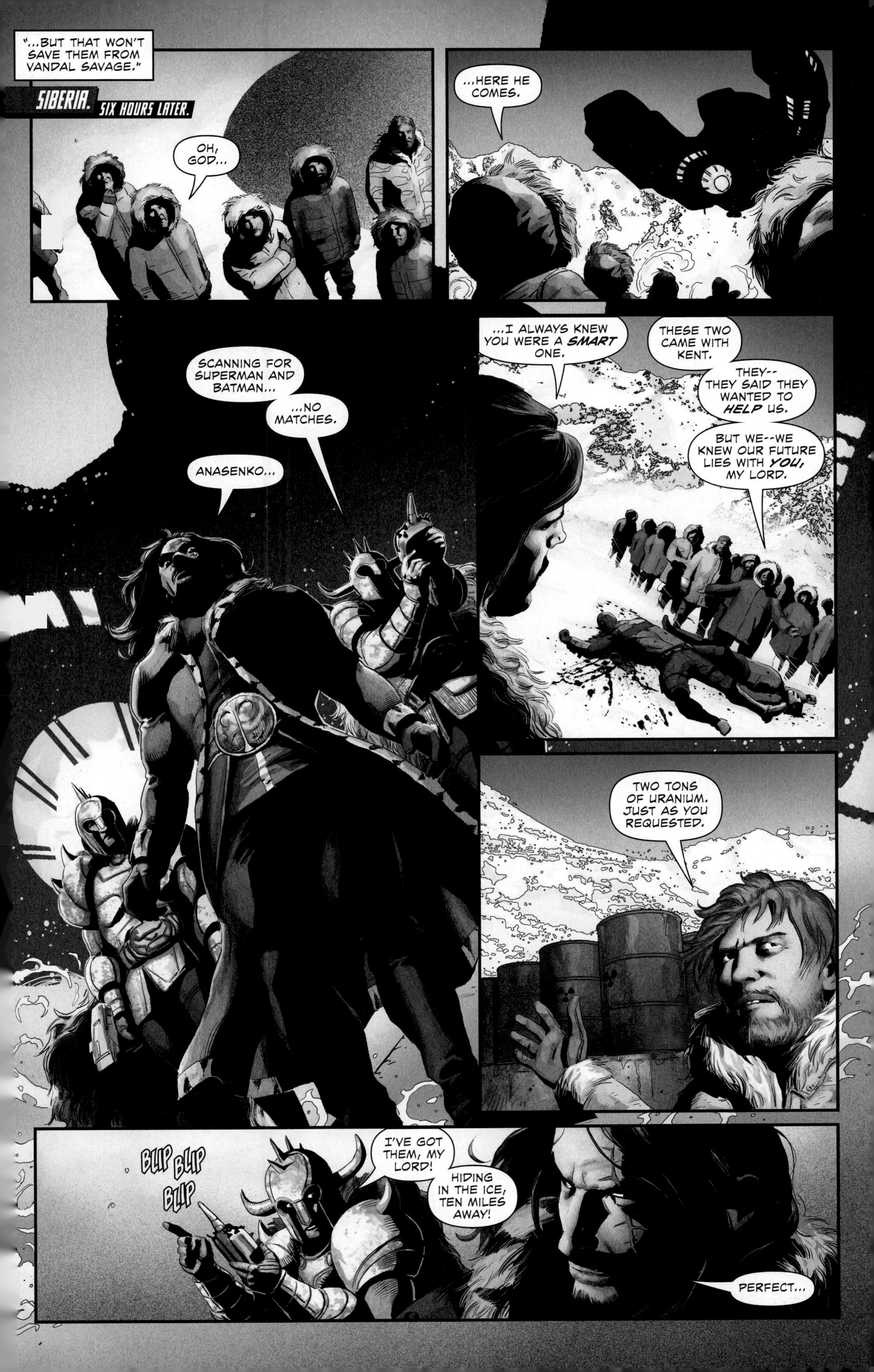
"...BUT THAT WON'T SAVE THEM FROM VANDAL SAVAGE."
SIBERIA. SIX HOURS LATER.
OH, GOD...
...HERE HE COMES.
SCANNING FOR SUPERMAN AND BATMAN...
...NO MATCHES.
ANASENKO...
...I ALWAYS KNEW YOU WERE A SMART ONE.
THESE TWO CAME WITH KENT.
THEY-- THEY SAID THEY WANTED TO HELP US.
BUT WE--WE KNEW OUR FUTURE LIES WITH YOU, MY LORD.
TWO TONS OF URANIUM. JUST AS YOU REQUESTED.
BLIP BLIP BLIP
I'VE GOT THEM, MY LORD!
HIDING IN THE ICE, TEN MILES AWAY!
PERFECT...

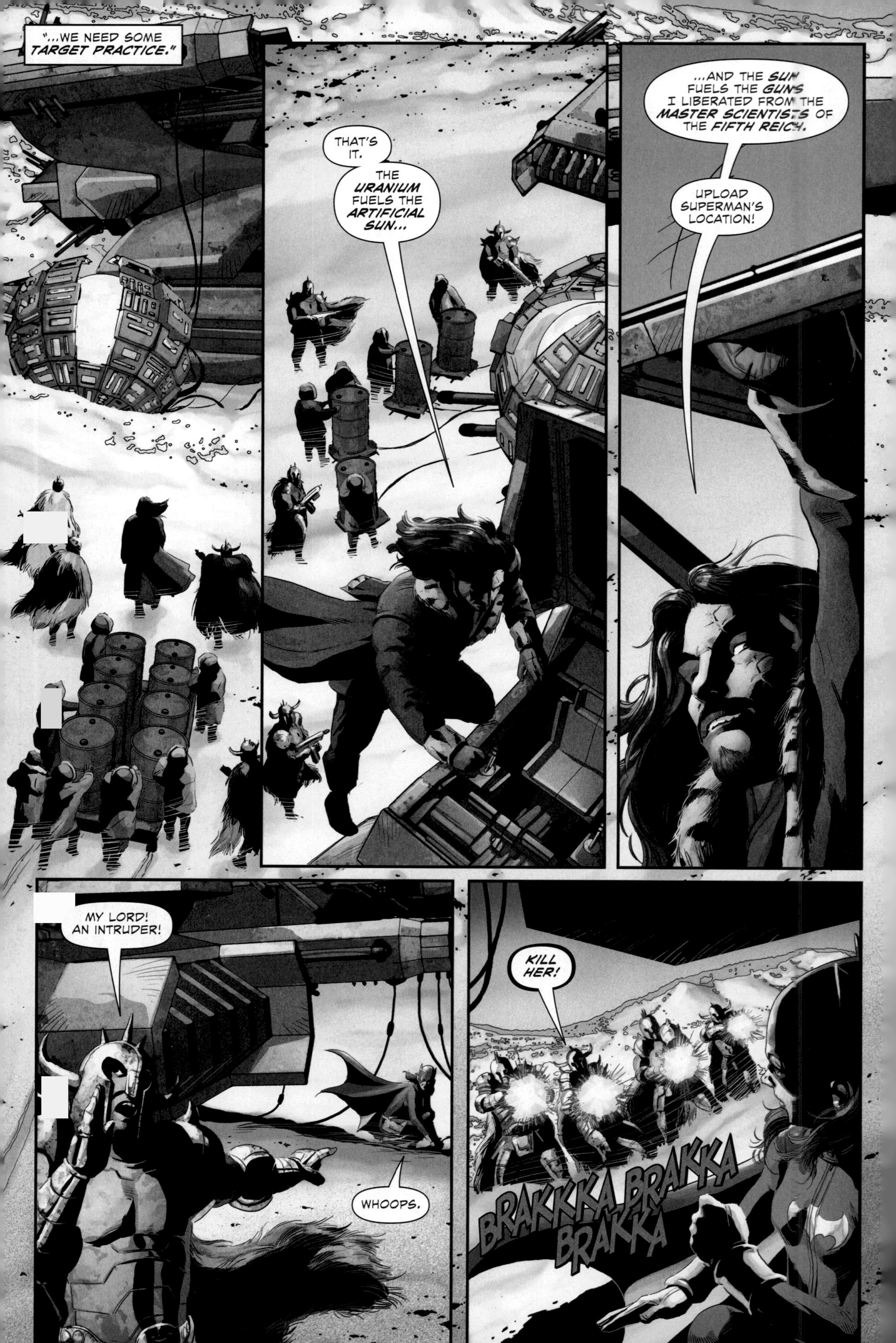
"...WE NEED SOME TARGET PRACTICE."
THAT'S IT.
THE URANIUM FUELS THE ARTIFICIAL SUN...
...AND THE SUN FUELS THE GUNS I LIBERATED FROM THE MASTER SCIENTISTS OF THE FIFTH REICH.
UPLOAD SUPERMAN'S LOCATION!
MY LORD! AN INTRUDER!
WHOOPS.
KILL HER!
BRAKKA BRAKKA BRAKKA

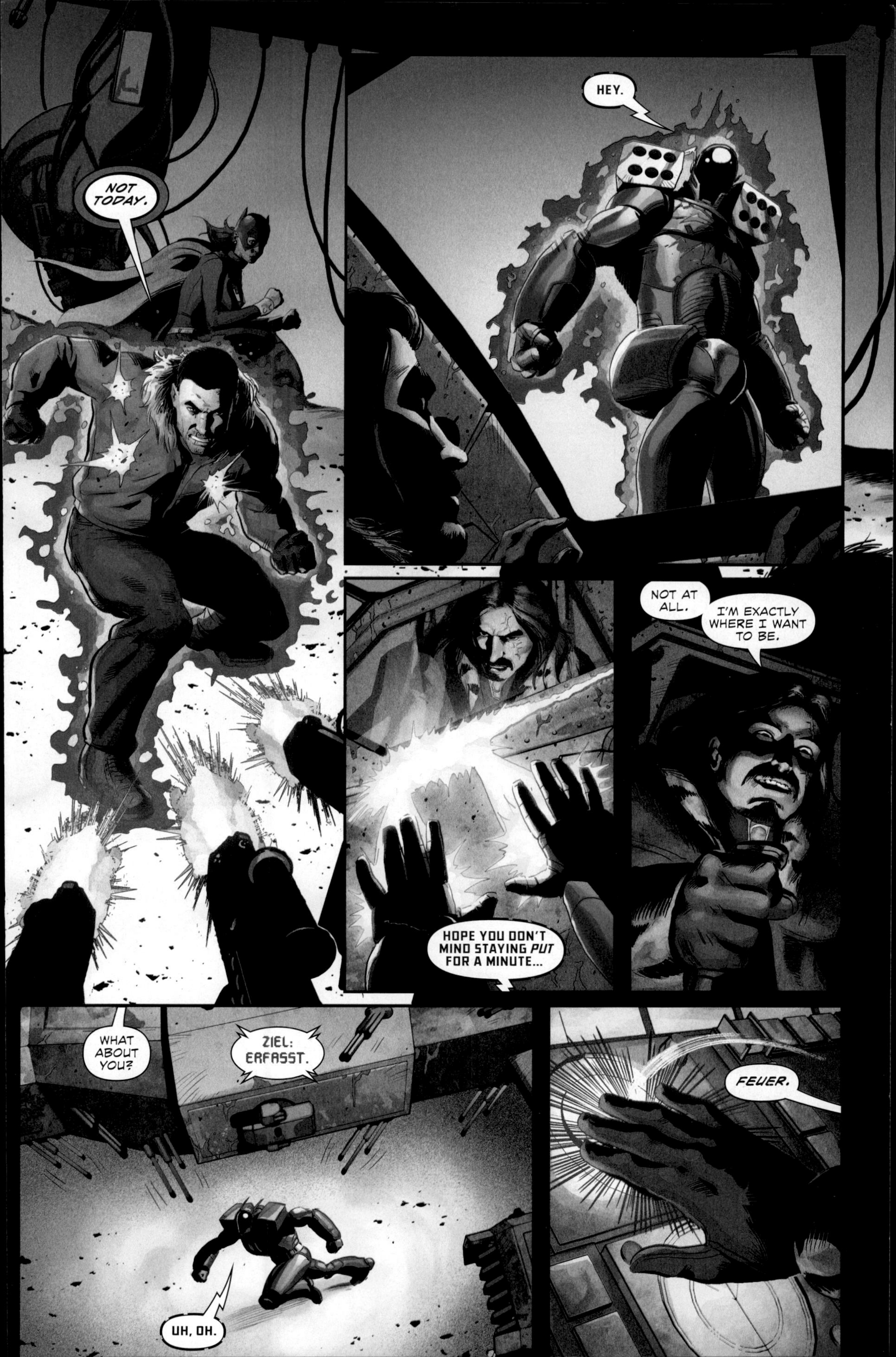
NOT TODAY.
HEY.
NOT AT ALL.
I'M EXACTLY WHERE I WANT TO BE.
HOPE YOU DON'T MIND STAYING *PUT* FOR A MINUTE...
WHAT ABOUT YOU?
ZIEL: ERFASST.
UH, OH.
FEUER.

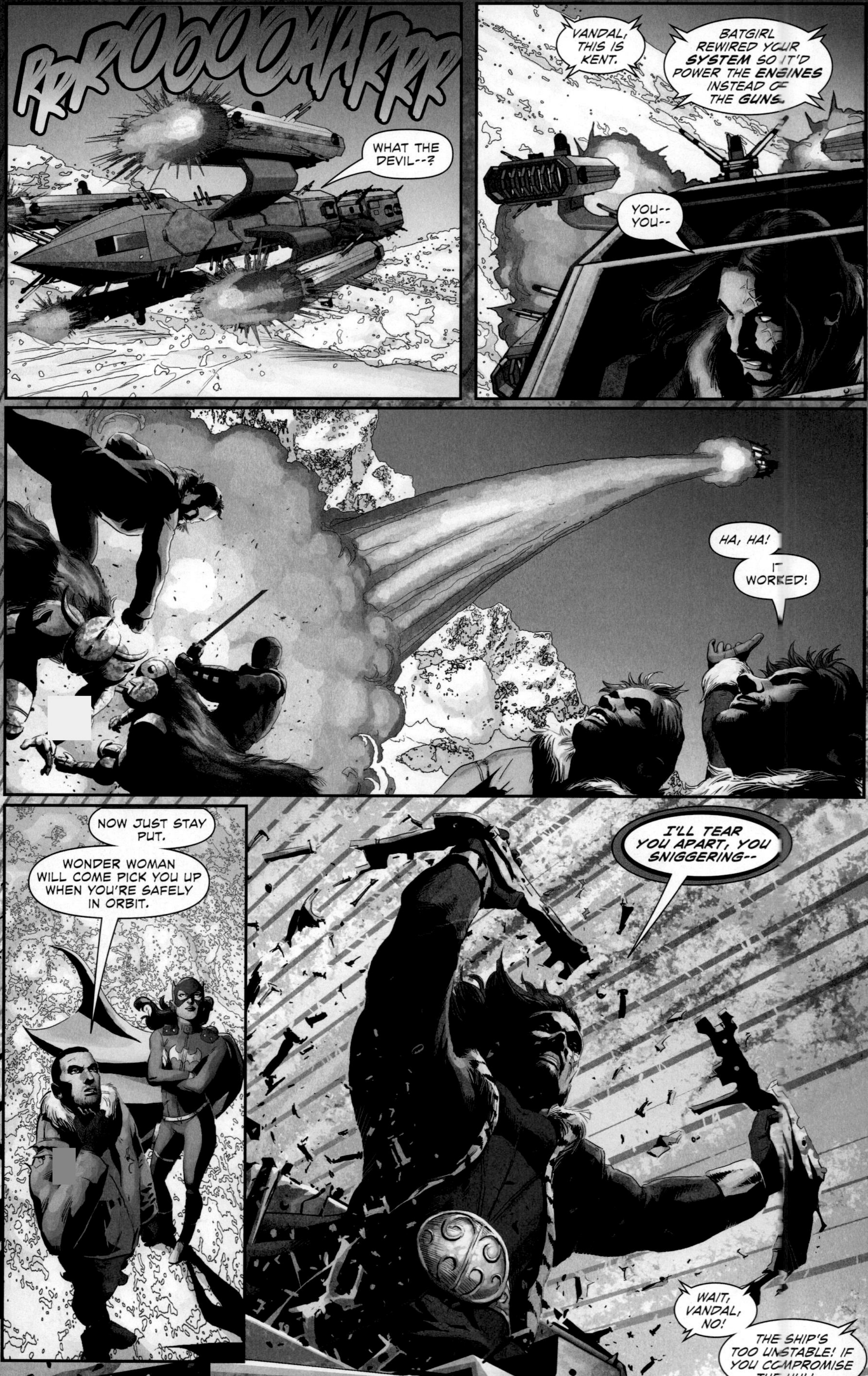
RRROOOOOWARRR
WHAT THE DEVIL--?
VANDAL, THIS IS KENT.
BATGIRL REWIRED YOUR SYSTEM SO IT'D POWER THE ENGINES INSTEAD OF THE GUNS.
YOU-- YOU--
HA, HA!
IT WORKED!
NOW JUST STAY PUT.
WONDER WOMAN WILL COME PICK YOU UP WHEN YOU'RE SAFELY IN ORBIT.
I'LL TEAR YOU APART, YOU SNIGGERING--
WAIT, VANDAL, NO!
THE SHIP'S TOO UNSTABLE! IF YOU COMPROMISE THE HULL--

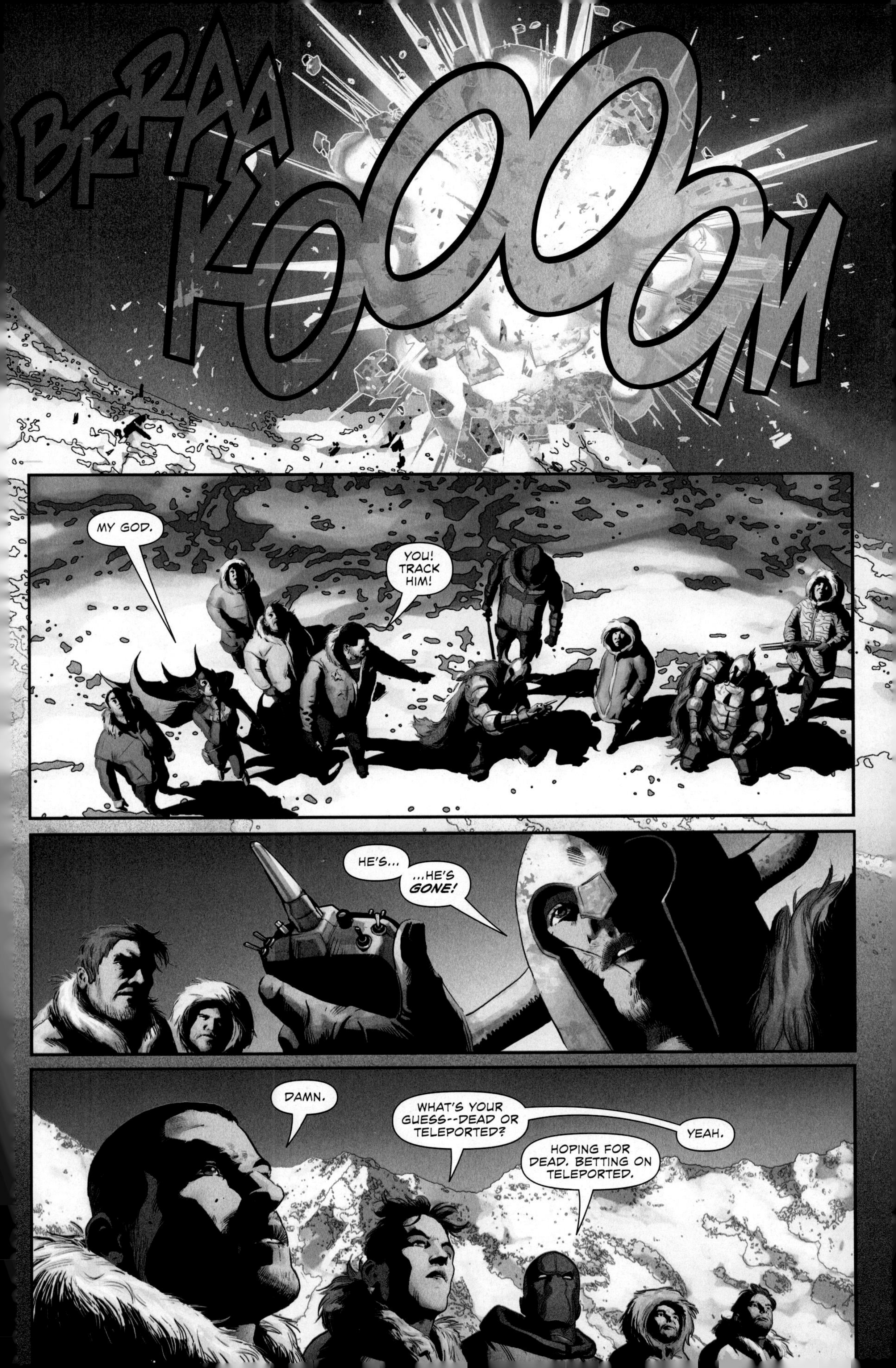
BRRAAKOOOOOM
MY GOD.
YOU! TRACK HIM!
HE'S...
...HE'S *GONE!*
DAMN.
WHAT'S YOUR GUESS--DEAD OR TELEPORTED?
YEAH.
HOPING FOR DEAD. BETTING ON TELEPORTED.

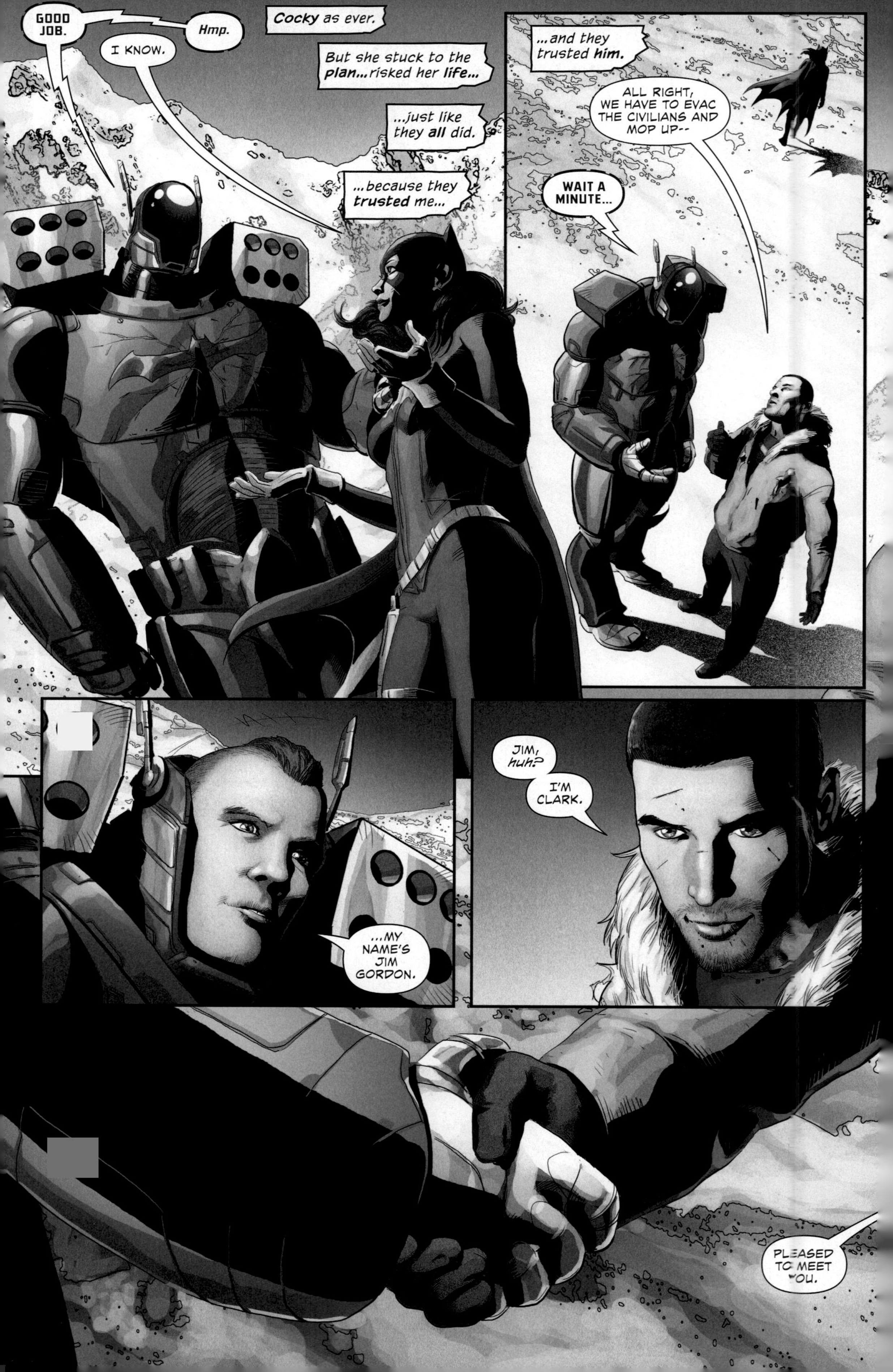
GOOD JOB.
I KNOW.
Hmp.
Cocky as ever.
But she stuck to the plan...risked her life...
...just like they all did.
...because they trusted me...
...and they trusted him.
ALL RIGHT, WE HAVE TO EVAC THE CIVILIANS AND MOP UP--
WAIT A MINUTE...
...MY NAME'S JIM GORDON.
JIM, huh?
I'M CLARK.
PLEASED TO MEET YOU.

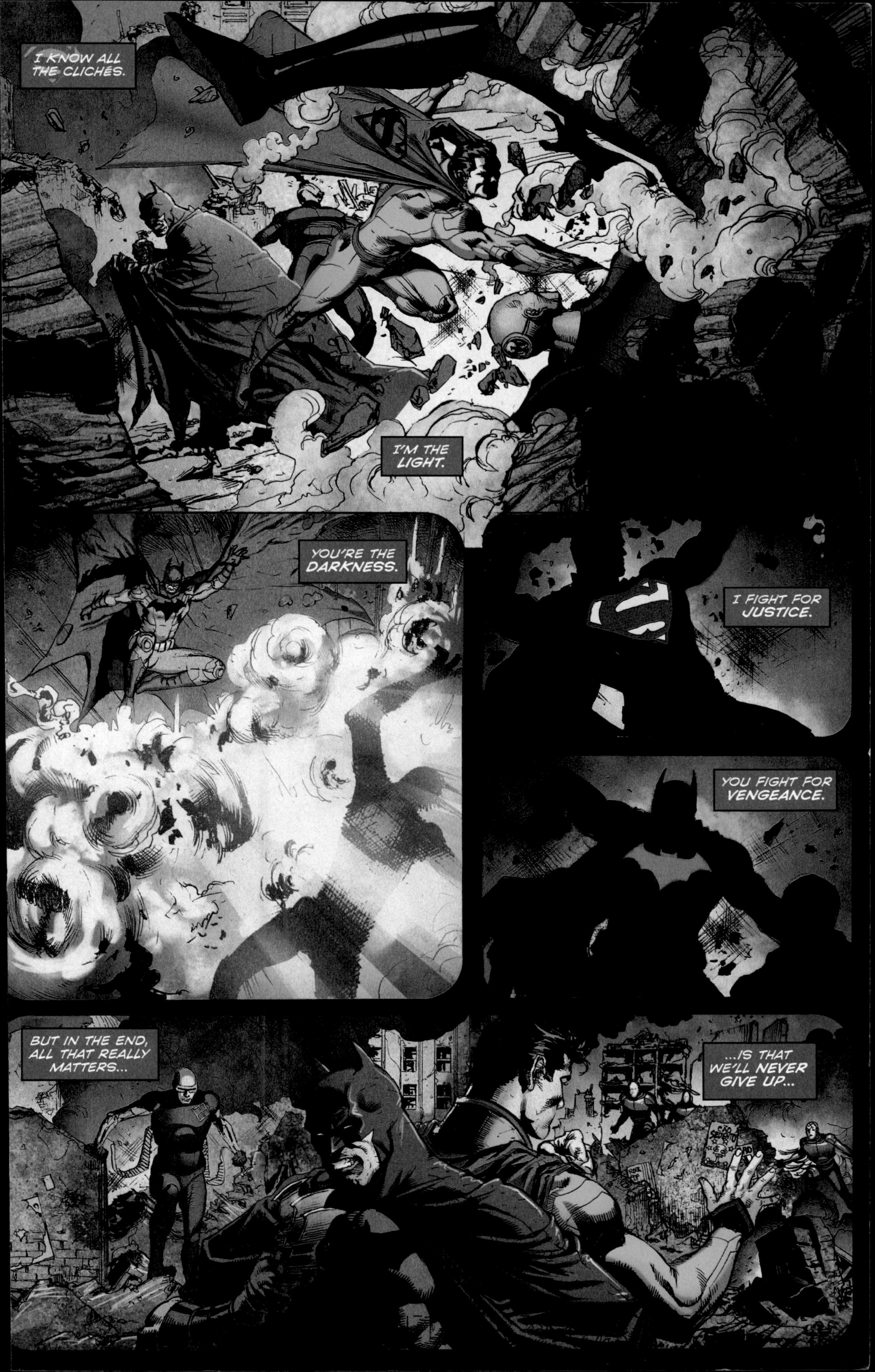
I KNOW ALL THE CLICHÉS.
I'M THE LIGHT.
YOU'RE THE DARKNESS.
I FIGHT FOR JUSTICE.
YOU FIGHT FOR VENGEANCE.
BUT IN THE END, ALL THAT REALLY MATTERS...
...IS THAT WE'LL NEVER GIVE UP...

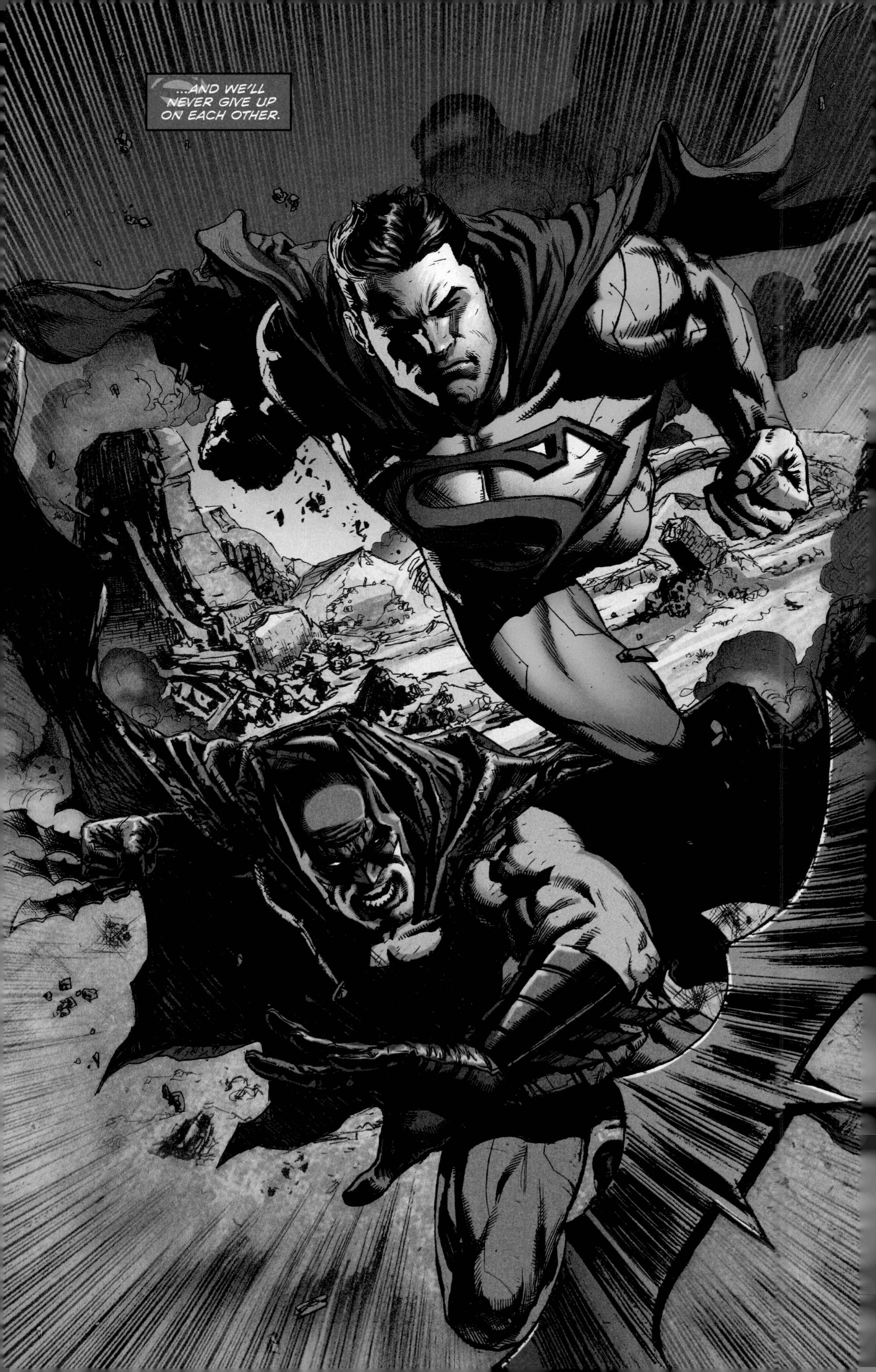
...AND WE'LL NEVER GIVE UP ON EACH OTHER.

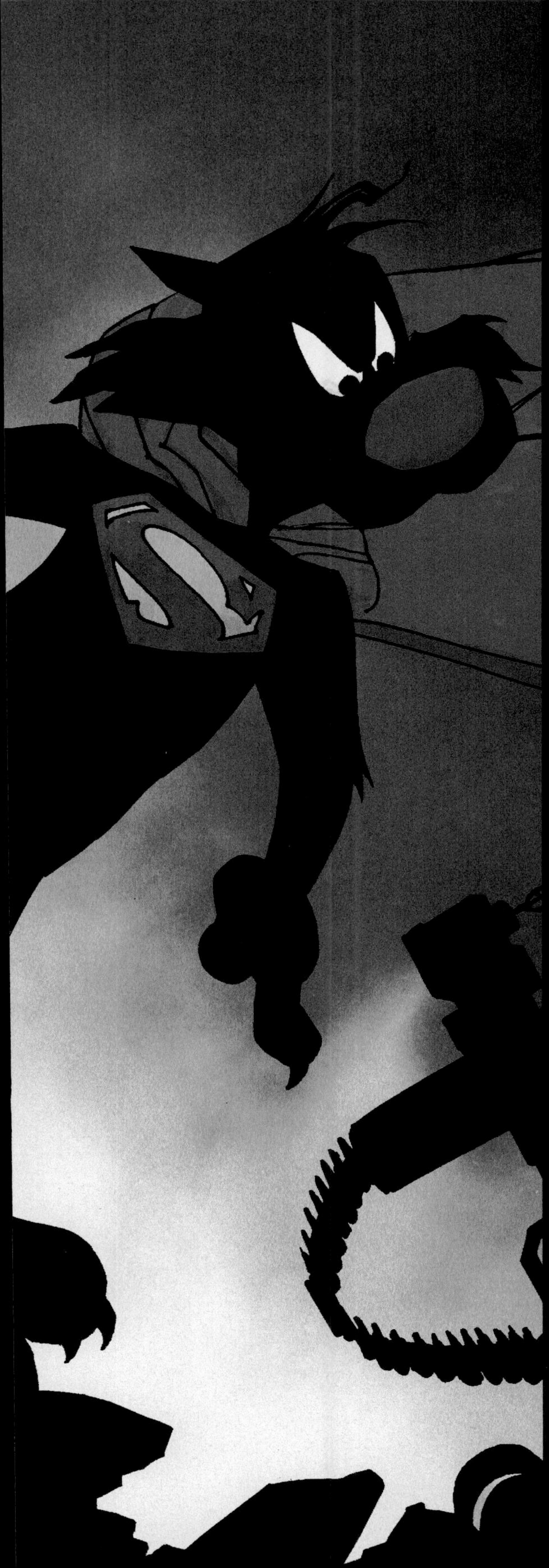

VARIANT COVER GALLERY

BATMAN/SUPERMAN #21
JOKER 75TH ANNIVERSARY
VARIANT BY JOCK

BATMAN/SUPERMAN #22
TEEN TITANS GO! VARIANT
BY DAN HIPP

BATMAN/SUPERMAN #23
BOMBSHELLS VARIANT BY DES TAYLOR

BATMAN/SUPERMAN #24
GREEN LANTERN 75TH ANNIVERSARY
VARIANT BY DAVE BULLOCK

BATMAN/SUPERMAN #25
MONSTER MONTH VARIANT
BY MICHAEL AVON OEMING

BATMAN/SUPERMAN #26
LOONEY TUNES VARIANT

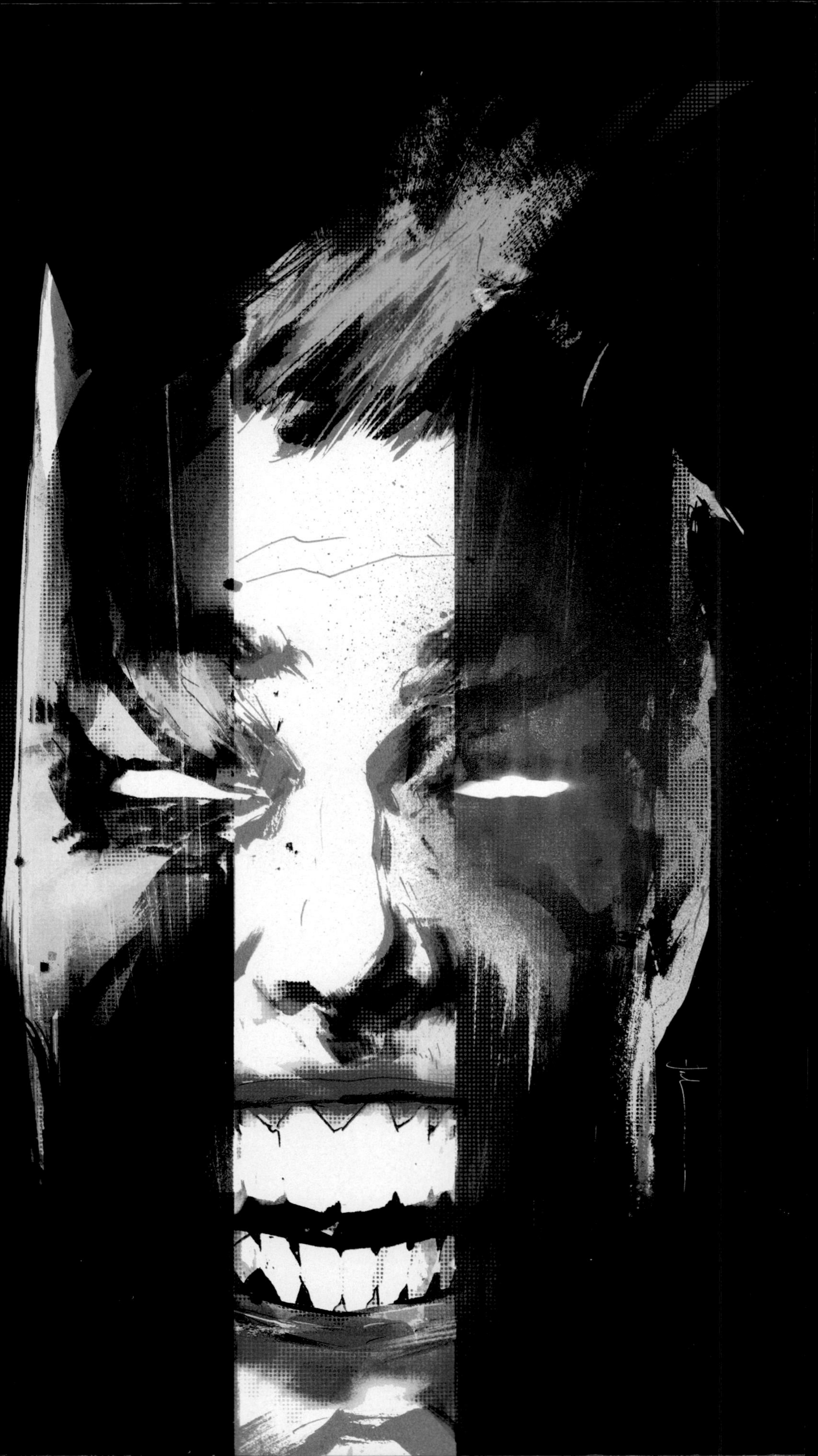

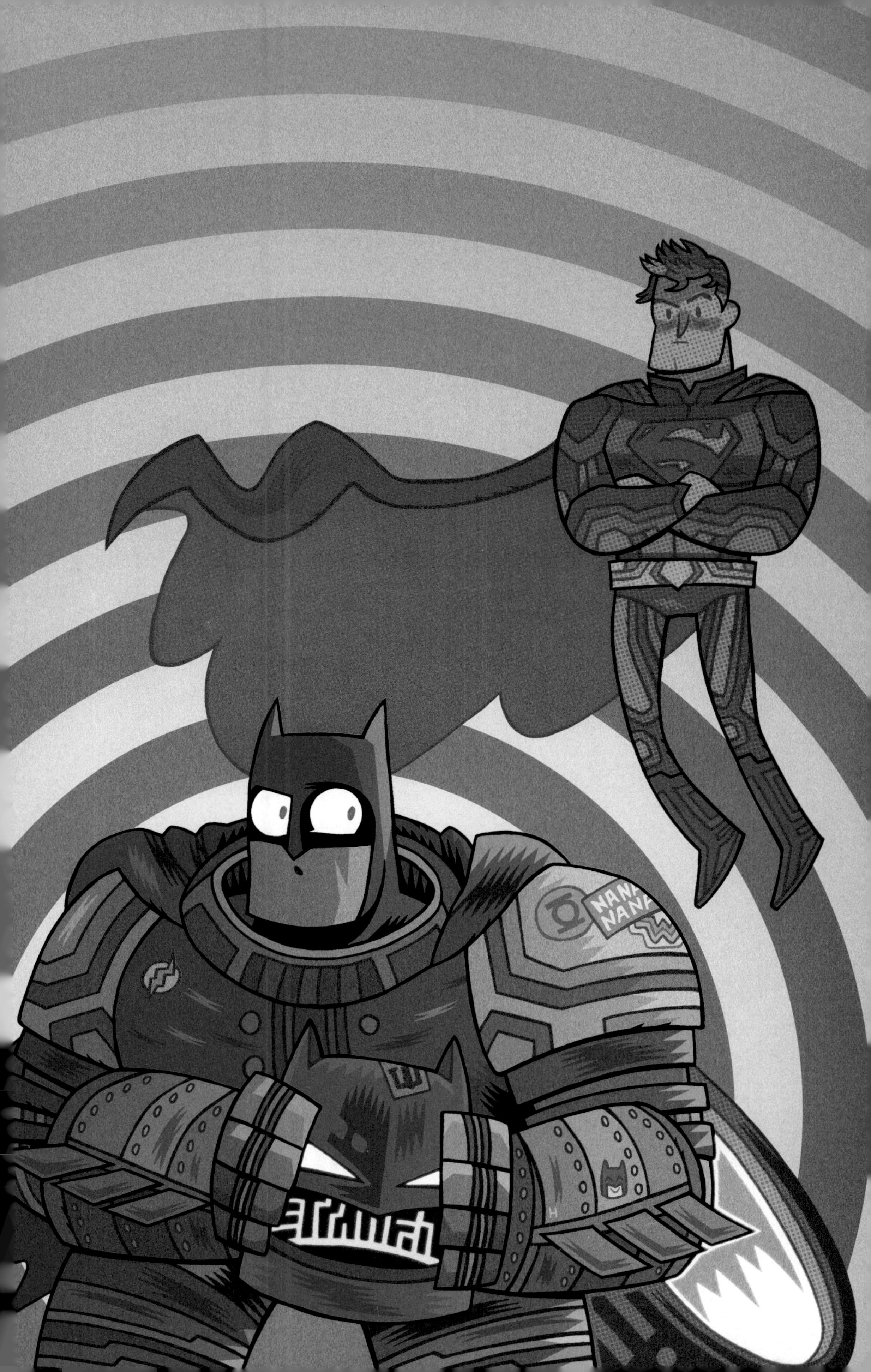
NANA
NANA

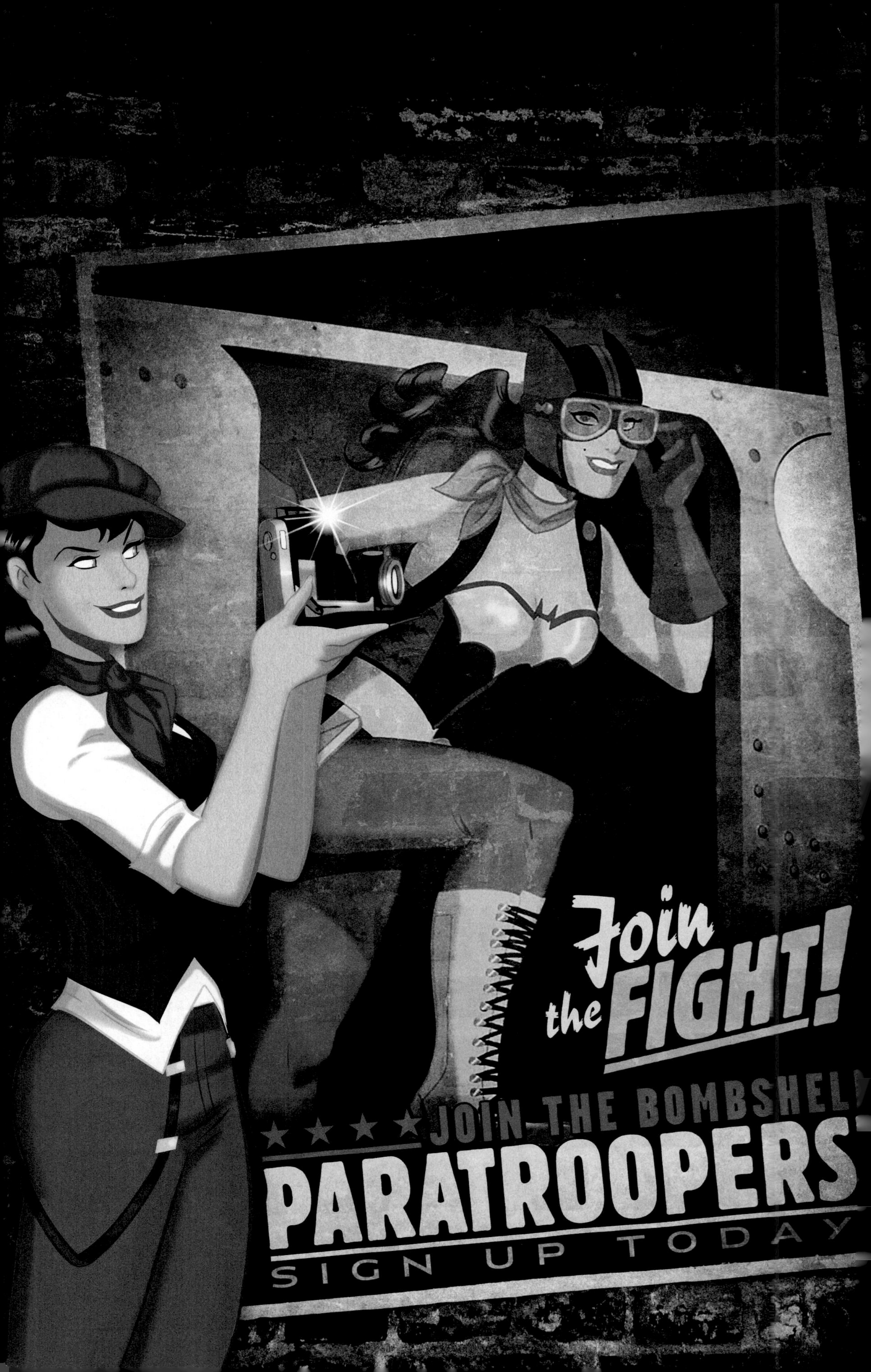
Join the FIGHT!
JOIN THE BOMBSHEL
PARATROOPERS
SIGN UP TODAY

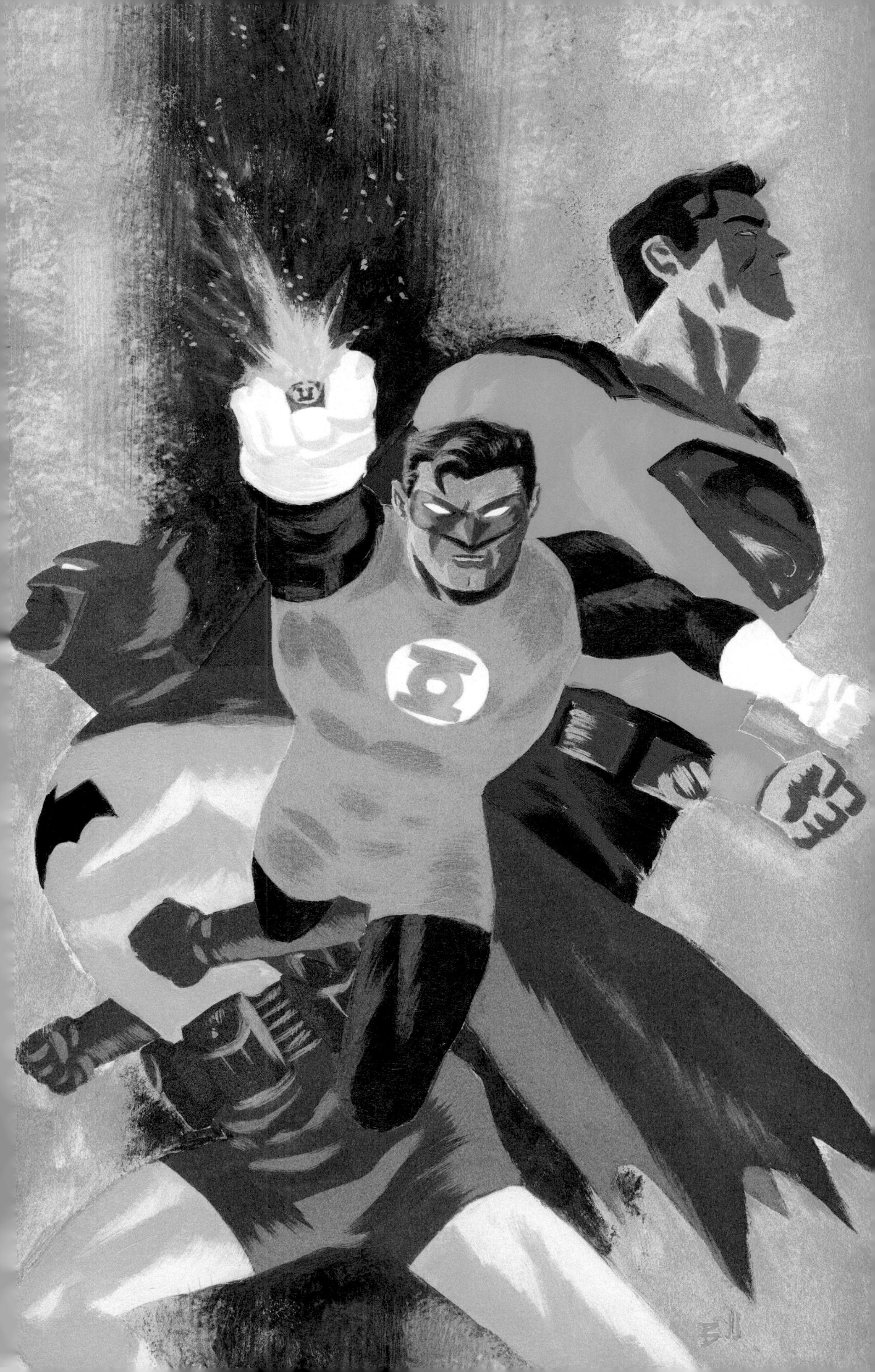

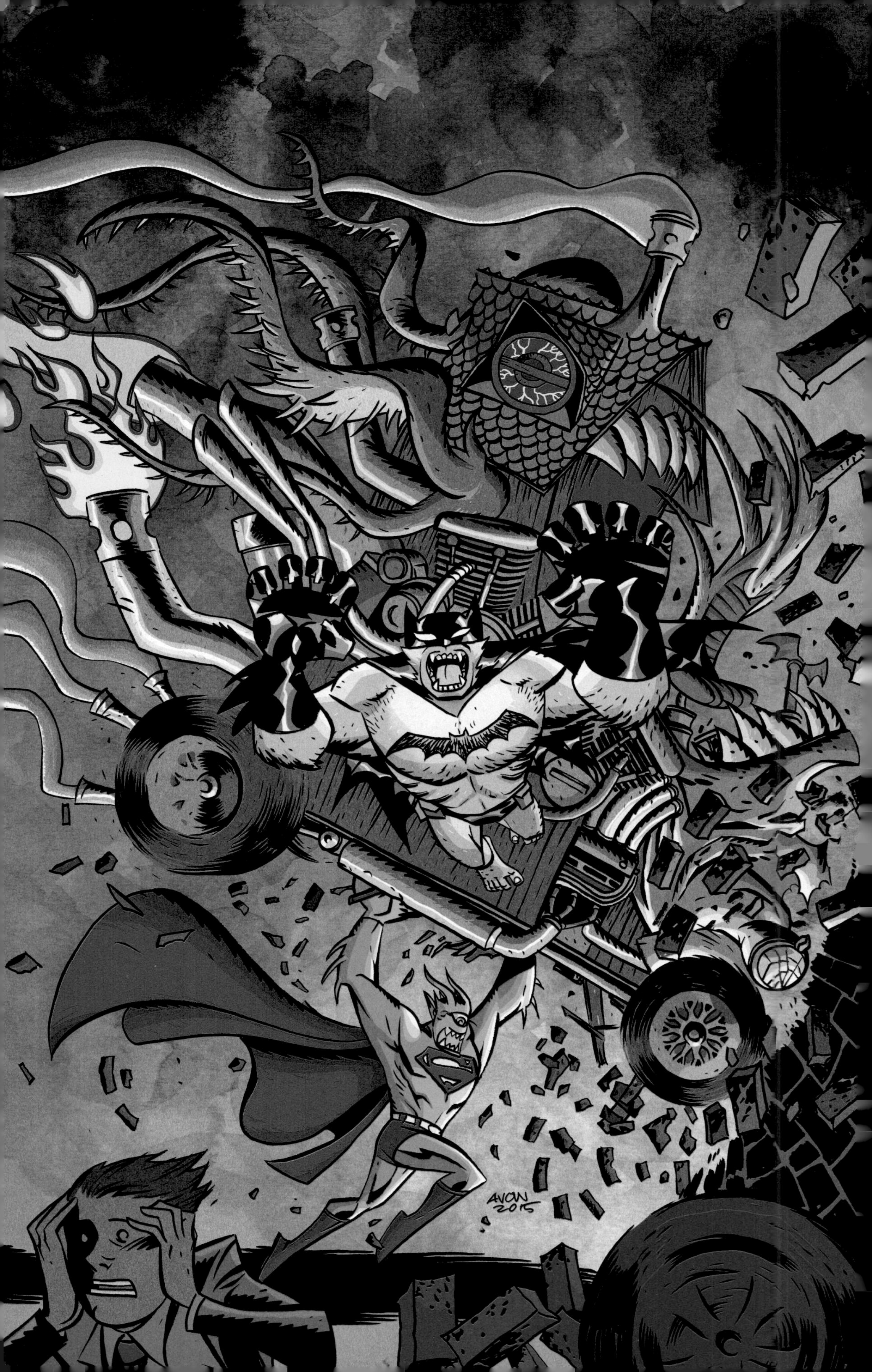
AVON
2015

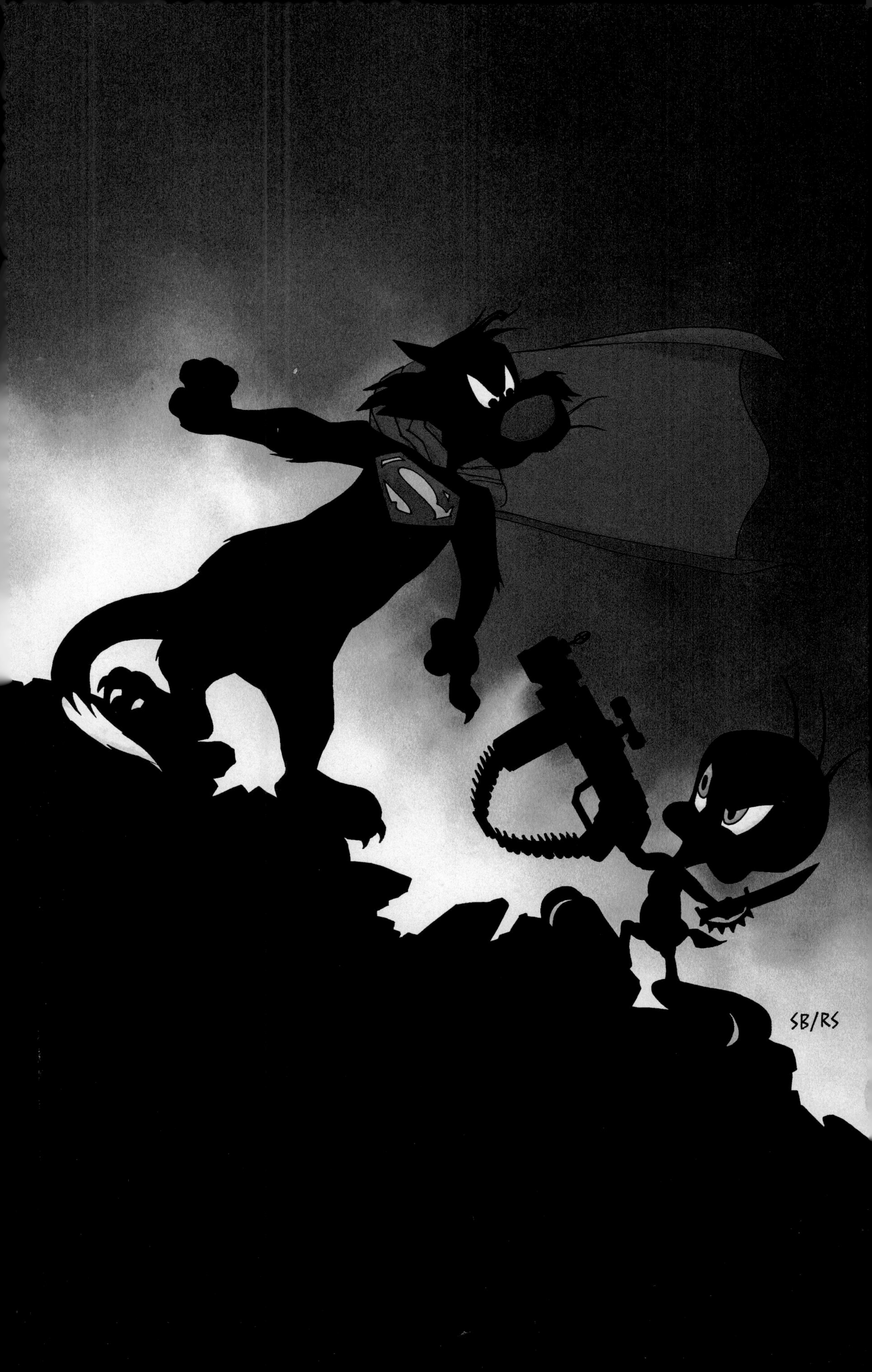
SB/RS

Pencils by Ardian Syaf for page 39

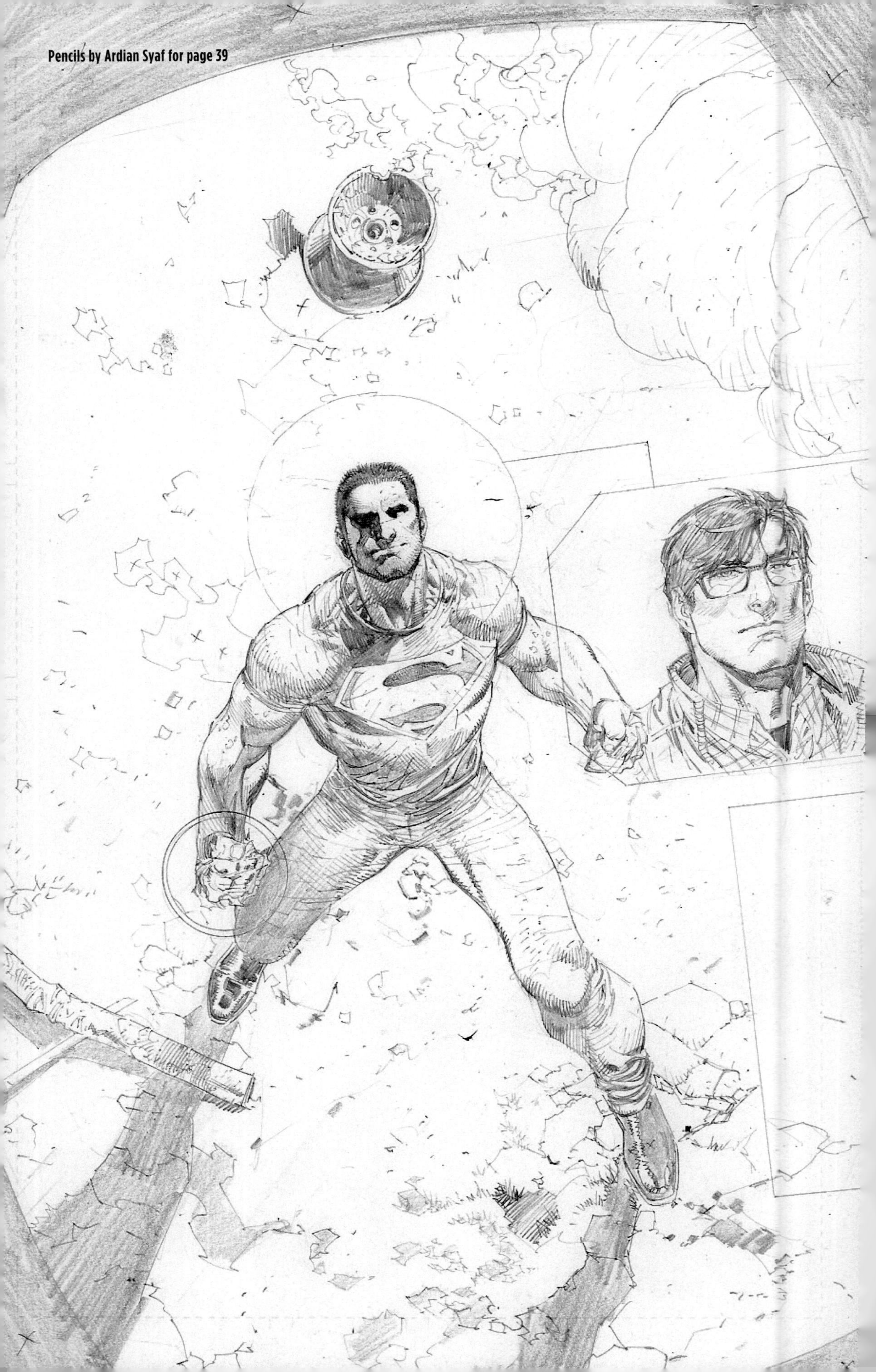

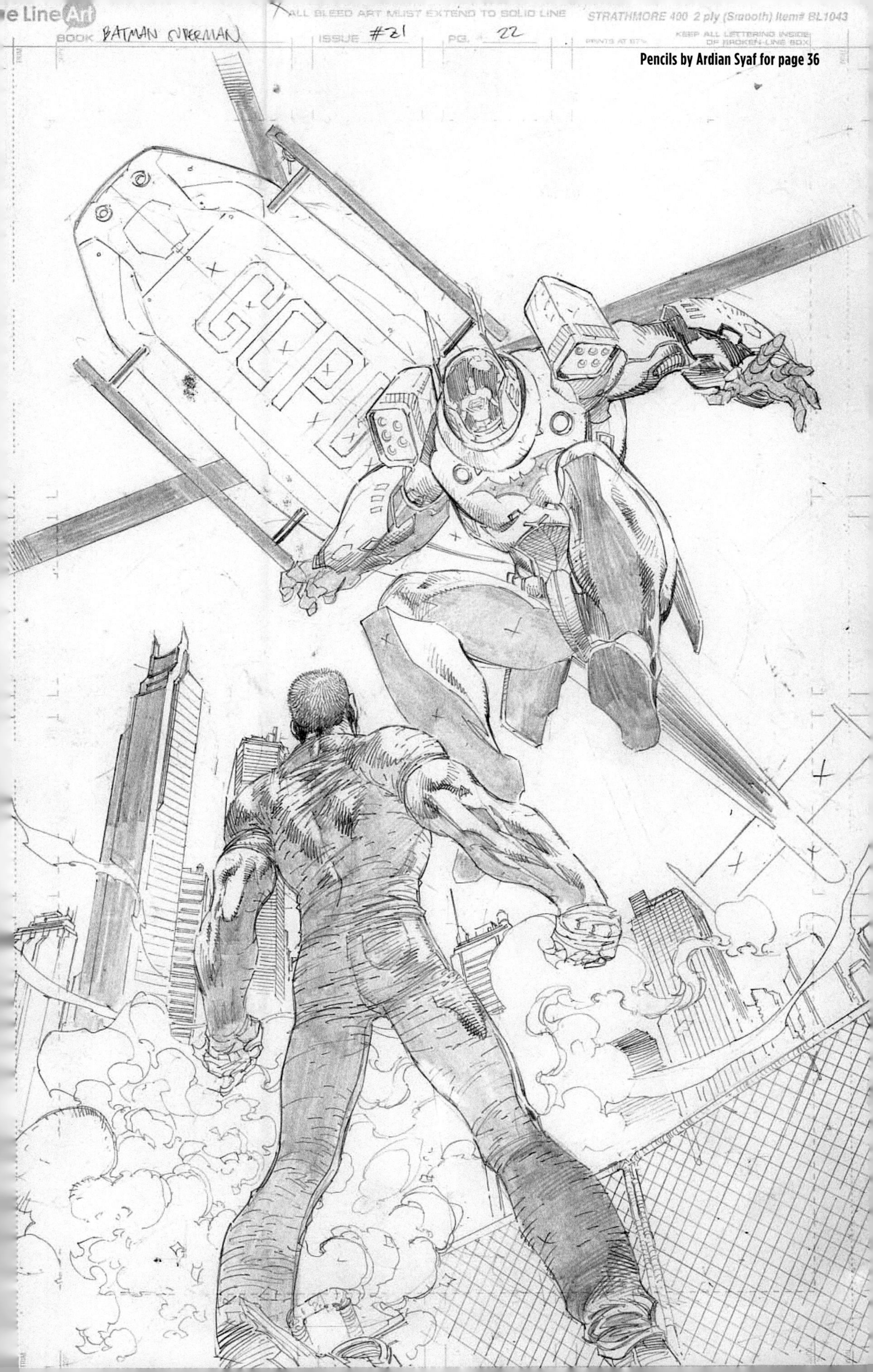
ALL BLEED ART MUST EXTEND TO SOLID LINE
STRATHMORE 400 2 ply (Smooth) Item# BL1043
BOOK BATMAN SUPERMAN
ISSUE #21
PG. 22
PRINTS AT 67%
KEEP ALL LETTERING INSIDE OF BROKEN-LINE BOX
GCPD

Pencils by Ardian Syaf for page 36

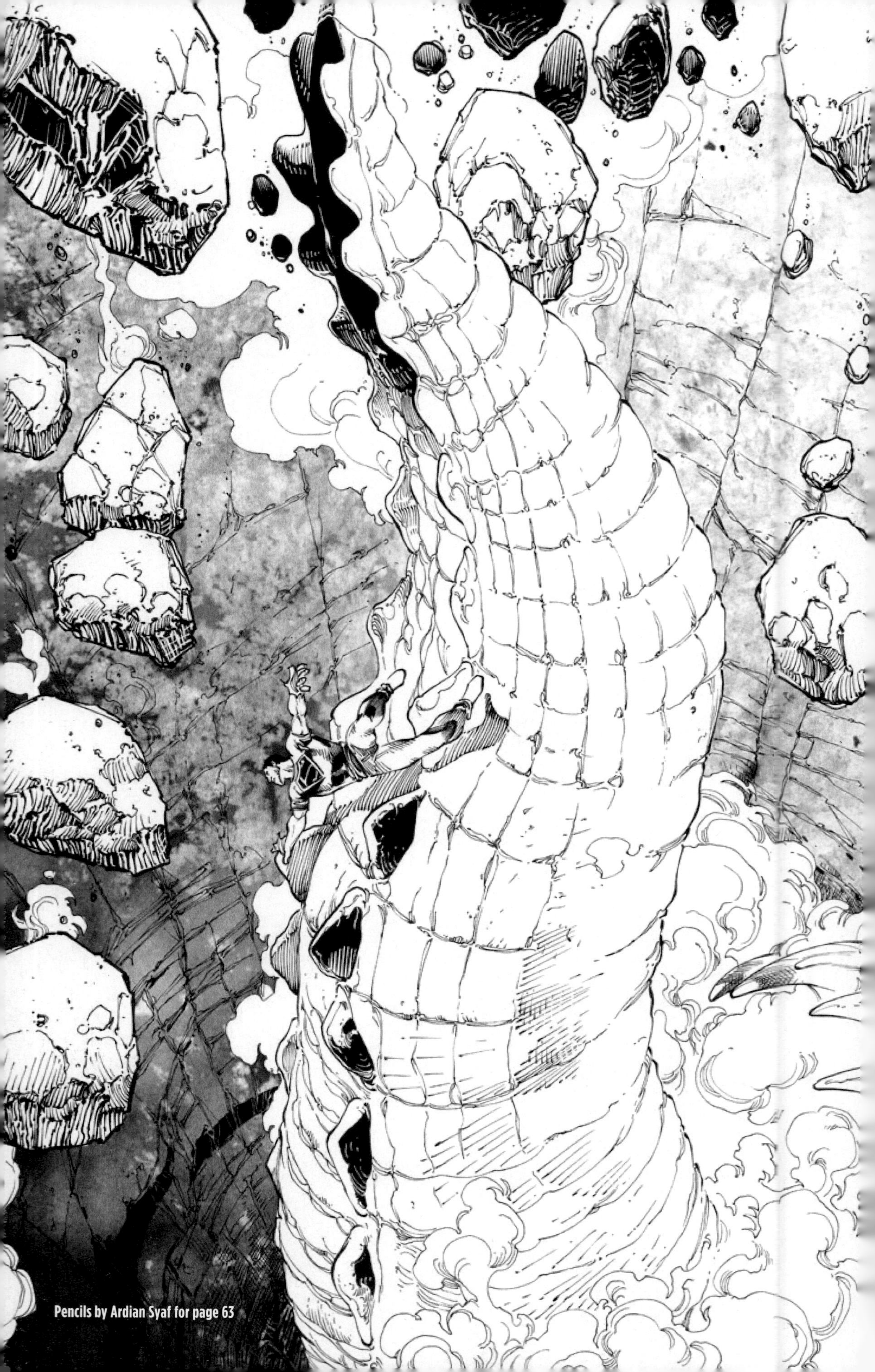

Pencils by Ardian Syaf for page 63